An Introduction to Syntax

This comprehensive new textbook is an engaging introduction to syntax. Clearly organized and accessible, it provides students with a thorough grounding in the analysis of syntactic structure using data from a typologically wide variety of languages. The book guides students through the basic concepts involved in syntactic analysis and goes on to prepare them for further work in any syntactic theory, using examples from a range of phenomena in human languages. It also includes a chapter on theories of syntax. Each chapter includes generous exercises and recommendations for further study. The emphasis on languages and data sets this book apart from other introductions to syntax.

This book is an essential text for undergraduate and graduate students on courses devoted to the study of syntax. It will also be very valuable to students in other cognitive science fields who are interested in language.

Robert D. Van Valin, Jr. is Professor and Chair at the Department of Linguistics, University at Buffalo, The State University of New York. He has published articles on syntax, universal grammar, language typology, and language acquisition. He is the editor of *Advances in Role and Reference Grammar* (1993) and also co-author of *Functional Syntax and Universal Grammar* (1984), and the co-author of *Syntax: Structure, Meaning and Function* (1997), both published by Cambridge University Press.

An Introduction to Syntax

ROBERT D. VAN VALIN, JR.

Department of Linguistics, University at Buffalo, The State University of New York

CAMBRIDGE
UNIVERSITY PRESS

CAMBRIDGE UNIVERSITY PRESS
Cambridge, New York, Melbourne, Madrid, Cape Town, Singapore, São Paulo

Cambridge University Press
The Edinburgh Building, Cambridge CB2 8RU, UK

Published in the United States of America by Cambridge University Press, New York

www.cambridge.org
Information on this title: www.cambridge.org/9780521631990

First published 2001
Fourth printing 2005

A catalogue record for this publication is available from the British Library

Library of Congress Cataloguing in Publication data

Van Valin, Robert D., Jr.
An Introduction to Syntax / Robert D. Van Valin, Jr.
p. cm.
Includes bibliographical references and index.
ISBN 0 521 63199 8 (hdbk.) — ISBN 0 521 63566 7 (pbk.)
1. Grammar, Comparative and general—Syntax. I. Title.

P291.V357 2001
415—dc21 00-062129

ISBN 978-0-521-63199-0 hardback
ISBN 978-0-521-63566-0 paperback

Transferred to digital printing 2007

For Anna, Alice and Bob

Contents

List of figures

Preface

If people encounter the term 'syntax', they usually think of 'grammar', and for many this term conjures up bad associations of schoolteachers' pronouncements about how one should and should not talk, of seemingly endless conjugations of verbs or declensions of nouns that must be mastered by rote, or of dreary repetitions of insipid phrases in a foreign-language class. This book is about *none* of these things. It is, rather, about the marvelous diversity of ways of expressing itself that the human mind has created during the evolution of human language. How does an Aborigine from central Australia, a Basque from Spain or an inhabitant of the island of Madagascar put a sentence together? Is it at all similar to the way an English speaker does it? Or a Spanish speaker? Or a Russian speaker? Or a Sioux speaker? Chinese and Japanese speakers use the same characters to write their respective languages; how similar is Chinese syntax to Japanese syntax? How does a scientist go about analysing the structure of all of these different languages?

These are just some of the questions that will be answered in this book. *An Introduction to Syntax* is first and foremost an exploration of the variety of human languages, with examples drawn from every part of the globe. It is also a guide to the analysis of these languages, teaching you the techniques that the practitioners of linguistic science use to reveal and understand the structure of human languages. This book also introduces you to some of the theories that have been proposed to explain how languages work. The study of language is one of the great intellectual challenges facing the cognitive sciences today, and it is an intellectual adventure of the highest order. This book takes you into the heart of one of the most important parts of this adventure, the investigation of the syntactic structure of human languages.

Acknowledgements

A lot of people have contributed to this book. First and foremost, I would like to thank the students in my Syntax 1 classes during the fall semesters of 1997, 1998 and 1999 at the University at Buffalo. They worked through successive versions of the manuscript, and their feedback has been invaluable. I would also like to thank the participants in my course at the Australian Linguistic Institute at the University of Melbourne for their comments and suggestions. I am also very grateful to my colleagues Jean-Pierre Koenig and Matthew Dryer, who read earlier drafts and gave me many helpful comments. I wish to thank Franz Müller-Gotama, Patrick Farrell, Irena Zovko, Balthasar Bickel, Joan Bresnan, Kiyoko Toritani and Nigel Vincent for their comments on earlier drafts, as well as two anonymous referees for theirs. I'm also indebted to the following people for their help with specific languages: Matthew Whelpton (Icelandic), Irena Zovko (Croatian), David Weber (Huallaga Quechua), Wolfgang Wölck (Ayacucho Quechua), Chris Yuen, Mei-Han Low (Cantonese) and K. P. Mohanan (Malayalam).

Note

The words in boldface in the text have entries in R. L. Trask's *Dictionary of Grammatical Terms in Linguistics* (London: Routledge, 1993); they are in boldface only for the first mention. I strongly recommend it as an accompaniment to this book.

Abbreviations

A	actor; transitive subject[1]
ABL	ablative
ABS	absolutive case
ACC	accusative case
ACD	accidental action
ACT	actor as nominative
ACTIVE	active voice
ADJ	adjective
AdjP	adjective phrase
ADV	adverb
AdvP	adverb phrase
AFF	affix
AGR	agreement
$AGR_O(P)$	object agreement (phrase)
$AGR_S(P)$	subject agreement (phrase)
AJT	adjunct
ALL	allative case
ANTI	antipassive
AOR	aorist tense
APL	applicative marker
ARG	argument
ART	article
ASP	aspect
AspP	aspect phrase
AUX	auxiliary verb
CIRC	circumstantial voice
CL	classifier
CLM	clause-linkage marker
CMPL	complement
CONJ	conjunction
COMP	complementizer
CP	complementizer phrase
DAT	dative case
DECL	declarative mood
DEF	definite(ness)
DEG	degree modifier
DEM	demonstrative
DET	determiner
dl incl	dual inclusive
DOBJ	direct object
DUAL	dual number
ERG	ergative case
F, FEM	feminine gender
FUT	future tense
GB	Government-Binding Theory
GEN	genitive case
GEND	gender
GL	goal as nominative
GPSG	Generalized Phrase Structure Grammar
HPSG	Head-driven Phrase Structure Grammar
ID	immediate dominance
IF	illocutionary force
IMPF	imperfective aspect
INAN	inanimate
IND	indicative mood
INF	infinitive

[1] Most of these terms have entries in Trask's *Dictionary*.

INFL	inflection
INST	instrumental case
IOBJ	indirect object
IP	inflection phrase
LFG	Lexical-Functional Grammar
LMT	Lexical Mapping Theory
LNK	linker
LOC	locative case
LP	linear precedence
LS	logical structure
M, MASC	masculine gender
MOD	modifier
N	noun; neuter gender
NEG	negation
NFUT	non-future tense
NM	noun marker
NOM	nominative case
NP	noun phrase
NTL	neutral case
NUC	nucleus
NUM	number
O	transitive direct object
OBJ	object
OBJ2	secondary object
OBJ_θ	semantically restricted object
OBL	oblique
PASS	passive voice
PAST	past tense
P	preposition/postposition
PER	person
pl, PL	plural number
PN	proper noun marker
POSS	possessor; possessive
PP	prepositional/ postpositional phrase
PrCS	precore slot
PRED, pred	predicate
PREP	preposition
PRES	present tense
PRFV	perfective aspect
PRO	pronoun
PROG	progressive aspect
PRT	particle
PS	phrase structure
PSA	privileged syntactic argument
PURP	purposive
Q	question particle, interrogative
QNT	quantifier
QP	quantifier phrase
RCP	recipient as nominative
RD	relational-dependency
REFL	reflexive
REL	relativizer
RelG	Relational Grammar
REP	reported speech
RRG	Role and Reference Grammar
S	intransitive subject; sentence
sg, SG	singular number
SPEC	specifier
SUBJ	subject
SUBRD	subordinator
SUF	suffix
TG	transformational grammar
TNS	tense
TP	tense phrase
U	undergoer
UND	undergoer as nominative
V	verb
VP	verb phrase
XP	phrase with head of category 'X'
1	subject in RelG
2	direct object in RelG
3	indirect object in RelG

Arabic numbers also represent noun classes in Swahili examples

CHAPTER 1

Syntax, lexical categories, and morphology

1.0 Introduction

This book is an introduction to the basic concepts of syntax and syntactic analysis. Syntax is a central component of human language. Language has often been characterized as a systematic correlation between certain types of gestures and meaning, as represented simplistically in Figure 1.1. For spoken language, the gestures are oral, and for signed language, they are manual.

GESTURES ⟵⟶ MEANING

Figure 1.1. *Language as a correlation between gestures and meaning*

It is not the case that every possible meaning that can be expressed is correlated with a unique, unanalyzable gesture, be it oral or manual. Rather, each language has a stock of meaning-bearing elements and different ways of combining them to express different meanings, and these ways of combining them are themselves meaningful. The two English sentences *Chris gave the notebook to Dana* and *Dana gave the notebook to Chris* contain exactly the same meaning-bearing elements, i.e. words, but they have different meanings because the words are combined differently in them. These different combinations fall into the realm of syntax; the two sentences differ not in terms of the words in them but rather in terms of their syntax. Syntax can thus be given the following characterization, taken from Matthews (1982:1):

> The term 'syntax' is from the Ancient Greek *sýntaxis*, a verbal noun which literally means 'arrangement' or 'setting out together'. Traditionally, it refers to the branch of grammar dealing with the ways in which words, with or without appropriate inflections, are arranged to show connections of meaning within the sentence.

First and foremost, syntax deals with how **sentences** are constructed, and users of human languages employ a striking variety of possible arrangements of the elements in sentences. One of the most obvious yet important ways in which languages differ is the order of the main elements in a sentence. In English, for example, the **subject** comes before the **verb** and the **direct object** follows the verb. In Lakhota (a Siouan language of North America), on the other hand, the subject and direct object both precede the verb, while in Toba Batak (an Austronesian language of Indonesia; Schachter 1984b), they both follow the verb. This is illustrated in (1.1), in which *the teacher*, *waų́spekhiye ki* and *guru i* function as subjects, and *a book*, *wówapi wą* and *buku* function as direct objects.

(1.1) a. The teacher is reading a book. English
b. Waų́spekhiye ki wówapi wą yawá. Lakhota
teacher the book a read
c. Manjaha buku guru i. Toba Batak
read book teacher the

The Lakhota and Toba Batak sentences also mean 'the teacher is reading the book', and in the Lakhota example the subject comes first followed by the direct object, whereas in the Toba Batak example the subject comes last in the sentence, with the direct object following the verb and preceding the subject. The **basic word order** in Toba Batak is thus the opposite of that in Lakhota. There are also languages in which the order of words is normally irrelevant to the interpretation of which element is subject and which is object. This is the case in the following Russian sentences.

(1.2) a. Učitel'nica čitaet knigu. Russian
teacher read book
b. Knigu čitaet učitel'nica.
book read teacher
c. Čitaet učitel'nica knigu.
read teacher book

Again, all three of these sentences mean 'the teacher is reading the book', and in these Russian examples the order of the words is not the key to their interpretation, as it is in the sentences from the other three languages. Rather, it is the form of the words that is crucial. The *-a* on the end of *učitel'nica* 'teacher' signals that it is the subject, and the *-u* on the end of *knigu* 'book' indicates that it is the direct object. If the word for 'teacher' were the direct object in a sentence, then it would end in *-u*, as in (1.3).

(1.3) a. Ženščina videla učitel'nic**u**. Russian
woman saw teacher
b. Učitel'nic**u** videla ženščina.
teacher saw woman
'The woman saw the teacher.'

These changes in the form of the words to indicate their function in the sentence are what Matthews referred to as 'inflections', and the study of the formation of words and how they may change their form is called **morphology**. These examples illustrate the important relationship between syntax and morphology: something which may be expressed syntactically in some languages may be expressed morphologically in others. Which element is subject and which is object is signalled syntactically in the examples from English, Lakhota and Toba Batak, while it is expressed morphologically in the Russian examples. Syntax and morphology make up what is traditionally referred to as **'grammar'**; an alternative term for it is **morphosyntax**, which explicitly recognizes the important relationship between syntax and morphology. Even though this book is focussed on syntax, morphology will nevertheless be an important part of the discussion.

Thus a more complex picture of the nature of language emerges than that given in Figure 1.1; it is summarized in Figure 1.2.

Figure 1.2. *Language as a correlation between gestures and meaning (revised)*

All of the examples looked at so far involve simple sentences, but one of the most important syntactic properties of language is that simple sentences can be combined in various ways to form complex sentences. In terms of Figure 1.2, one could say that syntax makes possible the formulation of expressions with complex meanings out of elements with simple meanings. One of the defining features of human language is its unlimited nature; that is, the number of meaningful expressions that can be produced by users of a human language is potentially infinite, and this expressive potential comes from the combination of the basic meaningful elements with syntactic principles. Much of the interest in language in psychology and cognitive science comes from what the study of the cognitive mechanisms underlying language use and acquisition can reveal about the human mind.

This book has three goals: first, to introduce the basic concepts of syntax; second, to elucidate the principles and tools of syntactic analysis, which make it possible for linguists to analyze the grammatical systems of human languages; and third, to give an overview of the typological range of phenomena found in human languages which syntacticians seek to describe. The content of this book is presupposed by more advanced courses in syntactic theory, and hence it is intended to prepare the reader for such courses. The perspective of the book is primarily **descriptive**, and theoretical issues will be raised only in chapter 6. To many people the term 'grammar' evokes bad memories of **prescriptive** rules learned in school, e.g. 'don't split infinitives!' Since the early part of the twentieth century, linguistics has rejected the prescriptive tradition which underlies school grammars and focusses instead on describing what users of human language actually do, not on prescribing what they should do.

A central part of the description of what speakers do is characterizing the **grammatical** (or **well-formed**) sentences of a language and distinguishing them from **ungrammatical** or (**ill-formed**) sentences. Grammatical sentences are those that are in accord with the rules and principles of the syntax of a particular language, while ungrammatical sentences violate one or more syntactic rules or principles. For example, (1.1a) is a grammatical sentence of English, while *Teacher the book a reading is* would not be. Ungrammatical sentences are marked with an asterisk, hence **Teacher the book a reading is.* This sentence is ungrammatical because it violates some of the word order rules for English, that is (i) basic word order in English clauses is subject–verb–object, (ii) **articles** like *the* and *a* precede the **noun** they modify, and (iii) **auxiliary verbs** like *is* precede the **main verb**, in this case *reading*. It is important to note that these are English-specific syntactic rules; this word order is perfectly grammatical in Lakhota, as (1.1b) shows, and if the Lakhota words were arranged in the English order, e.g. **Ki waų́spekhiye yawá wą wówapi* [the teacher reads a book], the result is thoroughly ungrammatical. Well-formed sentences are those that are in accord with the syntactic rules of the language; this does not entail that they always make sense semantically. For example, the sentence *the book is reading the teacher* is nonsensical in terms of its meaning, but it violates no syntactic rules or principles of English; indeed, it has exactly the same syntactic structure as (1.1a). Hence it is grammatical (well-formed), despite being semantically odd.

The organization of the book is as follows. In this chapter a number of distinctions that are relevant to the discussion in the remainder of the book are introduced. First, two aspects of syntactic structure are distinguished, one of which will be the main topic of chapters 2 and 3, and the other will be the main topic of chapter 4. Second, the traditional notion of parts of speech are reviewed, as these categories will be important throughout the book. Finally, a brief introduction to some of the basic concepts of morphology and morphological analysis is presented, with emphasis on those notions that will be especially pertinent to the discussion in the succeeding chapters.

The next three chapters present basic syntactic phenomena from two different analytic perspectives and introduce the concepts and analytic tools used in each. Many of the same grammatical phenomena will be analyzed from each perspective. In chapter 5 the basics of writing a grammar to describe syntactic phenomena will be presented; the formulation of rules to express the generalizations arising from syntactic analysis and the role of the lexicon in a grammar will be discussed. Different linguistic theories make different sets of assumptions about the nature of syntactic structure and accordingly employ different analytic principles and tools. In chapter 6 the basic ideas of four linguistic theories will be summarized, and their approaches to important grammatical phenomena, including the formation of information questions (e.g. *What did you see?*) and the **passive voice** (e.g. *The bread was eaten by the mouse*), will be compared and contrasted. These two phenomena are especially revealing for a comparison of theories, because the accounts given by the various theories highlight the conceptual and analytic differences among them.

1.1 Aspects of syntactic structure

In the syntactic structure of sentences, two distinct yet interrelated aspects must be distinguished. The first one has already been mentioned: the function of elements as subject and direct object in a sentence. 'Subject' and 'direct object' have traditionally been referred to as **grammatical relations**. Hence this kind of syntax will be referred to as '**relational structure**'. It includes more than just grammatical relations like subject and direct object; it also encompasses relationships like **modifier–modified**, e.g. *tall building* or *walk slowly* (*tall*, *slowly* = modifier, *building*, *walk* = modified) and **possessor–possessed**, e.g. *Pat's car* (*Pat's* = possessor, *car* = possessed). Relational structure will be the primary focus of chapters 2 and 3.

The second aspect concerns the organization of the units which constitute sentences. A sentence does not consist simply of a **string** of words; that is, in a sentence like *The teacher read a book in the library*, it is not the case that each word is equally related to the words adjacent to it in the string. There is no direct relationship between *read* and *a* or between *in* and *the*; *a* is related to *book*, which it modifies, just as *the* is related to *library*, which it modifies. *A* is related to *read* only through *a book* being the direct object of *read*, and similarly, *the* is related to *in* only through *the library* being the object of the **preposition** *in*. The words are organized into units which are then organized into larger units. These units are called **constituents**, and the hierarchical organization of the units in a sentence is called its **constituent structure**. This term will be used to refer to this second aspect of syntactic structure. Consider the eight words in the sentence *The teacher read a book in the library*. What units are these words organized into? Intuitively, it seems clear that the article *the* or *a* goes with, or forms a unit with, the noun following it. Is there any kind of evidence beyond a native speaker's intuitions that this is the case? Determining the constituent structure of sentences is the major topic of chapter 4, but a brief preliminary look at the kind of evidence needed follows.

If the article forms a unit with the noun that follows it, we would expect that in an alternative form of the same sentence the two would have to be found together and could not be split up. Thus in the passive version of this sentence, *A book was read by the teacher in the library*, the unit *a book* serves as subject, and the unit *the teacher* is the object of the preposition *by*. The constituent composed of a noun and an article is called a **noun phrase** [NP]; as will be shown later, NPs can be very complex. The preposition *in* and the NP following it also form a constituent in this sentence (*in the library*); it is called a **prepositional phrase** [PP]. The fact that the PP is a constituent can be seen by looking at another alternative form, *In the library the teacher read a book*. Finally, the verb plus the NP following it form a unit as well, as shown by a sentence like *I expected to find someone reading the book, and reading the book was a teacher*. The constituent composed of a verb plus following NP is called a **verb phrase** [VP]. As with NPs, VPs can be quite complex. In each of these alternative forms, a combination of words from the original sentence which one might intuitively put together in a single unit also occurs together as a unit, and this can be taken as evidence that they are in fact constituents. Using square brackets to group the words in constituents together, the constituent structure of *The teacher read a book in the library* may be represented as in (1.4). ('S' stands for 'sentence'.)

(1.4) $[_S\ [_{NP}$ The $[_N$ teacher$]]\ [_{VP}\ [_V$ read$]\ [_{NP}$ a $[_N$ book$]]\ [_{PP}\ [_P$ in$]\ [_{NP}$ the $[_N$ library$]]\ _{PP}]\ _{VP}]\ _S]$

Note the nesting of constituents within constituents in this sentence, e.g. the NP *the library* is a constituent of the PP *in the library* which is a constituent of the VP *read a book in the library*. In chapter 4 constituent structure will be explored in detail.

At the beginning of this section it was noted that the two aspects of syntactic structure, relational structure and constituent structure, are 'distinct yet interrelated', and it is possible now to see how this is the case. For example, a VP was described as being composed of a verb and the following NP, but it could alternatively be characterized as involving the verb and its direct object. Similarly, a PP is composed of a preposition and its object. NPs, on the other hand, involve modifiers, and accordingly the relation between *the* and *teacher* could be described as one of modifier–modified. Thus, these two aspects of syntactic structure are always present in a sentence, and when one or the other is emphasized, the sentence is being described from one of the two perspectives. It will be seen later that different grammatical phenomena seem to be more easily analyzed from one perspective rather than the other.

1.2 Lexical categories

In the discussion of the constituents of sentences, reference has been made to nouns and noun phrases, verbs and verb phrases, and prepositions and prepositional phrases. Nouns, verbs and prepositions are traditionally referred to as 'parts of speech' or 'word classes'; in contemporary linguistics they are termed **lexical categories**. The most important lexical categories are noun, verb, **adjective**, **adverb** and **adposition**, which subsumes prepositions and **postpositions**. In **traditional grammar**, lexical categories are given **notional definitions**, i.e. they are characterized in terms of their semantic content. For example, *noun* is defined as 'the name of a person, place or thing', *verb* is defined as an 'action word', and *adjective* is defined as 'a word expressing a property or attribute'. In modern linguistics, however, they are defined morphosyntactically in terms of their grammatical properties.

Nouns may be classified in a number of ways. There is a fundamental contrast between nouns that refer uniquely to particular entities or individuals and those that do not; the best example of the first kind of noun is a proper name, e.g. *Sam*, *Elizabeth*, *Paris* or *London*, and nouns of this type are referred to as **proper nouns**. Nouns which do not refer to unique individuals or entities are called **common nouns**, e.g. *dog*, *table*, *fish*, *car*, *pencil*, *water*. One of the important differences between proper and common nouns in a language like English is that common nouns normally take an article, while proper nouns do not, e.g. *The boy left* versus **The Sam left* (cf. **Boy left* versus *Sam left*). Common nouns may be divided into **mass nouns** and **count nouns**. Count nouns, as the name implies, denote countable entities, e.g. *seven chairs*, *six pencils*, *three dogs*, *many cars*. Mass nouns, on the other hand, are not readily countable in their primary senses, e.g. **two waters*, **four butters*, **six snows*. In order to make them countable, it is necessary to add what is sometimes called a 'measure word', which delimits a specific amount of the substance, e.g. *two glasses/bottles/drops of water*, *four pats/sticks of butter*, *six shovelfuls of snow*. Measure words can be used with count nouns only when they are plural, e.g. **six boxes of pencil* versus *six boxes of pencils*, **two cups of peanut* versus *three jars of peanuts*. **Pronouns** are closely related to nouns, as they both function as NPs. Pronouns are traditionally characterized as 'substitutes' for nouns or as 'standing for' nouns, e.g. *John went to the store, and <u>he</u> bought some milk*, in which *he* substitutes or stands for *John* in the second clause. This, however, is true only of **third-person** pronouns like *he*, *she*, *it*, or *they*; it is not true of **first-person** pronouns like *I* or **second-person** pronouns like *you*. First- and second-person pronouns refer to or index the speaker and addressee in a speech event and do not replace or stand for a noun.

Verbs can likewise be categorized along a number of dimensions. One very important dimension which will be discussed in detail in chapters 2 and 3 is whether a verb takes just a subject (an **intransitive** verb), or a subject and a direct object (a **transitive** verb), or a subject, direct object and **indirect object** (a **ditransitive** verb). This will be referred to as the 'valence' of the verb. Another dimension concerns the kind of situation it represents. Some verbs represent static situations which do not involve anyone actually doing anything, e.g. *know* as in *Chris knows the answer*, or *see* as in *Pat sees Dana over by the bookcase*. Some symbolize actions, e.g. *run* as in *Kim ran around the track*, or *sing* as in *Leslie sang a beautiful aria*. Others refer to a change of state, e.g. *freeze* as in *The water froze* (the change in the state of the water is from liquid to solid), or *dry* as in *The clothes dried quickly* (the change in the state of the clothes is from wet to dry). Some represent complex situations involving an action plus a change of state, e.g. *break* as in *Larry broke the window with a rock* (Larry does something with a rock [action] which causes the window to break [change of state]). This classification of verbs is quite complex and is more appropriately in the domain of semantics rather than syntax. However, some syntactically relevant aspects of the meaning of verbs will be investigated in chapter 2.

Some examples of adjectives in English include *red, happy, tall, sick, interesting, beautiful,* and many others. Adjectives typically express properties of entities, e.g. *a* red *apple, a* tall *woman, a* beautiful *sunset.* Some properties are inherent attributes of an entity; for example, some apples are red because they are naturally so, whereas some barns are red because they have been painted red, not because they are inherently red. Hence color is an inherent property of apples but not of barns. Some languages signal this distinction overtly. In Spanish, for example, the adjective *feliz* means 'happy', and whether it is an inherent or permanent property of the person referred to is signaled by the verb it is used with, i.e. *Maria es feliz* 'Maria is happy (a happy person)' versus *Maria está feliz* 'Maria is happy (now, at this moment but not necessarily always)'. Spanish has two verbs meaning 'be', *ser* and *estar,* and one of the differences between them is that *ser* plus adjective (*es* in this example) is used to signify inherent or permanent attributes, while *estar* plus adjective (*está* in this example) serves to indicate non-permanent, transitory attributes.

English adverbs typically, but not always, end in *-ly,* e.g. *quickly, happily, beautifully, rapidly* and *carefully. Fast* and *friendly* are exceptions; *fast* is an adverb without *-ly* (it can also be an adjective), and *friendly,* despite the admonitions of road signs in Texas to 'drive friendly', is an adjective, e.g. *a* friendly *waiter.* Adverbs modify verbs, adjectives and even other adverbs, and they can be classified in terms of the nature of this modification; manner adverbs, for example, indicate the manner in which something is done, e.g. *The detective examined the crime scene carefully,* or *The ballerina danced beautifully,* while temporal adverbs, as the name implies, express when something happened, e.g. *Kim talked to Chris yesterday,* or *Dana will see Pat tomorrow. Yesterday* and *tomorrow* do not end in *-ly* and have the same form when functioning as an adverb that they have when functioning as a noun, e.g. *Yesterday was a nice day, Tomorrow will be very special.* The most common adverbial modifiers of adjectives and adverbs are words like *very, extremely, rather,* e.g. *a very tall tree, the extremely clever student, rather quickly.* This class of adverbs is referred to as **degree modifiers**.

Prepositions are adpositions that occur before their object, while postpositions occur after their object. English and Spanish have only prepositions, e.g. English *in, on, under, to,* Spanish *en, a, con,* whereas Japanese and Korean have only postpositions. German has both: *<u>in</u> dem Haus* 'in the house' (preposition *in*) versus *dem Haus gegenüber* 'over across from the house' (postposition *gegenüber*).

There are a number of minor categories. The category of **determiners** includes articles like *a* and *the,* and **demonstratives** like *this* and *that.* Determiners modify nouns in relation to their referential properties. Articles indicate roughly whether the speaker believes her interlocutor(s) can identify the referent of the NP or not; an **indefinite article** like *a(n)* signals that the speaker does not assume the interlocutor(s) can identify the referent of the NP, while a **definite article** like *the* indicates that the speaker does assume that the interlocutor(s) can identify it. Demonstratives, on the other hand, refer to entities in terms of their spatial proximity to the speaker; English *this* refers to an entity close to the speaker, while *that* refers to one farther away. (*Which book do you mean? This one here or that one over there?* versus **This one over there or that one here?*) Many languages make a three-way distinction: close to the speaker (English *this*, Spanish *esta* [FEM]), away from the speaker but not far (English *that*, Spanish *esa* [FEM]), and farther away from the speaker (archaic English *yon*, Spanish *aquella* [FEM]). These distinctions are also expressed by locative demonstratives, e.g. English *here*, German *hier*, Spanish *aqui* versus English *there*, German *da*, Spanish *ahí* versus English *yonder*, German *dort*, Spanish *allí*. **Quantifiers**, as the label implies, express quantity-related concepts. English quantifiers include *every*, *each*, *all*, *many*, and *few*, as well as the numerals *one*, *two*, *three*, etc., e.g. *every boy*, *many books*, *the seven sisters*. **Classifiers** serve to classify the nouns they modify in terms of shape, material, function, social status and other properties. They are found in many East and Southeast Asian and Mayan languages, among others. They are similar in many respect to the measure words that occur with English mass nouns, but they occur with all nouns regardless of the count–mass distinctions, e.g. Cantonese *yāt būi séui* [one CL water] 'one cup of water versus *yāt jā séui* 'a jug of water', versus *yāt jēun séui* 'a bottle of water' with a mass noun, *nī ga dihnlóuh* [this CL computer] 'this computer' (classified as machine) versus *nī bouh dihnlóuh* 'this computer' (classified as model) versus *nī go dihnlóuh* 'this computer' (classified as object) with a count noun (Matthews and Yip 1994). **Conjunctions**, like *and*, *but* and *or*, serve to link the elements in a conjoined expression. There are conjoined NPs, e.g. *a boy and his dog*, conjoined verbs, e.g. *Leslie danced and sang*, and conjoined adjectives, e.g. *Lisa is tall and slender*. All major lexical categories can be linked by conjunctions to form conjoined expressions; this will be discussed in more detail in chapters 3 and 4. **Complementizers** mark the dependent clause is a complex sentence, e.g. English *that* as in *Sally knows that Bill ate the last piece of pizza*. The final category is **particles**, which is a classification often given to elements which do not fall into any of the other categories. Many particles have primarily **discourse** functions, e.g. English *indeed*, German *doch*, Spanish *entonces*.

There is an important opposition that divides lexical categories into two general classes, based on whether the membership of the class can readily be increased or not. Languages can usually increase their stock of nouns, for example, by borrowing nouns from other languages or creating new ones through **compounding** (e.g. *black* + *board* yields *blackboard*) or other morphological means (e.g. *rapid* + *-ly* = *rapidly*), but they do not normally create or borrow new adpositions, conjunctions or determiners. Lexical categories such as noun and verb whose membership can be enlarged are termed **open class** categories, whereas categories such as adposition, determiner or conjunction, which have small, fixed membership, are called **closed class** categories.

The definitions of lexical categories given so far are primarily the notional ones from traditional grammar. These definitions seem intuitively quite reasonable to speakers of Indo-European languages, and they seem to correlate nicely with the syntactic functions of the different parts of speech. Let us define three very general syntactic functions: **argument**, modifier and **predicate**. In a sentence like *the teacher read an interesting book*, *the teacher* and *an interesting book* are the arguments, *read* is the predicate, and *the*, *an* and *interesting* are modifiers. Similarly, in *Kim is tall*, *Kim* is the argument and *is tall* is the predicate. The term 'argument' here includes NPs and PPs functioning as subject, direct object or indirect object. The notions of predicate and argument will be discussed in more detail in the next chapter, but for now one can say simply that in a sentence the predicate expresses the state of affairs that the referents of the arguments are involved in. (The terms 'predicate' and 'argument' are also used in semantics with a different meaning; they are being used here and elsewhere to refer to syntactic notions, unless otherwise noted.) It is usual to distinguish 1-place, 2-place and 3-place predicates, depending on how many participants there are in the state of affairs depicted by the predicate. Being sick is a state of affairs involving only one participant, hence *be sick* is a 1-place predicate which takes one argument, e.g. *Kim is sick.* In *the teacher destroyed the note*, there is an action of destroying involving a teacher and a note. Destroying involves a destroyer and something destroyed; hence *destroy* is a 2-place predicate and takes two arguments. Finally, giving involves a giver, something given and a recipient, and therefore *give* is a 3-place predicate and takes three arguments, e.g. *The teacher gave an interesting book to Kim.* Given these distinctions, it seems intuitively clear that nouns would be arguments, verbs would be predicates and adjectives would be modifiers, and this is in fact the case very often.

But not always. Nouns and adjectives can function as part of a predicate, as in *Dana is a phonologist* and *Chris was sick.* Even though they are part of the predicate, they are still formally distinct from verbs; they do not take **tense suffixes** like verbs do, i.e. **Dana phonologists* or **Chris sicked.* The **copula** *be*, a kind of verb, carries these verbal inflections. Contrast this with the situation in Lakhota, in which nouns and adjective-like words do bear verbal inflections when functioning as predicates, in this instance **agreement** in **number** with the subject.

(1.5) a. Wičháša ki hená lową́-pi. Lakhota
man the those sing-PL
'Those men are singing.'[1]
a′. Lakhóta ki hená lową́-pi.
Sioux the those sing-PL
'Those Siouxs (Indians) are singing.'
b. Wičháša ki hená lakhóta-pi.
man the those Sioux-PL
'Those men are Siouxs (Indians).'
b′. Lakhóta ki hená wičháša-pi.
Sioux the those man-PL
'Those Siouxs (Indians) are men.'
c. Wičháša ki hená khúža-pi.
man the those sick-PL
'Those men are sick.'

[1] In most examples from languages other than English, there will be an interlinear **gloss** with a translation for each meaningful element in the sentence directly under it as well as a free translation into English in the third line. In the interlinear gloss, the translation will be lined up directly under the element being translated. Complex words will be broken up into their meaningful parts (see section 1.3 below) separated by hyphens, and the translation for each part will be joined to the translations for the other parts by hyphens and placed below the whole word. Thus in (1.5a), for example, *wičháša* means 'man', *ki* means 'the' and *hená* means 'those'; the last word, *lową́pi*, is broken up into two parts, *lową́* and *pi*, which are linked by a hyphen, and each part is translated (*lową́* means 'sing' and *pi* means 'plural subject'), with the translations linked by a corresponding hyphen and placed below the Lakhota word. If an element requires a translation involving more than one English word, the words will be joined by a '.', e.g. 'was.washed' in (2.4a). Finally, grammatical notions like tense and number are glossed using abbreviations which are listed at the beginning of the book.

Nouns in Lakhota do not normally carry any indication of number; the only way to tell that the NP containing *wičháša* 'man' is **plural** in (1.5a) is by means of the plural demonstrative *hená* 'those' (cf. *hé* 'that'). In particular, the plural suffix *-pi* is impossible on the noun *wičháša* in (1.5a); based on (1.5a), (1.5a′), one could conclude that it occurs only on verbs. But this would be incorrect, as the sentences in (1.5b, c) show. Nouns like *wičháša* 'man' do take *-pi* when they function as a predicate, rather than as an argument. Hence nouns in Lakhota seem to function readily as predicates, something their English counterparts do not do. Adjective-like words also function directly as predicates, as (c) illustrates; there is no copular element analogous to English *be* in either of these sentence types. Verbs and adjective-like words can also serve as arguments in Lakhota, as in (1.6).

(1.6) a. Hokšíla ki hená čhéya-pi. Lakhota
boy the those cry-PL
'Those boys are crying.'
b. Čhéya ki hená hokšíla-pi.
cry the those boy-PL
'The ones crying are boys.'
c. Khúža ki hená wičháša-pi. (cf. (1.5c))
sick the those man-PL
'The sick ones are men.'

The verb *čhéya* 'cry' serves as the predicate in (1.6a) and the argument in (1.6b). Note that in the English translation the verb *cry* cannot simply function as the subject; it must, rather, occur in a complex expression *the ones crying*. In Lakhota, by contrast, *hokšíla* 'boy' and *čhéya* 'cry' simply exchange positions in the sentence without any formal modification. The same is true of the noun *wičháša* 'man' and the adjective-like word *khúža* 'sick' in (1.6c). Thus, the expected correlations between noun and argument, verb and predicate and adjective and modifier are not as strong in Lakhota as they are in English.

An even more striking example of this lack of correlation between lexical class and syntactic function can be seen in Nootka, a Wakashan language spoken on Vancouver Island in British Columbia, Canada (Swadesh 1939).

(1.7) a. Wała:k-ma qo:ʔas-ʔi. Nootka
go-3sgPRES man-the
'The man is going.'
a′. Qo:ʔas-ma wała:k-ʔi.
man-3sgPRES go-the
'The one going is a man.'
a″. Qo:ʔas-ma.
man-3sgPRES
'He is a man.'
b. ʔi:ḥ-ma qo:ʔas-ʔi.
large-3sgPRES man-the
'The man is large.'
b′. Qo:ʔas-ma ʔi:ḥ-ʔi.
man-3sgPRES big-the
'The large one is a man.'

c. Ciqšƛ-ma ʔo:kwiɬ qo:ʔas-ʔi.
speak-3sgPRES to man-the
'He speaks to the man.'

c′. ʔi:ḥ-ma ciqšƛ-ʔi.
large-3sgPRES speak-the
'The one speaking is large.'

c″. ʔo:kwiɬ-ma qo:ʔas-ʔi.
to-3sgPRES man-the
'He is [in relation] to the man.'

d. Waɬa:k-ma ʔatḥiya.
go-3sgPRES night
'He is going at night.'

d′. ʔatḥiya-ma waɬa:k-ʔi.
night-3sgPRES go-the
'His going is at night.'

The basic pattern in these Nootka sentences is PREDICATE-*ma* ARGUMENT-*ʔi*, with *-ma* signalling both tense and subject agreement in terms of **person** and number. The sentences in (1.7a), (1.7a′) and (1.7b), (1.7b′) look like their Lakhota counterparts in (1.5) and (1.6). The striking examples are in (1.7c) and (1.7d). (1.7c) contains a preposition, *ʔo:kwiɬ* 'to', and in (1.7c″) it functions as the predicate, as indicated by its occurring first in the sentence with the suffix *-ma.* In (1.7d) there is an adverb, *ʔatḥiya* 'at night', and in (1.7d′) it is the predicate. Thus in Nootka, the expected correlations between lexical category and syntactic function appear to be even weaker than in Lakhota.

This has important implications for the traditional view of lexical categories. This view assumes that the semantics of words predict their category and hence their function. The examples from Lakhota and Nootka call this seriously into question, since functioning syntactically as predicate, argument or modifier does not follow from the meaning of words as expected in many instances. Moreover, the first link in the chain of inference, from meaning to category, does not even hold up from a cross-linguistic perspective. The notional account assumes, at least implicitly, that the major lexical categories are universal, but this turns out not to be true for all of them. Every language has noun and verb as lexical categories, even Nootka. This reflects the fundamental role of reference and predication in communication. One of the most important functions of language is to allow speakers to depict states of affairs in the world, and in order for them to do this, there must be linguistic devices which refer to the participant(s) in a state of affairs and other devices which denote the action, event or situation in a state of affairs. Lexical items specialized for the first task are nouns, those specialized for the second are verbs. Even though in examples from Lakhota and Nootka verbs function as arguments (and hence as referring expressions) and nouns as predicates, it is nevertheless the case that the basic use of words like *wičháša* 'man' in Lakhota and *qo:ʔas* 'man' in Nootka is as an argument; similarly, the basic use of words like *čhéya* 'cry' in Lakhota and *waɬa:k* 'go' in Nootka is as a predicate.

What about the other major lexical categories? There are languages which lack adpositions altogether; they express the semantic content of prepositions and postpositions by means of the kind of suffixes on nouns in the Russian examples in (1.2) and (1.3). The concepts expressed by these endings are called '**case**', and the endings are called 'case markers'. Case will be discussed a great deal throughout this book. Russian has both case suffixes and prepositions, but Dyirbal, an Australian Aboriginal language (Dixon 1972), has only case suffixes and no adpositions at all. Hence the lexical category 'adposition' is not universal. It also appears that adjective is not universal. In Lakhota, for example, the words expressing properties like 'red', 'tall', 'big', etc., are formally verbs and have basically the same morphosyntactic properties as verbs, as the examples in (1.6) showed in part. Hence there is no reason to posit a category 'adjective' distinct from that of 'verb'; the words corresponding to adjectives in a language like English, e.g. *khúža* 'sick' in (1.5) and (1.6), are really a subtype of verb in Lakhota. In Dyirbal and Quechua, spoken in the northern Andes mountains in South America (Wölck 1987), on the other hand, words of this type have the same morphosyntactic properties as nouns, and therefore they should be analyzed as a subtype of nouns. Finally, there has been much less research done on adverbs cross-linguistically than the other major categories, and therefore it is difficult to draw any conclusions about their universality.

Thus, it appears that noun and verb are universal lexical categories, but adposition and adjective are not. It is crucial to keep in mind that when it is claimed that adjective is not a universally valid lexical category, it does not mean that there are languages which lack words expressing properties like 'red', 'big', 'happy', etc. Rather, it means that the words expressing these notions behave morphosyntactically like members of one of the other classes (verb in Lakhota, noun in Dyirbal and Quechua).

In modern linguistics, the determination of the category of a word is not based on its meaning but rather on its morphosyntactic behavior, i.e. the elements it cooccurs with and the morphosyntactic environment(s) it occurs in. Meaning is not irrelevant to the function of a word, but it does not reliably predict it either. The term which is used to refer to classes based on their morphosyntactic properties is **form class**. Consider the similarities and differences between common and proper nouns in English, which was initially characterized semantically. They are both a type of noun, because they both occur in the major morphosyntactic environments which nouns (and NPs) occur in, e.g. as the subject or direct object of a verb, as the object of a preposition in a PP, and with *be* as a **predicate nominal** (*The girl gave a book to the teacher, Pat introduced Kim to Dana*; *Max is my lawyer, My lawyer is Max*). Other form classes cannot occur in these positions, e.g. **The yellow put a clumsily on the receive*. However, they differ in that common nouns can be modified by determiners and adjectives, while proper nouns cannot, e.g. *a tall girl* versus **a tall Dana*. Furthermore, common nouns, if they are count nouns, can take plural inflection, while proper nouns cannot, e.g. *the tall girls* versus **Danas*. Thus there are both syntactic and morphological differences between common and proper nouns which can be used to distinguish them as belonging to two distinct subclasses of the category noun.

English verbs can be differentiated from the other major classes by both morphological and syntactic criteria. Morphologically, only verbs take the suffixes *-ing* 'progressive', *-ed* 'past tense', or 'past participle', *-s* 'third-person singular subject–present tense' and *-en* 'past participle'. Syntactically, they occupy a unique position in a clause, and they may be modified by adverbs but not by adjectives or demonstratives. There are no consistent morphological properties that characterize English adjectives; there are distinctive endings that some adjectives carry, e.g. *-y* as in *slimy* (related to the noun *slime*) or *tricky* (related to the noun *trick*), and *-ic* as in *toxic* (related to the noun *toxin*) or *metric* (related to the noun *meter*). Many adjectives take *-er* for their **comparative** forms, e.g. *taller, faster,* and *-est* for their **superlative** forms, e.g. *tallest, fastest.* However, many do not, e.g. **beautifuler,* **beautifulest*; these adjectives take *more* and *most* to indicate their comparative (*more beautiful*) and superlative (*most beautiful*) forms. English adjectives occupy a specific position within NPs, i.e. DEM-QNT-ADJ-N, as in *the seven tall trees* (**tall the seven trees,* **the tall seven trees*), and they may function predicatively only in combination with the copula *be*, e.g. *The tree is tall,* **The tree talls*). Finally, English adverbs, as noted earlier, often (but not always) end in *-ly*; they function only as modifiers (but never of nouns), e.g. *the* extremely *quick rabbit, the rabbit ran* very quickly, **the* quickly *rabbit,* and never as predicates, e.g. **The rabbit is* quickly.

This brief discussion of the morphosyntactic properties of the major English classes has not been exhaustive, but it does illustrate how morphological and syntactic criteria can be used to characterize the form classes in a language. Even though the criteria for the classes are ultimately morphosyntactic, the labels for the classes reflect the traditional notional distinctions. That is, after having established the existence of a form class based on the morphosyntactic properties of its members, the semantic properties of the prototypical members of the class determine the name of the class. Hence if the prototypical members of a class include elements that function as the name of a person, place or thing, then the class will be given the label 'noun'.

1.3 Morphology

Even though this book is about syntax and syntactic analysis, it is not possible to get very far without some basic knowledge about morphology. It was already shown in section 1.0 that some languages use morphology to express what other languages express syntactically, and in the previous section it was noted that the inflectional properties of words are relevant to determining their category. In this section some basic concepts of morphology and the basic techniques of morphological analysis will be introduced; both will play a role in the syntactic analyses in later chapters. The discussion will be limited to those aspects of morphology which are relevant to syntactic analysis; this is not intended to be a general introduction to this complex and important part of linguistics.

Morphology is concerned with the structure of words, and morphological analysis is the process by which linguists break complex words down into their component parts. Consider the Lakhota word *wahi*, which means 'I arrive'. Just looking at it by itself, it is not possible to determine whether it is a simple or complex form. If it is compared with another form, *yahi* 'you [**singular**] arrive', it can be seen immediately that there is a common part to each of the words, *-i, -hi* or *-ahi*, and a different part in each, *wah-, wa-* or *w-* and *yah-, ya-* or *y-*. It is clear that these are complex forms made up of more than one component. There are two parts to each: one meaning 'arrive', which is *-i, -hi* or *-ahi*, and the other meaning first-person singular ('I') or second-person singular ('you') subject. It is not possible to tell from just these two forms, however, exactly what the two components are, since there are at least three ways to divide up these forms. Is the form for 'arrive' *-i, hi* or *ahi*? Is the form for first-person singular subject *wah-, wa-* or *w-*? The answer to this question becomes somewhat clearer when the form *ųhi* 'we [**dual inclusive**] arrive' (i.e. 'you [sg] and I arrive') is examined. The common parts to the three forms are *-i* or *hi*, and this would seem to eliminate the *-ahi* possibility. But we are still left with two possibilities for 'arrive' and for 'I' (*wah-* or *wa-*), 'you' (*yah-* or *ya-*) and 'we [dl incl]' (*ųh-* or *ų-*). In order to resolve the issue, it would useful to look at some other verbs, as in (1.8).

(1.8)	a.	*wa*lową	'I sing'	Lakhota
	a′.	*ya*lową	'you [sg] sing'	
	b.	*wa*čhį	'I want'	
	b′.	*ya*čhį	'you [sg] want'	
	c.	*wa*ʔu	'I come'	
	c′.	*ya*ʔu	'you [sg] come'	
	d.	na*wa*žį	'I stand'	
	d′.	na*ya*ži	'you [sg] stand'	
	e.	a*wa*phe	'I wait'	
	e′.	a*ya*phe	'you [sg] wait'	

In the first example in each pair the only common semantic element is first-person singular subject, and the only form common to all of them is *wa-*. Similarly, in the primed examples in the set the only common semantic element is second-person singular subject, and the only form common to all of them is *ya-*. Therefore *wa-* must mean 'I' and *ya-* must mean 'you [singular]'. If 'I' and 'you' are *wa-* and *ya-*, respectively, then 'arrive' must be *-hi*, not *-i*. Moreover, this means that 'we [dual inclusive]' must be *ų-*, not *ųh-*. Thus, the correct analysis of the first three forms is *wa-* 'I', *ya-* 'you [sg]', *ų-* 'we [dl incl]' and *-hi* 'arrive'. It may further be concluded that *lową* means 'sing', *čhį* means 'want', *ʔu* means 'come', *nažį* means 'stand' and *aphe* means 'wait'. Each of these words *wahi*, *yahi* and *ųhi*, as well as those in (1.8), is composed of two meaningful parts, which are called **morphemes**. Morphemes are the smallest meaningful units in language. *Hi* cannot be broken down into *h* + *i*, nor can *wa-* or *ya-* be broken down into *w-* or *y-* + *a*; these smaller forms have no meaning. Hence, *wa-*, *ya-* and *hi*, as well as *ų-*, are all morphemes in Lakhota, as are *lową*, *čhį*, *ʔu*, *nažį* and *aphe*.

The part of the complex form to which a morpheme is added is called the **stem**. In these examples, the stems are *hi*, *lową*, *čhį*, *ʔu*, *nažį*, and *aphe*. Morphemes like *wa-* and *ya-* which occur before the stem are called **prefixes**. Morphemes which occur after the stem are called suffixes; examples of suffixes can be found in the Russian sentences in (1.2) and (1.3), i.e. the markers *-a* and *-u*, and in the Lakhota examples in (1.5) and (1.6), i.e. *-pi* 'plural'. In (1.8d), (1.8e) *wa-* occurs within the stem itself; in these forms it is an **infix**. The general term which covers prefixes, infixes and suffixes is **affix**.

This example has been very simple, but it illustrates the basic principle used in breaking words down into their component morphemes: *look for recurring forms that correlate with consistent meanings*. In all of the Lakhota words examined above, the form *wa-* correlates with the meaning 'first-person singular subject', the form *ya-* correlates with the meaning 'second-person singular subject', and the form correlates *ų-* with the meaning 'first dual inclusive subject'. Similarly, in comparing (1.8a) and (1.8a′), the form *lową* consistently correlates with the meaning 'sing'.

The basic principle of morphological analysis stated above ('look for recurring forms that correlate with consistent meanings'), requires four very important qualifications.

The first is that a single meaning, e.g. plural, may be expressed by several different forms. Consider the following simple example from English.

(1.9) a. dog /dɔg/ a′. dogs /dɔgz/
b. cat /kæt/ b′. cats /kæts/
c. rose /roz/ c′. roses /rozəz/

The forms in the second column have a consistent semantic difference from the forms in the first column, but there does not appear to be a consistent formal distinction correlating with the semantic difference. Rather, there is /z/, /s/ and /əz/. However, if one looked at a large number of English nouns, one would find that nouns ending in a voiced sound take /z/ to indicate plural, that nouns ending in a voiceless, non-sibilant sound take /s/, and that nouns ending in a sibilant take /əz/. These forms are clearly related phonologically, and the form of the plural suffix is predictable from the phonological shape of the end of the word to which it is added. Hence these three forms may be viewed as conditioned variants of a single morpheme; they are referred to as its **allomorphs**. They are phonologically conditioned allomorphs, since the choice of allomorph is determined by the phonological shape of the stem. There are other allomorphs of the plural morpheme which are not phonologically conditioned. For example, the plural of *box* is *boxes*, but the plural of *ox* is *oxen*, not **oxes*. The plural of *ox* is said to be morphologically conditioned, because it is not phonologically predictable and is an idiosyncratic property of the word *ox*. Other examples of morphologically conditioned plurals in English include *mice* for *mouse* and *teeth* for *tooth*.

Words like *mice* and *teeth* illustrate the second qualification: meanings need not be represented by segmentable parts of words. With words like *dogs* (/dɔgz/) and *cats* (/kæts/), it is easy to break them up into two parts, one meaning 'dog' or 'cat' and the other meaning 'plural'. But it is not obvious that *mice* (/mays/) and *teeth* (/tiθ/) can be broken down into two comparable parts, one meaning 'mouse' or 'tooth' and the other meaning 'plural'. Forms like these have posed profound problems for morphological analysts and theorists alike. For the purposes of this book, it is enough to state that such a form is morphologically conditioned but unsegmentable (cf. *oxen*, which is morphologically conditioned but segmentable) and to state the meanings expressed by the form.

When there is a group of phonologically conditioned allomorphs like those of the English plural in (1.9), it is customary to select one of them as the basic allomorph to represent the morpheme. Typically, the allomorph occurring in the widest range of environments is taken as basic, although other factors may come into play. With respect to the three allomorphs in (1.9), /z/ occurs in the greatest number of environments, and therefore it is a good candidate for the basic allomorph.

As noted in the initial discussion in this section, there is a choice as to how to divide up a complex form. With respect to Lakhota *wahi* 'I arrive' and *yahi* 'you [sg] arrive', there were three initial hypotheses: *w-* 'I', *y-* 'you' and *-ahi* 'arrive', versus *wa-* 'I', *ya-* 'you' and *-hi* 'arrive', versus *wah-* 'I', *yah-* 'you' and *-i* 'arrive'. Given just these two forms, there is no reason to choose one analysis over the others, but when the form *ųhi* 'we [dl incl] arrive' is considered, the possibilities are reduced to two, *-hi* or *-i*, etc. Consideration of the data in (1.8) leads to the conclusion that the simplest analysis of all three forms is *wa-* 'I', *ya-* 'you', *ų-* 'we [dl incl]' and *-hi* 'arrive'. Why is this the simplest analysis? Because it avoids positing allomorphs for any of the morphemes.

If the analysis of 'arrive' as being *-i* were maintained, then one would have to claim that *wa-* 'I' has an allomorph *wah-* before the verb *-i*. While such an alternation is not impossible, positing it nevertheless results in a more complex account than the alternative analysis, which does not postulate any allomorphic variation for any of the morphemes. Hence, all things being equal, the simplest analysis is to be preferred, and one criterion for simplicity is positing the least amount of allomorphic variation compatible with the facts.

Not only can a single meaning be expressed by multiple forms, but a single form can express multiple meanings. This is the third qualification to the basic principle of morphological analysis. For example, in Russian the *-a* suffix on *učitel'nica* 'teacher' in (1.2) expresses three distinct concepts: **nominative** case, singular number, and **feminine gender**. The *-s* suffix on verbs in English likewise expresses three concepts: third-person subject, singular subject, present tense. Thus, even though there are simple instances in which a single form consistently pairs with a single meaning, the kinds of complexities involving allomorphic variation and multiple concepts in a single form are very common.

The fourth qualification is that structural patterns in a language may require the analyst to posit that a meaning is expressed by the *absence* of a form. Consider the following **paradigm** for the verb *hi* 'arrive' in Lakhota.

(1.10)	a. wahi	'I arrive'	Lakhota
	b. yahi	'you [sg] arrive'	
	c. hi	'he/she arrives'	
	d. ųhi	'we [dl incl] arrive'	
	e. ųhipi	'we [pl] arrive'	
	f. yahipi	'you [pl] arrive'	
	g. hipi	'they arrive'	

It has already been established that *wa-* signals first-person singular subject, *ya-* second-person subject and *ų-* first-person dual inclusive subject, and in (1.5) and (1.6) it was shown that *-pi* indicates plural, which is the case here as well. What, then, signals third person singular subject? The absence of *-pi* in (1.10a)–(1.10d) indicates that the subject is non-plural, and it is the absence of *wa-*, *ya-* and *ų-* that signals that the forms in (1.10c) and (1.10g) are third person. Thus, third person is marked by the absence of a prefix, and it is customary to represent this by '∅'. Hence the form for 'he/she arrives' would be *∅-hi*. This meaningful absence of a phonological form is called a **zero** morpheme. Zero morphemes are normally posited only within paradigms such as that in (1.10) in which one form is distinctive by virtue of the absence of an affix.

Morphemes may be divided into two general classes: **lexical morphemes**, which have substantive semantic content, e.g. English *dog*, *rose*, *cat*, or Lakhota *hi* 'arrive', and **grammatical morphemes**, which lack substantive semantic content and express grammatical notions like person, number, gender, tense or case, e.g. English *-s* on verbs, Lakhota *wa-*, or Russian *-a*. The lexical versus grammatical opposition correlates with the earlier distinction made between open and closed classes: typically, lexical morphemes are open-class items, while grammatical morphemes are closed-class items. This opposition also relates to another important contrast, that between **free morphemes** and **bound morphemes**. Free morphemes are elements that can stand alone as independent words, e.g. *dog*, *car*, *to*, *the* and *or*, whereas bound morphemes cannot occur by themselves as independent words, e.g. *-s*, *-ing*, *-ed* in English. Bound morphemes are usually grammatical morphemes, while free morphemes may be both lexical and grammatical, as the above examples from English illustrate. There are languages in which lexical morphemes can be considered bound morphemes, in that they cannot occur without an accompanying grammatical morpheme. In Russian, for example, *vide-* means 'see', which makes it a lexical morpheme, but it is not a free morpheme, since it cannot occur as a complete word without the addition of a suffix indicating its tense and subject agreement, e.g. *-l-a* 'PAST-FEMsg', yielding *videla* 'saw'. These distinctions are summarized in Table 1.1.

Table 1.1. *Types of morphemes*

	Free	Bound
Lexical	*dog*, *sing*; Lakhota *hokšíla*, *čhéya*	Russian *vide-*
Grammatical	*the*, *a*; Lakhota *ki*, *hená*	*-s*, *-ing*, *-ed*; Lakhota *wa-*, *-pi*

Since the focus of this book is on syntax, primary concern will be given to grammatical morphemes which express syntactic notions, e.g. subject, or syntactically relevant notions, e.g. person agreement on a verb.

In the next chapter, the notion of subject and grammatical relations in general will be examined.

Notes and suggested readings

For an excellent overview of systems of lexical categories across languages, see Schachter (1985). Hopper and Thompson (1984), Langacker (1991) and Croft (1991) argue for the universality of noun and verb as lexical categories based on the fundamental role of reference and predication in language. Jacobsen (1979) takes a detailed look at Nootkan languages and argues that there is evidence in favor of postulating noun and verb as lexical categories in these languages. Dixon (1977a) investigates the category 'adjective' cross-linguistically.

An excellent introduction to morphological analysis is Nida (1946); two more recent texts, which include discussion of morphological theory, are Bauer (1988) and Spencer (1991).

Exercises

1. Pretend the italicized nonsense words in the following sentences are real words of English. Identify the form class of each one, and state the morphosyntactic properties of each that lead you to assign it to a particular category. [section 1.2]

   (1) a. The dog *wugged* the ball.
   b. The dog is *wugging* the ball.
   c. The dog likes to *wug* the ball.
   d. The dog gently *wugged* the ball.
   e. *The *wug* kicked the ball.
   f. *The dog chased the *wug* cat.

(2) a. The tall *blick* sat by the river.
b. The *blicks* played in the park.
c. Mary sent a present to her favorite *blick*.
d. Sam is not a *blick*.
e. *Max *blicked* the cat.
f. *The *blick* animal ran away.

(3) a. A *nork* person walked by the car.
b. Mary is very *nork*.
c. *Sam *norks*.
d. *The *nork* called me yesterday.

(4) a. *Li* cat slept by the fire.
b. I bought *li* three interesting books.
c. Mary didn't like *li* one.
d. I don't care for *li*.
e. *Two *li* dogs barked at the cat.
f. *Sam *lis* every day.

(5) a. Max walked *blishly* down the corridor.
b. Max walked down the corridor *blishly*.
c. *Blishly*, Max walked down the corridor.
d. Sam did so extremely *blishly*.
e. *Pat is *blishly*.
f. *The *blishly* woman looked unhappy.

(6) a. Larry placed the book *za* the table.
b. *Za* the table Sam found his glasses.
c. **Za* green book fell on the floor.
d. *I don't like *za*.
e. *Sam *zas* every day.
f. *Sam found his gloves *za*.

(7) a. Anna bought *nace* rare books.
b. I liked *nace* of them.
c. *Nace* left the party early.
d. I thought she bought too *nace*.
e. *Anna bought rare *nace* books.
f. *Sam *naces* every morning.
g. *The tall red *nace* fell off the shelf.

2. In the following verse from Lewis Carroll's famous poem *Jabberwocky*, identify the form class of each of the italicized words. State the morphosyntactic properties that lead you to assign it to a particular category. Give two different analyses of the words in the last line. [section 1.2]

'Twas *brillig*, and the *slithy toves*
  Did *gyre* and *gimble* in the *wabe*;
All *mimsy* were the *borogroves*,
  And the *mome raths outgrabe*.

3. Consider the following examples from English:
(1) The **break** is just above the knee.
(2) Please **maple syrup** your pancakes from the dispenser on the table. (sign in a cafe in Adelaide, South Australia)
(3) The **climb** up the north face is very difficult and dangerous.
(4) Kinko's, the new way to **office**. (advertisement)

(5) The referee **book**ed the player for the foul.
(6) A good **cry** often makes you feel better.

What are the implications of examples like these for the discussion of English lexical categories in section 1.2? Compare these with the examples from Nootka and Lakhota; is English as flexible in terms of the functions of its lexical categories as these languages? [section 1.2]

4. In the following Italian sentences, what formal properties do the nouns, articles, adjectives, adverbs and verbs have? Do they have any special morphological marking indicating their category? Do they have any specific or special syntactic properties? With respect to the latter, assume simple **declarative** utterances and ignore **elliptical** answers to questions, e.g. Q: *How does Fred run?* A: *Slowly*, and **vocative** expressions, e.g. *'Hey man!'*. [section 1.2]

(1)	La bella ragazza parla rapidamente.	'The pretty girl speaks rapidly.'
(2)	Il giovane ragazzo parla chiaramente.	'The young boy speaks clearly.'
(3)	Le belle ragazze parlano chiaramente.	'The pretty girls speak clearly.'
(4)	I giovani ragazzi parlano rapidamente.	'The young boys speak rapidly.'
(5)	Parlano.	'They speak.'
(6)	*I parlano.	
(7)	Parlano rapidamente.	'They speak rapidly.'
(8)	*Bella ragazza parla.	
(9)	Una bella ragazza parla.	'A pretty girl speaks.'
(10)	*Bella parla.	
(11)	La macchina rapida arriva.	'The fast car arrives.'
(12)	Le macchine rapide arrivano.	'The fast cars arrive.'
(13)	Il ragazzo povero arriva.	'The poor boy arrives.'
(14)	Chiaramente parla.	'He/she speaks clearly.'
(15)	La bella arriva.	'The pretty one arrives.'
(16)	Il giovane parla.	'The young one speaks.'
(17)	*Bella.	
(18)	*I.	
(19)	*Chiaramente.	
(20)	Parla.	'He/she speaks.'
(21)	Arrivano.	'They arrive.'
(22)	*Ragazzo.	
(23)	*Macchina.	

5. Break down the following words from Ayacucho Quechua (Parker 1969) into their constituent morphemes and state their meaning. [section 1.3]

(1)	Rimani.	'I speak.'
(2)	Warmita rikun.	'He/she sees the woman.'
(3)	Runtuta mikurqani.	'I ate an egg.'
(4)	Runa rimarqa.	'The man spoke.'
(5)	Warmi rikun.	'The woman sees him/her.'
(6)	Runakuna rimarqaku.	'The men spoke.'
(7)	Runata rikuni.	'I see the man.'
(8)	Warmikuna rimanku.	'The women speak.'
(9)	Runtuta mikuni.	'I eat an egg.'
(10)	Runa hatun.	'The man is big.'
(11)	Warmikunata rikurqani.	'I saw the women.'
(12)	Runa daliwan.	'The man hits me.'
(13)	Rimarqani.	'I spoke.'
(14)	Runtu hatun.	'The egg is big.'

(15)	Warmi rikurqawa.	'The woman saw me.'
(16)	Rikurqa.	'He/she saw him/her.'
(17)	Riman.	'He/she speaks.'
(18)	Warmikuna rikurqawaku.	'The women saw me.'
(19)	Warmi runtuta dalirqa.	'The woman hit an egg.'
(20)	Mikurqaku.	'They ate.'

What would the following forms mean:
(21) Mikun.
(22) Warmi runata rikurqa.
(23) Runata dalirqani.
(24) Runa rikurqawa.

How would you say the following in Ayacucho Quechua?
(25) The men saw an egg.
(26) The woman ate an egg.
(27) The women hit [PAST] the man.
(28) The men see the woman.

6. Break down the words in the following sentences from Hungarian (de Groot 1989) into their constituent morphemes and state their meaning. If a morpheme has more than one allomorph, give all of them. [section 1.3]

(1)	János a könyvet Marinak adta.	'John gave the book to Mary.'
(2)	A könyv az asztal alatt van.	'The book is under the table.'
(3)	Mari Jánosnak adta az órát.	'Mary gave the clock to John.'
(4)	A gyerek látta Marit.	'The child saw Mary.'
(5)	Az óra az asztal fölött van.	'The clock is above the table.'
(6)	Mari látja Jánost.	'Mary sees John.'
(7)	A gyerek tette az órát az asztalhoz.	'The child put the clock near the table.'
(8)	Mari Jánosnak adja a könyvet.	'Mary gives the book to John.'
(9)	A level az asztal alatt van.	'The letter is under the table.'
(10)	János a könyvet az asztalra tette.	'John put the book on the table.'
(11)	Mari látta a gyereket.	'Mary saw the child.'
(12)	A könyv van az asztal mögött.	'The book is behind the table.'
(13)	Mari írja a levelet.	'Mary writes the letter.'
(14)	Mari a gyereknek adta az órát.	'Mary gave the clock to the child.'
(15)	János írta a levelet.	'John wrote the letter.'

CHAPTER 2

Grammatical relations

2.0 Introduction

Chapter 1 introduced the notion of relational structure, which concerns primarily the role of concepts like subject, direct object and indirect object in grammatical systems, and in this chapter the focus is on this aspect of syntax. The three grammatical relations played a very important role in traditional grammar, and they are a significant component of a number of contemporary syntactic theories, as will be seen in chapter 6. The reason for this is that many important morphosyntactic phenomena appear to involve grammatical relations, and consequently these notions would be important for the description and ultimately for the explanation of these phenomena. One of the things that will become apparent in this chapter is that the roles that notions like subject and direct object play in the grammars of different languages is surprisingly variable.

As an example of the role that grammatical relations can play in syntactic description, consider **finite** verb agreement in English. It is traditionally described as being **triggered** by the subject of the sentence. It is exemplified in (2.1).

(2.1) a. The boy knows the answer.
b. The boys know the answers.

How does one know that it is the subject NP rather than the direct object NP which triggers agreement? After all, in (2.1a) both NPs are singular and in (2.1b) both are plural. The answer can be seen clearly in (2.2).

(2.2) a. The boy knows/*know the answers.
b. The boys know/*knows the answer.

In (2.2a), the subject NP is singular and the direct object NP is plural, and the verb shows singular rather than plural agreement; similarly in (2.2b), the subject NP is plural and the direct object is singular, and the verb shows plural rather than singular agreement. Hence it must be the subject, not the direct object, which triggers agreement. Suppose one were to say that it is not necessarily the subject which is the trigger but rather the first NP in the sentence; how would one show that this is not the correct analysis? The crucial examples which argue against this hypothesis are given in (2.3).

(2.3) a. Those boys Chris does/*do not like.
a′. That boy the girls do/*does not like.
b. Which teacher do/*does the girls like?
b′. Which students does/*do the teacher like?

In these sentences the verb does not agree with the first NP in the sentence; rather, it agrees with the subject. When the initial NP is plural and the subject NP singular, as in (2.3a), (2.3b′), the verb shows singular agreement. Similarly, when the initial NP is singular and the subject plural, as in (2.3a′), (2.3b), the verb shows plural agreement. Note that the sentences in (2.3b), (2.3b′) show that the rule is not simply 'the verb agrees with the immediately preceding NP'; while that is true in (2.1), (2.2) and (2.3a), (2.3a′), it is not true in these two sentences. Hence the simplest and most straightforward hypothesis is the initial one: in English a tensed verb agrees with the subject.

In the remainder of this chapter grammatical relations will be investigated. In section 2.1, syntactic or grammatical relations will be distinguished from the **semantic roles** (also called '**thematic relations**' or '**theta roles**') that the arguments bear to the predicate. In section 2.2, the properties that define the different grammatical relations will be examined, and in section 2.3 languages whose systems of grammatical relations are rather different from the ones found in the familiar Indo-European languages will be discussed.

2.1 Grammatical relations versus semantic roles

In English and many other languages, it is possible to express an event in more than one way using the same words. For example, if one wanted to report the state of affairs in which a woman had used soap and water to make some clothes clean, one could say either *The woman washed the clothes* or *The clothes were washed by the woman*. In both sentences the woman is the doer of the action, the washer, and the clothes are the thing affected by the action, the washed; but they differ in how the NPs referring to the woman and to the clothes are realized syntactically. In the first sentence, the NP referring to the doer of the action is the subject and the NP referring to the thing affected is the direct object, while in the second the NP referring to the thing affected is the subject and the NP referring to the doer of the action is the object of the preposition *by*. This contrast is captured in the notion of 'voice': the first sentence is in **active** voice, while the second is in passive voice. Another example of the active–passive contrast can be found in the following examples from Malagasy, an Austronesian language spoken on Madagascar (Keenan 1976a). As in a Toba Batak sentence with a transitive verb (see (1.1)), the basic word order in Malagasy is VOS, with the subject (*ny vehivavy* 'the woman') following the verb (*nanasa* 'washed') and the direct object (*ny lamba* 'the clothes') in (2.4a).

(2.4) a. Nanasa ny lamba ny vehivavy. Malagasy
washed the clothes the woman
'The woman washed the clothes.'
b. Nosasan-ny vehivavy ny lamba.
was.washed-the woman the clothes
'The clothes were washed by the woman.'

The NP referring to the doer of the washing will be termed the '**agent**' and the NP referring to the entity being washed will be termed the '**patient**'. Hence in the active sentence in (2.4a) and its English translation, the agent (*ny vehivavy* 'the woman') is the subject and the patient (*ny lamba* 'the clothes') is the direct object, whereas in the passive sentence in (2.4b) and its English translation, the patient is the subject and the agent is not the subject. The subject NP of (2.4a), *ny vehivavy* 'the woman', is compounded with the verb in the passive sentence in (2.4b); there is no preposition analogous to English *by* marking it. Agent and patient are semantic roles and are an important part of the meaning of the sentence; because *ny vehivavy* 'the woman' is the agent and *ny lamba* 'the clothes' is the patient, the sentences in (2.4) refer to a state of affairs in the world in which a specific woman was engaged in the activity of washing some specific clothes. This state of affairs can be referred to by either the active or the passive form of the sentence. Thus, grammatical relations like subject and direct object are independent of semantic roles like agent and patient: in both English and Malagasy, the subject of a sentence can be the agent (active voice) or the patient (passive voice), the agent can be subject or non-subject, and the patient can be direct object or subject.

There are, then, different types of relations holding between a predicate and its argument(s) in a sentence: grammatical relations like subject and direct object, and semantic roles like agent and patient. (There is no agreement among syntacticians or semanticists as to the 'correct' set of semantic roles; hence this discussion should not be taken as definitive but rather as introducing the most commonly used semantic roles.) Each verb or other predicate has a certain number of arguments, each of which bears a distinct semantic role; this will be referred to as a verb's **argument structure**. The Malagasy verb *sasan* 'wash' can have a third argument, *ny savony* 'the soap', as in (2.5a).

(2.5) a. Manasa ny lamba amin-ny savony ny vehivavy. — Malagasy
washes the clothes with the soap the woman
'The woman washes the clothes with the soap.'
b. Anasan-ny vehivavy ny lamba ny savony.
be.washed.with-the woman the clothes the soap
'The soap is washed the clothes with by the woman,' (literal) or
'The soap is used by the woman to wash the clothes.'

This NP does not function as subject, direct object or indirect object in (2.5a), and it is marked by the preposition *amin* 'with'. Its semantic role is usually termed '**instrument**'. It can function as subject in a special voice form, as (2.5b) shows; this voice form is distinct from the passive, both morphologically and in terms of the argument which occurs as subject, and it is known as the '**circumstantial**' voice. Thus, the verb *sasan* 'wash' can have three semantic arguments (agent, patient, instrument), and any of the three can serve as subject of a particular voice form. The argument structure of *sasan* 'wash' would be represented as *sasan* 'wash' <Agent Patient (Instrument)>. Parenthesis indicates that the instrument is optional, as (2.4a) shows.

It would be useful to make two terminological distinctions at this point. NPs functioning as subject, direct object or indirect object will be referred to as '**terms**'. Those NPs not bearing one of these grammatical relations will be referred to as 'non-terms'. In (2.5a), *ny vehivavy* 'the woman' and *ny lamba* 'the clothes' are terms, while *ny* *savony* 'the soap' is a non-term. In (2.5b), on the other hand, *ny savony* 'the soap' and *ny lamba* 'the clothes' are terms, and *ny vehivavy* 'the woman' is a non-term. The second distinction is between direct and **oblique** arguments. Direct arguments are those which are not marked by an adposition, while oblique arguments are so marked. Hence in (2.5a), *ny vehivavy* 'the woman' and *ny lamba* 'the clothes' are direct arguments, while *ny savony* 'the soap' is an oblique argument, as it is marked by the preposition *amin* 'with'. Terms tend strongly to be direct arguments, but there are exceptions. In an English sentence like *Chris gave the notebook to Dana*, for example, the indirect object *Dana* is an oblique argument, since it is marked by the preposition *to.* In Malagasy sentences with three terms, e.g. (2.47a), all three NPs are direct.

While there are only three grammatical relations, there are many semantic roles, and which semantic role an NP has depends upon the meaning of the verb it occurs with. Agents are typically animate and normally instigate the actions they perform and do so wilfully and intentionally. Some verbs, e.g. *murder*, require the agent to act intentionally (**Sam murdered his neighbor accidentally*), whereas others allow both intentional and unintentional agents, e.g. *kill, break* (*Sam killed his neighbor intentionally/ accidentally*). A patient argument is either in a state or condition or undergoes a change of state or condition, e.g. *The bird is dead* (state) versus *The bird died* (change of state). Semantically similar to patients are **theme** arguments, which refer to entities which are located or which undergo a change of location; they also denote entities which are possessed or which undergo a change of possession. In *Chris gave the notebook to Dana, the notebook* is a theme, not a patient, because it undergoes a change of possession, not a change of state. Similarly in *Pat put the book on the table*, *the book* is a theme, not a patient, because it undergoes a change of location. Patient arguments typically occur with verbs like *kill, smash, break, crush, wash,* and *destroy*, while themes typically occur with verbs like *put, place, give, send,* and *buy*. The role of *Dana* in *Chris gave the notebook to Dana* is **recipient**. Recipient arguments can appear syntactically as an indirect object, as in this sentence, or as a subject, in a sentence like *Sandy received the message from Kim.*

Examples of additional semantic roles are given in (2.6).

(2.6)	a. The book is lying *on the table.*	*the table* = **location**
	a′. Pat put the book *on the table.*	*the table* = **goal**
	b. Kim sent the package *to Philadelphia.*	*Philadelphia* = goal
	c. The child ran *from the playground.*	*the playground* = **source**
	c′. The child took the book *from Kim.*	*Kim* = source
	d. The dog ran *through the garden.*	*the garden* = **path**
	e. Dana bought some flowers *for Pat.*	*Pat* = **benefactive**
	f. Jesse knows *that Chris lied.*	*that Chris lied* = content

Goal differs from recipient in that it refers to the endpoint of a change of location, while recipient refers to the endpoint of a transfer of possession. Goals, locations, recipients and sources cooccur with themes, because the theme argument refers to the entity which is located, possessed or undergoing a change of location or possession. They typically do not cooccur with patients. These roles are a function of the meaning of the verb in the following sense. An event of putting, for example, necessarily involves a participant who initiates the change of location (agent), an entity which moves (theme), and a place where the moved entity ends up (goal). In the same way, in an event of running, it is typically the case that there is a runner (agent), and the runner starts from a specific place (source), moves through some area (path), and ends up in a specific place (goal).

However, the particular properties of verbs cannot be explained simply by reference to the states of affairs in the world that they depict. Consider the sentences in (2.7).

(2.7)
a. *Pat put the book.
a′. *Pat put on the table.
a″. Pat put the book on the table.
b. The dog ran.
b′. The dog ran from the house.
b″. The dog ran from the house to the creek.
b‴. The dog ran from the house through the garden to the creek.
c. Leslie gave the flowers.
c′. *Leslie gave to Chris.
d. Kim drank a beer quickly.
d′. Kim drank quickly.

Putting involves three elements, as noted above, and the English verb *put* requires that all three occur in a sentence, as the ungrammaticality of (2.7a), (2.7a′) shows. Running may involve a runner and three places, but the English verb *run* requires only that the runner be specified in a sentence in which it occurs; specification of any or all of the places is optional. An act of giving involves a giver, something given and a recipient, but the English verb *give* seems to require only the giver and the thing given be expressed, as (2.7c) and (2.7c′) illustrate. Finally, an event of drinking involves a drinker and something being imbibed, but the English verb *drink* demands only that the drinker be specified, as in (2.7d′). Thus, while examining the states of affairs in the world that a verb denotes can reveal something about a verb's meaning, it is the specific lexical properties of the verb that determine which arguments are obligatory and which are optional.

Most of the examples discussed thus far involve transitive verbs. What about the single argument of intransitive verbs? From a semantic point of view, it must have one of these semantic roles. It is easy to see that some intransitive subjects are agents. To begin with, some verbs have alternating transitive and intransitive forms, such as *drink* in (2.7), and if the subject NP *Kim* in the transitive sentence in (2.7d) is an agent, then *Kim* must also be an agent in the intransitive form in (2.7d′), since in both sentences the referent of *Kim* is doing the drinking. Evidence that the subjects of some intransitive verbs are patients comes from a transitivity alternation different from the one mentioned above; it is given in (2.8).

(2.8)
a. The boy broke the clock.
a′. The clock broke.
b. The rock shattered the window.
b′. The window shattered.
c. The submarine sank the ship.
c′. The ship sank.

In (2.8a), (2.8b) and (2.8c) there are transitive verbs, and the subject is an agent and the direct object a patient. In the (a′, b′, c′) examples, the verb is intransitive, and the argument corresponding to the patient in the transitive version appears as the intransitive subject. Hence these intransitive subjects are patients, e.g. in both (2.8b) and (2.8b′) the referent of *the window* undergoes shattering. If the transitive sentences are paraphrased as in (2.9), the semantic identity of the transitive direct object and the intransitive subject becomes explicit.

(2.9) a. The boy caused the clock to break. (= (2.8a))
b. The rock caused the window to shatter. (= (2.8b))
c. The submarine caused the ship to sink. (= (2.8c))

In these rough paraphrases, the verbs in question occur in their intransitive forms, and the identity of the patient in the two forms is overt.

All of the transitive verbs discussed so far code actions and take agents as subjects. What about verbs that do not code actions, such as *see*, *know*, *believe*, and *love*? Their subjects are poor answers to the question '*What did X do?*', which asks about an agent's action.

(2.10) a. What did the boy do?
b. ??He saw a fox.
c. ??He knew that the world is round.
d. ??He loved his first-grade teacher.

This suggests that their subjects are not agents like those of *kill*, *hit*, *smash*, *put* and *give*. The verb in (2.10b) is a perception verb, the one in (c) is a cognition verb, and the one in (d) is an emotion verb. The subjects of these verbs may be referred to as perceivers, cognizers and emoters, respectively. English treats these arguments just like agents in most respects, but this is not true in other languages. In Avar, a Daghestanian language spoken in the Caucasus in Russia (Černý 1971), agents of transitive verbs appear in the **ergative** case, as in (2.11a). All Avar verbs of perception and cognition (Černý 1971: 47, 50), on the other hand, have their perceiver and cognizer arguments in the **locative** case, as in (2.11b), whereas 'all verbs having the general meaning of "liking" or "wanting", etc. have the "subject" in the **dative** case' (47), as in (c). The objects of all of these verbs appear in what is called the **absolutive** case. (See section 2.2.1 for discussion of these different cases.)

(2.11) a. Inssu-cca çul-∅ qoṭ-ula. Avar
father-ERG wood-ABS chop-PRES
'The father chops wood.'
b. Inssu-da ɬimer-∅ wix̄-ana.
father-LOC child-ABS see-PAST
'The father saw the child.'
c. Inssu-je ɬimer-∅ bok'-ula.
father-DAT child-ABS love-PRES
'The father loves the child.'

Other verbs taking locative subjects include *biç̌ç̌ize* 'understand', *ḳoç̌ene* 'forget' and *ɬaze* 'know'. Thus, Avar gives one kind of special treatment to perceiver and cognizer arguments and another to the emoter argument of emotion verbs; none of these arguments are coded like agents. Some languages give these arguments differential treatment from agents without, however, distinguishing among perceivers, cognizers and emoters.

Such is the case in Lezgian, a Nakho-Daghestanian (North-East Caucasian) language spoken in the eastern Caucasus in Russia and Azerbaijan (Haspelmath 1993). Clauses with agents, like (2.12a), follow the same ergative–absolutive pattern as in Avar, but clauses with perception, cognition and emotion verbs follow a different pattern. In such clauses, the subject is in the dative case, and the direct object, if there is one, is in the absolutive case.

(2.12) a. Alfija-di maq̄ala-∅ kx̂e-na. Lezgian
Alfija-ERG article-ABS write-AOR
'Alfija wrote an article.'
b. Muʔminata-z Ibrahim-∅ aku-na.
Mu'minat-DAT Ibrahim-ABS see-AOR
'Mu'minat saw Ibrahim.'
c. Mašin-ar-∅ xürü-w agaq'-na.
car-PL-ABS village-ALL reach-AOR
'The cars reached the village.'
d. Ada-z gišin-zawa žedi.
it-DAT hungry-IMPF PRT
'It (the bird) is probably hungry.'

The verb *aku-* 'see' in (2.12b) is a perception verb, while the verb *gišin-* 'be hungry' in (2.12d) is a verb of internal sensation; both take dative subjects. The following verbs are listed as among those taking dative subjects (Haspelmath 1993: 280–1): *akun* 'see', *žuğun* 'find', *k'an* 'want, love', *či-* 'know', *begenmiš x̂un* 'like', *x̂is x̂un* 'think', *kič'e x̂un* 'be afraid of', *bejkef x̂un* 'be angry about' (*x̂un* 'become' is an auxiliary verb). There are verbs from all of the classes mentioned above, and one way of capturing the fact that the subjects of these verbs are treated alike is to posit that the dative-marked argument of these verbs bears the same semantic role, which is usually called '**experiencer**'. This semantic role subsumes perceivers, emoters, cognizers and other roles of this type. It appears that in Lezgian, subjects which are experiencers receive dative case, whereas transitive subjects which are not experiencers receive ergative case. The verb in (2.12d) is intransitive, and its subject is an experiencer. In (2.12c) the intransitive subject is not an experiencer, and therefore it appears in the absolutive case (see table 2.1 in section 2.2.1).

Expressing experiencer arguments in the dative case is not a property of so-called 'exotic' languages alone; it also happens in many Indo-European languages. The following examples from Spanish, German and Croatian (Dahm-Draksic 1997) illustrate this.

(2.13) a. Te gusta-∅ la músic-a modern-a? Spanish
2sgDAT like-3sgPRES the.Fsg music-Fsg modern-Fsg
'Do you like modern music?'
b. Nos interesa-n las teorí-as lingüístic-as.
1plDAT interest-3plPRES the.Fpl theory-Fpl linguistic-Fpl
'We are interested in linguistic theories.'

(2.14) a. Der Vorschlag gefäll-t mir. German
the.MsgNOM suggestion please-3sgPRES 1sgDAT
'I like the suggestion,' or 'The suggestion is pleasing to me.'

a′. Ich mag den Vorschlag.
1sgNOM like.PRES the.MSGACC suggestion
'I like the suggestion.'

b. Mir ist kalt.
1sgDAT be.3sgPRES cold
'I'm cold,' or 'I feel cold.'

(2.15) a. Sandr-i se sviđ-a Zagreb-∅. Croatian
Sandra-FSGDAT REFL please-3sg Zagreb-MSGNOM
'Sandra likes Zagreb.'

b. Žen-ama je neugodn-o.
woman-FplDAT be.3sg uncomfortable-Nsg
'The women are embarrassed.'

In all three languages there are verbs meaning 'please, like' which take the liker or the one pleased in the dative case (the (a) examples). German also has the verb *mögen* 'like' which has a nominative subject and an **accusative** direct object, as illustrated in (2.14a′). The Spanish verb *interesar* 'to interest' takes its experiencer in the dative as well, and these German and Croatian expressions of internal sensation likewise take the experiencer in the dative case. Thus, many languages may express experiencers and related arguments differently from agents with both transitive and intransitive verbs.

In talking about the verbs in (2.7), the subject in each sentence was described as a runner, giver or drinker, but they could with equal accuracy have been described as an agent, since they are in each instance the doer of the running, giving or drinking, analogous to the doer of the washing in (2.4). Hence it is possible to talk about the semantic role of the arguments of these verbs in verb-specific terms, e.g. runner, giver, drinker or washer, and more general terms, e.g. agent. The same thing can be said with respect to object arguments. In (2.4) there is the entity washed and in (2.7d) the entity imbibed, both of which may also be described as patients. In (2.7a) there is the entity placed, and in (c), the entity given; both can be characterized as themes as well. With respect to the perception, cognition and emotion verbs discussed in (2.11)–(2.15), the subject arguments can be described as see-er, hearers, and tasters, as well as perceivers; the subject arguments of cognition verbs can be characterized as knowers and thinkers, as well as cognizers; and the subjects of emotion verbs can be described as lovers, likers and haters, as well as emoters. Moreover, perceivers, cognizers and emoters can be grouped together as experiencers.

Semantic roles have been discussed at two levels of generality or specificity: in terms of verb-specific roles, like runner or entity broken, and in more general terms, like agent, experiencer and patient. In order to distinguish the two types of roles terminologically, roles like runner and hearer will be referred to as 'verb-specific semantic roles', and roles like agent, instrument, experiencer and theme will be referred to as 'thematic relations'. The relationship between the two types of semantic roles is captured in Figure 2.1.

Thematic relations are generalizations across verb-specific roles, and the contrast between cognizer, perceiver and emoter, on the one hand, and experiencer, on the other, shows that more than one level of generality is possible. It should be noted that not all of the thematic relations discussed in the text are represented in Figure 2.1.

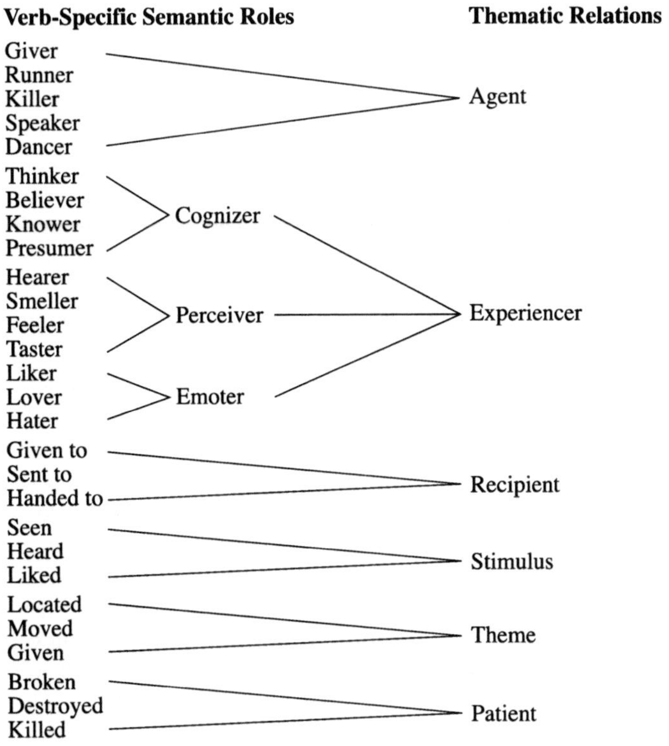

Figure 2.1. *Verb-specific semantic roles and thematic relations*

Are there any other levels of generality with respect to semantic roles that are linguistically relevant? It appears that there is at least one more. Consider the range of thematic relations that can function as subject and direct object in English.

		Subject	Direct object
(2.16)	a. The farmer killed the duckling.	Agent	Patient
	b. The rock broke the window.	Instrument	Patient
	c. The lawyer received the summons.	Recipient	Theme
	d. Many tourists saw the accident.	Experiencer	Stimulus
	e. Sally presented Bill with the award.	Agent	Recipient
	f. The mugger robbed Sam of $50.	Agent	Source
	g. The clown amused the child.	Agent	Experiencer

(2.17) a. The duckling was killed by the farmer.
b. The window was broken by the rock.
c. The summons was received by the lawyer.
d. The accident was seen by many tourists.
e. Bill was presented with the award by Sally.
f. Sam was robbed of $50 by the mugger.
g. The child was amused by the clown.

To the right of each example in (2.16) is listed the thematic relation of the subject followed by the thematic relation of the direct object. There is a range, sometimes overlapping, of thematic relations that can serve as subject and direct object; the subject can be an agent, instrument, experiencer or recipient, while the direct object can be a patient, theme, stimulus, recipient, source or experiencer. The passive versions of these sentences are given in (2.17), and the very same grouping of thematic relations that functions as the direct object in (2.16) serves as the subject in (2.17), and similarly, the same grouping of thematic relations that functions as the subject in (2.16) appears as the object of *by* in the passive versions. The grammatical relations are different in (2.16) and (2.17), and yet the groupings of thematic relations are the same. This shows that these groupings do not constitute a grammatical relation but rather another, more general type of semantic role. The role of the subject of an active voice transitive verb and the object of *by* in a passive construction will be referred to as '**actor**,' and the role of the direct object of an active voice transitive verb and the subject of a passive verb will be referred to as '**undergoer**.' Actor and undergoer together will be termed 'semantic macroroles,' because each represents a grouping of thematic relations. The single argument of an intransitive verb is either an actor, as with verbs like *run*, or an undergoer, as with verbs like *die*.

This discussion brings out one of the important generalizations that the notions of actor and undergoer capture. It is very simple to describe active and passive voice in English using macroroles: in the active voice, the actor is subject and the undergoer is direct object, whereas in the passive voice, the undergoer is the subject and the actor is an oblique non-term. Now, imagine trying to state the same thing using verb-specific semantic roles! Even if one uses thematic relations, the result is less than elegant: in the active voice, the agent, instrument, experiencer or recipient is subject and the patient, theme, experiencer, stimulus, recipient or source is direct object, whereas in the passive voice, the patient, theme, experiencer, stimulus, recipient or source is the subject and the agent, instrument, experiencer or recipient is an oblique non-term. Clearly, a generalization is being missed in these statements. The more roles that are recognized, the longer and more inelegant this formulation becomes. Hence actor and undergoer are very useful concepts that permit the elegant expression of important linguistic generalizations.

An important concept embodied in Figure 2.1 is the notion of neutralization. Once one moves to thematic relations like cognizer, experiencer or patient, distinctions among verb-specific semantic roles become neutralized. For example, in grouping see-er, hearer, feeler, taster and smeller together as perceiver, the mode of perception is necessarily lost. The more general the roles are, the more semantic contrasts are neutralized, and the macroroles of actor and undergoer represent extensive neutralizations. Actor and undergoer are themselves neutralized in the notion of subject in languages like English and Malagasy. The finite verb in English, for example, agrees with the subject regardless of whether the subject is the actor of a transitive verb, the undergoer of a passive verb, the actor of an intransitive verb, or the undergoer of an intransitive verb. Thus, the grammatical relation of subject represents a neutralization of these semantic contrasts. These neutralizations are summarized in Figure 2.2.

It was mentioned that the thematic relations that can serve as actor overlap to some extent with those that can serve as undergoer, and in Figure 2.2 experiencer and recipient are represented as being a possible actor or a possible undergoer. How can the same thematic relation be an actor in one instance and an undergoer in another?

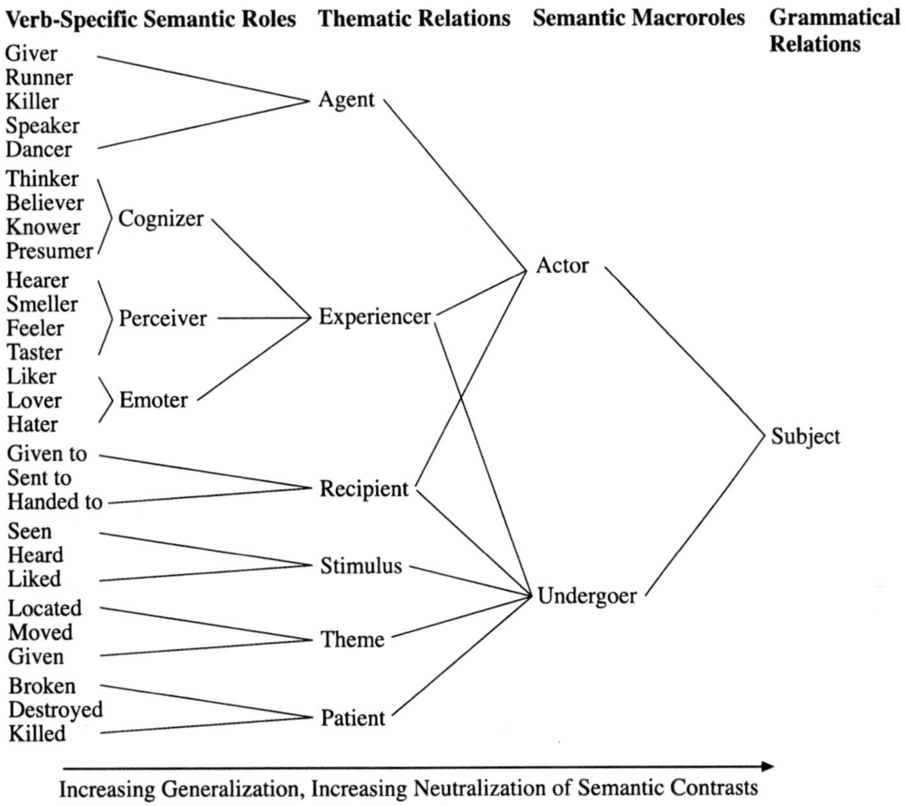

Figure 2.2. *Continuum from verb-specific semantic roles to grammatical relations*

The answer has to do with a verb's argument structure. The examples from (2.16) and (2.17) involving experiencers and recipients are repeated below, along with the argument structure of each verb.

(2.18) a. The lawyer received the summons. <Recipient, Theme>
a′. The summons was received by the lawyer.
b. Sally presented Bill with the award. <Agent, Theme, Recipient>
b′. Bill was presented with the award by Sally.

(2.19) a. Many tourists saw the accident. <Experiencer, Stimulus>
a′. The accident was seen by many tourists.
b. The clown amused the child. <Agent, Experiencer>
b′. The child was amused by the clown.

Recipient and experiencer function as actor in the (a) (a′) examples and function as undergoer in the (b) (b′) examples. Why can the recipient be the actor with *receive* but not with *present*? Why can the experiencer be the actor with *see* but not with *amuse*? In order to answer this question, it is necessary to look at the relationships among the various thematic relations. In (2.20), the two hierarchies relate thematic relations to macroroles; the thematic-relations labels used could be replaced by lists of the appropriate verb-specific semantic roles.

(2.20) a. Actor hierarchy
Agent > Instrument > Experiencer > Recipient
b. Undergoer hierarchy
Patient > Theme > Stimulus > Experiencer > Recipient/Goal/Source/Location

The prototypical actor argument would be an agent, since it is a potentially willful, instigating doer of an action, and the prototypical undergoer would be a patient, since it undergoes a change of state or condition. These hierarchies reflect how 'agent-like' or 'patient-like' the other thematic relations are. The most agent-like argument of a verb will be the actor, and the most patient-like argument is the default choice for undergoer. Agent and patient are at the top of the hierarchies, meaning that if a verb takes an agent argument, it will be the actor, and if one takes a patient argument, it will be the undergoer. If the verb does not have an agent but does have an instrument, as in (2.16b), then the instrument will be actor. If there is no agent or instrument, then an experiencer, as in (2.19a), or a recipient, as in (2.18a), can function as actor. The ranking is absolute; a lower ranking role cannot be selected as actor over a higher ranking role. This is why sentences like **The key opened the door by/with Bill* are quite impossible. The situation is somewhat different with respect to the Undergoer hierarchy; it reflects only the default ranking, and it is possible for a lower ranking argument to be selected as undergoer over a higher ranking one. Examples of this can be seen in (2.21).

(2.21) a. The president presented the award to Leslie.
a′. The president presented Leslie with the award.
a″. Leslie was presented with the award by the president.
b. The company supplied uniforms to the team.
b′. The company supplied the team with uniforms.
b″. The team was supplied with uniforms by the company.

In (2.21a) and (2.21b), the higher ranking non-agent argument, the theme, is the undergoer, whereas in (2.21a′) and (2.21b′) the lower ranking argument, the recipient, functions as undergoer. As (2.21a″) and (2.21b″) clearly show, the issue is undergoer and not direct object here; the recipient–undergoer is the subject in both examples.

It is now possible to answer the question of why the recipient is actor with *receive* but undergoer with *present* and why the experiencer is the actor with *see* but the undergoer with *startle*. *Receive* is a two-argument verb, having recipient and theme arguments; the only candidate for actor is the recipient. *Present*, on the other hand, is a three-argument verb, having agent, recipient and theme arguments. The agent is the highest ranking role in (2.21a) and therefore would be actor; the recipient is outranked by the agent. With respect to undergoer, on the other hand, the default choice is the theme, as in (2.21a), but the recipient is a possible choice, as (2.18a′) shows. *See* is also a two-argument verb, taking experiencer and stimulus arguments; in this argument structure, the experiencer will be the actor and the stimulus the undergoer. *Amuse* is likewise a two-argument verb, but its two arguments are agent and experiencer; this can be seen clearly in the paraphrase of (2.19b) as 'the clown (agent) caused the child (experiencer) to be amused'. Since this verb has an agent argument, it must function as actor, leaving the experiencer to function as undergoer.

The semantic function of some arguments is best described in terms of two thematic relations. Consider the subjects of *give* and *take* in (2.22).

(2.22) a. Pat gave the book to Chris.
b. Chris took the book from Pat.

If these two sentences are analyzed solely with respect to the transfer they express, it is clear that *Pat* is the source, the starting point of the transfer, *the book* is the theme, the item transferred, and *Chris* is the recipient, the endpoint of the transfer. In other words, both of these sentences code a transfer of possession of the book from Pat to Chris. Where they differ is in the expression of the initiator of the transfer; in (a) Pat is coded as initiating the transfer, whereas in (b) Chris is. Thus, it would be appropriate to say that in (2.22a) the NP *Pat* has both agent and source thematic relations, and that in (b) the NP *Chris* has both agent and recipient thematic relations. The same could be said for *the clown* in (2.19b): it bears both agent and stimulus thematic relations. Is there any linguistic evidence that these arguments are agents in addition to being a recipient, source or stimulus? One piece of evidence is that they all readily take adverbs like *intentionally*, which express agency.

(2.23) a. The clown intentionally amused the child.
b. Pat intentionally gave the book to Chris.
c. Chris intentionally took the book from Pat.

The subjects (actors) of *receive* and *see* are not agents, in addition to being recipients and experiencers, respectively, because they cannot cooccur with adverbs like *intentionally*.

(2.24) a. *Many tourists intentionally saw the parade.
a′. Many tourists intentionally watched/looked at the parade.
b. *The lawyer intentionally received the summons.
b′. The lawyer intentionally accepted the summons.

The experiencer with *watch* or *look at*, in contrast to that of *see*, can be an agent, as the grammaticality of (2.24a′) shows. The same holds for the recipient of *accept* as opposed to that of *receive*, as (b′) shows. Thus, recipients, stimuli and experiencers may also be agents with certain verbs. When an argument has a double thematic relation, e.g. agent–experiencer as in (2.24a′), it counts as an agent for the purposes of the hierarchies in (2.20).

2.2 Properties of grammatical relations

The question of how to identify grammatical relations is a fundamental analytic issue for approaches to syntactic description which take an essentially relational view of syntax (see chapter 6). Of the three relations, subject is by far the most important, as more syntactic phenomena involve subjects than direct objects or indirect objects. A word of caution is required at the outset. There is no single morphosyntactic phenomenon (or single group of phenomena) which uniquely and consistently identifies each of the grammatical relations cross-linguistically. Rather, there are strong tendencies for certain phenomena to involve a particular relation, and examples of the most likely **constructions** to pick out subjects, direct objects or indirect objects will be presented.

It is useful to make a distinction between the coding and behavioral properties of grammatical relations. Coding properties are primarily, but not exclusively, morphological, while behavioral properties are syntactic; the latter refers to the involvement of a particular relation in different grammatical constructions. It should be noted that in this section attention will be restricted to languages in which the subject of an active transitive verb is an actor, the direct object of an active transitive verb is an undergoer, and the indirect object of an active ditransitive verb is a recipient or goal. This is, of course, the pattern found in many Indo-European languages and in many other languages around the world.

2.2.1 *Coding properties*

The primary coding properties are verb agreement, case marking and (in languages with very rigid word order) the position of an argument in the sentence, which may serve to express a particular grammatical relation. The first two are morphological and the third syntactic. Finite verb agreement was discussed briefly at the beginning of this chapter, and based on the data in (2.1)–(2.3) it was argued that it must be triggered by the subject in English. While this is a unique property of subjects in English, it is not in other languages. In Lakhota, for example, transitive verbs agree with both subject and direct object. (The verb *naxʔų́* 'hear' takes its subject and object markers as infixes.)

(2.25) a. (Miyé) mathó ki hená na-wíčha-wa-xʔų. Lakhota
(1sg) bear the those stem-3plOBJ-1sgSUBJ-hear
'I heard those bears.'
b. Mathó ki hená (miyé) na-má-∅-xʔų-pi.
bear the those (1sg) stem-1sgOBJ-3SUBJ-hear-PL
'Those bears heard me.'

The independent pronoun *miyé* 'I' is optional and would only be used for emphasis. The verb shows agreement for both of its terms, and accordingly in languages like Lakhota being the trigger for verb agreement is not a unique property of subjects. There are even languages in which there is agreement with all three terms in a sentence with a ditransitive verb; the following examples are from Basque (Laka 1997).

(2.26) a. Ni-k hi-ri liburu-∅ bat oparitu d-i-a-t. Basque
1sg-ERG 2sg-DAT book-ABS one give.as.gift 3sgDOBJ-have-2sgIOBJ-1sgSUBJ
'I have given you a book (as a present).'
b. Hi-k ni-ri liburu-∅ bat oparitu d-i-da-k.
2sg-ERG 1sg-DAT book-ABS one give.as.gift 3sgDOBJ-have-1sgIOBJ-2sgSUBJ
'You have given me a book (as a present).'

The agreement morphemes occur on the auxiliary verb *ukan* 'have' (which appears as *-i-* in these two examples), and all three terms are expressed there. Thus while triggering verb agreement is a unique property of terms, it is not a unique property of subjects in many languages. The most one can say is that if a language has verb agreement with only one term, the trigger is almost certainly the subject; there are very few exceptions to this generalization.

In languages with case marking on NPs, such as Russian, German, Turkish, Hungarian, Quechua (South America) and Telugu (Dravidian, India), the nominative case normally codes the subject, and it corresponds to the **citation form** for nouns. That is, if one asked a Russian speaker how to say 'book', he or she would respond with *kniga*, the nominative singular form, not *knigu* (accusative singular) or *knige* (dative singular). Similarly, if one asked a speaker of Ayacucho Quechua the word for 'rock', the response would be *rumi* (nominative), not *rumita* (accusative) or *rumiwan* (**instrumental**) (Parker 1969). Direct objects are normally expressed in the accusative case and indirect objects in the dative case. Examples of all three cases from Russian, Hungarian, Korean (Yang 1994) and Telugu (Prakasam 1985) are given in (2.27).

(2.27) a. Učitel'nic-a da-l-a knig-u ženščin-e. Russian
teacher-FSGNOM give-PAST-FSG book-ACC woman-DAT
'The teacher gave the book to the woman.'
a′. Ženščin-a/učitel'nic-a govori-l-a/umer-l-a.
woman-/teacher-FSGNOM talk-PAST-FSG/die-PAST-FSG
'The woman/the teacher talked/died.'
b. Mari-∅ a gyerek-nek ad-ta az órá-t. Hungarian
Mary-NOM the child-DAT give-3sgPAST the clock-ACC
'Mary gave the clock to the child.'
c. Chelswu-ka Swunhi-eykey chayk-ul cwu-ess-ta. Korean
Chelsoo-NOM Soonhi-DAT book-ACC give-PAST-DECL
'Chelsoo gave the book to Soonhi.'
d. Atanu-∅ da:n-ni tana pella:ni-ki icc-a:du. Telugu
3MSG-NOM 3NSG-ACC self wife-DAT give-PAST.3sgM
'He gave it to his (own) wife.'

The nominative case is the case of the subject in Russian, and the accusative case is the case of the direct object. With intransitive verbs, as in (2.27a′), the subject is nominative, as with transitive verbs. In the initial analysis of a language, the following rules of thumb can help the analyst recognize the three main cases, nominative, accusative and dative. With respect to the nominative, first, it is normally the same as the citation form for nouns, as noted earlier; second, it is the case of the single argument of an intransitive verb; and third, it translates as the actor argument of an active voice transitive verb. With respect to the accusative, first, it normally only occurs in clauses with transitive verbs and does not correspond to the citation form for nouns, and second, it translates as the undergoer of an active voice transitive verb. With respect to the dative, it does not correspond to the citation form for nouns, and with verbs like *give* it translates as the recipient argument.

The pattern illustrated in (2.27), the nominative–accusative pattern, represents one of the two major case-marking patterns found in the world's languages. The other major case-marking pattern is the ergative–absolutive pattern, exemplified in (2.12) from Lezgian and in (2.28) from Yalarnnga, an Australian Aboriginal language (Blake 1977).

(2.28) a. Kupi-ŋku milŋa-∅ tiaca-mu. Yalarnnga
fish-ERG fly-ABS bite-PAST
'The fish bit the fly.'
b. Milŋa-ŋku kupi-∅ tiaca-mu.
fly-ERG fish-ABS bite-PAST
'The fly bit the fish.'
c. Milŋa-∅/kupi-∅ waka-mu.
fly-/fish-ABS fall-PAST
'The fly/the fish fell.'

The ergative case is the case of the actor of a transitive verb in a language of this type, and the absolutive case is the case of the undergoer of a transitive verb; the subject of an intransitive verb, as in (2.28c), is likewise in the absolutive case. The two case-marking patterns are summarized in Table 2.1.

Table 2.1. *Case-marking patterns*

		Case Pattern	
Term		Nominative–Accusative	Ergative–Absolutive
Subject of transitive verb	[A]	Nominative	Ergative
Subject of intransitive verb	[S]	Nominative	Absolutive
Direct object of transitive verb	[O]	Accusative	Absolutive

It is customary in discussions of case marking, following Dixon (1972), to use S, A and O as abbreviations for the relevant grammatical relations (although some scholars use 'P' instead of 'O' for transitive object). Nominative–accusative systems are often referred to simply as 'accusative systems', and in such systems the O argument receives distinctive case marking, the S and A normally being in the citation form. In an ergative system, on the other hand, the A argument receives distinctive case marking, the S and O normally being in the citation form. This may be represented more generally as in Figure 2.3.

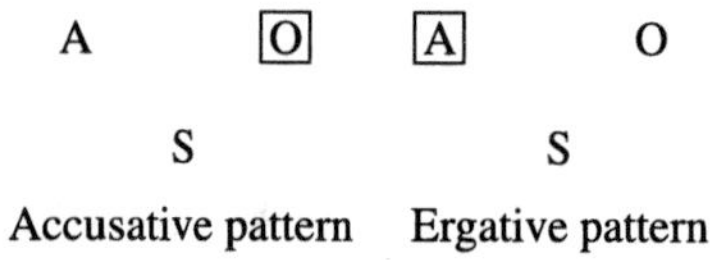

Figure 2.3. *Accusative versus ergative patterns*

The box around one of the grammatical relations indicates that it is the one that receives distinctive treatment in the pattern. The syntactic consequences of this contrast will be discussed in section 2.3.2.

Rules of thumb for identifying the absolutive and ergative cases are analogous to those for nominative and accusative. With respect to the absolutive case, first, it is normally the same as the citation form for nouns; second, it is the case of the single argument of an intransitive verb; and third, it translates as the undergoer argument of a transitive verb. With respect to the ergative case, first, it normally only occurs in clauses with transitive verbs and does not correspond to the citation form for nouns, and second, it translates as the actor of a transitive verb.

Nominative, accusative, ergative and absolutive are used to mark the most syntactically important arguments in a clause, including, most importantly, the subject. Indirect objects are typically in the dative case, as illustrated in the three examples from accusative languages in (2.27) and in the two examples from Georgian (Harris 1981) and Dyirbal (Dixon 1972) below.

(2.29) a. Nino-m ačvena surat-eb-i gia-s. Georgian
Nino-ERG showed pictures-PL-ABS Gia-DAT
'Nino showed the pictures to Gia.'
b. Balam miraɲ-∅ baŋgul yaɽa-ŋgu wugan bagul Dyirbal
NM.ABS beans-ABS NM.ERG man-ERG gave NM.DAT
ɖugumbil-gu.
woman-DAT
'The man gave beans to the woman.'

Other cases, such as instrumental and **genitive**, function analogously in both systems. An important use of the instrumental case is, as the label implies, to mark instrument arguments.

(2.30) a. Ženščin-a napisa-l-a karandaš-em. Russian
woman-NOM write-PAST-FSG pencil-INST
'The woman wrote with a pencil.'
b. Bala yugu-∅ baŋgul yaɽa-ŋgu nudin baŋgu bari-ŋgu. Dyirbal
NM.ABS tree-ABS NM.ERG man-ERG cut NM.INST axe-INST
'The man cut down the tree with an axe.'

Genitive case is used primarily to mark possession within NPs; it may also be used to mark arguments of the verb (see (2.32b) below).

(2.31) a. Ich hab-e das Auto des Mann-es gesehen. German
1sgNOM have-1sgPRES the.ACC car the.GEN man-GEN seen
'I saw the man's car.'
b. Bayi waŋal-∅ baŋun ɖugumbil-ŋu baŋgul Dyirbal
NM.ABS boomerang-ABS NM.GEN woman-GEN NM.ERG
yaɽa-ŋgu buɽan.
man-ERG saw
'The man saw the woman's boomerang.'

The genitive case on *des Mannes* 'the man's' indicates that it is the possessor of *das Auto* 'the car' in the German example, and likewise in the Dyirbal sentence, the genitive case on *baŋun ɖugumbilŋu* 'the woman's' signals that it is the possessor of *bayi waŋal* 'boomerang'. Thus, the contrast between accusative and ergative case marking concerns the marking of the most syntactically important terms, and the cases which code indirect objects and non-terms function basically the same way in both systems.

While these correlations of subject with nominative case, direct object with accusative case and indirect object with dative case in languages with an accusative case-marking system are valid in many instances, it is nevertheless not always possible to correlate case with grammatical relations in this way. In Russian, German, Latin and many other Indo-European languages, many verbs take a second argument in something other than the accusative case, as illustrated in (2.32); the Latin example is from Michaelis (1993).

(2.32) a. Učitel'nic-a pomog-l-a ženščin-e/*ženščin-u. Russian
teacher-NOM help-PAST-FSG woman-DAT/woman-ACC
'The teacher helped the woman.'
b. Vivor-um memin-i. Latin
living-GEN remember-1sg
'I remember the living.'

The Russian verb *pomoč'* 'help' takes its second argument in the dative case, while the verb *memini* 'remember' in Latin takes its second argument in the genitive case. Some languages may mark both direct and indirect objects with the same case, as in (2.31) from Icelandic, Korean (Yang 1994) and Ancash Quechua (Wölck 1987).

(2.33) a. Ég skila-ð-i henn-i pening-un-um. — Icelandic
1sgNOM return-PAST-1sg 3Fsg-DAT money-DEF-DAT
'I returned her the money.'
b. Chelswu-ka Swunhi-lul chayk-ul cwu-ess-ta. — Korean
Chelsoo-NOM Soonhi-ACC book-ACC give-PAST-DECL
'Chelsoo gave Soonhi the book.'
c. Warmi-∅ Pablo-ta kashki-ta qu-rqa-n. — Ancash Quechua
woman-NOM Pablo-ACC soup-ACC give-PAST-3
'The woman gave Pablo soup.'

In the Icelandic example, both direct and indirect objects appear in the dative case with the verb *skila* 'return'; other ditransitive verbs, e.g. *gefa* 'give', govern the case pattern in (2.27). In the Korean and Ancash Quechua sentences both objects are in the accusative case; Korean also marks indirect objects with dative, as in (2.27c), but in Ancash Quechua (2.33c) is the only option. Hence it is not possible to conclude that a NP is direct object or indirect object simply because it is in the accusative or dative case. An example of a non-nominative subject was given in (2.12d) from Lezgian, and further examples of 'mismatches' between case and grammatical relations will be found in section 2.3.

Case may be **instantiated** morphologically in a number of ways within a NP. In all of the examples looked at so far, it is realized by a suffix on the noun. This is by far the most common pattern when case is expressed by a bound affixal element. There are very few examples of languages in which case is realized by a prefixal element. Two such languages are Shuswap, a Salishan language spoken in Canada (Kuipers 1974) and Modern Hebrew (Berman 1978).

(2.34) a. n-k°úk°p'y ɣ-cítx°-s — Shuswap
LOC-chief ABS-house-3GEN
'to the chief's house'
b. lə 'to' + yéled 'boy' → ləyéled 'to a boy' — Modern Hebrew
b′. lə 'to' + ha 'the' + yéled 'boy' → layéled 'to the boy'

The Shuswap prefix *n-* indicates location or goal, while Hebrew *lə* expresses dative case and forms a single phonological unit with the word that follows.

Case may also be signaled by adpositions or on articles. In Japanese (Kuno 1973), all case markers are postpositions, while in Tagalog (Schachter 1976) they are prepositions (the labels on the prepositions in (b) are provisional, as Tagalog will be discussed further in section 2.3). In German, case is expressed primarily on the article, not on the **head** noun in the NP, as illustrated in (2.35c, c′).

(2.35) a. Hanako ga Taroo ni hon o yat-ta. — Japanese
Hanako NOM Taroo DAT book ACC give-PAST
'Hanako gave a book to Taroo.'

b. Nagbigay ng libro sa bata ang lalake. Tagalog
gave ACC book DAT child NOM man
'The man gave a book to the child.'

c. Der Mann hat der Frau einen Kuß German
the.MSgNOM man has the.FSgDAT woman one.MSgACC kiss
gegeben.
given
'The man gave the woman a kiss.'

c′. Die Frau hat dem Mann einen Kuß gegeben.
the.FSgNOM woman has the.MSgDAT man one.MSgACC kiss given
'The woman gave the man a kiss.'

The only difference between the form of the NPs meaning 'the man' and 'the woman' in the two German sentences is the form of the article; the nouns themselves do not change their form, unlike nouns in Russian or Hungarian, for example. In genitive NPs in German, on the other hand, the head noun does show case (if it is masculine or neuter gender), as in (2.31a). One of the most unusual ways of expressing case is found in Maasai, a Nilotic language spoken in east Africa; in this language it is the tone on the last syllable of a noun which indicates whether it is nominative or accusative (Welmers 1973).

(2.36) a. Cǐle pɔ̀ntét. Maasai
look.at old.man
'He's looking at the old man.'

b. Cǐle pɔ̀ntet.
look.at old.man
'The old man's looking at him.'

In (2.36a) there is a high tone on the last syllable of the noun, and this signals that it is the direct object of the verb, while in (2.36b), the absence of a high tone on the last syllable of the noun signals that it is the subject of the verb.

Languages need not have verb agreement or case marking; in languages without them, the only coding property is position in the clause. Cantonese (Matthews and Yip 1994) is a good example of a language with neither case nor agreement. This is illustrated in the following examples.

(2.37) a. Ngóh/ngóhdeih jūngyi kéuih/kéuihdeih. Cantonese
1sg/1pl like 3sg/3pl
'I/we like him~her/them.'

a′. Kéuih/kéuihdeih jūngyi ngóh/ngóhdeih.
3sg/3pl like 1sg/1pl
'He~she/they like(s) me/us.'

b. Jek māau gin léuhng jek gáu.
CL cat see two CL dog
'The cat sees two dogs.'

b′. Léuhng jek gáu gin jek māau.
two CL dog see CL cat
'Two dogs see the cat.'

In these examples, the verb does not change form depending upon the number or person of the subject, and neither nouns nor pronouns change their form depending upon whether they serve as subject or direct object. Position of an NP in the clause is the signal for its grammatical relation. Several examples of the role of position in signalling grammatical relations have been given from English, Toba Batak, and Lakhota in (1.1) and from Malagasy in (2.4). In English, the subject is typically the NP occurring before the verb, while the direct object is the direct NP immediately following the verb. In the default order in Lakhota, the subject NP precedes the direct object NP, and the verb follows both of them. In both Toba Batak and Malagasy, the subject is clause-final, and the direct object follows the verb but precedes the subject. Note that while there is a special position in the clause for the subject and direct object, it is not the same position in these four languages. In English and Lakhota the subject is clause-initial, while in Toba Batak and Malagasy it is clause-final. The direct object precedes the verb in Lakhota but follows it in the other three languages. There are also languages with verb–subject–object order, e.g. Welsh, Kwakwala (Wakashan, Canada), Zapotec (Oto-Manguean, Mexico), object–verb–subject order, e.g. Hixkaryana (Carib, Brazil), and object–subject–verb order, e.g. Xavante (Gê, Brazil) (Derbyshire and Pullum 1991). Thus, there is no single position which consistently expresses the subject or direct object in the various languages which use position to code them. There is, however, a very strong tendency for the subject to precede the direct and indirect objects; hence languages like English, Kwakwala and Lakhota are much more common than ones like Toba Batak and Malagasy.

Looking at coding properties universally, it can be seen that there is no coding property which uniquely identifies any grammatical relation. With respect to languages that signal the identity of terms by position in a sentence, there is no position associated consistently with subject, direct object or indirect object cross-linguistically. Within individual languages, however, there may be consistent correlation of terms with positions, as in Cantonese and Malagasy. With respect to case marking, the nominative case marks subject in all of the examples discussed so far, but in section 2.3 it will be shown that there are languages in which the case corresponding to the citation form of nouns does not always code the subject. Similarly, there are examples from Icelandic, Korean and Ancash Quechua in which accusative or dative marks both direct and indirect objects. Hence, from a cross-linguistic perspective, one cannot conclude simply because an NP is nominative, accusative or dative that it is a subject, direct object or indirect object, respectively. However, within particular languages, such consistent correlations may well hold. In German, for example, the NP in the nominative case with which the finite verb agrees is always the subject.

2.2.2 *Behavioral properties*

The behavioral properties of terms are the range of constructions that they may be involved in. If a construction uniquely targets a specific term in a language, then involvement in that construction is a property of the particular grammatical relation in that language. Relational syntactic analysis looks for restrictions that make one type of argument privileged with respect to a particular construction, e.g. the only argument that can trigger verb agreement, as in the English examples in (2.1)–(2.3). In the case of English finite verb agreement, subject is the privileged syntactic argument with respect to the construction. If there were a construction that universally and exclusively targeted a specific grammatical relation, then that construction would be a universal property of that grammatical relation. Unfortunately, no such universal properties exist for any of the three types of term. However, there are some very strong tendencies cross-linguistically, and in individual languages each grammatical relation often has quite distinctive properties. In the following sections, each term relation will be discussed in terms of its behavioral properties in simple sentences first and then in complex sentences.

2.2.2.1 *Subject*

As mentioned in section 2.2, subject is by far the most important grammatical relation, and accordingly there are many more syntactic phenomena which target subject than the other relations. A construction which seems to come close to universally targeting subjects is **imperative** formation. In this construction the second-person subject is normally omitted and is interpreted as the addressee, and the verb is in a special, usually tenseless form, as illustrated in (2.38).

(2.38) a. Open the door!
b. Gmor/gimru! — Modern Hebrew
Finish! (MSG/MPL addressee)
b′. Gimri/gmórna!
Finish! (FSG/FPL addressee)
c. Govori/govorite! — Russian
Speak! (sg/pl addressee)
d. Iyáyaye/iyáyayo! — Lakhota
Go away! (FEM/MASC speaker)
e. Jām būi chàh béi ngóh lā! — Cantonese
pour cup tea for me PRT
'Pour me a cup of tea!'

In all of these commands the addressee is understood to be the subject of the verb, and it is reasonable to expect that this would be the case everywhere. Malagasy presents a very unusual, albeit very interesting, type of imperative.

(2.39) a. Manasa ny lamba! — Malagasy
wash the clothes
'Wash the clothes!'
b. Sasao ny lamba!
be.washed the clothes
'The clothes be washed!'

The first example looks similar to those in (2.38), but the second one is strikingly different. It is a *passive* imperative, in which *ny lamba* 'the clothes' is the syntactic subject, just as in (2.4b). (For sociolinguistic reasons, it is the preferred form.) In (2.39b) it cannot be the case that the addressee is the subject, since *ny lamba* 'the clothes', the subject, is not the addressee. Rather, the addressee is the understood agent of the verb *sasan-* 'wash'. Hence being the addressee of an imperative is normally (but not necessarily) a property of subjects, and therefore this construction can be used as a useful test for subjecthood in a language. However, it is not an exclusive property of subjects universally, as the Malagasy examples in (2.39) show; additional examples of this will be presented in section 2.3.

Another construction that involves subjects is reflexivization. The issue here is which argument can be the **antecedent** of the reflexive pronoun. Examples from Norwegian (Hellan 1988) and English are given below.

(2.40) a. Jon fortal-te meg om seg selv. Norwegian
John tell-PAST 1sgACC about self
'John told me about himself.'
b. *Vi fortal-te Jon om seg selv.
1plNOM tell-PAST John about self
*'We told John about himself.'

(2.41) a. $James_i$ saw $himself_i$. Antecedent = subject
a′. $James_i$' $sister_j$ saw $herself_j$/*$himself_i$.
b. Sam_i told $Miriam_j$ about $herself_{j/*i}$. Antecedent = direct object
b′. Sam_i told $Miriam_j$'s $brother_k$ about $himself_{i/k}$/*$herself_j$.
c. $Miriam_i$ talked to Sam_j about $himself_{j/*i}$. Antecedent = indirect object
c′. $Miriam_i$ talked to Sam_j's $sister_k$ about $herself_{i/k}$/*$himself_j$.
d. $Miriam_i$ talked with Sam_j about $himself_{j/*i}$. Antecedent = non-term
d′. $Miriam_i$ talked with Sam_j's $sister_k$ about $herself_{i/k}$/*$himself_j$.

The class of arguments that can be the antecedent for reflexive pronouns in a language always includes subjects, and in some languages, e.g. Norwegian, there is a reflexive pronoun (in Norwegian, *seg selv*) that can only have a subject as an antecedent, as (2.40) illustrates. In such a language, the ability to be the antecedent of such a reflexive pronoun would be a significant subject property. However, in other languages, such as English, it is not a unique property of subjects, as (2.41) clearly shows. While the antecedent can be one of these grammatical relations or even a non-term as in (d), the possessor of a term or non-term cannot serve as an antecedent within a clause, as the primed examples show. (A possessor can be the antecedent of a reflexive within an NP, e.g. *Mary's picture of herself.*) The fact that English reflexive pronouns express gender allows one to see clearly that the antecedent in (2.41a′) must be *sister*, not the possessor *James'*, since English reflexive pronouns must agree with their antecedent in person, number and gender. The other three primed sentences are ambiguous, because either the subject or the other argument can be construed as the antecedent; in none of them can a possessor be so interpreted, however. Hence the strongest generalization one can make is that subjects are universally among the possible antecedents of reflexive pronouns, but again this is not an exclusive property of subjects.

One clarification is in order. It is often the case that a language has more than one way of realizing a particular phenomenon, and this claim applies to the phenomenon as a whole and not to every way it is manifested. A concrete example of this can be seen in reflexivization. In some languages, there is more than one reflexive pronoun, and different ones may have different conditions on their potential antecedents. Consider the following additional examples from Norwegian.

(2.42) a. Vi fortal-te Jon om ham selv. Norwegian
1plNOM tell-PAST John about self
'We told John about himself.'

b. *Jon snakk-er om ham selv.
John talk-PRES about self
'John talks about himself.'

Norwegian has a complex system of reflexive elements, and two are of interest here, *seg selv* and *ham selv*. As the examples in (2.40) show, *seg selv* must be bound by the subject of the sentence, whereas *ham selv* cannot be bound by the subject; it must be bound by a non-subject, normally the direct object, as in (2.42). If one looked only at *ham selv*, one might think that Norwegian reflexivization contradicted the claim made above, because the antecedent of *ham selv* must not be a subject but rather one of the other terms. However, when one looks at reflexivization as a whole in the language, it becomes clear that this generalization is not contradicted, because there is a different reflexive pronoun that is restricted to subject antecedents only, namely *seg selv*.

Imperative formation and reflexivization are good tests for subjecthood, since they always target subjects, albeit not always exclusively. The next two constructions are somewhat the opposite: they are normally unrestricted, but when they are restricted to a single term type, it is always subject. The constructions are WH-question and **cleft** formation. In English, WH-question formation is unconstrained with respect to grammatical relations, and the same is true with respect to cleft formation. Examples are given below in (2.43) and (2.44).

(2.43) WH-question formation

a. Who ate my sandwich?	*who* = subject
b. Who did Pat see?	*who* = direct object
c. Who did Leslie give the tickets to?	*who* = indirect object
d. With whom did Kim go to the party?	*whom* = object of preposition *with*
e. Whose car did Dana drive?	*whose* = possessor
f. Who is Chris taller than?	*who* = object of comparative *than*

(2.44) Cleft formation

a. It was Pat who ate my sandwich.	*Pat* = subject of *ate*
b. It was Pat who Chris saw.	*Pat* = direct object of *saw*
c. It was Pat who Leslie gave the tickets to.	*Pat* = indirect object of *gave*
d. It was with Pat that Kim went to the party.	*Pat* = object of preposition *with*
e. It was Pat whose car Dana drove.	*Pat* = possessor of *car*
f. It was Pat who Chris was taller than.	*Pat* = object of comparative *than*

There are clear parallels between the two constructions. The NP *Pat* in (2.44) may be referred to as the clefted NP. Because the WH-expression or clefted NP or PP occurs in a position different from its canonical position in a simple declarative sentence, these constructions are sometimes referred to as **extraction** constructions.

In Malagasy, on the other hand, WH-question formation and cleft formation are highly constrained: if the WH-word and the clefted NP are direct arguments, they must always be the subject of the sentence. This is illustrated in the following examples.

(2.45) a. Nanasa ny lamba ny vehivavy. Malagasy
washed the clothes the woman
'The woman washed the clothes.'
b. Iza no nanasa ny lamba?
who PRT washed the clothes
'Who washed the clothes?'
c. Inona no nanasa ny vehivavy?
what PRT washed the woman
'*What did the woman wash?' (OK: 'What washed the woman?')

The third example, in which the WH-word *inona* 'what' would be interpreted as the direct object, is impossible. This is a striking restriction; does it mean that speakers of Malagasy cannot ask the equivalent of 'What did the woman wash?'? Not at all. In order to ask this, the passive voice would have to be used, yielding the Malagasy equivalent of 'What was washed by the woman?', as in (2.46b).

(2.46) a. Nosasan-ny vehivavy ny lamba. Malagasy
was.washed-the woman the clothes
'The clothes were washed by the woman.'
b. Inona no nosasan-ny vehivavy?
what PRT was.washed-the woman
'What was washed by the woman?'

Malagasy has additional voices which allow arguments other than the direct object to serve as subject, and these are crucial for WH-question formation. This is illustrated in (2.47).

(2.47) a. Manolotra ny vary ny vahiny ny vehivavy. Malagasy
offers the rice the guests the woman
'The woman offers the guests the rice.'
a′. Iza no manolotra ny vary ny vahiny?
who PRT offers the rice the guests
'Who offers the rice to the guests?'
b. Atolo-ny vehivavy ny vahiny ny vary.
be.offered.to-the woman the guests the rice
'The rice is offered to the guests by the woman.'
b′. Inona no atolo-ny vehivavy ny vahiny?
what PRT be.offered.to-the woman the guests
'What is offered to the guests by the woman?'
c. Tolorana-ny vehivavy ny vary ny vahiny.
be.offered-the woman the rice the guests
'The guests are offered the rice by the woman.'
c′. Iza no tolorana-ny vehivavy ny vary?
who PRT be.offered-the woman the rice
'Who is offered the rice by the woman?'

The verb *tolor-* 'offer' is ditransitive and therefore takes two objects, *ny vary* 'the rice' and *ny vahiny* 'the guests'. As the examples in (2.47) show, there is a different voice form which allows each of these arguments to serve as the subject, and each voice form is required for the formation of a WH-question when one of the objects of (2.47a) is to be questioned. Keenan (1976a) refers to the voice in (2.47b) as the 'intermediary voice'. The voice in (2.47c) is the passive, the same as in (2.46a). When the argument to be questioned does not serve as a direct argument of the verb in a declarative sentence, then it may, but need not, be subject in the question. This is exemplified in (2.48).

(2.48) a. Manasa ny lamba amin-ny savony ny vehivavy. Malagasy
washes the clothes with the soap the woman
'The woman washes the clothes with the soap.'
b. Amin-inona no manasa ny lamba ny vehivavy?
with-what PRT washes the clothes the woman
'With what does the woman wash the clothes?'
c. Anasan-ny vehivavy ny lamba ny savony.
be.washed.with-the woman the clothes the soap
'The soap is washed the clothes with by the woman.' (literal) or
'The soap is used by the woman to wash the clothes.'
d. Inona no anasan-ny vehivavy ny lamba?
what PRT be.washed.with-the woman the clothes
'What is washed the clothes with by the woman.' (literal) or
'What is used by the woman to wash the clothes?'

The NP *ny savony* 'the soap' is the object of the preposition *amin* 'with' and is neither subject, direct object, nor indirect object in (2.48a). It may be questioned directly, as in (2.48b), or it may occur as subject with the circumstantial voice as in (2.48c), in which case the resulting question in (2.48d) is parallel to the questions in (2.45)–(2.47).

Given the parallels between WH-question formation and cleft formation, it is not surprising that the same restrictions that apply to WH-question formation in Malagasy also apply to cleft formation. Specifically, if the clefted NP is a term argument, then it must be subject; if it is a non-term, then the PP may function directly as the clefted element, or the circumstantial voice may be used to make it subject. Examples of cleft sentences are given in (2.49).

(2.49) a. Manasa ny lamba amin'ity savony ity Rasoa. Malagasy
washes the clothes with-this soap this Rasoa
'Rasoa is washing the clothes with this soap.'
b. Rasoa no manasa ny lamba amin'ity savony ity.
Rasoa PRT washes the clothes with-this soap this
'It is Rasoa who is washing the clothes with this soap.'
c. Ny lamba no sasan-dRasoa amin'ity savony ity.
the clothes PRT be.washed-Rasoa with-this soap this
'It's the clothes that are being washed with this soap by Rasoa.'
c′. *Ny lamba no manasa amin'ity savony ity Rasoa.
the clothes PRT washes with-this soap this Rasoa
*'It's the clothes that Rasoa is washing with this soap.'
d. Amin'ity savony ity no manasa lamba Rasoa.
with-this soap this PRT washes clothes Rasoa
'It's with this soap that Rasoa is washing clothes.'
d′. Ity savony ity no anasan-dRasoa lamba.
this soap this PRT be.washed.with-Rasoa clothes
'It's this soap that is used by Rasoa to wash the clothes.'

The basic sentence is given in (2.49a), and a variant with the subject NP *Rasoa* clefted is given in (b). In order for the undergoer NP *ny lamba* 'the clothes' to appear as the clefted NP, the passive voice must be used, as in (2.49c); the result is ungrammatical if the direct object NP appears as the clefted NP, as in (c′). When the element is an oblique non-term, then it may directly appear as a clefted PP, as in (2.49d), or the circumstantial voice may be used, so that the instrument NP *ity savony ity* 'this soap' is the subject, as in (d′). Thus, among term arguments, only subjects may serve as the WH-expression in a question and the clefted NP in a cleft construction. A similar situation can be found in Kwakwala, a Wakashan language spoken in British Columbia, Canada (Anderson 1984). This restriction on extraction constructions is not very common cross-linguistically, but when it is found in a language, it always targets subjects. A number of the languages to be discussed in section 2.3 have this restriction.

With respect to imperative formation, reflexivization and two extraction constructions, subject has been found to be the most important grammatical relation, when there are restrictions on which terms can be involved in the construction. These facts have led a number of syntacticians to propose the grammatical relations hierarchy given in (2.50).

(2.50) Grammatical relations hierarchy:
SUBJECT > DIRECT OBJECT > INDIRECT OBJECT > NON-TERMS

This hierarchy embodies the claim that if a syntactic phenomenon is restricted to a single term type, then it will always be restricted to subjects. In other words, if there is a single privileged syntactic argument in a construction, it is the subject. If there are two privileged arguments, they are subject and direct object. If there are three, then they are subject, direct object and indirect object. Hence if a syntactic phenomenon targets more than one term type, it will always include subjects. This has been true for the the phenomena examined in this section. The addressee of imperative constructions is normally a subject cross-linguistically, and subjects are either the exclusive (Norwegian *seg selv*) or the preferred (English) antecedent for reflexive pronouns. Where restrictions on extraction constructions exist, the subject is the privileged argument.

Table 2.2 below summarizes the subject properties in simple sentences discussed in this section.

Complex sentences provide some of the most important subject tests, and the first one to be examined is **relative clause** formation. In a relative clause, a sentence is typically

Table 2.2. *Subject properties in simple sentences*

Simple sentences	Subject only	Terms only	No restriction
Coding properties			
Verb agreement	English	Lakhota, Basque	
Nominative case marking	Russian, Hungarian, etc.		
Behavioral Properties			
Reflexivization	Norwegian (*seg selv*)	English (incl. obl. args)	
WH-question formation	Malagasy		English
Cleft formation	Malagasy		English

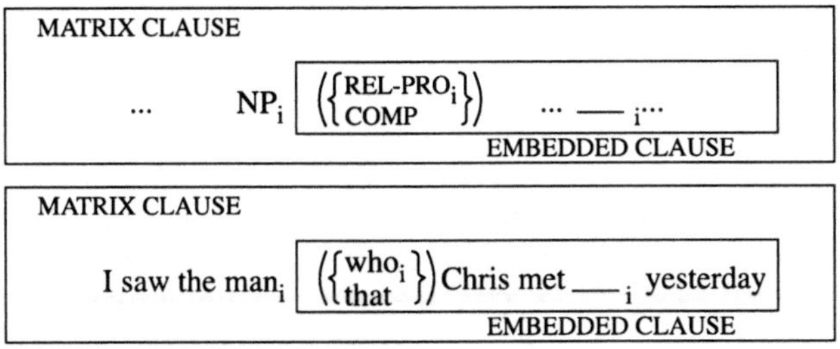

Figure 2.4. *Structure of relative clauses*

used as a modifier of an NP, and the modified NP is referred to as the 'head' of the relative clause. The structure of relative clauses is represented in Figure 2.4.

In Figure 2.4, 'NP_i' in the matrix clause is the head noun, and the relative clause follows it. In some languages, e.g. Japanese and Turkish, the relative clause precedes the head noun. The relative clause is missing a phrase, and the head noun is interpreted as having the function of the missing phrase inside the relative clause. Relative clauses may have a **relative pronoun**, a complementizer, or no marker at all; English exhibits all three possibilities. (The relative clause is in square brackets; the head is the italicized NP immediately preceding it.)

(2.51) a. I talked to *the person* [who bought the house on the corner]. — Head = subject of *bought*
a′. I talked to *the person* [that bought the house on the corner].
a″. *I talked to *the person* [bought the house on the corner].
b. I talked to *the person* [who the police interviewed]. — Head = direct object of *interview*
b′. I talked to *the person* [(that) the police interviewed].
c. I talked to *the person* [to whom the police sent a summons]. — Head = indirect object, object of prep. *to*
c′. I talked to *the person* [(that) the police sent a summons to].
c″. *I talked to *the person* [to that the police sent a summons].
d. I talked to *the person* [whose house burned down]. — Head = possessor of *house*
d′. *I talked to *the person* [(that) her house burned down].
e. I talked to *the person* [who Chris is taller than]. — Head = object of comparative *than*
e′. I talked to *the person* [(that) Chris is taller than].

Relative clauses with external heads are another kind of extraction construction. This is clearest when relative pronouns are involved. The relative pronouns in English are the same WH-expressions that occur in the WH-questions in (2.43), and as in WH-questions the relative pronoun occurs clause-initially and not in the canonical position in which the corresponding non-WH-expression would occur in a simple declarative utterance. Even if there is no relative pronoun, as in the primed examples in (2.51), the interpretive problem is the same: the head NP is outside of the relative clause and yet is interpreted as having a syntactic function in it. In the primed examples, *that* is not a relative pronoun; rather, it is a complementizer, akin to its function in sentences like *I know that Chris bought a new house*. This can be seen most clearly in the contrast among the sentences in (2.51c), (2.51c′) and (2.51c″). The relative pronoun *who(m)* can serve as the object of the preposition *to*, as in (c), but the complementizer *that* cannot, as (c″) shows. The grammatical equivalent of (c) with *that* is (c′) in which the preposition *to* is stranded at the end of the relative clause. *That* is also impossible in constructions involving heads functioning as a possessor in the relative clause, as in (2.51d′). This is to be expected if *that* is a complementizer rather than a pronoun, because only the latter would have a possessive form in English.

Grammatical relations do not play a significant role in extraction constructions in English. This has already been seen with respect to WH-questions in (2.43) and to cleft constructions in (2.44) (which involve relative clauses), and the examples in (2.51) show that the same is mostly true with respect to relativization. If relative pronouns are used, then grammatical relations are irrelevant. If relative pronouns are not used, as in the primed examples, then they are relevant with respect to the possibility of omitting the complementizer *that*: if the head functions as the subject within the relative clause, as in (2.51a′), then *that* is obligatory, as (2.51a″) shows. Given the parallels among extraction constructions and the importance of grammatical relations for WH-questions and clefting in Malagasy, it is to be expected that grammatical relations will be equally important for relativization in this language, and this is in fact the case. Examples of Malagasy relative clauses are given below; *izay* is an optional complementizer analogous to English *that*.

(2.52) a. Manasa ny lamba amin'ity savony ity ny zazavavy. — Malagasy
washes the clothes with-this soap this the girl
'The girl is washing the clothes with this soap.'

b. ny zazavavy (izay) manasa ny lamba — Head = subject (actor)
the girl (COMP) washes the clothes
'the girl who is washing the clothes'

b′. *ny lamba (izay) manasa amin'ity savony ity ny zazavavy — *Head = direct object (undergoer)
the clothes (COMP) washes with-this soap this the girl
Intended: 'the clothes that the girl washed with this soap'

b″. *ity savony ity (izay) manasa ny lamba amin ny zazavavy — *Head = non-term (instrument)
this soap this (COMP) washes the clothes with the girl
Intended: 'this soap that the girl washed the clothes with'

Given a simple sentence like the one in (2.52a), it is possible to form only one relative clause, the one in (b) in which the head is interpreted as the subject of the relative clause; it cannot be construed as the direct object (undergoer), as in (b′), or as an oblique non-term (instrument), as in (b″). In order to form a relative clause with the head interpreted as the undergoer, the verb in the relative clause must be in the passive voice, as in (2.53a). The resulting relative clause in (2.53b) is grammatical.

(2.53) a. Sasan'ny zazavavy amin'ity savony ity ny lamba. Malagasy
be.washed-the girl with-this soap this the clothes
'The clothes are washed with this soap by the girl.'
b. ny lamba (izay) sasan'ny zazavavy amin'ity Head = subject
the clothes (COMP) be.washed-the girl with-this (undergoer)
savony ity
soap this
'the clothes that are washed with this soap by the girl'

Finally, in order to form a relative clause in which the head is interpreted as an instrument, the circumstantial voice must be used within the relative clause, yielding the relative clause in (2.54b).

(2.54) a. Anasan'ny zazavavy ny lamba ity savony ity. Malagasy
be.washed.with-the girl the clothes this soap this
'The soap is used by the girl to wash the clothes.'
b. ity savony ity (izay) anasan'ny zazavavy Head = subject
this soap this (COMP) be.washed.with-the girl (instrument)
ny lamba
the clothes
'the soap that is used by the girl to wash the clothes'

Thus, in all three extraction constructions in Malagasy, there is a restriction to the effect that if the extracted or displaced element is a term, it must be the subject of the relevant sentence, and accordingly, grammatical relations play a very important role in these constructions in Malagasy, unlike English. If a language has a restriction on extraction like that found in Malagasy, then these constructions constitute a good test for subjecthood in such a language.

Another construction which involves an element occurring in other than its canonical position is what will be called a '**matrix**-coding construction'; it is also known as a '**raising**' construction. There are two types in English, and they are illustrated in (2.55).

(2.55) a. It seems (that) the students have forgotten the assignment.
a′. The students seem to have forgotten the assignment.
b. Leslie believes (that) the students have forgotten the assignment.
b′. Leslie believes the students to have forgotten the assignment.

In (2.55a) the NP *the students* is the subject of the embedded clause *that the students have forgotten the assignment*, whereas in (a′) it is is the subject of the matrix clause headed by *seem*, which agrees with it. The embedded clause is now a tenseless **infinitive**, marked by *to*. The structure of these sentences is given in Figure 2.5.

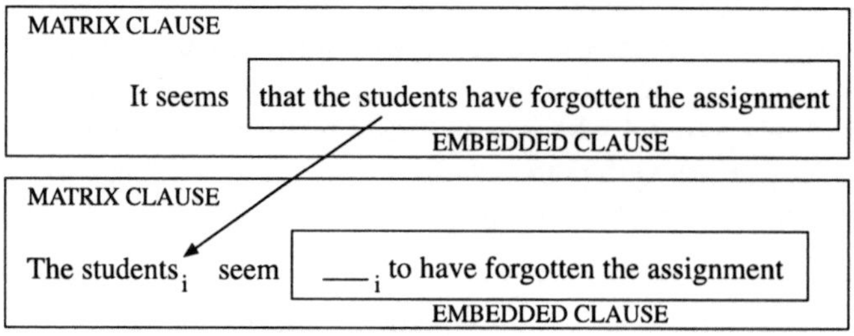

Figure 2.5. *Structure of matrix-coding-as-subject construction*

In (2.55b), as in (a), the NP *the students* is the subject of the embedded clause, while in (b′) it is the direct object of the matrix verb *believe* and again the embedded clause is an infinitive. The structure of these sentences is given in Figure 2.6.

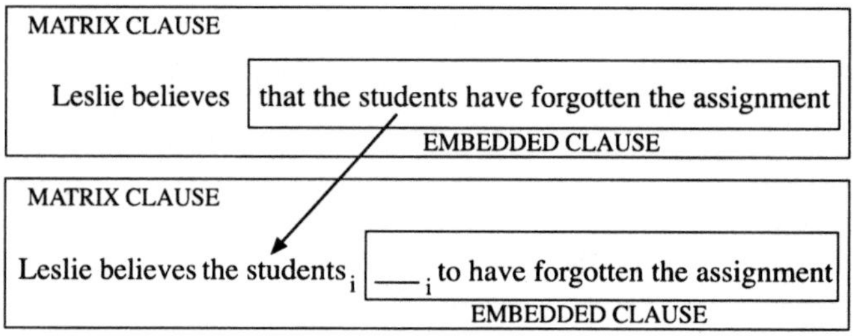

Figure 2.6. *Structure of matrix-coding-as-object construction*

There is no change in the semantic role of the NP *the students* in (2.55a′) and (2.55b′) from (2.55a) and (2.55b): in all four sentences the NP *the students* is the actor of *forget*; in particular, it is not the undergoer of *believe* in (b), (b′), because in both examples what Leslie believes is 'the students forgot the assignment' (see (2.64)–(2.66) below). It is clear that *the students* is the subject of the matrix clause in (2.55a′), since it occurs in the preverbal subject position and triggers verb agreement. What is the evidence this NP is the direct object of *believe* in (b′)? Three pieces of evidence are usually given. First, if *the students* is replaced by a pronoun in (b), it is a nominative pronoun, whereas if the same replacement is done in (b′), the pronoun is accusative.

(2.56) a. Leslie believes (that) they/*them have forgotten the assignment.
b. Leslie believes them/*they to have forgotten the assignment.

Second, in English a reflexive pronoun must be in the same clause as its antecedent, as illustrated in (2.57). (The 'k', 'l' subscripts on *him* and *her* refer to possible discourse antecedents outside of the sentence.)

(2.57) Sam$_i$ believes that Mary$_j$ embarrassed him$_{i/k}$/*himself$_i$/her$_{*j/l}$/herself$_j$.

The subject of the embedded clause in (2.55b), *the students*, cannot be replaced by a reflexive pronoun, whereas it is possible to replace *the students* by a reflexive pronoun in (b′). Since the reflexive must be in the same clause with its antecedent, this shows that *themselves* must be in the same clause as *the students* in (b) but not (a).

(2.58) a. The students$_i$ believe (that) they$_i$/*themselves$_i$ have forgotten the assignment.
b. The students$_i$ believe themselves$_i$/*them$_i$ to have forgotten the assignment.

Third, in a passive construction the argument that is the direct object in the active voice form appears as the subject in the passive voice form. *The students* in (2.55b′) can serve as the subject of a passive matrix clause, as illustrated in (2.59b).

(2.59) a. *The students were believed by Leslie have forgotten the assignment.
b. The students were believed by Leslie to have forgotten the assignment.

Passivizing (2.55b) yields the ungrammatical (2.59a). Hence it appears that the NP *the students* in (2.55b′) is the direct object of *believe* in the matrix clause.

The question to be asked now is, which argument of the embedded clause can be matrix-coded? That is, which argument of the embedded verb can serve as the subject of *seem* or the direct object of *believe*? Let's look at the matrix-coding-as-subject construction with *seem* first. Consider the following sentences; the matrix-coding version is given first and the non-matrix-coding version below in the primed examples.

(2.60) a. Chris seems to be doing the assignment.
a′. It seems that Chris is doing the assignment.
b. Chris seems to be running.
b′. It seems that Chris is running.
c. Chris seems to be sad.
c′. It seems that Chris is sad.
d. *Chris$_i$ seems the police to have arrested $\_\__i$.
d′. It seems that the police have arrested Chris.
e. Chris seems to have been arrested by the police.
e′. It seems that Chris has been arrested by the police.

In (2.60a), the NP *Chris* is interpreted as the subject of the lower clause and as the actor of its verb. In (b) it is likewise construed as the subject and actor of the lower clause. Note that there are two hypotheses that could account for these first two sentences; one is that the matrix-coded NP must be interpreted as the subject of the embedded clause, and the other is that it must be construed as the actor of the verb in the embedded clause. Both hypotheses account for (2.60a) and (2.60b), but only one accounts for (2.60c). In this sentence, the NP *Chris* is interpreted as the subject of the embedded clause but as the undergoer of the predicate *be sad.* Hence it is not the case that the matrix-coded NP must be the actor of the embedded clause. The sentences in (d) and (e) further support this conclusion. The example in (2.60d) is ungrammatical, and as (d′) shows, the matrix-coded NP is interpreted as the direct object and undergoer in the lower clause. The problem is not that it is an undergoer, however, as (c) shows. If the lower clause is passive, as in (e), then the construction is perfectly grammatical, and in (e) *Chris* is interpreted as the subject and the undergoer of the embedded clause. Thus, it does not matter whether the matrix-coded NP is the actor or undergoer of the lower clause; what matters is that it be interpreted as the *subject* of the embedded clause.

The matrix-coding-as-object construction with *believe* is governed by the very same constraint. It is exemplified in (2.61).

(2.61) a. Leslie believes Chris to be doing the assignment.
a′. Leslie believes that Chris is doing the assignment.
b. Leslie believes Chris to be running.
b′. Leslie believes that Chris is running.
c. Leslie believes Chris to be sad.
c′. Leslie believes that Chris is sad.
d. *Leslie believes $Chris_i$ the police to have arrested $\_\__i$.
d′. Leslie believes that the police have arrested Chris.
e. Leslie believes Chris to have been arrested by the police.
e′. Leslie believes that Chris has been arrested by the police.

The pattern of grammaticality and ungrammaticality in (2.61) is identical to that in (2.60), and therefore it may be concluded that the crucial restriction on this construction is that the matrix-coded NP, in this instance the direct object of *believe*, must be interpreted as the subject of the embedded clause.

Malagasy has both of these constructions, and they are both constrained by the subject-only requirement. The matrix-coding-as-subject construction is illustrated in (2.62).

(2.62) a. Toa manasa lamba Rasoa. — Malagasy
seem wash clothes
'Rasoa seems to be washing clothes.'
b. *Toa manasa Rasoa ny lamba.
seem wash the clothes
*'The clothes seem Rasoa to be washing.'
c. Toa sasan'dRasoa ny lamba.
seem be.washed-Rasoa the clothes
'The clothes seem to be being washed by Rasoa.'

The verb meaning 'seem' in Malagasy is *toa*, and in this construction its subject must be interpreted as the subject of the embedded verb. In (b), in which the subject of *toa*, *ny lamba* 'the clothes', is to be interpreted as the direct object of *manasa* 'wash', the result is ungrammatical. In order for this NP to be the subject of *toa* 'seem', the embedded verb must be passive, as in (c). This parallels the English examples in (2.60d) and (2.60e). The matrix-coding-as-object construction is exemplified in (2.63).

(2.63) a. Nanantena Rasoa fa nanasa ny zaza ny vehivavy. — Malagasy
hoped COMP washed the child the woman
'Rasoa hoped that the woman washed the child.'
b. Nanantena ny vehivavy ho nanasa ny zaza Rasoa.
hoped the woman COMP washed the child
'Rasoa hoped the woman to have washed the child.'
c. Nanantena ny zaza ho nanasa ny vehivavy Rasoa.
hoped the child COMP washed the woman
*'Rasoa hoped the child the woman to have washed.' (OK: 'Rasoa hoped the child to have washed the woman.')
d. Nanantena ny zaza ho sasan'ny vehivavy Rasoa.
hoped the child COMP be.washed-the woman
'Rasoa hoped the child to have been washed by the woman.'

The change from the non-matrix coding construction in (2.63a) to the matrix-coding construction in (b) is much more dramatic than in English: in (a) the subject of the embedded clause, *ny vehivavy* 'the woman', occurs at the end of the embedded clause, whereas in (b) *ny vehivavy* 'the woman' appears immediately after the matrix verb and before the embedded clause, which separates it from the subject of the matrix clause. The immediately postverbal NP in the matrix clause is interpreted as the subject of the embedded clause. The matrix subject occurs before the embedded *fa*-clause, but in the matrix-coding construction it occurs in its usual sentence-final position. In (c) the sentence is grammatical, but the postverbal NP, *ny zaza* 'the child' must be interpreted as the subject and not as the direct object of the embedded clause. This shows that the subject-only constraint is in effect. The only way to have *ny zaza* 'the child' appear in the matrix clause and be interpreted as the undergoer of the embedded verb is for the embedded verb to be passive, as in (2.63d). If one wanted to form sentences like 'the soap seems to be used by the woman to wash the clothes' or 'Rasoa hopes the soap to be used by the woman to wash the clothes', then the circumstantial voice would have to be used in the embedded clause, just as in the extraction constructions.

Cross-linguistically, matrix-coding-as-subject constructions are much more common than matrix-coding-as-object constructions. If a language had one or both of them, and the matrix-coded NP could have only one function in the embedded clause, then the grammatical relations hierarchy in (2.50) predicts that the construction(s) should be restricted to subjects only. Hence in such a language, e.g. Malagasy and English, the ability to be matrix-coded in one of these constructions would be a distinctive property of subjects.

The constructions investigated so far all involve an element not occurring in its canonical position in a sentence. The next two constructions to be examined have rather different properties: in them, an element that would normally appear in a simple clause is missing, and the crucial question is, which element can be omitted? The first construction looks superficially similar to the matrix-coding constructions; it is illustrated in (2.64) and is known as a **control structure** (also known as '**equi-NP-deletion**').

(2.64) a. Pat tried to open the window.
a′. *Pat tried (for) Kim to open the window.
b. Dana persuaded Pat to open the window.
b′. *Dana persuaded Pat (for) Kim to open the window.

In this construction, there is an argument which is obligatorily missing from the embedded clause, as the ungrammatical primed examples show. The structure of (2.64a) is given in Figure 2.7.

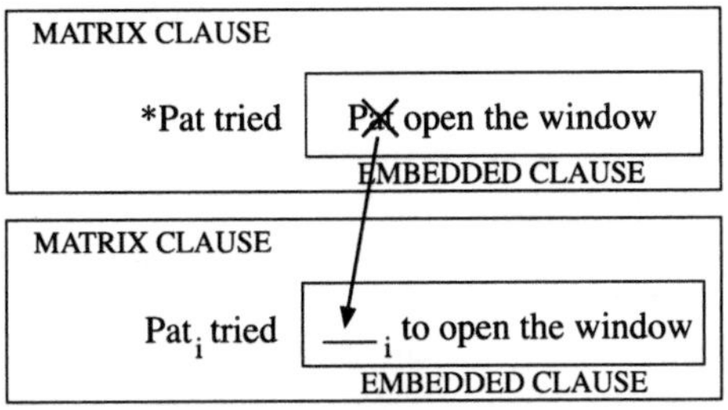

Figure 2.7. *Structure of control construction in (2.64a)*

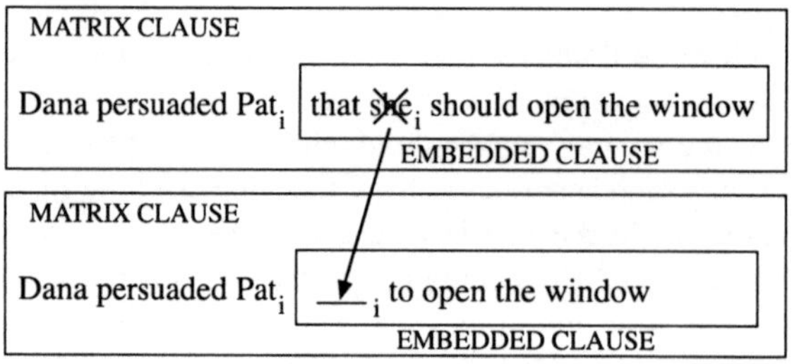

Figure 2.8. *Structure of control construction in (2.64b)*

The structure of the control construction in (2.64b) is given in Figure 2.8.

The control construction in (2.64a) looks rather like the matrix-coding-as-subject construction in (2.60a), and analogously, the control construction in (2.64b) bears a strong resemblance to the matrix-coding-as-object construction in (2.61a); in both types of construction the embedded clause is an infinitive and appears to be missing an argument. There is, however, a very important difference between the two construction types. In matrix-coding constructions, the matrix-coded NP is not an argument of the matrix verb semantically; that is, in (2.60a) *Chris* is not a semantic argument of *seem* but rather the actor of *do* only, and in (2.61a) *Chris* is not the undergoer of *believe*. In (2.64a), on the other hand, *Pat* is interpreted semantically as both the actor of *try* and the actor of *open*, and similarly in (2.64b) *Pat* is semantically the undergoer of *persuade* and the actor of *open*. Evidence for this comes from the following contrasts.

(2.65) a. Pat seems to have opened the window.
a′. The window seems to have been opened by Pat.
b. Pat tried to open the window.
b′. *The window tried to be opened by Pat.

(2.66) a. Kim believed Pat to have opened the window.
a′. Kim believed the window to have been opened by Pat.
b. Kim persuaded Pat to open the window.
b′. *Kim persuaded the window to be opened by Pat.
c. Kim believed the doctor to have examined Pat.
c′. Kim believed Pat to have been examined by the doctor.
d. Kim persuaded the doctor to examine Pat.
d′. Kim persuaded Pat to be examined by the doctor.

In the sentences with *seem* and *believe*, the meaning of the sentence is not substantially affected by the choice of active or passive voice in the embedded clause, and both possibilities are grammatical. That is, if it is true that Kim believes Pat to have opened the window, then it is also true that Kim believes the window to have been opened by Pat. This contrasts sharply with the sentences involving *try* and *persuade*; only the versions with active voice in the embedded clause are grammatical in (2.65b), (2.65b′) and (2.66b), (2.66b′). The reason for this is that *try* requires an **animate** actor as its subject, and an **inanimate** NP like *the window* cannot satisfy this requirement. Similarly, *persuade* requires an undergoer which refers to an entity that is persuadable, i.e. animate and sentient, and again the inanimate NP *the window* fails to satisfy this requirement of the verb. Since neither *Pat* nor *the window* are semantic arguments of *seem* or *believe*, either can occur as subject with *seem* or direct object with *believe*. The ungrammaticality of (2.65b′) and (2.66b′) shows that the subject of *try* is semantically its actor and that the direct object of *persuade* is semantically its undergoer. This can also be seen in the final four examples in (2.66). The two matrix-coding sentences, (2.66c), (2.66c′) mean the same thing; if (2.66c) is true, then (2.66c′) is also true. The two control sentences in (2.66d), (2.66d′) do not mean the same thing; in (2.66d) it is the doctor who is persuaded, but in (2.66d′) it is Pat who is persuaded. The first one could be true and the second one false, and vice versa.

Thus, control constructions differ fundamentally from matrix-coding constructions, but the question to be raised is the same: which argument in the embedded infinitive is pivotal for the construction? The following examples, parallel to those in (2.60) and (2.61), provide the relevant evidence.

(2.67) a. Pat tried to do the assignment.
b. Pat tried to run.
c. Pat tried to sleep.
d. *Pat$_i$ tried (for) Kim to see __$_i$.
e. Pat tried to be seen by Kim.

(2.68) a. Kim persuaded the students to do the assignment.
a′. Kim persuaded the students that they should do the assignment.
b. Kim persuaded the students to run.
b′. Kim persuaded the students that they should run.
c. Kim persuaded the students to sleep.
c′. Kim persuaded the students that they should sleep.
d. *Kim persuaded the students$_i$ (for) the doctor to examine __$_i$.
d′. Kim persuaded the students that the doctor should examine them.
e. Kim persuaded the students to be examined by the doctor.
e′. Kim persuaded the students that they should be examined by the doctor.

The pattern of grammatical and ungrammatical sentences is the same as it was in (2.60) and (2.61). It does not matter whether the omitted argument is an actor, as in the (a) and (b) examples, or is an undergoer, as in the (c) and (e) sentences; rather, what matters is whether the omitted argument would be the subject, if the embedded clause were complete, as in the primed examples. Hence the crucial feature of these constructions for our discussion is that the missing argument in the embedded clause must be the subject.

Malagasy has a control construction corresponding to (2.67) but not to (2.68). Not surprisingly, the missing argument in the embedded clause must be the subject, the same subject-only restriction found in all of the other Malagasy constructions discussed in this chapter.

(2.69) a. Mikasa hanasa ny zaza ny vehivavy. Malagasy
intends wash the child the woman
'The woman intends to wash the child.'
a′. Mikasa hanasa ny vehivavy ny zaza.
intends wash the woman the child
*'The child$_i$ intends (for) the woman to wash __$_i$.' (OK: 'The child intends to wash the woman.')

b. Mikasa hosasan-ny vehivavy ny zaza.
intends be.washed-the woman the child
'The child intends to be washed by the woman.'

In (2.69a) *ny vehivavy* 'the woman' is the actor of *kasa-* 'intend' and is interpreted as the actor and subject of *sasa-* 'wash'. In (a′) only one interpretation is possible, namely the one in which *ny zaza* 'the child' is the subject and therefore the actor of the embedded clause; it cannot be interpreted as the actor of *kasa-* and the undergoer of *sasa-* in this sentence. In order to express this meaning, it is necessary to passivize the embedded clause, as in (2.69b). Thus here again there is a restriction to subjects in Malagasy, and as in the matrix-coding constructions, it parallels the situation in English.

The final construction to be examined in this section involves an omitted argument in a **coordinate** construction. The construction contains two or more clauses, and each of the clauses except the first is missing an argument. It is often referred to as '**conjunction reduction**'. Again, the questions is, which argument can be left out? Examples from English are given in (2.70) and (2.71).

(2.70) a. Sally$_i$ saw Pam$_j$, and she$_{i/j}$ greeted her$_{j/i}$.
b. Sally$_i$ saw Pam$_j$, and __$_{i/*j}$ greeted her.
c. *Sally$_i$ saw Pam$_j$, and she$_j$ greeted __$_i$.
d. Sally$_i$ saw Pam$_j$, and __$_{i/*j}$ was greeted by her.

(2.71) a. John$_i$ got mad at Bill$_j$, and he$_{i/j}$ punched him$_{j/i}$.
b. John$_i$ got mad at Bill$_j$, and __$_{i/*j}$ punched him.
c. *John$_i$ got mad at Bill$_j$, and he$_j$ punched __$_i$.
d. John$_i$ got mad at Bill$_j$, and __$_{i/*j}$ was punched by him.

The first sentence in each group contains two clauses and no missing arguments in the second clause. In the (b) examples, the subject of the second clause is omitted, and the result is grammatical, if the missing subject is interpreted as coreferential with the subject of the first clause. The structure of (2.70b) is given in Figure 2.9.

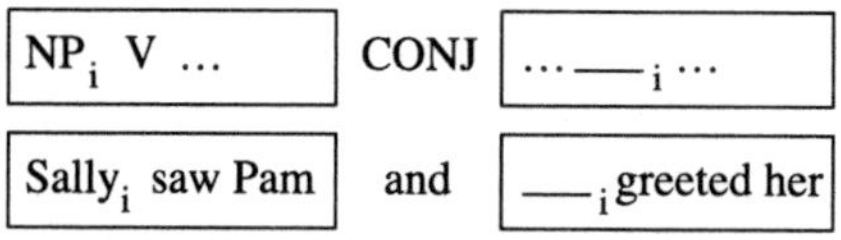

Figure 2.9. *Structure of conjunction-reduction construction in (2.70b)*

In the (c) examples, on the other hand, the direct object of the second clause is missing, and the result is quite ungrammatical. As in the matrix-coding and control constructions, the problem with the (c) sentences can be remedied by having the second clause in the passive voice, so that the NP coreferential with the subject of the first clause would be the subject of the second clause.

Malagasy has a conjunction-reduction construction, and as in all of the other constructions, the subject is the crucial argument. Two examples are given in (2.72).

(2.72) a. Misotro taoka Rabe ary mihinam-bary. Malagasy
drinks booze Rabe and eats-rice.
'Rabe is drinking booze and is eating rice.'

b. Nahita ny vehivavy Rasoa ary nanasa ny zaza.
saw the woman Rasoa and washed the child
'Rasoa saw the woman and washed the child.'

These are parallel to the English examples above. If the identical argument in the second clause is not the actor, it may not be omitted, as (2.73a) and (2.73a′) show. As in English, passive is required in the second clause, if the conjunction-reduction construction is to be used.

(2.73) a. Nahita ny zaza Rasoa ary nanasa ny vehivavy. Malagasy
saw the child Rasoa and washed the woman
*'Rasoa$_i$ saw the child and the woman washed __$_i$.' (OK: 'Rasoa saw the child and washed the woman.')
a′. Nahita ny zaza Rasoa ary nanasa izy ny vehivavy.
saw the child Rasoa and washed 3sg the woman
'Rasoa saw the child and the woman washed her.'
b. Nahita ny zaza Rasoa ary nosasan'ny vehivavy.
saw the child Rasoa and was.washed-the woman
'Rasoa saw the child and was washed by the woman.'

There is one additional question that can be asked about the control and conjunction-reduction constructions. In both of them, there is a missing argument in an embedded (control) or non-initial clause (conjunction reduction), and the interpretation of the omitted argument is derived from one of the arguments of the matrix clause (control) or initial clause (conjunction reduction). Which argument in the matrix or initial clause can serve as the **controller** (or antecedent) of the missing argument in the embedded or following clause? In control constructions with verbs like English *try* in (2.67) and Malagasy *kasa-* 'intend' in (2.69), the controller is the subject of the matrix verb. This is not surprising, since there is only one NP in the matrix clause, and therefore it is the only possible controller. In control constructions with verbs like *persuade* in (2.68), on the other hand, the controller is the direct object, not the subject. In conjunction-reduction constructions, the controller in the first clause is always the subject. In (2.70b) and (2.71b), the person doing the greeting or punching must be the subject of the first clause; that is, (2.70b), for example, cannot mean that Pam greeted Sally. The same is true in Malagasy: (2.72b) must be interpreted with Rasoa, not the woman, being the one washing the child. Thus in both languages the controller in the first clause of the missing argument in the second clause must be the subject.

Not all languages show the same restrictions on control constructions that English and Malagasy do. Tindi, a Dagestanian language spoken in the Caucasus region of Russia (Kibrik 1985), is an example of a language in which there is no restriction to subject in terms of which argument can be omitted in the embedded clause.

(2.74) a. Wač̄uła [jač̄i hēła] q'očā hiḳ'i. Tindi
brother.DAT sister.ABS see want not
'Brother doesn't want to see sister.' Omitted NP = subject
b. Jač̄uła [wač̄$_0$i L$_0$'eła] q'očā hiḳ'i.
sister.DAT brother.ERG beat want not
'Sister$_i$ doesn't want brother to beat __$_i$.' Omitted NP = direct object

In (2.74a), the omitted argument in the embedded clause (in square brackets) is the subject, but in (b) it is the direct object. There is no passive voice in this language; it is the direct object of an active-voice verb which is omitted in (2.74b), something which is impossible in English or Malagasy. This is also possible in the Tindi equivalent of conjunction reduction. This is illustrated in (2.75).

(2.75) a. Wac̄i wo?o, jac̄i hāwo. Tindi
brother.ABS came sister.ABS saw
'Brother came and saw sister.' Omitted NP = subject
b. Wac̄i wo?o, jac̄$_{o}$i buRo.
brother.ABS came sister.ERG hit
'Brother$_i$ came and sister hit __$_i$.' Omitted NP = direct object

The first sentence is very much like its English and Malagasy counterparts, but the second is quite different. In it the direct object of the second clause is omitted, a possibility not available in English or Malagasy. Tindi is like these two languages in having the subject of the first clause be the controller of the missing argument in the second clause, as illustrated in (2.76a); as in English and Malagasy, a pronoun must be used in order to interpret a non-subject in the first clause as the subject of the second, as in (2.76b).

(2.76) a. Wac̄uba jac̄i hāwo, woLo. Tindi
brother.LOC sister.ABS saw left.
'Brother saw sister and left.' Controller = subject
NOT: 'Brother saw sister$_i$ and __$_i$ left.'
b. Wac̄uba jac̄i hāwo, oj jeLo.
brother.LOC sister.ABS saw 3sgFEM left.
'Brother saw sister, and she left.'

The Tindi sentences in (2.74)–(2.76) illustrate interesting 'mismatches' between case and grammatical relations (cf. section 2.2.1). Like Avar in (2.11), the actor with a perception verb like 'see' occurs in the locative case, as (2.76) shows, and the actor of the verb 'want' appears in the dative case, as (2.74a) shows; non-experiencer actors occur in the ergative case, as in (2.74b) and (2.75b) with the verbs 'beat' and 'hit'. In the control constructions in (2.74), the dative NPs act as controllers, just like subject NPs in English and Malagasy, and the omitted arguments are the actor in the locative case in (2.74a) and undergoer in the absolutive case in (2.74b). In the conjunction-reduction constructions in (2.75) and (2.76), the omitted NP in the second clause in (2.75a) is the actor in the locative case, and in (2.76a) the controller in the first clause of the missing argument in the second clause is the actor in the locative case. Thus in Tindi, actors in the dative and locative case can be subjects in control and conjunction-reduction constructions, and this illustrates very well the point made in section 2.1.1 that it is impossible in many languages to find consistent correlations between case and grammatical relations.

A number of properties of subjects in both simple and complex sentences have been presented. This is not an exhaustive list of possible subject properties, but the ones discussed are sufficient to permit the identification of subject in a wide range of languages. While not every language will have all of these phenomena, it is usually the case that enough of them are found in a language to make it possible to identify subjects. The properties are summarized in Table 2.3.

Table 2.3. *Subject properties*

	Subject only	Terms only	No restriction
Simple sentences			
Coding properties			
Verb agreement	English	Lakhota, Basque	
Nominative case marking	Russian, Hungarian, etc.		
Behavioral properties			
Reflexivization	Norwegian (*seg selv*)	English (incl. obl. objs)	
WH-question formation	Malagasy		English
Cleft formation	Malagasy		English
Complex sentences			
Relative clause formation	Malagasy		English
Matrix-coding ('raising')	English, Malagasy		
Control–omitted argument ('equi-NP-deletion')	English, Malagasy	Tindi	
Conjunction reduction–omitted NP	English, Malagasy	Tindi	
Conjunction reduction–controller	English, Malagasy, Tindi		

If one of these constructions exists in the language and, crucially, involvement in the construction is limited to a single type of argument, then the grammatical relations hierarchy in (2.50) predicts that the argument in question will be a subject. Hence these tests are very valuable under these conditions, which are in fact common cross-linguistically.

2.2.2.2 *Direct object*

Direct objects are difficult to characterize universally, because they have few unique or exclusive attributes. With respect to coding properties, they are typically in the accusative case, but, as shown in the examples in (2.32) and (2.33), this is not a consistent cue to the identity of direct objects, since some languages have objects in cases other than the accusative (e.g. Russian, Latin, Icelandic) and others may mark both direct and indirect objects with the accusative (e.g. Korean, Quechua). If the verb agrees with two terms, then the agreement should be with the subject and the direct object, according to the hierarchy in (2.50). Hence neither coding property represents a consistent characteristic of direct objects, although in many languages accusative case is a reliable feature, e.g. German.

In semantic role terms, the kind of neutralization found with subjects is not found with direct objects. In the discussion of subjects, it was shown that in some languages, e.g. English, the subject can be the actor of a transitive verb, the actor of an intransitive verb, the undergoer of a transitive verb (in a passive construction), or the undergoer of an intransitive verb; the examples in (2.60) and (2.61) show this clearly. Direct objects are normally features of clauses with active-voice transitive verbs, and the direct object is always an undergoer semantically. There is no neutralization of actor and undergoer with respect to direct object, but there is neutralization with respect to the thematic relations of the argument. As (2.16) showed, the undergoer can be a patient, theme, recipient, stimulus, source or experiencer, in thematic-relations terms (this list should not be taken as exhaustive). Hence with respect to the notion of direct object, the semantic neutralization is in terms of thematic relations, not in terms of macroroles.

There is one consistent behavioral property of direct objects: if a language has a passive construction, then the NP which would be the direct object in the active voice can appear as the subject in the passive voice. Numerous examples of this from English and Malagasy have already been presented. However, what Malagasy also shows is that being able to be the subject of a non-active voice construction is not a unique attribute of direct objects. It could be argued that these examples are misleading, because there is one voice form for erstwhile direct objects (undergoers) to be subject and other voice forms (circumstantial, intermediary voices) for other arguments (instruments, non-undergoer themes). There are languages in which the same voice construction permits either the direct or indirect object of the corresponding active sentence to be subject. This is exemplified by Japanese (Kuno 1973) in (2.77).

(2.77) a. Hanako ga Taroo ni kunsyoo o atae-ta. Japanese
Hanako NOM Taroo DAT medal ACC give-PAST
'Hanako gave Taroo a/the medal' Or 'Hanako gave a/the medal to Taroo.'
b. Kunsyoo ga Hanako ni yotte Taroo ni atae-rare-ta.
medal NOM Hanako DAT by Taroo DAT give-PASS-PAST
'A/the medal was given to Taroo by Hanako.'
c. Taroo ga Hanako ni kunsyoo o atae-rare-ta.
Taroo NOM Hanako DAT medal ACC give-PASS-PAST
'Taroo was given a/the medal by Hanako.'

In the active-voice sentence in (2.77a), *Hanako* is the subject (actor) in the nominative case, *Taroo* is the indirect object (recipient) in the dative case, and *kunsyoo* 'medal' is the direct object (undergoer) in the accusative case. Two possible passive sentences can be formed: in (2.77b) the undergoer, the direct object in (2.77a), is the subject, while in (2.77c), the recipient, the indirect object in (2.77a) is the subject. Note that in (2.77c) the direct object (undergoer) is in the accusative case, just as in (2.77a). Japanese is exceptional in this regard; in the vast majority of languages with a single non-active voice construction, only the argument which appears as the direct object in the corresponding active sentence, i.e. the undergoer, can serve as the subject in a passive construction. However, Japanese does not contradict the above generalization about direct objects, because the direct object can appear as the subject of the passive.

Many languages have constructions in which arguments which would not normally appear as a direct object are allowed to be realized as a direct object. English exhibits four alternations of this kind. The first involves the indirect object and is usually referred to as **'dative shift'**. It is illustrated in (2.78), along with the corresponding passive versions; an abstract schema of the alternation is given in (2.78c) and (2.78c′), in which *Chris* = NP_1, *the package* = NP_2 and *Pat* = NP_3.

(2.78) a. Chris sent the package to Pat. Direct object = undergoer (theme)
a′. The package was sent to Pat by Chris.
a″. *Pat was sent the package to by Chris.

b.	Chris sent Pat the package.	Direct object = undergoer (recipient)
b′.	Pat was sent the package by Chris.	
b″.	(*)The package was sent Pat by Chris.	
c.	NP_1 V NP_2 *to*-NP_3	(= (2.78a))
c′.	NP_1 V NP_3 NP_2	(= (2.78b))

There is little agreement among syntacticians regarding the analysis of this English construction, even with respect to which NP is the direct object and which is the indirect object in (2.78b); some argue that *Pat* is the indirect object and *the package* the direct object (which equates the thematic relations recipient with indirect object and theme with direct object), while others argue that *Pat* is the direct object and *the package* is a secondary object (see section 2.2.2.4). Given the active voice sentence in (2.78a), the only passive that can be formed is (a′) in which *the package*, the direct object of (a), is subject. The only passive form of (2.78b) that all English speakers accept is (b′) in which *Pat*, the direct object in (b), is subject. The fact that many speakers find (2.78b″) ungrammatical suggests that *the package* is not the direct object in (b), since it cannot be the subject of the corresponding passive. An alternation similar to dative shift was presented in (2.21) and is repeated below; an abstract schema for it is given in (2.79e), (2.79e′).

(2.79)	a.	The president presented the award to Leslie.	Direct object = undergoer (theme)
	a′.	The award was presented to Leslie by the president.	
	b.	The president presented Leslie with the award.	Direct object = undergoer (recipient)
	b′.	Leslie was presented with the award by the president.	
	c.	The company supplied uniforms to the team.	Direct object = undergoer (theme)
	c′.	Uniforms were supplied to the team by the company.	
	d.	The company supplied the team with uniforms.	Direct object = undergoer (recipient)
	d′.	The team was supplied with uniforms by the company.	
	e.	NP_1 V NP_2 *to*-NP_3	(= (2.79a, c))
	e′.	NP_1 V NP_3 *with*-NP_2	(= (2.79b, d))

The primary difference between this alternation, which may be termed the 'transfer alternation', and dative shift is that the theme argument is marked by *with* when it is not undergoer, whereas in the dative-shift construction it is not marked by a preposition. *Present* and *supply* are verbs of transfer like *give* and *send*, which are canonical dative-shift verbs. Hence there is a basic similarity between these two alternations, and in all of the sentences in (2.78) and (2.79), the non-oblique NP immediately following the verb is the undergoer and direct object, when the verb is in active voice.

The third alternation is known as the 'locative alternation', and it is illustrated in (2.80).

(2.80) a. Dana sprayed the fertilizer on the plants. — Direct object = undergoer (theme)
a′. The fertilizer was sprayed on the plants by Dana.
b. Dana sprayed the plants with the fertilizer. — Direct object = undergoer (location)
b′. The plants were sprayed with the fertilizer by Dana.
c. Kim loaded the boxes onto the truck. — Direct object = undergoer (theme)
c′. The boxes were loaded onto the truck by Kim.
d. Kim loaded the truck with the boxes. — Direct object = undergoer (location)
d′. The truck was loaded with the boxes by Kim.
e. NP_1 V NP_2 *on/onto*-NP_3 (= (2.80a, c))
e′. NP_1 V NP_3 *with*-NP_2 (= (2.80b, d))

The locative alternation is very similar to the transfer alternation, in that the theme argument is marked by *with* when it is not undergoer in both constructions. The final alternation involves instrument NPs and verbs like *hit*; it is exemplified in (2.81); it may be termed the 'instrumental alternation'.

(2.81) a. Leslie hit the table with the stick. — Direct object = undergoer (location)
a′. The table was hit with the stick by Leslie.
b. Leslie hit the stick on the table. — Direct object = undergoer (instrument)
b′. The stick was hit on the table by Leslie.
c. NP_1 V NP_2 *with*-NP_3 (= (2.81a))
c′. NP_1 V NP_3 *on*-NP_2 (= (2.81b))

In all four of these alternations, either of the non-subject (non-actor) arguments in the active-voice forms can serve as subject in the passive, depending on which non-actor argument serves as undergoer in the corresponding active.

These alternations are found in other languages, but unlike English, most other languages which have them indicate the alternation in some way in the morphology of the verb. Bantu languages, which are spoken in subSaharan Africa, have a very productive means for allowing arguments to appear as direct object; it is called an '**applicative**' construction. Examples from Swahili (Driever 1976, Vitale 1981) are given in (2.82)–(2.83). (Numbers refer to the **noun class** of the agreement affix.)

(2.82) a. Badru a-li-andik-a barua (%kwa Juma). — Swahili
Badru 1-PAST-write-IND letter to Juma
'Badru wrote a letter (to Juma).' — Direct object = undergoer (patient)
a′. Barua i-li-andik-w-a na Badru (%kwa Juma).
letter 9-PAST-write-PASS-IND by Badru to Juma
'The letter was written (to Juma) by Badru.'
b. Badru a-li-mw-andik-i-a Juma barua.
Badru 1-PAST-1-write-APL-IND Juma letter
'Badru wrote Juma a letter.' — Direct object = undergoer (recipient)

b′. Juma a-li-andik-i-w-a barua na Badru.
Juma 1-PAST-write-APL-PASS-IND letter by Badru
'Juma was written a letter by Badru.'

b″. *Barua i-li-mw-andik-i-w-a Juma na Badru.
letter 9-PAST-1-write-APL-PASS-IND Juma by Badru
'The letter was written Juma by Badru.'

c. NP_1 V NP_2 (*kwa*-NP_3) (= (2.82a))

c′. NP_1 V+APL NP_3 NP_2 (= (2.82b))

('%' signals that this PP is possible only for some speakers.) Swahili has eighteen noun classes (analogous to genders in Indo-European languages), and the subject-agreement prefix on the verb agrees with the subject in noun class. Hence in (2.82a) the subject NP *Badru* is class 1, and the agreement prefix is also for class 1. There is object agreement for animate arguments, and it too shows class agreement, as in (2.82b). In (2.82a), the direct object (undergoer) is the patient argument *barua* 'letter'. The recipient, *Juma*, is optionally expressed in a PP headed by *kwa*. In (2.82b), the applicative suffix *-i* has been added to the verb, and in this example the recipient *Juma* is the undergoer and direct object. Swahili permits only the undergoer, the direct object in the active voice, to appear as the subject of a passive, as (2.82a′), (2.82b′) and (2.82b″) show. In (2.82a′) *barua* 'letter' is the subject, while in (2.82b) only *Juma*, the undergoer–recipient, can be the subject of a passive of an applicative verb; as (b″) shows, *barua* 'letter' cannot be subject. The following sentences illustrate the use of applicative constructions with instruments.

(2.83) a. Juma a-li-bomo-a ukuta kwa nyundo. Swahili
Juma 1-PAST-pull.down-IND wall with hammer
'Juma pulled down the wall with the hammer.' Direct object = undergoer (patient)

a′. Ukuta u-li-bomo-w-a na Juma kwa nyundo.
wall 11-PAST-pull.down-PASS-IND by Juma with hammer
'The wall was pulled down with the hammer by Juma.'

b. Juma a-li-bomo-le-a nyundo ukuta.
Juma 1-PAST-pull.down-APL-IND hammer wall
'Juma used the hammer to pull down the wall.' Direct object = undergoer (instrument)
(literal: 'Juma pulled-down-with the hammer the wall.')

b′. Nyundo i-li-bomo-le-w-a ukuta na Juma.
hammer 9-PAST-pull.down-APL-PASS-IND wall by Juma
'The hammer was used by Juma to pull down the wall.'

b″. *Ukuta u-li-bomo-le-w-a nyundo na Juma.
wall 9-PAST-pull.down-APL-PASS-IND hammer by Juma
'The wall was pulled-down-with the hammer by Juma.'

c. NP_1 V NP_2 *kwa*-NP_3 (= (2.83a))

c′. NP_1 V+APL NP_3 NP_2 (= (2.83b))

In (2.83a) the instrument *nyundo* 'hammer' is marked by the preposition *kwa*, and *ukuta* 'wall' is the direct object (undergoer). In the passive sentence in (a′), the undergoer *ukuta* is the subject. In the applicative construction in (2.83b), *nyundo* 'hammer' now functions as the direct object (undergoer), and in the passive voice only *nyundo* and not *ukuta* 'wall' can be subject, as (2.83b′), (2.83b″) show clearly. Thus, in Swahili, only the direct object (undergoer) of an active voice sentence can appear as the subject in a passive construction, and therefore when an alternative choice is made for direct object (undergoer), as in (2.82b) and (2.83b), only the alternative argument functioning as undergoer can occur as subject of the corresponding passive construction.

Not all Bantu languages are as restricted as Swahili, however. Kinyarwanda (Kimenyi 1980) presents a different situation: the Kinyarwanda equivalents of both (2.82b″) and (2.83b″) are completely grammatical. There is no constraint on expressing recipients akin to that in Swahili in (2.82), and the applicative construction is not used for coding recipients. In sentences with both direct and indirect objects, as in (2.84), both arguments can be subject in a passive.

(2.84) a. Umugabo y-a-haa-ye umugóre igitabo. Kinyarwanda
man 1-PAST-give-ASP woman book
'The man gave the woman the book.'
b. Igitabo cy-a-haa-w-e umugóre n'ûmugabo.
book 7-PAST-give-PASS-ASP woman by-man
'The book was given to the woman by the man.'
b′. Umugóre y-a-haa-w-e igitabo n'ûmugabo.
woman 1-PAST-give-PASS-ASP book by-man
'The woman was given the book by the man.'

As in the Japanese example in (2.77), both non-subject (non-actor) arguments of a ditransitive verb can appear as subject in a passive construction. This also applies to the added object in an applicative construction. The examples in (2.85) involve an added benefactive argument.

(2.85) a. Umukoôbwa a-ra-andik-a íbárúwa. Kinyarwanda
girl 1-PRES-read-ASP letter
'The girl is writing a letter.'
a′. Íbárúwa i-ra-andik-w-a n'umukoôbwa.
letter 9-PRES-write-PASS-ASP by-girl
'The letter is written by the girl.'
b. Umukoôbwa a-ra-andik-ir-a umuhuûngu íbárúwa.
girl 1-PRES-write-APL-ASP boy letter
'The girl is writing a letter for the boy.'
b′. Umuhuûngu a-ra-andik-ir-w-a íbárúwa n'umukoôbwa.
boy 1-PRES-write-APL-PASS-ASP letter by-girl
'The boy is having the letter written for him by the girl.'
b″. Íbárúwa i-ra-andik-ir-w-a umuhuûngu n'umukoôbwa.
letter 9-PRES-write-APL-PASS-ASP boy by-girl
'The letter is being written for the boy by the girl.'
c. NP_1 V NP_2 (= (2.85a))
c′. NP_1 V+APL NP_3 NP_2 (= (2.85b))

The addition of the applicative morpheme *-ir* in (2.85b) permits the expression of a benefactive NP *umuhuûngu* 'boy'. When the sentence is passivized, either postverbal NP can appear as subject, as (b′) and (b″) indicate, just as in (2.84) with a ditransitive verb. The same is true when an instrument is involved, as illustrated in (2.86).

(2.86) a. Umukoôbwa a-ra-andik-a íbárúwa n'ííkárámu. Kinyarwanda
girl 1-PRES-write-ASP letter with-pen
'The girl is writing a letter with the pen.'
b. Umukoóbwa a-ra-andik-iish-a íbárúwa íkárámu.
girl 1-PRES-write-APL-ASP letter pen
'The girl is writing a letter with the pen.'
b′. Íbárúwa i-ra-andik-iish-w-a íkárámu n'umukoôbwa.
letter 9-PRES-write-APL-PASS-ASP pen by-girl
'The letter is written with a pen by the girl.'
b″. Íkárámu i-ra-andik-iish-w-a íbárúwa n'umukoôbwa.
pen 9-PRES-write-APL-PASS-ASP letter by-girl
'The pen is used by the girl to write the letter.'
c. NP_1 V NP_2 *n*'NP_3 (= (2.86a))
c′. NP_1 V+APL NP_3 NP_2 (= (2.86b))

The applicative morpheme for instruments is *-iish*, and here again either the original direct object or the applicative object can occur as subject in a passive construction. Kinyarwanda and other Bantu languages like it pose an interesting issue for theories of grammatical relations. While it might possibly be plausible to say for (2.84) and (2.85) that Kinyarwanda is like Japanese in allowing either direct or indirect objects to serve as subject of the corresponding passive sentences, the sentences with instruments in (2.86) do not readily yield to such an analysis, since instrument NPs are not normally analyzed as indirect objects. Moreover, locations, manner adverbs and possessors of the direct object can also appear as direct objects in applicative constructions, and accordingly the indirect-object analysis is inadequate. Some linguists have suggested that Kinyarwanda allows more than one direct object, analyzing both of the postverbal direct NPs as direct objects. This is rather controversial, since it has long been assumed that there can be only one subject or one direct object per sentence. In any case, applicative constructions, dative shift and the locative and instrument alternations in English all point to the importance of direct object in the grammar of some languages, and consequently, being the object in one of these constructions can be taken to be an important property of direct objects in these languages.

Another construction which has also a 'derived' direct object is the matrix-coding-as-object construction in English and Malagasy illustrated in, for example, (2.55b′) and (2.63b). Since this construction permits the subject of the embedded clause to appear as the direct object of the matrix verb, the syntactic properties of the matrix NP which is interpreted as the subject of the embedded clause are properties of direct objects in languages which have this construction.

There are two other constructions which may single out direct objects in some languages. The first is reflexivization. In English, direct objects are possible antecedents of reflexive pronouns, as in (2.41b), and in Norwegian, there is a reflexive pronoun *ham selv* which cannot have a subject antecedent and takes a direct-object antecedent, as in (2.42b). In both languages the ability to be the antecedent for a reflexive pronoun is a property of direct objects, albeit not a unique one. The second construction is the control construction with verbs like *persuade* in (2.68). In it the direct object of the matrix verb is the controller of the omitted argument in the embedded infinitive. This is an important property of direct objects, because this construction is relatively common cross-linguistically.

The final property of direct objects involves relativization. In the previous section it was shown that there are languages like Malagasy which require that the head of the relative clause function as the subject of the relative clause. There are languages, however, which permit the head to function as subject or direct object, and in these languages, e.g. Swahili, Welsh, Indonesian and Finnish, the ability to be the head of a relative clause could be construed as a direct-object property. This is illustrated with the following Swahili examples (Hinnebusch 1979, Givón 1979). The relative clause marker occurs on the verb after the tense marker. The head noun as subject is exemplified in (2.87) and as direct object in (2.88).

(2.87) a. Mwa-namke a-na-twang-a mahindi. Swahili
1-woman 1-PRES-pound-IND maize
'The woman is pounding maize.'
b. Mwa-namke a-na-ye-twang-a mahindi ni m-zee.
1-woman 1-PRES-REL-pound-IND maize be 1-old
'The woman who is pounding maize is old.'

(2.88) a. A-na-wa-on-a wa-nawake. Swahili
1-PRES-2-see-IND 2-women
'He sees the women.'
b. Wa-nawake a-na-o-wa-on-a ni wa-zee.
2-women 1-PRES-REL-see-IND be 2-old
'The women who he sees are old.'

The verb in Swahili shows agreement for subject and in some instances for direct object, and since the verb in the relative clause must agree with the head, the head is limited to just these two possible functions. From this follows the restriction on interpreting the head as subject or direct object in Swahili. What happens when it is necessary to interpret the head as something other than subject (actor) or direct object (undergoer) with a multi-argument verb, for example, a recipient, as in *the woman to whom I gave the book*? In this case the applicative construction is used to make the argument the undergoer and therewith the direct object. This is illustrated in (2.89).

(2.89) a. A-li-tum-a barua kwa mwa-namke. Swahili
1-PAST-send-IND letter to 1-woman
'He sent a letter to the woman.'
a′. A-li-m-tum-i-a mwa-namke barua.
1-PAST-1-send-APL-IND 1-woman letter
'He sent the woman a letter.'
b. Mwa-namke a-li-ye-m-tum-i-a barua ni m-zee.
1-woman 1-PAST-REL-1-send-APL-IND letter be 1-old
'The woman whom he sent a letter is old.'
b′. *Mwa-namke a-li-ye-tum-a barua ni m-zee.
1-woman 1-PAST-REL-send-IND letter be 1-old

In (2.89a) *mwanamke* 'woman', the recipient of *-tum-* 'send', is an oblique core argument marked by the preposition *kwa* 'to', whereas in (a′) with the applicative form of the verb it is the undergoer and direct object; note that the verb shows direct object agreement with it in (a′) but not in (a). It is possible to form a relative clause with *mwanamke* 'woman' as the head noun based on (a′); it is given in (2.89b). Such a relative clause is

Table 2.4. *Direct object properties*

	Direct object only	Subject and direct object only	Direct object and indirect object	Other
Simple sentences				
Coding properties				
Verb agreement		Lakhota		Basque
Accusative case	German		Korean, Quechua	
Behavioral properties				
Reflexivization		Norwegian (*ham selv*)		English
Passive subject	Swahili		Japanese	Kinyarwanda
Dative shift, etc.	English			
Applicative	Swahili			
Complex sentences				
Matrix-coding-as-object	English, Malagasy			
Control in persuade-type control construction	English			
Relativization		Swahili		

impossible with the plain form of the verb, as (b′) shows. In the earlier discussion of Swahili it was shown that the applicative construction permits a non-patient/theme to function as undergoer, which makes it possible for it to be the subject in a passive construction (see (2.82), (2.83)). In (2.89a′), the applicative enables a recipient to function as undergoer (direct object) and therefore makes it possible for it to serve as the head of a relative clause, as in (2.89b). Thus in languages of this type, the ability to serve as the head of a relative clause is a property of direct objects, albeit not an exclusive one.

The direct object properties discussed in this section are summarized in Table 2.4.

Passive, dative shift, applicative and matrix-coding-as-object constructions all target direct objects, but most languages lack one or more of these constructions; many lack all of them. As with subjects, it is virtually impossible to come up with any universally valid morphosyntactic criteria for identifying direct objects, but the properties in Table 2.4 make it possible to pinpoint direct objects in languages with some or all of these constructions.

2.2.2.3 *Indirect object*

The main property that indirect objects share is semantic, not morphosyntactic: they typically code the recipient argument of a ditransitive verb. Grammatically speaking, they fall into three groups: (1) they are treated the same as direct objects, e.g. Kinyarwanda; (2) they are treated the same as oblique arguments, e.g. English; and (3) they receive distinctive coding, e.g. Russian. As shown in (2.84), Kinyarwanda indirect objects have basically the same syntactic properties as direct objects, and this is true in a variety of languages, for example, Lakhota, Tepehua (Totonacan, Mexico), Huichol

(Uto-Aztecan, Mexico), Hausa (Chadic, Africa), and Lahu (Tibeto-Burman, Thailand). This will be discussed further in the next section.

Indirect objects in English behave like other oblique PPs with respect to, for example, WH-question formation, clefting and relativization in (2.43), (2.44) and (2.51). Recipients can be realized as direct objects in dative-shift and transfer alternations, as in (2.78b) and (2.79), but the same can be said of location and instrument arguments, as shown in (2.80) and (2.81). Hence alternating with the direct object is not a unique property of indirect objects. Finally, not even the ability to be an antecedent for a reflexive pronoun is unique to indirect objects as opposed to other oblique NPs, as (2.41d) showed. Thus, indirect objects do not constitute a unique argument type in English, and indeed some linguistic theories do not even recognize a notion of indirect object for English.

The final type of indirect object was illustrated by the dative NPs in the sentences in (2.27) from Russian, Hungarian and Telugu. In these languages the primary properties of indirect objects are that they occur in the dative case and that they are not the subject or direct object. They cannot be the subject in a passive construction, for example (Japanese is exceptional in this regard). In Romance languages, there is a distinct set of **clitic** pronouns for indirect objects (e.g. *le* in Spanish, *lui* in French) which express recipients, benefactives and some experiencers.

Given that there are three main types of indirect objects cross-linguistically, it is clear that there could not be a consistent morphosyntactic characterization of this relation, unlike the semantic one given above. Hence this grammatical relation is not of great importance descriptively or theoretically, and some theories do without this notion completely.

2.2.2.4 *Primary versus secondary objects*

It was noted in the last section that in some languages indirect objects have the same properties as direct objects. This statement actually covers two different situations. The first is the Kinyarwanda-type situation, in which multiple non-actor arguments behave syntactically like a direct object in the same sentence, e.g. (2.84). The second is a situation in which the recipient argument with a ditransitive verb functions as direct object and has the same properties as the direct object of a plain transitive verb; in other words, in such languages only the equivalent of the English *Chris sent Pat the package* is possible, never *Chris sent the package to Pat.* Malagasy and Lakhota are examples of languages of this type. The Malagasy ditransitive examples in (2.47) are repeated below, along with examples with a plain transitive verb.

(2.90) a. Manolotra ny vary ny vahiny ny vehivavy. Malagasy
offers the rice the guests the woman
'The woman offers the guests the rice.'

a′. Tolor-ana-ny vehivavy ny vary ny vahiny.
offered-PASS-the woman the rice the guests
'The guests are offered the rice by the woman.'

b. Manasa ny lamba ny vehivavy.
washed the clothes the woman
'The woman is washing the clothes.'

b′. Sas-an-ny vehivavy ny lamba.
wash-PASS-the woman the clothes
'The clothes are being washed by the woman.'

The ditransitive verb in (2.90a) takes three terms, all of which are direct NPs. The final NP, *ny vehivavy* 'the woman' is the subject; which of the other NPs is the direct object? One test would be passivization using the same passive suffix, *-an(a)*, which is employed with plain transitive verbs, as in (2.90b′). When this suffix is added to a ditransitive verb, it is the recipient NP, *ny vahiny* 'the guests', which appears as the subject, not the theme NP, *ny vary* 'the rice'. In order for *ny vary* 'the rice' to function as subject, a different voice form, the intermediary voice, must be used (see (2.47b)). Thus, the recipient NP, not the theme NP, is treated the same way as the direct object of a plain transitive verb, and therefore it must be the direct object in (2.90a).

The Lakhota situation is somewhat simpler. The verb in Lakhota agrees with the subject and direct object, and therefore the question arises, which argument, the theme or the recipient, does a ditransitive verb agree with? It agrees with the recipient, not the theme.

(2.91) Wį́yą ki hokšíla ki hená igmú wą   Lakhota
woman the boy the those cat a
wičhá-∅-k'u/*∅-∅-k'ú.
3plOBJ-3sgSUBJ-give/*3sgOBJ-3sgSUBJ-give
'The woman gave those boys a cat.'

The theme is *igmú wą* 'a cat', and the recipient is *hokšíla ki hená* 'those boys', and it is clear from the agreement on the verb *k'u* 'give' that it agrees with the plural recipient NP and not the singular theme NP. This is the same as the direct-object agreement in (2.25a) with a plain transitive verb. Thus in both Malagasy and Lakhota the recipient argument is treated as the direct-object argument of ditransitive verbs, and there is no alternative coding pattern in these languages in which the theme, rather than the recipient, functions as direct object.

In a Malagasy sentence like (2.90a) and its English translation, if the recipient (*ny vahiny* 'the guests') is the direct object, then what grammatical relation does the other non-subject NP (*ny vary* 'the rice') have? Calling it the indirect object would be rather strange, since it is not a recipient semantically. It has been suggested that the direct–indirect object contrast is not appropriate for languages of this kind and that a different distinction is required, namely **primary object** (the recipient of ditransitive verbs or the usual direct object of plain transitive verbs) versus **secondary object** (the theme of ditransitive verbs). From this perspective English could be viewed as a language which exhibits both contrasts: direct versus indirect object in *Chris sent the package to Pat*, and primary versus secondary object in *Chris sent Pat the package.* Henceforth the term 'secondary object' will be used for the theme argument with ditransitive verbs.

2.2.3 *Summary*

Even though there do not seem to be any universally valid properties which subjects and direct objects each possess exclusively, there are enough constructions to provide tests which should enable a linguist to identify these grammatical relations in many languages. Relations which appear to be rather straightforward in familiar Indo-European languages turn out to be much more varied and problematic when a wider range of languages is examined. In the next section, languages which present particularly striking analytic problems will be investigated.

2.3 Other systems of grammatical relations

In this section the focus is on two different systems of grammatical relations: the first is the Philippine type, exemplified by Tagalog (Schachter 1976, 1977), and the second is the ergative type, exemplified by Dyirbal and Yidiɲ, Australian Aboriginal languages (Dixon 1972, 1977b). The point of this discussion is not to propose a definitive analysis of these types, as there is considerable controversy regarding the analysis of them, but rather to highlight the analytic challenges they present.

2.3.1 *The Philippine system*

Philippine languages are part of the Austronesian language family, and as such are related to Malagasy and Indonesian. Tagalog will be taken as representative of this system, with the acknowledgement at the outset that there is considerable variation among Philippine languages; it should not be assumed that other Philippine languages parallel Tagalog in every detail. Nevertheless, Tagalog exemplifies clearly the problems that languages of this type raise.

An example from Tagalog was presented earlier in (2.35b). The basic Tagalog clause is given in (2.92). The preposition *ang* will be glossed as 'nominative', *ng* as 'neutral' and *sa* as 'dative'. The terms NPs normally follow the verb and can occur in any order.

(2.92) a. Mag-bibigay ang babae ng bigas sa bata. Tagalog
ACT-will.give NOM woman NTL rice DAT child
'The woman will give some rice to a/the child.'
b. I-bibigay ng babae ang bigas sa bata.
UND-will.give NTL woman NOM rice DAT child
'A/the woman will give the rice to a/the child.'
c. Bibigy-an ng babae ng bigas ang bata.
will.give-RCP NTL woman NTL rice NOM child
'A/the woman will give some rice to the child.'

In each of these examples, the verb bears an affix which signals the semantic role of the NP in the nominative case: in these examples, *mag-* if it is the actor, *i-* if it is the undergoer, and *-an* if it is the recipient. This could be construed as a kind of agreement, with the trigger being the nominative NP. Three of the behavioral subject properties discussed in section 2.2.2.1 will be examined: addressee of an imperative, antecedent of a reflexive, and functioning as the head of a relative clause. The following sentences are imperatives; the addressee may be overt in Tagalog, and it need not be the nominative NP.

(2.93) a. Mag-bigay ka sa kaniya ng kape! Tagalog
ACT-give 2sgNOM DAT 3sgNTL NTL coffee
'Give him some coffee!'
b. I-bigay mo sa kaniya ang kape!
UND-give 2sgNTL DAT 3sgNTL NOM coffee
'Give him the coffee!'
c. Bigy-an mo siya ng kape!
give-RCP 2sgNTL 3sgNOM NTL coffee
'Give him some coffee!'

In all of these sentences the addressee is the actor, and it is the nominative argument only in (2.93a). This suggests that the actor argument is the subject, at least as far as imperatives are concerned. The sentences in (2.93b) and (2.93c) are analogous to the passive-voice imperative in Malagasy in (2.39b).

The next construction is reflexivization; as discussed earlier, the ability to be the antecedent of a reflexive pronoun is a property of subjects, albeit not an exclusive one.

(2.94) a. Nag-iisip sila sa kanilang sarili. Tagalog
ACT-think.about 3plNOM DAT 3plGEN self
'They think about themselves.'
b. In-iisip nila ang kanilang sarili.
GL-think.about 3plNTL NOM 3plGEN self
'They think about themselves.'

The essential feature of these two sentences for this discussion is that the actor is the antecedent of the reflexive pronoun, regardless of the form of the verb. The reflexive pronoun is marked by *ang* in (2.94b), which would make it a nominative reflexive, something which is very rare cross-linguistically. In this respect Tagalog is quite different from Malagasy, in which the antecedent must be the actor and the subject, as shown in (2.95).

(2.95) a. Namono tena Rabe. Malagasy
killed body Rabe
'Rabe killed himself.'
b. *Novonoin'ny tena ny Rabe.
was.killed-the body the
*'Rabe was killed by himself.'
b′. *Novonoin-Rabe ny tena.
*'Himself was killed by Rabe.'

The facts in (2.94) are in accord with those in (2.93) and point to the actor NP as the subject, regardless of its case.

Relativization is governed by the Tagalog analog of the subject-only constraint in Malagasy: the head must be interpreted as the nominative argument in the relative clause. This is illustrated in (2.96), based on the examples in (2.92).

(2.96) a. ang babae-ng mag-bibigay ng bigas sa bata. Tagalog
woman-LNK ACT-will.give NTL rice DAT child
'the woman who will give some rice to a/the child'
a′. *ang babae-ng i-bibigay ang bigas sa bata.
woman-LNK UND-will.give NOM rice DAT child
a″. *ang babae-ng bibigy-an ng bigas ang bata
woman-LNK will.give-RCP NTL rice NOM child
b. ang bigas-an i-bibigay ng babae sa bata.
rice-LNK UND-will.give NTL woman DAT child
'the rice that a/the woman will give to a/the child'
b′. *ang bigas-an mag-bibigay ang babae sa bata
rice-LNK ACT-will.give NOM woman DAT child

b″. *ang bigas-an bibigy-an ng babae ang bata
rice-LNK will.give-RCP NTL woman NOM child
c. ang bata-ng bibigy-an ng babae ng bigas
child-LNK will.give-RCP NTL woman NTL rice
'the child that a/the woman will give some rice'
c′. *ang bata-ng mag-bibigay ang babae ng bigas
child-LNK ACT-will.give NOM woman NTL rice
c″. *ang bata-ng i-bibigay ng babae ang bigas
child-LNK UND-will.give NTL woman NOM rice

In each of the grammatical examples, the head is interpreted as the nominative argument within the relative clause; the form of the verb signals the semantic role of the missing NP within the relative clause. In this construction, then, the nominative NP counts as the subject; since it is the only function in the relative clause that the head can have, the nominative NP must be the subject in terms of the grammatical relations hierarchy in (2.50).

An interesting situation arises when these constructions are combined. Consider the examples in (2.97) involving relativization and reflexivization.

(2.97) a. B-um-ili ang babae ng bigas para sa kaniyang sarili. Tagalog
ACT-bought NOM woman NTL rice for DAT 3sgGEN self
'The woman bought rice for herself.'
b. B-in-ili ng babae ang bigas para sa kaniyang sarili.
UND-bought NTL woman NOM rice for DAT 3sgGEN self
'A/the woman bought the rice for herself.'
c. Binilh-an ng babae ng bigas ang kaniyang sarili.
bought-RCP NTL woman NTL rice NOM 3sgGEN self
'A/the woman bought rice for herself.'
d. ang babae-ng b-um-ili ng bigas para sa kaniyang sarili
woman-LNK ACT-bought NTL rice for DAT 3sgGEN self
'the woman who bought rice for herself'
e. ang bigas-na b-in-ili ng babae para sa kaniyang sarili
rice-LNK UND-bought NTL woman for DAT 3sgGEN self
'the rice that the woman bought for herself'

The sentences in (2.97a)–(2.97c) are analogous to those in (2.92); in (a) the nominative NP is the actor, in (b) it is the undergoer, and in (c) it is the benefactive. The crucial examples are the relative clauses in (2.97d) and (2.97e): *babae* 'woman' in (d) and *bigas* 'rice' in (e) are the heads of the relative clauses and therefore are interpreted as the nominative NP within the relative clauses. *Babae* 'woman' is the antecedent of the reflexive NP in both sentences. In (2.97d) both reflexivization and relativization pick out *babae* 'woman' as the subject of the embedded clause, but this is not the case in (e). The relativization construction identifies *bigas* 'rice' as the subject of the embedded clause, as does verb agreement, whereas the reflexive construction points to *babae* 'woman' as the subject of the embedded clause. Which NP is the subject of the embedded clause in (2.97e)? There appear to be two subjects, and this is precisely the problem which Philippine-type systems raise. The subject properties discussed in section 2.2.2.1 often converge on a single NP in a clause as the subject, but in this language type they need not. There appear to be two subjects in a clause like (2.97e).

Only a brief glimpse at the Philippine system has been presented here, but the essential problem stands out. Some constructions identify the nominative (*ang*) NP as the subject, while other constructions pick out the actor NP, regardless of whether it is marked by *ang* or *ng*, as the subject. Exactly how to analyze a system with split subject properties like Tagalog is a very controversial issue, but what is not contentious is that it presents a grammatical system which differs in important and revealing ways from the familiar Indo-European systems.

2.3.2 *Syntactic ergativity*

In Table 2.1, on page 36, the contrast between nominative–accusative and ergative–absolutive case marking patterns was introduced.

This contrast is found not only in case marking but also in the syntactic behavior of the arguments. It is useful to distinguish morphological coding and syntactic behavior here. Ergative coding patterns, whether in case marking or agreement, will be referred to as 'morphological ergativity'. In a syntactically accusative construction, S and A are treated alike and O is treated differently; many examples of this were given in section 2.2.2.2, especially with respect to control, matrix-coding and conjunction-reduction constructions. In a syntactically ergative construction, S and O are treated alike, and A receives different treatment. This phenomenon will be referred to as 'syntactic ergativity'. It can be illustrated by relativization in Dyirbal (Dixon 1972); the relative clauses are in square brackets.

(2.98) a. Baŋgul yaɽa-ŋgu balan ɖugumbil-∅ [ɲina-ŋu-∅] — Dyirbal
NM.ERG man-ERG NM.ABS woman-ABS sit-REL-ABS
buɽa-n.
see-NFUT
'The man saw the woman who was sitting down.' — Head = S

b. Baŋgul yaɽa-ŋgu bayi yuɽi-∅ [baŋgun
NM.ERG man-ERG NM.ABS kangaroo-ABS NM.ERG
ɖugumbi-ɽu baga-ŋu-∅] buɽa-n.
woman-ERG spear-REL-ABS see-NFUT
'The man saw the kangaroo that the woman speared.' — Head = O

c. *Baŋgul yaɽa-ŋgu balan ɖugumbil-∅ [bayi
NM.ERG man-ERG NM.ABS woman-ABS NM.ABS
yuɽi -∅ baga-ŋu-∅] buɽa-n.
kangaroo-ABS spear-REL-ABS see-NFUT
'The man saw the woman who speared the kangaroo.' — *Head = A

As in Malagasy and Tagalog, there is no relative pronoun in Dyirbal, and the NP identical to the head is simply omitted within the relative clause, which agrees with the head in case. Since the verb in the relative clause in (2.98a) is intransitive, there is no NP in it, and the head is interpreted as the S. In (2.98b), the verb in the relative clause is transitive, and the NP in it is in the ergative case, indicating that it is the A (actor). The head is interpreted as the O (undergoer) of the verb. In (2.98c), the verb in the relative clause is transitive, and the NP in it is in the absolutive case, indicating that it is the O (undergoer). The head must, therefore, be interpreted as the A, which is impossible in Dyirbal. Does this mean it is impossible to interpret the head as the actor of the verb in a relative clause? The answer is 'no', and the way languages like Dyirbal get around this restriction is analogous to the way English and Malagasy get around the problem of interpreting the missing argument in the embedded clause in a control construction as an undergoer: they employ a special voice construction. There are two ways to express 'the woman (actor) speared the kangaroo (undergoer)' in Dyirbal; they are given in (2.99).

(2.99) a. Bayi yuɽi-∅ ba-ŋgu-n ɖugumbi-ɽu baga-n. Dyirbal

Bayi	yuɽi-∅	ba-ŋgu-n	ɖugumbi-ɽu	baga-n.
NM.ABS	kangaroo-ABS	NM-ERG	woman-ERG	spear-NFUT

'The woman speared the kangaroo.'

b. Balan ɖugumbil-∅ ba-gu-l yuɽi-gu bagal-ŋa-ɲu.

Balan	ɖugumbil-∅	ba-gu-l	yuɽi-gu	bagal-ŋa-ɲu.
NM.ABS	woman-ABS	NM-DAT	kangaroo-DAT	spear-ANTI-NFUT

'The woman speared the kangaroo.'

In both sentences the NP referring to the woman is the actor and the NP referring to the kangaroo is the undergoer. In (2.99a), which is the default, active-voice form, the undergoer appears as the O in the absolutive case, and the actor occurs as the A in the ergative case. In (2.99b), on the other hand, the actor appears as the S of a derived intransitive verb and is in the absolutive case, while the undergoer is realized as a non-term in the dative case. The construction in (2.99b) is called an **antipassive** construction. If it is used in the relative clause, it is then possible to say 'the man saw the woman who speared the kangaroo', as in (2.100).

(2.100)

Baŋgul	yaɽa-ŋgu	balan	ɖugumbil-∅	[bagul
NM.ERG	man-ERG	NM.ABS	woman-ABS	NM.DAT

yuɽi-gu	bagal-ŋa-ŋu-∅]	buɽa-n.
kangaroo-DAT	spear-ANTI-REL-ABS	see-NFUT

'The man saw the woman who speared the kangaroo.' Head = S

This use of the antipassive in the relative clause here is exactly analogous to the use of the passive in the embedded clauses in the matrix-coding and control constructions in English in (2.60), (2.61), (2.67) and (2.68) and to the use of the different voice constructions in the extraction, matrix-coding and control constructions in Malagasy in (2.45)–(2.48), (2.49), (2.52), (2.62), (2.63) and (2.69). In these syntactically accusative languages, the special syntactic treatment of the O (undergoer) is that it cannot be directly involved in these constructions and must be realized as the S of a passive construction in order to be matrix-coded, omitted, etc. In syntactically ergative languages, the special syntactic treatment of the A is that it cannot be directly involved in this and other constructions and must be realized as the S of an antipassive construction in order (in this instance) for the head to be interpreted as the actor of the verb in the relative clause. In terms of the subject properties in Table 2.3, one would have to conclude that relativization picks out the absolutive NPs, that is, the S and O, as the subject, and this means that in a simple transitive clause like (2.99a) in Dyirbal the undergoer, not the actor, is the subject. This difference between accusative and ergative syntactic systems may be summarized as in Table 2.5.

Yidiɲ, another Australian Aboriginal language (Dixon 1977b), also exhibits syntactic ergativity in a number of complex sentence constructions. Like Dyirbal, it has an antipassive construction; it is illustrated in (2.101).

Table 2.5. *Subject defaults in accusative and ergative systems*

Syntactic system	Default choice for subject	Choice for subject requiring special construction
Accusative	Actor	Undergoer [Passive]
Ergative	Undergoer	Actor [Antipassive]

(2.101) a. Mayi-∅ guŋgambu-du maḏa-:ɲ. Yidiɲ
food-ABS butterfly-ERG suck-PAST
'The butterfly was sucking nectar [from a flower].'
b. Guŋga:mbuɽ-∅ mayi-: maḏa-:ḏi-ɲu.
butterfly-ABS food-LOC suck-ANTI-TNS
'The butterfly was sucking nectar [from a flower].'

(The locative case on *mayi* 'food' is indicated by the lengthening of the final vowel.) The undergoer *mayi* 'food' appears in the absolutive case and the actor *guŋga:mbuɽ* 'butterfly' in the ergative case in the basic active voice sentence in (2.101a). In the antipassive construction in (b), the actor *guŋga:mbuɽ* 'butterfly' occurs in the absolutive case and the undergoer *mayi* 'food' in the locative case. In certain types of subordinate clauses, an NP coreferential with an NP in the matrix clause is omitted if both NPs are in S or O function; it cannot be omitted if it or the NP in the matrix clause functions as A. This is illustrated in the following examples; the subordinate clauses are in square brackets.

(2.102) a. Ŋuŋu-∅ buɲa-∅ ḏuŋga-ŋ [maŋga-ɲunda]. Yidiɲ
that-ABS woman-ABS run.along-PAST laugh-SUBRD
'That woman ran along while laughing.' S = S
b. Wuguḏa-ŋgu wawa-:l miɲa mugiɲ-∅ [biḏu-:ŋ
man-ERG see-PAST animal mouse-ABS eaglehawk-ERG
buga-ɲunda].
eat-SUBRD
'The man saw the mouse while the eaglehawk ate [it].' O = O
c. Wuguḏa-∅ maŋga-ɲu [buɲa-:ŋ nambil-ɲunda].
man-ABS laugh-PAST woman-ERG hold-SUBRD
'The man was laughing while the woman held [him].' S = O
d. Buɲa-:ɲ wuguḏa-∅ nambi-:l [maŋga-ɲunda].
woman-ERG man-ABS hold-PAST laugh-SUBRD
'The woman held the man while [he/*she] was laughing.' O = S, *A = S

The first example involves two clauses with intransitive verbs, and therefore the only possibility is the matrix S as the controller of the missing S argument in the subordinate clause. In the second example, both clauses have transitive verbs, and the O of the matrix clause, *miɲa mugiɲ* 'mouse' is the controller of the missing O of the subordinate clause. In (2.102c) the first verb is intransitive, and accordingly its single argument (S) must be the controller of the missing O in the subordinate clause. Finally, in the last example the O, not the A, of the matrix clause is the controller of the missing S in the embedded clause. In this construction S and O are possible controllers and missing arguments, while A cannot serve as either. Hence S and O are treated alike syntactically to the exclusion of A, which is the ergative pattern in Figure 2.3. Hence Yidiɲ, like Dyirbal, exhibits ergative syntax, or syntactic ergativity, in one of its complex sentence types. This construction picks out the undergoer as the subject of a clause with an active-voice transitive verb.

If one wanted to say 'the man was laughing while holding the woman' or 'the woman held the man while [she] laughed', it is necessary to antipassivize the transitive verbs, as in (2.103).

(2.103) a. Wuguḏa-∅ maŋga-ɲu [buɲa-: nambi-:ḏi-ɲu:n]. Yidiɲ
man-ABS laugh-PAST woman-LOC hold-ANTI-SUBRD
'The man was laughing while holding the woman.' S = S
b. Buɲa-∅ wuguḏa-la nambi-:ḏi-ɲu [maŋga-ɲunda].
woman-ABS man-LOC hold-ANTI-PAST laugh-SUBRD
'The woman held the man while [she] laughed.' S = S

The requirement of antipassivization is the special treatment given to A arguments; in these examples the actor appears as the S of a detransitivized verb.

None of the sentences have involved pronouns, because the syntax of these constructions when they involve pronouns is quite different. To begin with, pronouns show a nominative–accusative pattern in terms of their form. That is, for first-person singular, for example, *ŋayu* is used for S and A, while *ŋaɲaɲ* is used for O; hence *ŋayu* is labelled the nominative form and *ŋaɲaɲ* the accusative form. With respect to complex constructions, the pattern of controllers and omitted arguments is likewise accusative, as (2.104a) illustrates; that is, the controller must be S or A, and the omitted argument must be S or A. The sentence in (2.104b) illustrates the same construction with full NPs, and in it the pattern is ergative, as in the other constructions above. (Clause boundaries are indicated by '/'.)

(2.104) a. Ŋayu guri:li-∅ gala-: baga-:li-ɲu / miɲa-∅ Yidiɲ
1sgNOM wallaby-ABS spear-INST spear-go-PAST animal-ABS
baḏa-:ɽ / biɽi gunḏi-:ɲ. A = A = S
leave-PAST PRT return-PAST
'I went and speared a wallaby with a spear, [then] left the meat [lying there] and went home.'
b. Ŋuɲu-∅ buɲa-∅ gaba-:ɲḏa ḏana-:ɲ / ŋuɲḏu-:ŋ
that-ABS woman-ABS road-LOC stand-PAST that-ERG
waguḏa-ŋgu gunda-:ḏi-ɲu baŋga-:lda.
man-ERG cut-ACD-PAST axe-INST S = O
'That woman was standing in the road, and the man accidentally cut [her] with his axe.'

(The suffix *-:ḏi* signals that the action was accidental in (2.104b); this is not an antipassive construction, as can be seen clearly from the fact that the actor NP is in the ergative case.) The pattern of omission and coreference is exactly the same in the Yidiɲ example and its English translation in (2.104a), which is quite different from the examples and their translations in (2.102) and in (2.104b). In the second example, the O in the second clause is omitted under coreference with the S of the first clause, yielding the same ergative pattern seen in the earlier examples. Both sentences in

(2.104) are conjunction-reduction constructions, and the crucial difference between them is that the coreferential subjects in (a) are pronominal, while those in (b) are not pronominal. Thus Yidiɲ has accusative syntax as well as ergative syntax.

The example in (2.104) brings up two very important points about languages with ergative syntax. First, these languages almost always have split case-marking systems, with pronouns usually having an accusative pattern and nouns an ergative pattern; there is a great deal of variation across individual languages with respect to the details of the split. Second, while many languages are consistently accusative, no language is consistently ergative; all languages which have constructions that show an ergative pattern also have constructions that exhibit an accusative pattern. Hence these systems are split syntactically as well as morphologically.

Syntactic ergativity is not very common among the world's languages. It is found primarily in Mayan languages in Mexico and Central America, in a number of Australian languages, in some Philippine languages, in some Tibeto-Burman languages, and in Eskimo (Inuit). Morphological ergativity is much more common, and this means that most morphologically ergative languages are in fact syntactically accusative. This can be illustrated with data from Mparntwe Arrernte, an Australian Aboriginal language spoken around Alice Springs in central Australia (Wilkins 1989).

(2.105) a. Ampe nhenhe-le artwe kngerre-∅ are-ke. — Mparntwe Arrernte
child this-ERG man big-ABS see-PAST
'This child saw a big man.'
b. Artwe kngerre re-le ampe nhenhe-∅ are-ke.
man big DEF-ERG child this-ABS see-PAST
'The big man saw this child.'
c. Ampe nhenhe-∅ unthe-ke.
child this-ABS wander-PAST
'This child wandered around.'

The case-marking pattern for nouns is clearly ergative, just as in Yidiɲ and Dyirbal. There is optional number agreement on the verb, and it is sensitive to the number of the S and A arguments, not S and O; hence it has an accusative pattern.

(2.106) a. Artwe therre-le nwerne-nhe twe-rlenerre-ke. — Mparntwe Arrernte
man two-ERG 1pl-ACC hit-DUAL-PAST
'The two men hit us all.' — Agreement with A
a′. *Artwe therre-le nwerne-nhe twe-rrirre-ke.
man two-ERG 1pl-ACC hit-PL-PAST — *Agreement with O
b. Nwerne-∅ re-nhe awe-rrirre-ke.
1pl-NOM 3sg-ACC hear-PL-PAST
'We all heard it.' — Agreement with A
c. Artwe therre-∅ lhe-rre-me.
man two go-DUAL-PRES
'The two men are walking away.' — Agreement with S

There are two NPs in (2.106a), the A having dual number and the O being plural, and the verb shows agreement with the dual A, not the plural O, as the contrast between (a) and (a′) clearly shows. Thus despite having case marking for nouns on an ergative pattern, verb agreement has an accusative pattern. The overall syntax of the language works on the same accusative pattern as verb agreement. This is illustrated by the purposive constructions in (2.107); the issue here is which NP can be omitted in the purpose clause.

(2.107) a. The merne-∅ ine-ke re-nhe arlkwe-tyeke. Mparntwe Arrernte
1sgA food-ABS get-PAST 3sg-ACC eat-PURP
'I got food in order to eat it.' A = A
b. Ayenge lhe-ke kere-∅ arlkwe-tyeke.
1sgS go-PAST meat-ABS eat-PURP
'I went to eat meat.' S = A
c. Artwe yanhe-∅ petye-ke angke-tyeke.
man that-ABS come-PAST speak-PURP
'That man came to speak.' S = S
d. Arlhe yanhe-le door-∅ altywe-rile-ke irrpe-tyeke.
woman that-ERG door-ABS open-CAUSE-PAST go.into-PURP
'That woman opened the door in order to enter.' A = S
e. The kere-∅ knge-tye-ke unte re-nhe arlkwe-tyeke.
1sgA meat take-come-PAST 2sgA 3sg-ACC eat-PURP
'I brought meat in order for you to eat it.'

The omitted argument in the purpose clause is in every instance an S or A, and the controller in the matrix clause is always an S or A. In both (2.107a) and (e) there is coreference between the O NPs in the two clauses, but the second one cannot be omitted, as it would be in Yidiɲ or Dyirbal in this construction; it must occur overtly, normally as a pronoun as in these examples. There is no omitted argument in the purpose clause in (e), because there is no coreference between the A arguments of the two verbs. Thus, despite its ergative case marking, Mparntwe Arrernte is syntactically accusative, and this is, in fact, the most common situation in languages with ergative morphology.

2.3.3 *Summary*

In this section languages with systems of grammatical relations rather different from those discussed in section 2.2 have been examined, namely, Philippine and syntactically ergative systems. The significance of the Philippine system for discussions of grammatical relations is that they show that the subject properties in Table 2.3 need not always converge on a single NP in a sentence; it is possible for different properties to pick out distinct NPs within a single sentence. This is potentially a problem for the traditional view that there is a single notion of e.g. subject running through the whole grammar and that only one occurrence of each grammatical relation is possible in a particular sentence. The issue of possible multiple occurrence of a single grammatical relation also arises in the context of the Kinyarwanda applicative construction, in which there appears to be more than one direct object in a single sentence.

Languages with ergative syntax show that subject is not necessarily linked to the semantic role of actor universally, even though this is the most common association. These languages also call into question the universality of the subject–direct–object opposition. Hence it has been proposed that these languages should be viewed as having a distinct set of grammatical relations, usually termed 'absolutive' for [S, O] and 'ergative' for [A], with the terms 'subject' and 'direct object' reserved for [S, A] and [O], respectively.

Languages like Mparntwe Arrernte which have ergative case-marking and accusative syntax reinforce the point made in section 2.2.1 that there is no necessary correlation between cases and grammatical relations; that is, it is not possible to assume that because an NP is in the absolutive case with a transitive verb, it is the subject. This would be true in Dyirbal and Yidiŋ but not in Mparntwe Arrernte. Indeed, subjects in this language are not uniformly case marked. If a noun is the subject (A) of a transitive verb, it will appear in the ergative case, but if it is the subject (S) of an intransitive verb, it will appear in the absolutive case.

Finally, the fact that no language is consistently syntactically ergative shows that the uniformity found in many accusative languages is not a universal feature of languages. Rather, syntactic systems may be split, with some constructions having an ergative pattern and others an accusative pattern. Thus, some languages could be said to have two systems of grammatical relations.

2.4 Conclusion

This chapter has explored an aspect of relational structure, namely grammatical relations, and it has been shown both how important subject and direct object are for many languages and yet how problematic it can be to identify them in some languages. Many of the assumptions of traditional grammar about grammatical relations apparently fail to hold in languages like Tagalog, Kinyarwanda and Yidiŋ, for example. A number of properties of subjects and direct objects have been presented, and it has been demonstrated how they can be used as tests to identify grammatical relations in specific languages. Semantic roles were distinguished from grammatical relations, and it was found that different syntactic systems can be characterized in terms of how the semantic (macro)roles of actor and undergoer map into subject and direct object. Semantic roles represent an important, morphosyntactically relevant facet of the meaning of verbs, and most theories of syntax employ them in some way.

Grammatical relations may thus be considered an important, if sometimes problematic, part of the descriptive and theoretical arsenal that linguists bring to bear in analyzing particular languages and postulating theories of **universal grammar**. In the next chapter relational structure will be investigated further, with the focus on other types of dependency relations and on developing means for formally representing grammatical relations in particular and dependency relations in general.

Notes and suggested readings

Palmer (1994) is devoted to the topic of semantic roles and grammatical relations. Other general discussions of grammatical relations include Keenan (1976b), Andrews (1985), Comrie (1989), Bhat (1991), Van Valin (1993b), Dixon (1994), Müller-Gotama (1994), Kibrik (1997) and Van Valin and LaPolla (1997). The subject properties discussed in section 2.2.2 come primarily from Keenan (1976b). The labels 'term' and 'non-term' come from **Relational Grammar** (e.g. Perlmutter 1980). Gary and Keenan (1977) analyse Kinyarwanda multiple-object constructions and argue that they represent multiple direct objects in a single clause; Dryer (1983) offers an alternative analysis. Relational constraints on relativization and a grammatical-relations hierarchy are proposed in Keenan & Comrie (1977). Faltz (1978) is one of the few investigations of indirect objects cross-linguistically, and the conclusions presented herein come from his analysis. The primary object–secondary object distinction was proposed in Dryer (1986). Hudson (1993) presents a thorough discussion of English ditransitive constructions. The classic discussion of Philippine languages is Schachter (1976, 1977); analyses of this type of grammatical system are proposed in Foley and Van Valin (1984), Andrews (1985) and Kroeger (1993). General discussions of ergativity can be found in Anderson (1976), Comrie (1978), Dixon (1979, 1994), Van Valin (1981), Kibrik (1985), Manning (1996) and Van Valin and LaPolla (1997). There is a rich literature on semantic roles, e.g. Fillmore (1968, 1977), Jackendoff (1972, 1976, 1990), Foley and Van Valin (1984), Andrews (1985), Palmer (1994), Van Valin and LaPolla (1997). The notions of actor and undergoer are taken from **Role and Reference Grammar** (Foley and Van Valin 1984, Van Valin 1993b), while Jackendoff has been the primary developer of the theory of thematic relations. The basic ideas of Relational Grammar and Role and Reference Grammar (along with those of two other theories) will be presented in Chapter 6.

Exercises

1. Identify the thematic relations of the arguments of the English verbs in the examples below. For each verb, list the thematic relations that it takes; use the format 'verb <ThR$_1$ . . . ThR$_n$>', e.g. 'give <Agent Theme Recipient>', and put the thematic relations which are optional in the data in parenthesis. State which NP is the actor and the undergoer in each sentence, as appropriate, along with its thematic relation. [section 2.1]

(1) a. The repairman drained the water from the pool.
b. The repairman drained the pool of its water.

(2) a. Chris jogged from his house through the park to the lake.
b. Chris jogged through the park.
c. Chris jogged to the lake.
d. Chris jogged.

(3) a. The baby smeared the strained peas on the wall.
b. The baby smeared the wall with the strained peas.

(4) a. Dana taught the students Swahili.
b. Dana taught Swahili to the students.

(5) a. The child cracked the window.
b. The child cracked the window with a rock.
c. The rock cracked the window.

(6) a. The girl drank.
b. The girl drank two beers.

(7) a. The gangsters robbed the bank of $1,000,000.
b. The gangsters stole $1,000,000 from the bank.

(8) a. Kim saw the picture.
b. Leslie showed Kim the picture.
c. Leslie showed the picture to Kim.

(9) a. The ship sank.
b. The submarine sank the ship.

2. Identify the subject, direct object and indirect object in each of the grammatical German sentences in (1)–(5). What are the coding properties of each grammatical relation? What behavioral evidence is there with respect to the identification of each grammatical relation? In addition, identify the actor and undergoer in each sentence in (1)–(5); where a sentence appears more than once with different word orders, specify the macroroles only once. [section 2.2]

(1) Der Mann ha-t den Hut gekauft.
the.MSgNOM man have-3sgPRES the.MSgACC hat bought
'The man bought the hat.'

(2) a. Der Mann hat die Bücher gekauft.
the.ACCpl books
'The man bought the books.'

a′. *Der Mann hab-en die Bücher gekauft.
have-3plPRES

b. Die Bücher hat der Mann gekauft.
'The man bought the books.'

b′. *Die Bücher haben der Mann gekauft.

(3) a. Die Männer haben das Haus gekauft.
the.NOMpl men the.NSgACC
'The men bought the house.'

b. Das Haus haben die Männer gekauft.

(4) Die Frau hat dem Mann den Hut geschenkt.
the.FSgNOM woman the.MSgDAT given.as.present
'The woman gave the hat to the man.'

(5) a. Der Hut wurd-e von dem Mann gekauft.
become-3sgPAST by
'The hat was bought by the man.'

b. Der Hut wurde dem Mann von der Frau geschenkt.
the.FSgDAT
'The hat was given to the man by the woman.'

c. *Der Mann wurde den Hut von der Frau geschenkt.
'The man was given the hat by the woman.'

(6) a. Der Lehrer$_i$ hat dem Schüler$_j$ ein-e Geschichte über sich$_{i/*j}$ erzählt.
teacher pupil one-FSgACC story about 3.self told
'The teacher$_i$ told the pupil$_j$ a story about himself$_{i/*j}$.'

b. Der Lehrer$_i$ hat dem Schüler$_j$ eine Geschichte über ihn$_{*i/j}$ erzählt.
3MSgACC
'The teacher$_i$ told the pupil$_j$ a story about him$_{*i/j}$.'

c. Der Lehrer$_i$ sah den Schüler$_j$ sich$_{*i/j}$ verletzen.
saw hurt
'The teacher$_i$ saw the pupil$_j$ hurt himself$_{*i/j}$.'

3. Describe the Malayalam case-marking system, based on the sentences below. Malayalam is a Dravidian language spoken in India (Mohanan 1982, Asher and Kumari 1997). Identify the morphemes in the data: nouns, verbs, adjectives, possessive pronouns, and the morphemes for 'want', 'while' and passive. Ignore the tense morphemes on the verbs. First, identify the cases illustrated in the data and state the morphemes that mark each one. Second, give the behavioral evidence that leads you to postulate specific grammatical relations. Third, how well does case correlate with grammatical relations in this language? [section 2.2]

(1)	Kuṭṭi ammakkə aanaye koṭuṯṯu.	'The child gave the elephant to the mother.'
(1′)	Ammakkə kuṭṭi aanaye koṭuṯṯu.	'The child gave the elephant to the mother.'
(1″)	Koṭuṯṯu ammakkə aanaye kuṭṭi.	'The child gave the elephant to the mother.'
(1‴)	Kuṭṭi aanaye ammakkə koṭuṯṯu.	'The child gave the elephant to the mother.'
(2)	Kuṭṭi aa paṯṯə waliya aanakaḷe kaṇṭu.	'The child saw those ten big elephants.'
(2′)	Aa paṯṯə waliya aanakaḷe kuṭṭi kaṇṭu.	'The child saw those ten big elephants.'
(2″)	Kaṇṭu aa paṯṯə waliya aanakaḷe kuṭṭi.	'The child saw those ten big elephants.'
(2‴)	Kuṭṭi kaṇṭu aa paṯṯə waliya aanakaḷe.	'The child saw those ten big elephants.'

(3)	Aana kuṭṭiye kaṇṭu.	'The elephant saw the child.'
(3′)	*Aana kuṭṭi kaṇṭu.	
(4)	Kuṭṭi ammaye ikkiḷiyaakki waṭi koṇṭə.	'The child tickled the mother with a stick.'
(4′)	Kuṭṭi waṭi koṇṭə ammaye ikkiḷiyaakki.	'The child tickled the mother with a stick.'
(4″)	*Kuṭṭi amma ikkiḷiyaakki waṭi koṇṭə.	
(5)	Amma aa kaṭṭilil kiṭan̲n̲u.	'The mother lay on that bed.'
(6)	Amma san̲t̲ooṣiccu.	'The mother was happy.'
(6′)	*Ammakkə san̲t̲ooṣiccu.	
(7)	Kuṭṭikkə wišan̲n̲u.	'The child was hungry.'
(7′)	*Kuṭṭi wišan̲n̲u.	
(8)	Pakṣi paran̲n̲u.	'The bird flew.'
(9)	Amma kuṭṭiye waṭiyaal ikkiḷiyaakki.	'The mother tickled the child with a stick.'
(9′)	Amma waṭiyaal kuṭṭiye ikkiḷiyaakki.	'The mother tickled the child with a stick.'
(9″)	Waṭiyaal kuṭṭiye amma ikkiḷiyaakki.	'The mother tickled the child with a stick.'
(9‴)	Amma ikkiḷiyaakki kuṭṭiye waṭiyaal.	'The mother tickled the child with a stick.'
(10)	Amma ii pakṣiye kaṇṭu.	'The mother saw this bird.'
(10′)	*Amma ii pakṣi kaṇṭu.	
(11)	Uran̲n̲i ii ceriiya kuṭṭi.	'This small child slept.'
(12)	Kuṭṭikaḷ waliya kaṭṭil kaṇṭu.	'The children saw the big bed.'
(12′)	*Kuṭṭikaḷ waliya kaṭṭile kaṇṭu.	
(13)	Ceriiya kuṭṭi kaṇṭu waliya waṭi.	'The small child saw the big stick.'
(14)	Roṭṭi paz̧ayat̲ə aaṇə.	'The bread is stale.'
(15)	Ṣarṭṭə paz̧ayat̲ə aaṇə.	'The shirt is old.'
(15′)	Paz̧ayat̲ə aaṇə ṣarṭṭə.	'The shirt is old.'
(15″)	*Aaṇə paz̧ayat̲ə ṣarṭṭə.	
(16)	Amma waayiccu pust̲akam kuṭṭikkə weeṇṭi.	'The mother read the book for the child.'
(16′)	Pust̲akam amma waayiccu kuṭṭikkə weeṇṭi.	'The mother read the book for the child.'
(16″)	Amma kuṭṭikkə weeṇṭi pust̲akam waayiccu.	'The mother read the book for the child.'
(17)	Pust̲akam paz̧ayat̲ə aaṇə.	'The book is old.'
(18)	Kuṭṭi n̲allawan aaṇə.	'The child is good.'
(19)	Pakṣi ceriiya roṭṭi t̲in̲n̲u.	'The bird ate the small bread.'
(19′)	*Pakṣi ceriiya roṭṭiye t̲in̲n̲u.	
(20)	Amma coorə t̲in̲n̲u.	'The mother ate the rice.'
(21)	Coorə paz̧ayat̲ə aaṇə.	'The rice is stale.'
(22)	Kuṭṭikkə roṭṭi t̲innaṇam.	'The child wants to eat the bread.'
(23)	Aana amma aaṇə.	'The elephant is a mother.'
(24)	Aanaye kuṭṭi n̲uḷḷi.	'The child pinched the elephant.'
(25)	Ammakkə n̲uḷḷaṇam kuṭṭiye.	'The mother wants to pinch the child.'
(26)	Kuṭṭi aanaye aar̃aad̲hiccu.	'The child worshipped the elephant.'
(27)	Aana kuṭṭiyaal aar̃aad̲hikkappeṭṭu.	'The elephant was worshipped by the child.'
(28)	Aanakkə kuṭṭiyaal aar̃aad̲hikkappeṭaṇam.	'The elephant wants to be worshipped by the child.'
(29)	Amma kuṭṭikkə pust̲akam koṭuṭṭu.	'The mother gave the book to the child.'
(30)	Pust̲akam kuṭṭikkə ammayaal koṭukkappeṭṭu.	'The book was given to the child by the mother.'
(31)	*Kuṭṭi pust̲akam ammayaal koṭukkappeṭṭu.	'The child was given the book by the mother.'

(32)	Kuṭṭi swaṉṯam aanaye ṉuḷḷi.	'The child$_i$ pinched his$_{i/*j}$ (own) elephant.'
(33)	Kuṭṭi awante aanaye ṉuḷḷi.	'The child$_i$ pinched his$_{*i/j}$ elephant.'
(34)	Kuṭṭikkə swaṉṯam aanaye ṉuḷḷaṇam.	'The child$_i$ wants to pinch his$_{i/*j}$ (own) elephant.'
(35)	Peṇṇə ammaye swaṉṯam waṭiyaal ikkiḷiyaakki.	'The woman$_i$ tickled the mother$_j$ with her$_{i/*j}$ stick.'
(36)	Peṇṇə ammaye awaḷuṭe waṭiyaal ikkiḷiyaakki.	'The woman$_i$ tickled the mother$_j$ with her$_{*i/j}$ stick.'
(37)	Kuṭṭiye ṉuḷḷikoṇṭə, amma pusṯakam waayiccu.	'While __$_i$ pinching the child, the mother$_i$ read the book.'
(38)	Kaṭṭilil kiṭaṉṉukoṇṭə, amma kuṭṭikkə pusṯakam koṭuṯṯu.	'While __$_{i/*j}$ lying on the bed, the mother$_i$ gave the book to the child$_j$.'
(39)	Kaṭṭilil kiṭaṉṉukoṇṭə, kuṭṭiye amma ṉuḷḷi.	'While __$_{i/*j}$ lying on the bed, the mother$_i$ pinched the child$_j$.'
(40)	Cuuṭə piṭiccukoṇṭə, kuṭṭi coorə iḷakki.	'While __$_{i/*j}$ getting hot, the child$_i$ stirred the rice$_j$.'
(41)	Pusṯakam waayiccukoṇṭə, kuṭṭikkə uraŋŋaṇam.	'While __$_i$ reading the book, the child$_i$ wanted to sleep.'
(42)	Wišaṉṉukoṇṭə, kuṭṭi pusṯakam waayiccu.	'While __$_i$ being hungry, the child$_i$ read the book.'
(43)	*Amma pusṯakam koṭuṯṯukoṇṭə, kuṭṭi aanaye ṉuḷḷi.	'While the mother gave __$_i$ the book, the child$_i$ pinched the elephant.'
(44)	Ammayaal ṉuḷḷappeṭṭukoṇṭə, kuṭṭi aanaye ṉuḷḷi.	'While __$_i$ being pinched by the mother, the child$_i$ pinched the elephant.'
(45)	Kaṭṭilil kiṭaṉṉukoṇṭə, kuṭṭi ammayaal ṉuḷḷappeṭṭu.	'While __$_{i/*j}$ lying on the bed, the child$_i$ was pinched by the mother$_j$.'

4. Describe the case-marking system for lexical NPs found in Tongan, a Polynesian language of the Austronesian family (Chung 1978), based on (1)–(8) below. The case markers are not glossed. How do grammatical relations pattern in this language? What evidence do (9)–(15) provide? [section 2.3]

(1)	'Oku fu'u hela'ia 'a Ālani. PRES very tired Alan	'Alan is very tired.'
(2)	Na'e lolotonga puna 'a e vakapuna. AUX fly ART airplane	'The airplane was flying.'
(3)	'Oku fa'u 'e hoku tokoná 'a e tēpile. make my brother table	'My brother is making a table.'
(4)	Na'e taa'i 'e Mele 'a Sione. PAST hit Mary John	'Mary hit John.'
(5)	Na'e ilo 'e Sione 'a e tangatá 'i he 'ana. find man cave	'John found a man in the cave.'
(6)	'Oku manako 'a Sione 'i he ta'ahiné. like ART girl	'John likes the girl.'
(7)	Na'e tō mai 'a 'uha ki he motu. fall here rain island	'Some rain fell on the island.'
(8)	Na'e sio 'a Mele ki he fo'i manupuna. see one bird	'Mary saw a bird.'
(9)	Pea na'e 'alu 'a e tangatá 'o folau mama'o. then go CONJ sail far	'Then the man went and sailed away.'
(10)	Na'e tu'u hake 'a Mele 'o 'alu. stand up	'Mary stood up and went.'

(11) Na'e 'alu 'a e tangatá 'o taa'i 'a e kūli.   'The man went and hit the dog.'
(12) Na'e taa'i 'e Mele 'a Sione 'o mate.   'Mary hit John and [he/*she] died.'
(13) Na'e 'alu 'a e ta'ahiné 'o ala   ki he pēpē.   'The girl went and touched the baby.'
                                    touch   baby
(14) *Na'a ku puna atu   'o ne ma'u.   'I jumped up and he grabbed [me].'
         1sg jump away   3sg catch
(14′) Na'a ku puna atu 'o ne ma'u au.   'I jumped up and he grabbed me.'
(15) *Na'a nau omi 'o mau fakamālō.   'They came, and we thanked [them].'
         3pl come 1pl thank
(15′) Na'a nau omi 'o mau fakamālō ki ai.   'They came, and we thanked them.'

5. Describe verb agreement in the Jakaltek sentences in (1)–(10); Jakaltek is a Mayan language
    spoken in Guatemala (Craig 1977). Does it pattern ergatively or accusatively? What conclu-
    sions regarding the notion of subject in Jakaltek can you reach on the basis of (11)–(25)?
    (Elements glossed 'SUF' are irrelevant to the problem.) [section 2.3]

(1)   X-Ø-to-pax   heb naj winaj.   'The men returned.'
      PAST-3-go-back PL CL man
(2)   Ch-in   aẍni.   'I bathe.'
      PRES-1sg bathe
(3)   Xc-ach   to-yi.   'You went.'
      PAST-2sg go-SUF
(4)   X-Ø-aw-il   naj winaj.   'You saw the man.'
      PAST-3-2sg-see
(5)   Ch-in   haw-il-a.   'You see me.'
      PRES-1sg 2sg-see-SUF
(6)   Ch-ach   y-oche naj winaj.   'The man likes you.'
      PRES-2sg 3-like
(7)   X-Ø-w-il   naj winaj.   'I saw the man.'
      PAST-3-1sg-see
(8)   Xc-ach   w-abe.   'I heard you.'
      PAST-2sg 1sg-hear
(9)   Ch-Ø-aẍni.   'He/she bathes.'
      PRES-3-bathe
(10) a. Ch-Ø-y-oche naj winaj ix ix.   'The man likes the woman.'
          PRES-3-3-like   CL woman
      b. Ch-Ø-y-oche ix ix naj winaj.   'The woman likes the man.'
(11) Ha' heb naj winaj x-Ø-to-pax.   'It's the men who returned.'
(12) Ha' ix ix ch-Ø-aẍni.   'It's the woman who is bathing.'
(13) Ha' ix ix x-Ø-y-il naj winaj.   'It's the woman who the man saw.'
                                                    (*'It's the woman who saw the man.')
(14) Ha' ix ix x-Ø-'il-ni naj winaj.   'It's the woman who saw the man.'
                                                    (*'It's the woman who the man saw.')
(15) Mac x-Ø-to-pax?   'Who returned?'
(16) Mac ch-Ø-aẍni?   'Who is bathing?'
(17) Mac x-Ø-y-il naj winaj?   'Who did the man see?' (*'Who saw
                                                    the man?')
(18) Mac x-Ø-'il-ni naj winaj?   'Who saw the man?' (*'Who did the
                                                    man see?')
(19) Mac ch-Ø-y-oche ix ix?   'Who does the woman like?'
                                                    (*'Who likes the woman?')

(20) Mac ch-∅-oche-ni ix ix? — 'Who likes the woman?' (*'Who does the woman like?')

(21) a. Xc-ach to sajch-oj. — 'You went to play.'
play-SUF

b. *Xc-ach to ha-sajchi.
2sg-

c. X-∅-to ix ix aẍn-oj. — 'The woman went to bathe.'

d. *X-∅-to ix ix y-aẍni.
3-

(22) a. Ch-∅-y-oche naj winaj cañalw-oj. — 'The man likes to dance.'
dance-SUF

b. *Ch-∅-y-oche naj winaj s-cañalwi.
3-

(23) a. Ch-in to hach hin-col-o'. — 'I go to help you.'
2sg 1sg-help-SUF

b. *Ch-in to col-o' hach.

c. *Ch-in to hach col-o'.

(24) a. Xc-in to hin ha-col-o'. — 'I went for you to help me.'

b. *Xc-in to ha-col-o'.

c. Xc-in to hin-col-lax-i. — 'I went to be helped.'
1sg-help-PASS-SUF

d. *Xc-in to col-lax-oj.

(25) a. Ch-∅-y-oche naj winaj hayoñ s-col-o'. — 'The man likes to help us.'
1pl 3-

b. *Ch-∅-y-oche naj winaj hayoñ col-o'.

c. Ch-∅-y-oche naj winaj s-col-lax-i. — 'The man likes to be helped.'

d. *Ch-∅-y-oche naj winaj col-lax-i.

CHAPTER 3

Dependency relations

3.0 Introduction

In section 1.1 two distinct facets of syntactic structure, namely relational structure and constituent structure, were distinguished, and in this chapter and the next the two main approaches to describing syntactic structure, namely **dependency grammar** and constituent-structure grammar, will be presented. Dependency grammar concentrates on the relational aspect of syntax, while constituent-structure grammar focuses on the constituent-structure aspect. The grammatical relations discussed in the previous chapter express a kind of **dependency** holding between the verb (or other predicating element) and the NPs and/or PPs in the clause. Other types of dependencies exist as well, for example, the dependence of a modifier on the element it modifies, and in this chapter these other types of dependency relations will be examined.

At the end of the discussion of lexical categories in section 1.2, it was mentioned that in modern linguistics lexical categories are defined not in terms of their meaning but in terms of their morphosyntactic properties. With respect to determining the form class of an item, the important questions to ask are 'what elements can it cooccur with?' and 'what morphosyntactic environment(s) can it occur in?' The relation that a morphosyntactic element has to the elements it cooccurs with is termed a **syntagmatic relation**, and it is one of the two fundamental relations that underlie language as a structural system. The relation holding between article and noun, subject and verb, verb and direct object, possessor NP and possessed N, or adposition and object are all examples of syntagmatic relations. The other fundamental relation is termed a **paradigmatic relation**, and it refers to the relation holding among elements which can be substituted for each other in a specific morphosyntactic environment. For example, given the morphosyntactic frame 'ART+__+N', there is a class of elements that can occupy this position, e.g. *tall*, *red*, *happy*, *interesting*, etc., and they constitute the class of **attributive** adjectives in English. In the Lakhota verb paradigm in (1.10), the prefixes *wa-*, *ya-* *Ø-* and *u̧-* are in a paradigmatic relation to each other, since each can be substituted for the other. In exercises 1, 2 and 4 at the end of Chapter 1, you were asked to characterize the syntagmatic relations that defined each of the form classes found in the data. The reason that syntagmatic and paradigmatic relations are fundamental to the structure of language can be seen in the simple English NP example above. It can be schematically represented as 'ART+ADJ+N', and it consists of three form classes in syntagmatic relations to each other, each form class being composed of a group of elements in a paradigmatic relation to each other. Thus, a syntagmatic relation is one of cooccurrence among elements, whereas a paradigmatic relation is one of substitution among elements.

The primary topic of syntax is the characterization of syntagmatic relations (note the obvious etymological connection between 'syntax' and 'syntagmatic'). The grammatical relations discussed in the previous chapter are syntagmatic relations. In the next section different types of dependency relations, their properties, and how they are coded in languages will be investigated. In the final section, the dependency relations in some of the constructions discussed in this and the previous chapter will be represented in a formal notation.

3.1 Syntactic dependencies

If two or more elements cooccur in a syntactic arrangement, some kind of dependency exists between or among them. Typically, there is one dominant element which is the primary determinant of the properties of the arrangement; it is referred to as the *head*, and the other elements are its *dependent(s)*. For example, in an adpositional phrase, the adposition is the head and its object is the dependent, and in a clause, the verb is the head and the term arguments are its dependents. Why are the adposition and the verb the heads? The reason is that they select their dependents and may determine their morphosyntactic and other properties. In many languages, for example, an adposition determines the case of its object. The verb not only determines the case of its direct term arguments, it also specifies the number of dependents and in many instances some of their properties. For example, a verb like English *think* requires that its subject be an animate, sentient being, while a verb like English *elapse* takes a subject which refers to some period of time. The Lakhota verb *kabléčha* 'break by striking' requires that its undergoer be a flat, brittle object, whereas the verb *kawéga* 'crack by striking' specifies that its undergoer be a long, thin, brittle object. These requirements, which a verb imposes on its arguments, are called **selectional restrictions**. Adpositions and verbs determine properties of their arguments, not the other way around, and therefore they are the heads. Table 3.1 presents a list of syntactic constructs with the head and dependent(s) specified.

In general, modifiers are dependents, and the elements modified are the heads.

Syntagmatic relations are cooccurrence relations, and it is important to keep in mind that cooccurrence does not entail adjacency. In the English NP example mentioned above, all of the elements in the NP occur adjacent to each other, as do an adposition and its object normally. But there are other examples of syntagmatic relations in English that do not involve adjacency. For example, in a question like *Who did you give the book to?*, the object of the preposition *to* occurs separated from it at the beginning of the

Table 3.1. *Heads and dependents*

Construct	Head	Dependent(s)
Clause	Verb	Terms
Adpositional phrase	Adposition	Object
Noun phrase	Noun	Modifier(s)
Possessive NP	Possessed N	Possessor NP

sentence; yet they are in the same syntagmatic relation as in *Pat gave the book to Dana* despite the lack of adjacency between the preposition and its object. **Preposition stranding** like this is very rare cross-linguistically: English and Dutch are the primary examples of languages permitting it. It is also rare for the modifiers of a noun to be separated from the noun they modify, but it does happen. In Croatian and Serbian (South Slavic), the verb *je* 'is' must occur in second position in a clause. What is unusual in this situation is that second position (sometimes known as **Wackernagel's position**) may be defined as being after the first NP in the clause or after the first word in the clause. The two possibilities are exemplified in (3.1), from Barac-Kostrenčić *et al.* (1993).

(3.1) a. Naš-a učionic-a je udobn-a. — Croatian
our-FSGNOM classroom-FSGNOM be.3SGPRES comfortable-FSGNOM
'Our classroom is comfortable.'
b. Naša je učionica udobna.
our is classroom comfortable
'Our classroom is comfortable.'

In (3.1a) the verb *je* 'is' occurs after the subject NP *naša učionica* 'our classroom', but this is not the form preferred by native speakers. What speakers prefer is (3.1b), in which *je* 'is' appears between *naša* 'our' and *učionica* 'classroom', thereby separating the modifier from the head it modifies; in this example, *je* 'is' occurs after the first word in the clause, *naša* 'our', rather than after the first NP, as in (3.1a). Nevertheless, the two sentences mean the same thing. Even more dramatic examples of modifiers separated from their heads can be found in Australian Aboriginal languages, as in the following sentences from Kalkatungu (Blake 1979) and Yidiɲ.

(3.2) a. Ṉa-ci japacara-ṯu kuḷa-ji ḻaji ṯuar-∅ maḻṯa-∅. — Kalkatungu
1sg-DAT clever-ERG father-ERG kill snake-ABS mob-ABS
'My clever father killed the snakes.'
a′. Ṉa-ci kuḷa-ji ḻaji ṯuar-∅ maḻṯa-∅ japacara-ṯu.
1sg-DAT father-ERG kill snake-ABS mob-ABS clever-ERG
'My clever father killed the snakes.'
(*'My father killed the clever snakes.')
b. Ṉayu ŋuŋu-∅ munil-∅ wawa-:l. — Yidiɲ
1sgNOM that-ABS vine-ABS see-PAST
'I saw that Munil vine.'
b′. Ṉayu ŋuŋu-∅ wawa-:l munil-∅.
1sgNOM that-ABS see-PAST vine-ABS
'I saw that Munil vine.'

(The dative case is used to mark possession in Kalkatungu.) Both of these languages have free phrase order (i.e. free ordering of NPs and PPs with respect to each other and to the verb), which is not at all uncommon cross-linguistically, but they also allow the modifiers of a noun to occur separated from the noun, which is very unusual; this may be termed **'free word order'**. In the second Kalkatungu example, the adjective *japacara* 'clever', which modifies *kuḷa* 'father', appears at the end of the sentence separated from it by the verb and the absolutive NP. Because modifiers agree with their head in case, there is no possibility of interpreting this sentence as meaning that the snakes are clever, not the father; *japacara-ṯu* 'clever-ERG' has an ergative case suffix in these sentences, indicating that it modifies *kuḷa-ji* 'father-ERG', which is also in the ergative case, and not *ṯuar-∅* 'snake-ABS', which is in the absolutive case. The situation in the Yidiɲ example is much the same: a noun modifier occurs separated from the noun it modifies. In (3.2b′) the demonstrative *ŋuŋu* 'that' precedes the verb, while the noun it modifies, *munil* 'Munil vine', follows the verb; they agree in case. Thus, it is possible in some languages for a modifier to appear separated from the head noun it modifies; in the Serbian and Croatian situation, the verb *je* 'is' intervenes between them, whereas in Kalkatungu and Yidiɲ (and in many other Australian Aboriginal languages as well) the modifier and its head noun may appear in different parts of the clause separated by a number of other elements. Hence while syntagmatic relations between modifiers and the head modified typically involve adjacency, they do not always require it.

3.1.1 *Types of dependencies*

Dependencies may be classified into three general types: bilateral, unilateral and coordinate. In a bilateral dependence, the occurrence of each element is dependent upon the occurrence of the other; that is, the head cannot occur without the dependent, and the dependent cannot occur without the head. Two very good examples of this are subject–verb and preposition–object in English. In a simple sentence the verb normally cannot occur without a subject, and the subject cannot occur without the verb. Hence the dependence between them is bilateral. The same is true with respect to prepositional phrases. Prepositions normally cannot stand alone without an object; even in a sentence like *Who did you give the book to?* the preposition *to* has an object, namely the WH-word *who.* An object of a preposition cannot be such without the preposition; hence each requires the presence of the other in a prepositional phrase. In a unilateral dependence, on the other hand, the head can occur without any dependents. Accordingly, while the dependents require the head for their occurrence, the head is not subject to the corresponding restriction and can occur alone. This is best illustrated in English with various kinds of modifier. Consider the sentence *The very tall women like basketball a lot. Very*, an adverb, modifies *tall*, and *the* and *very tall* modify *women*; *a lot* modifies *like. The* cannot occur by itself, and neither can *very tall*; but *tall* can occur without *very*, as in *The tall women like basketball a lot. Women* can occur without any modifiers, as in *Women like basketball a lot.* The verb *like* can also appear without any modifiers, as in *Women like basketball.* Hence in the adjective phrase *very tall*, *very* is the dependent and *tall* is the head, and they are in a unilateral dependence. In the NP *the very tall women*, the head is *women* and *the* and *(very) tall* are dependents; they are in a unilateral dependence with the head. The adverb *a lot* is a modifier of *like*, and they too are in a unilateral dependence. The types of dependencies are summarized in Table 3.2; parenthesis means that the element is not obligatorily.

Table 3.2. *Types of dependencies*

Bilateral	Head	Dependent
Unilateral	Head	(Dependent)
Coordinate	Head	Head

Possessive constructions pose an interesting problem with respect to the type of dependence involved. Possessor NPs are a kind of modifier, and so it might be reasonably assumed that the dependence would be unilateral, as with other modifiers. However, if the possessor NP is omitted, the construction is no longer a possessive construction. That is, if *Mary's* is dropped from *Mary's books*, leaving *books*, the result is still an NP (as in *Books can be found in aisle 2*), but it is not a possessive NP. Hence the possessor NP is an obligatory part of a possessive construction, and consequently the dependence between the possessor NP and the possessed N is bilateral. The possessed N is unequivocably the head of the construction. First, it, and not the possessor NP, is the argument of the verb; as such, it satisfies the selectional restrictions of the verb, as exemplified in (3.3).

(3.3) a. Mary's dog saw the chipmunk.
b. Mary's rock saw the chipmunk.

The verb *see* requires that the referent of its subject be an animate, sentient being, and the referent of *Mary's dog* but not of *Mary's rock* satisfies this requirement, despite the fact that the referent of the possessor NP, Mary, does satisfy it in both sentences. Second, the finite verb agrees with the number of the possessed N, not that of the possessor NP, indicating that it is the head of the overall NP.

(3.4) a. The boys' dog is/*are barking.
b. The boy's dogs are/*is barking.

In (3.4a) the possessor NP is plural and the possessed N is singular, and the verb shows singular agreement. In (3.4b), on the other hand, the possessor NP is singular and the possessed N is plural, and the verb shows plural agreement. Hence it is the number of the possessed N which determines the number of the NP as a whole, not the number of the possessor NP. Third, only the possessed N, not the possessor NP can be the antecedent of a reflexive pronoun in a clause, as shown in (2.41). Thus, the possessed N is the head of the possessive NP.

The final type of dependence is coordinate, and in it both or all of the elements are of equal status; in other words, they all count as heads. Any kind of conjoined phrase is of this type: *the girl and the boy* (conjoined NPs), *the happy and prosperous couple* (conjoined adjectives), *Chris cooked and ate the fish* (conjoined verbs). Note the contrast between *Kim saw Chris and Dana* and *Kim saw Chris with Dana.* In the former, *Chris* and *Dana* are both heads in a coordinate relationship, whereas in the latter *Chris* is the head and *with Dana* is a modifying PP, with *with* as the head and *Dana* as the dependent. It should be noted that coordinate constructions need not have a linking element like a conjunction. Consider the contrast between the Yidiɲ coordinate construction involving clauses in (2.104b), repeated below in (3.5a), and its English translation in (3.5b).

(3.5) a. Ŋuŋu-∅ buɲa-∅ gaba-:ɲɖa ɖana-:ɲ / ŋuɲɖu-:ŋ Yidiɲ
that-ABS woman-ABS road-LOC stand-PAST that-ERG
waguɖa-ŋgu gunda-:ɖi-ɲu baŋga-:lda.
man-ERG cut-ACD-PAST axe-INST
b. That woman was standing in the road, and the man accidentally cut [her] with his axe.
b′. That woman was standing in the road; the man accidentally cut [her] with his axe.

Both sentences are coordinate constructions made up of two clauses, but there is no conjunction in Yidiɲ, whereas there is one in the English translation in (3.5b). It is possible to have a construction in English analogous to the one in Yidiɲ; it is represented in (3.5b′). In English orthography, this is expressed by the use of a semi-colon. Coordination without a conjunction, as in (3.5a), (3.5b′) is known as **parataxis**.

Parataxis is also possible within the NP in some languages. The following examples are from Pitjantjatjara, a morphologically ergative Aboriginal language of central Australia (Bowe 1990).

(3.6) a. Wati-∅, tjitji-∅, minyma-∅ kunyu paltjatjiratja ngari-ngu. — Pitjantjatjara
man-ABS child-ABS woman-ABS REP hungry lie.down-PAST
'The man, the child and the woman reportedly went to sleep hungry.'

a′. *Wati-∅, tjitji-∅, kunyu minyma-∅ paltjatjiratja ngari-ngu.
man-ABS child-ABS REP woman-ABS hungry lie.down-PAST

b. Wati-ngku, tjitji-ngku, minyma-ngku kunyu, kuka-tjiratja-ngku, mai ngalku-nu.
man-ERG child-ERG woman-ERG REP meat-because.without-ERG bread eat-PAST
'The man, child and woman reportedly ate bread due to a lack of meat.'

b′. *Wati-ngku, kunyu tjitji-ngku, minyma-ngku, kuka-tjiratja-ngku, mai ngalku-nu.
man-ERG REP child-ERG woman-ERG meat-because.without-ERG bread eat-PAST

c. Wati tjitji minyma-ngku-n̠i nya-ngu.
man child woman-ERG-1sgACC see-PAST
'The man, child and woman saw me.'

c′. *Wati-n̠i tjitji minyma-ngku nya-ngu.
man-1sgACC child woman-ERG see-PAST

c″. *Wati-ngku-n̠i, tjitji-ngku, minyma-ngku nya-ngu.
man-ERG-1sgACC child-ERG woman-ERG see-PAST

In (3.6a) the three NPs *wati* 'man', *tjitji* 'child' and *minyma* 'woman' form a coordinate NP; they all occur in the absolutive case, as they are the S argument of the verb. The word *kunyu* 'reportedly' is a second position element like the verb *je* 'is' in Serbian and Croatian; it must occur in the second syntactic position in the clause, i.e. after the first constituent. (Pitjatjantjara does not permit the kind of variation found in Serbian and Croatian illustrated in (3.1).) This is evidence that the three NPs count as a single coordinate NP; note the ungrammaticality of (3.6a′) in which *kunyu* occurs between two of the NPs rather than after all three. In (3.6b), (3.6c) the three NPs are the A argument of a transitive verb, and therefore they take the ergative case. Because the three NPs form a single A argument, the ergative case marker can appear either on each NP, as in (3.6b), or just on the coordinate NP as a whole, in which case it appears only on the final NP, as in (3.6c). As in (3.6a′), the occurrence of *kunyu* 'reportedly' between two NPs within the coordinate NP is ungrammatical, as (3.6b′) shows. There is another second-position element in (3.6c), *-n̠i* '1sgACC'. It must appear attached to the NP as a whole, which is realized as being linked to the last NP in the coordinate construction;

otherwise the result is ungrammatical, as in (3.6c′), (3.6c″). In coordination, then, there are two or more elements functioning as co-heads; none of them is a modifier of the other(s).

3.1.2 *Valence*

The concept of valence (or, in British English, **valency**) refers to the number of dependents that a head may take. In the context of grammatical relations, the notions of transitive and intransitive refer to the valence of verbs, and it is the valence of verbs and other predicates that is of primary concern here. Consider the English sentence in (3.7).

(3.7)	a. Chris	gave the present	to Pat	at the party	yesterday.
	Subject	Direct Object	Ind Object		
	Agent	Theme	Recipient	Location	Temporal
	b. Chris gave the present to Pat.				
	c. Chris gave the present (at the party).				

There are five dependents in (3.7a), i.e. the NPs *Chris* and *the present*, the PPs *to Pat* and *at the party* and the adverb *yesterday*, but there is an important difference between the PP *at the party* and the adverb *yesterday* and the other dependents. The other dependents are semantically arguments of the verb *give* and syntactically are terms; *at the party* and *yesterday* are neither semantic arguments of *give* nor terms syntactically, as they denote not a participant in the event of giving but rather the location where the event as a whole took place and the time when it took place. *At the party* and *yesterday* are therefore not arguments of *give*, semantically or syntactically, but rather are **adjuncts** in the clause. There is, then, a fundamental distinction between arguments and adjuncts, and the term 'the valence of a verb' refers to the number of arguments that it takes. The contrast between terms and non-terms was introduced in chapter 2, and it overlaps but is not identical to the argument–adjunct opposition. Terms (i.e. subject, direct object, indirect object) are almost always arguments (the main exception being the **dummy** subjects with weather expressions in some languages), but non-terms can be either arguments or adjuncts. The locative PP with *put* is an argument but a non-term, while all adjuncts are non-terms. The French tradition of valence theorists, following Tesnière, uses the terms 'actant' and 'circonstant' for (syntactic) argument and adjunct, respectively, while others use '**complement**' and 'adjunct' for this distinction. The terms 'argument' and 'adjunct' will continue to be used in this book.

But what kind of arguments? As shown in (3.7a), the arguments in the sentence can be described in both syntactic and semantic terms, and therefore it is appropriate to talk about the syntactic valence of a verb, that is the number of terms it may have, and the semantic valence of a verb, i.e. the number of semantic roles associated with it. The semantic valence of a verb was termed its 'argument structure' in section 2.1. As (3.7c) and the examples in (2.7) show, the syntactic and semantic valences of a verb need not be the same in every instance. *Eat*, for example, has two arguments semantically (hence a semantic valence of 2), but only one syntactic argument, the subject, is required to occur with it (hence a syntactic valence of 1 or 2). *Give*, as in (3.7), has a semantic valence of 3, but only two arguments are required, as in (3.7c). Hence *give* has a semantic valence of 3 and a syntactic valence of 2 or 3. **Weather verbs** like *rain*

Table 3.3. *Semantic versus syntactic valence*

Verb	Semantic valence	Syntactic valence
rain, snow	0	1
die	1	1
break (transitive)	2	2
eat	2	1 or 2
put	3	3
give	3	2 or 3

and *snow* illustrate the opposite discrepancy between the two valence types. Such verbs have no arguments semantically, but because English requires that all clauses in simple sentences have subjects, they take a dummy subject *it.* Hence they have a semantic valence of 0 but a syntactic valence of 1. This is summarized in Table 3.3.

Because verbs like *eat* and *give* have variable syntactic valence, it is necessary to distinguish between obligatory syntactic arguments and optional syntactic arguments. Adjuncts are always optional. Semantic arguments normally appear as syntactic arguments, but there is one significant exception. In a passive construction, the actor NP, which is a semantic argument of the verb, appears as an optional adjunct, if it is not omitted; it is marked by an oblique case, e.g. instrumental as in Malayalam, or by an adposition, for example *by* in English, *von* in German, *par* in French and *ni* in Japanese.

What are the criteria for deciding whether a given NP or PP is an argument or an adjunct? As the discussion in the previous paragraph shows, this is not a simple question, and it is necessary in the first place to ask the question separately with respect to syntactic arguments and semantic arguments. The usual criterion that has traditionally been proposed to determine whether an NP or PP is a syntactic argument is omissibility; if an NP or PP is obligatorily present in a clause, then it is an argument of the verb, whereas optional NPs or PPs are adjuncts. While it is certainly true that obligatory NPs or PPs are arguments and that adjuncts are always optional, it is not the case that all optional NPs or PPs are adjuncts. If all optional elements were adjuncts, then the direct object of verbs like *eat* and *drink* (e.g. *Chris ate (fish)*, *Pat drank (beer)*) would be an adjunct, which is hardly credible. It would also mean that the indirect object of *give* in (3.7) is also an adjunct, again an implausible result. What distinguishes the direct objects of *eat* and *drink* and the indirect object PP with *give* from adjuncts like *yesterday* and *at the party* in (3.7a)? The usual answer is the same one that is given in the preceding paragraph: *fish*, *beer* and *to Pat* are semantic arguments of *eat*, *drink* and *give*, while *yesterday* and *at the party* are not. This answer is satisfactory only if there are criteria for determining whether an NP or PP is a semantic argument of a verb, that is, whether it is part of its argument structure.

The usual way the issue of semantic argumenthood is approached is to say that the NPs and PPs which refer to participants which are conceptually necessary to the meaning of the verb are arguments, and those which refer to participants which are not conceptually necessary are not. Thus with *eat* and *drink*, in order to have an event of eating it is necessary to have an eater (drinker) and something eaten (imbibed), and consequently the NPs referring to the eater (drinker) and the eaten (imbibed) are semantic arguments. Translated into thematic relations, this means that the argument structure of *eat* or *drink* is <Agent (Patient)>, with the agent being the eater (drinker) and the patient being the eaten (imbibed). Similarly, an act of giving necessarily involves a giver, something given and a receiver, and consequently the argument structure of the verb *give* is <Agent Theme (Recipient)>, with the agent being the giver, the theme the thing given and the recipient being the receiver. So far so good. But what about instrumental *with*-PPs? Are they conceptually necessary? Consider the examples in (3.8).

(3.8) a. The boy broke the window (with a rock).
a′. The rock broke the window.
b. The girl ate the pasta (with a fork).
b′. *The fork ate the pasta.

The *with*-PP is optional in both (3.8a) and (3.8b), and one could imagine arguments both for and against its conceptual necessity with each verb. However, there is an important difference between the two. The instrument *rock* can be the subject (actor) with *break*, as in (3.8a′), while the instrument *fork* cannot be the subject (actor) with *eat*, as (3.8b′) clearly shows. Since the rock can be the subject (actor) of *break*, it must be a semantic argument of the verb. This contrast shows that the instrument is a semantic argument with *break*, whereas the instrument is an adjunct with *eat*.

A similar variation occurs with location PPs. With *put*, the location PP is an argument because it is obligatory, as in (3.9).

(3.9) a. Dana put the book on the table.
b. *Dana put the book.

Some intransitive verbs take an optional location PP, as in (3.10).

(3.10) a. Leslie arrived at the office.
a′. Leslie arrived.
a″. *At the office, Leslie arrived.
b. Kim sat on the sofa.
b′. Kim sat.
b″. ?On the sofa, Kim sat.
c. Dana read *The New York Times* in the kitchen.
c′. In the kitchen, Dana read *The New York Times*.

The location PP with arrive in (3.10a) is optional, as in (a′), but it is nevertheless an argument semantically; an arrival event necessarily involves an entity that comes to be in a place, and consequently the NP referring to the entity and the PP to the place are semantic arguments of *arrive*. Its argument structure would be <Theme (Location)>. In (3.10b), sitting necessarily involves an entity in a particular posture in a specific location; hence in (3.10) *Kim* and *sofa* are the semantic arguments of *sit*. Its argument structure would be the same as for *arrive*. Compare the semantic function of the location PPs in (3.9a), (3.10a) and (3.10b) with that of the PP in (3.10c). (The PP *in the kitchen* is not part of the NP; the intended meaning is not '*The New York Times* which is in the kitchen'.) In the first three sentences the location PP specifies the location of one of the participants but not the location of the event as a whole; this is particularly clear in (3.9a), where *on the table* specifies the location of the book but not Dana's location. In contrast, the location PP in (3.10c) expresses where the event as a whole took place, and by doing so it indicates the location of both the subject and the direct object. All events take place in space and time, and therefore it is always possible to specify the time and place of an event. Hence the elements expressing the spatio-temporal coordinates of an event are never semantic arguments of the verb, since they are never distinctive. The location PP in (3.10c) is therefore an adjunct. In general, if a location PP expresses the location of a participant (normally the one referred to by the theme NP), then it is a semantic argument, as in (3.9a), (3.10a), (3.10b), and because it is a semantic argument, it will also be a syntactic argument. If, on the other hand, a location PP indicates the location of the event as a whole, as in (3.10c), then it is not a semantic argument and is an adjunct. In English, adjunct PPs readily occur sentence-initially, as in (3.10c′), while argument location PPs typically do not, as (3.10a″), (3.10b″) show. In the end, the question of whether an NP or PP is a semantic argument or not is ultimately a theoretical issue, and different theories take a variety of stances on this issue.

Thus far only the valence properties of verbs have been discussed, but other categories can take arguments and therefore have a valence. The most obvious example is adpositions, which are traditionally said to take an object. While it is reasonable to take the default valence for an adposition to be 1, there are prepositions in English which appear to lack an object. Consider the following examples.

(3.11) a. Kim ran down the stairs.
a′. Down the stairs ran Kim.
b. Kim put the book down.
b′. *Kim put the book down the table.
c. Kim ran away.
c′. Away ran Kim.
c″. *Kim ran away the house.
d. Kim put the book away.
d′. *Kim put the book away the box.

The directional preposition *down* takes an object in (3.11a) and (3.11a′) but not in (3.11b) or (3.11b′); hence it seems to be somewhat like *eat* in sometimes taking an object and sometimes not. *Away*, on the other hand, never seems to take an object, as the last five examples in (3.11) show. It has a valence of 0. Adjectives, when functioning predicatively, also take arguments. While the most common use would be as 1-place predicates, there are also instances of optionally 2-place adjectives such as *angry* and *proud.*

(3.12) a. Leslie is tall.
b. Dana is angry.
b′. Dana is angry at Kim.
c. Chris is very proud.
c′. Chris is very proud of Robin.

In (3.12a) *Leslie* is a patient semantically and the subject syntactically; hence the semantic and syntactic valence of *tall* is 1. *Tall* in (3.12a) is a predicate adjective, and it, not *be*, is the semantic predicate. In many languages there is nothing equivalent to the English verb *be* and the adjective functions directly as a predicate, as in the Lakhota example in (1.5c). Hence the argument structure of English *be tall* is <Patient>; Lakhota *khúža* 'be sick' in (1.5c) would have the same argument structure. In (3.12b) and (3.12b′), *angry* can have one or two arguments, and in (3.12c) and (3.12c′) *proud* may also have one or two arguments. Hence the argument structure for predicative *angry* and *proud* is <Experiencer (Stimulus)>. Adjectives can have two arguments in English only when they function predicatively; an attributive expression like **the very proud of his son parent* is quite impossible. Finally, certain nouns can be said to have optional arguments, for example **deverbal** nominals (i.e. nouns derived from verbs) and nouns referring to kinship relations and royalty.

(3.13) a. the gift
b. the gift of money to the library by the philanthropist
c. the gift of money
d. the gift to the library
e. the gift by the philanthropist
f. the gift to the library by the philanthropist

(3.14) a. the Queen (of England)
a′. the Prince (of Wales)
b. the father (of my best friend)
b′. the mother (of my wife)

The noun *gift* is related to the verb *give*, but unlike *give*, it can occur alone without any arguments, as in (3.13a). The optional arguments all occur in PPs, and some or all of them can be present, as in (3.13b). Each of these corresponds to one of the three semantic arguments of *give*, i.e. *the philanthropist* = agent, *the money* = theme, and *the library* = recipient. Since all of them are optional, they may occur in combinations not possible with *give*. Royalty and kinship expressions like those in (3.14) have a structure similar to (3.13), and it is reasonable to analyze *England* and *my wife* as being optional arguments of *Queen* and *mother*, respectively.

3.1.3 *Coding*

The coding properties of grammatical relations were discussed in section 2.2.1, and the range of coding options presented there is the same as for dependency relations in general. Hence only a brief review is needed here.

Word order is a common means of signalling grammatical relations, and it is also relevant in many languages to the relation between adpositions and their objects, since the object must immediately follow (preposition) or precede (postposition) the adposition. Modifiers are often in a strict ordering relation to the head they modify. In English, articles and other determiners must precede the noun they modify, and adjectives and quantifiers must as well.

Dependency relations are also expressed by morphological means, specifically case and agreement. Examples of the different ways case can be expressed were given in section 2.2.1 in the discussion of how case is used to code grammatical relations, and examples of verb agreement with subject only, with subject and direct object only, and with all three terms were also presented. In languages with case systems, the dependence of a modifier on its head is signalled by agreement in case, number and/or gender with the head. This is illustrated in Russian and German in (3.15a) and (3.15b); in Kalkatungu modifiers (but not possessors) agree with their head in case only, as in (3.2a).

(3.15) a. Molod-aja učitel'nic-a da-l-a nov-uju — Russian
young-FSGNOM teacher-FSGNOM give-PAST-FSg new-FSGACC
knig-u star-oj ženščin-e.
book-FSGACC old-FSGDAT woman-FSGDAT
'The young teacher gave a/the new book to an/the old woman.'

b. Der klein-e Mann ha-t den — German
the.MSGNOM small-MSGNOM man have-3SGPRES the.MSGACC
groß-en Hut gekauft.
big-MSGACC hat bought
'The small man bought the big hat.'

In Swahili and other Bantu languages, noun modifiers must agree with their head in class; this is exemplified in the following example from Hinnebusch (1979).

(3.16) Wa-tu ha-wa wa-zuri wa-na-vi-nunua vi-ti vi-le vi-kubwa — Swahili
2-person this-2 2-nice 2-PRES-8-buy 8-chair 8-that 8-big
duka-ni hu-mu.
store-18 this-18
'These nice people are buying those big chairs in this store.'

In Swahili, class 2 is for plural human referents, class 8 is for plural things, and class 18 is for locations. The head noun comes first in the Swahili NP, bearing a class affix, and the following modifiers must also carry this affix. Note that it is the same affix that occurs on the verb to signal subject and direct-object agreement.

In addition to marking term arguments, case is also important for signalling the dependence of an adpositional object on its adposition, as in (3.17), and for indicating possession in a possessive NP, as in (3.18). Many languages have a case whose primary function is signalling possession; it is usually called the genitive case, as discussed in section 2.1.

(3.17) a. um den Hut — German
around the.MSGACC hat
'around the hat'

b. in dem Hut
in the.MSGDAT hat
'in the hat'

b′. in den Hut
in the.MSGACC hat
'into the hat'

c. wegen des Hut-es
because the.MSGGEN hat-GEN
'because of the hat'

(3.18) a. das Auto des Mannes — German
the.MSGN car the.MSGGEN man-GEN
'the man's car'

b. bayi wagal-Ø ba-ŋu-n ḑugumbil-ŋu — Dyirbal
NM.ABS boomerang-ABS NM-GEN woman-GEN
'the woman's boomerang'

c. Hanako no tomodati — Japanese
GEN friend
'Hanako's friend'

The examples in (3.17) illustrate the case-marking properties of three German prepositions: *um* 'around' assigns accusative case to its object, as in (a); *in* 'in, into' assigns dative case when it signifies static location, as in (3.17b), or accusative when it signifies motion, as in (b′); and *wegen* 'because of' assigns genitive case, as in (c). Possessive NPs from three languages are given in (3.18); in German and Dyirbal, the possessor occurs in the genitive case, whereas in Japanese the possessor is linked to the possessed noun by the genitive postposition *no.*

In most of these coding examples, the relation between the head and dependent has been coded on the dependent; that is, arguments of the verb carry case assigned by the verb, objects of adpositions carry case assigned by the adposition, and possessor NPs bear genitive case. This is not the only possibility, however; in some languages, the relation between head and dependent is coded on the head, not on the dependent. In the Swahili sentence in (3.16), for example, the subject and direct object carry no case at all, but the verb has markers indicating that the subject is a class 2 NP and the direct object is a class 8 NP. Hence the fact that *watu hawa wazuri* 'these nice people' is the subject and *viti vile vikubwa* 'those big chairs' is the direct object is coded morphologically on the verb, which is the head of the construction, not on the dependents, as in the Russian and German examples in (3.15). An important consequence of this is that the inflected verb can stand alone in place of the whole clause; that is, *wanavinunua* 'they [human] bought them [things]' is a complete sentence by itself, unlike the German and Russian examples in (3.15), in which **dala* 'gave' (Russian) and **hat gekauft* 'bought' (German) could not count as complete clauses on their own. In Swahili, on the other hand, the subject and direct object NPs are in a unilateral dependence on the verb, since the verb can occur without them. Another example of this can be seen in the Lakhota example in (2.25), repeated below. (The verb *naxʔų́* 'hear' takes its subject and object markers as infixes.)

(3.19) a. (Miyé) mathó ki hená na-wíčha-wa-xʔų. — Lakhota
(1sg) bear the those stem-3plOBJ-1sgSUBJ-hear
'I heard those bears.'

a′. Nawíčhawaxʔų.
'I heard them.'

b. Mathó ki hená (miyé) na-má-Ø-xʔų-pi.
bear the those (1sg) stem-1sgOBJ-3SUBJ-hear-PL
'Those bears heard me.'

b′. Namáxʔųpi.
'They heard me.'

In (3.19a′), *nawíčhawaxʔų* 'I heard them' is a complete sentence in Lakhota, and in (3.19b′), *namáxʔųpi* 'they heard me' is likewise a complete sentence. Thus, the verb alone forms a complete clause and therefore can stand by itself as an independent utterance, just as in Swahili.

This pattern, which is called **head marking**, is also found in adpositional phrases and possessive NPs. The following examples of head-marking PPs and possessive NPs are taken from Yagua, an indigenous language of Peru (Payne 1986).

(3.20) a. sa-jų̨noonú Pedro   Yagua
3sg-mother
'Pedro's mother'
a′. sa-jų̨noonú
'his mother'
b. sa-rą́jvą̨ą̨ jíryonu
3sg-poison bushmaster
'bushmaster's poison'
b′. sa-rą́jvą̨ą̨
'his poison'
c. ríí-va ra-myudasúy
INAN-on 1sg-pants
'on my pants'
c′. ríí-va
'on them/it'
d. rá-viimú jų̨muñú
INAN-inside canoe
'inside the canoe'
d′. rá-viimú
'inside it.'

The phrases in (3.20a) and (3.20b) are possessive phrases, and the possessor NPs, *Pedro* and *jíryonu* 'bushmaster' [a kind of snake], bear no case akin to the genitive illustrated in (3.18); rather, the possessed Ns, *jų̨noonú* 'mother' in (a) and *rą́jvą̨ą̨* 'poison' in (b), carry a prefix indicating that there is a third-person singular possessor. Hence possession is marked on the possessed N, the head, rather than on the possessor NP, the dependent. This has important consequences for the syntax of these phrases. It was argued above that in possessive phrases in languages like German, Dyirbal and English the dependence between the possessor (dependent) and possessed (head) is bilateral, because if the possessor is omitted, the phrase ceases to count as a possessive construction. In (3.20a′) and (3.20b′), however, the possessor NP is not present, and yet the expression still counts as a possessive construction, due to the possessive prefix on the possessed noun. Thus the relation between the possessor NP and the possessed noun in Yagua is unilateral, not bilateral. The same is true with respect to the adpositional phrases in (3.20c) and (3.20d): the adposition bears a prefix which signals its object, and the object NP can be omitted, as in (c′) and (d′), with the resulting expression still counting as a PP. Thus head marking in clauses, possessive phrases and adpositional phrases sharply contrasts with the **dependent-marking** constructions in English, German, Dyirbal and Russian. Languages in which the head-marking pattern is predominant are called 'head-marking languages', and other languages of this type in addition to Swahili, Kinyarwanda and Lakhota are Acehnese (Durie 1985) and Jakaltek. Languages in which the dependent-marking pattern is dominant are called 'dependent-marking languages', and examples of this type include Yalarnnga, Kalkatungu, Yidiɲ, Avar, Telugu, Malayalam, Icelandic, Korean, Japanese, and Tongan.

This opposition is not absolute, for several reasons. First, there are languages to which it simply does not apply, e.g. Cantonese, which lacks case and agreement altogether (see (2.37)). Second, some languages have some properties of both types. Basque is an example of what is called a 'double-marking language'; the example in (2.26a) is repeated below.

(3.21) a. Ni-k hi-ri liburu-∅ bat oparitu d-i-a-t. — Basque
1sg-ERG 2sg-DAT book-ABS one give.as.gift 3sgDOBJ-have-2sgIOBJ-1sgSUBJ
'I have given you a book (as a present).'
b. Oparitu d-i-a-t.
give 3sgDOBJ-have-2sgIOBJ-1sgSUBJ
'I have given it to you (as a present).'

As noted in chapter 2, up to three terms can be cross-referenced on the auxiliary verb in Basque, and this is an essential feature of head-marking languages. In addition, independent NPs and pronouns carry case, just as in a dependent-marking language. However, unlike a typical dependent-marking language, Basque allows the independent NPs and pronouns to be omitted, and the result is a complete clause, just as in Swahili. Other double-marking languages encountered thus far include Hungarian and Tindi. A number of Indo-European languages have agreement for subject which allows the subject to be omitted, but no other arguments can be left out; such languages are often referred to as **'pro-drop'** languages. The following example is from Latin.

(3.22) a. Natur-a nōs ab cēter-īs animāl-ibus — Latin
nature-FsgNOM 1plACC from other-NplABL animal-NplABL
separāv-it.
separate-3sgPAST
'Nature separated us from the other animals.'
b. Nōs ab cēter-īs animāl-ibus separāv-it.
'It separated us from the other animals.'

Latin has canonical features of a dependent-marking language, e.g. verbs and prepositions assign case to their objects, and possessors carry genitive case. But it has one head-marking feature: subject agreement which permits the subject NP or independent pronoun to be omitted. No other arguments are cross-referenced on the verb, and no others can be freely omitted. Unlike Basque, Latin is basically a dependent-marking language with one head-marking feature. Other languages of this type discussed in chapter 2 are Spanish and Mparntwe Arrernte.

Third, the mere existence of agreement morphology in a language does not guarantee that the argument indexed by the agreement can be omitted. In German, for example, there is agreement for subject, but the subject NP or independent pronoun cannot be omitted.

(3.23) a. Ich geh-e. — German
1sgNOM go-1sgPRES
a′. *Gehe.
b. Du geh-st.
2sgNOM go-2sgPRES
'You go.'

b′. *Gehst.
c. Die Frau/ Sie geh-t.
the.FsgNOM woman/3FsgNOM go-3sgPRES
'The woman/She goes.'
c′. *Geht.

Even though the present-tense verb forms are distinct for the three persons in the singular, the subject cannot be omitted in German the way it can be left out in Latin, Lakhota or Swahili.

3.1.4 *Summary*

In this section one way of characterizing the syntagmatic relations that hold between a head and its dependent(s) has been presented, namely, in terms of dependency relations. There are three kinds of dependencies, i.e. bilateral, unilateral and coordinate, and attention has been focussed on the first two. In a bilateral dependence, neither the head nor the dependent(s) can occur without the other(s). Examples of bilateral dependencies include clause, PP and possessive-phrase constructions in English, German, and Russian. In a unilateral dependence, the head can occur without dependents in a particular type of construction, but the dependents cannot occur without the head. Examples of unilateral dependencies can be seen in modifier–modified constructions in all of the languages discussed in this chapter, clauses in Swahili, Kinyarwanda, Basque and Lakhota, and in PPs and possessive constructions in Yagua. The contrast between the two types of clause, PP and possessive constructions underlies the important typological distinction between languages with head marking and dependent marking. Languages of both types have coordinate constructions. This is summarized in the following table.

Table 3.4. *Dependencies in head-marking and dependent-marking languages*

Language type	Syntactic construct	Dependence type	Examples
Head-marking	Clause	Unilateral	Swahili, Lakhota
	PP	Unilateral	Yagua
	Possessive NP	Unilateral	Yagua
Dependent-marking	Clause	Bilateral	English, German
	PP	Bilateral	English, German
	Possessive NP	Bilateral	German, Dyirbal

In the next section, a way of formally representing dependency relations will be presented.

3.2 Dependency representations

An important part of syntactic analysis is representing the results of the analysis. That is, once a sentence has been broken down into its parts and the categories of the parts and the relations among them identified, these elements and interrelations are presented in a formal notation which makes them explicit. Different approaches to the analysis of dependency relations employ distinct notations, and the representational schema to be used here takes the sentence to be analyzed as the starting point and adds arrows to indicate the dependencies. This method is employed in Matthews (1982) and Hudson's (1984) **Word Grammar**, although there are differences in their approaches. The preliminary representation of the English sentence *A girl handed a blue toy to the baby* is given in Figure 3.1 below. The arrows indicate the relation from head to dependent.

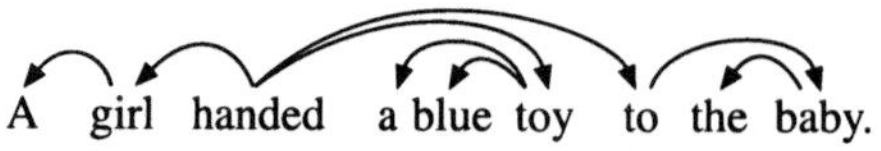
A girl handed a blue toy to the baby.

Figure 3.1. *Preliminary dependency representation*

The arrows indicate that *a* is a dependent of the head *girl*, while *girl* is a dependent of the head *handed*; *a* and *blue* are dependents of *toy*, while *toy* is a dependent of *handed*; and finally, *the* is a dependent of *baby*, which is a dependent of the preposition *to*, which is a dependent of *handed*. There is no indication, however, of the type of dependence (unilateral or bilateral) or of the grammatical relations involved. Both types of information can be added to the diagram. For indicating the type of dependence, a single-headed arrow will be used to indicate a unilateral dependence of the dependent on the head and a double-headed arrow will be used to indicate a bilateral dependence between them. These notations are summarized in Table 3.5.

Table 3.5. *Arrows indicating types of dependencies*

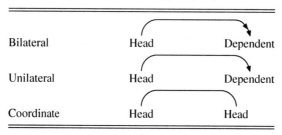

Bilateral	Head	Dependent
Unilateral	Head	Dependent
Coordinate	Head	Head

In addition, notations for subject, direct object, and indirect object can be added. The revised representation is given in Figure 3.2.

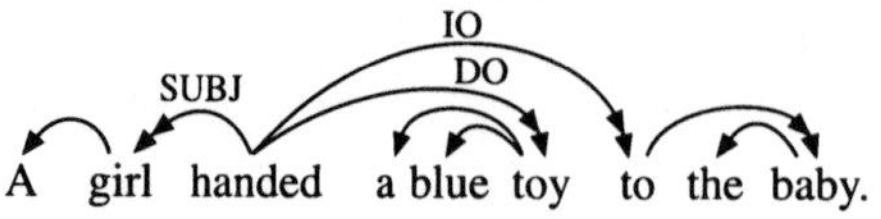
IO
DO
SUBJ
A girl handed a blue toy to the baby.

Figure 3.2. *Enhanced representation*

The three term arguments are presented as being in bilateral dependencies with the verb, and *baby* is in a bilateral dependence with *to*; in addition, the modifiers *a*, *blue* and *the* are portrayed as being in unilateral dependencies with the heads that they modify. This means that it is possible to make explicit the structural contrast between head-marking and dependent-marking constructions. Compare the representation of *to the baby* in Figure 3.2 with that in Figure 3.3 of the Yagua PP in (3.20d), *ráviimú jųmuñú* 'in the canoe'.

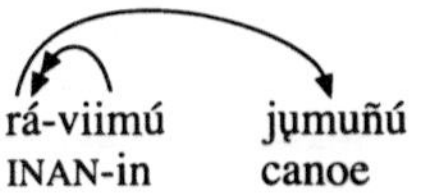
rá-viimú jųmuñú
INAN-in canoe

Figure 3.3. *Yagua head-marking PP 'in the canoe'*

The Yagua PP *ráviimú jųmuñú* literally means 'in-it$_i$ (the) canoe$_i$', and the grammatical element that is the object of the adposition *-viimú* 'in' is the pronominal prefix *rá-* 'it'. Hence the bilateral dependence is between these two elements. The NP *jųmuñú* 'canoe' is actually **in apposition to** the pronominal prefix *rá-*, and this is a unilateral dependence, in which *jųmuñú* is an omissible element. The same is true in clausal head-marking structures. Figure 3.4 represents a simplified version of the Swahili sentence in (3.16), *Watu wanavinunua viti* 'The people are buying the chairs'.

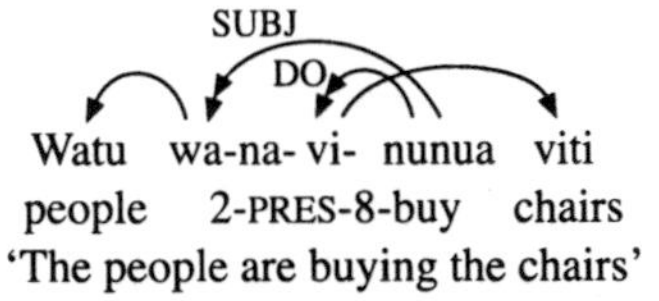
SUBJ
DO
Watu wa-na- vi- nunua viti
people 2-PRES-8-buy chairs
'The people are buying the chairs'

Figure 3.4. *Swahili head-marking clause in (3.16)*

The elements in a bilateral dependence with the verb *nunua* 'buy' are the agreement prefixes *wa-* (class 2) and *vi-* (class 8); as we noted earlier, they cannot occur without the verb and the verb cannot occur without them. They and the verb, plus the tense morpheme, constitute a complete clause, *wanavinunua* 'they are buying them'. The independent NPs, *watu* 'people' and *viti* 'chairs', are in apposition to the agreement morphemes on the verb and need not appear for there to be a complete clause. Hence their relation to their heads is a unilateral dependence, just as in the Yagua PP. This is strikingly different from the relation of the NPs in the English clause and PP in Figure 3.2; in both the verb and its arguments and the preposition and its object are in bilateral dependencies.

This type of representation also readily captures structures like the Kalkatungu sentence in (3.2a′) with the displaced noun modifier, or the Croatian sentence in (3.1b) with the verb intervening between a noun modifier and the noun it modifiers. The representation of (3.2a′) is given in Figure 3.5.

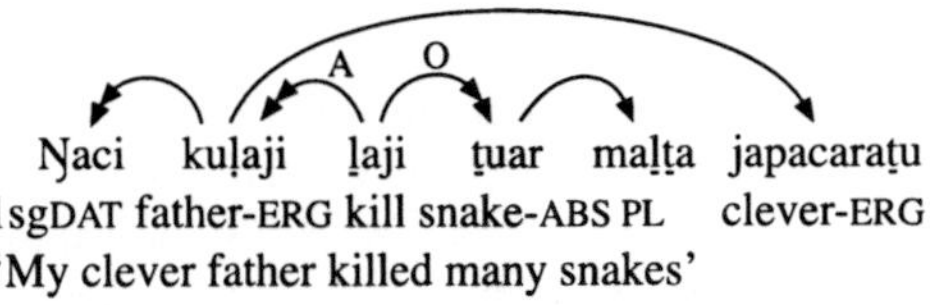
A O
Ŋaci kuḷaji ḷaji ṭuar maḷṭa japacaraṭu
1sgDAT father-ERG kill snake-ABS PL clever-ERG
'My clever father killed many snakes'

Figure 3.5. *Representation of Kalkatunga sentence in (3.2a′)*

This diagram explicitly represents the fact that *japacara-ṯu* 'clever-ERG' is a dependent modifier of the head noun *kuḷa-ji* 'father-ERG' and that it occurs in a different part of the clause from it. The Croatian example in (3.1b) is depicted in Figure 3.6.

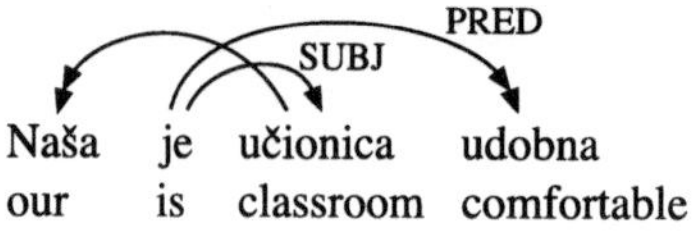
PRED
SUBJ
Naša je učionica udobna
our is classroom comfortable

Figure 3.6. *Representation of Croatian sentence in (3.1b)*

The dependence between *je* 'is' and *učionica* 'classroom' is unilateral, because Croatian is like Latin and allows subject NPs to be omitted; hence *udobna je* 'it is comfortable' is a complete clause in Croatian.

Coordinate dependencies are represented by an arc without any arrowheads, indicating that the elements joined by it are of equal status. Representations for *The boy and the girl sang* and *The boy cooked and ate the fish* are given in Figure 3.7.

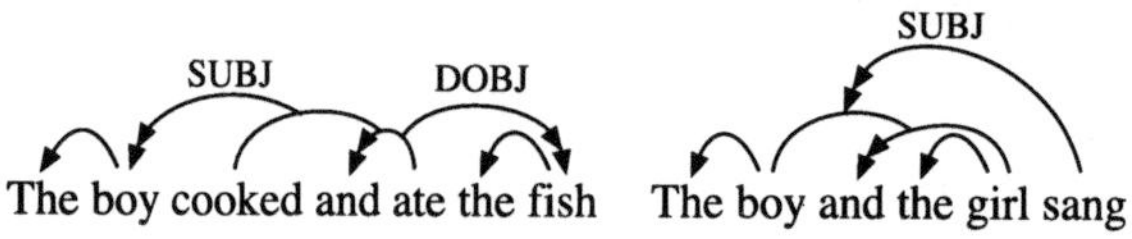
SUBJ
DOBJ
The boy cooked and ate the fish
SUBJ
The boy and the girl sang

Figure 3.7. *Coordination of NPs and Vs*

The arc in the right diagram unites the head nouns *boy* and *girl*, and they collectively serve as the subject of the verb *sang*. In the left diagram, the arc links the two verbs *cooked* and *ate*, and the arrows signal that *the boy* is the subject of both verbs and *the fish* is the direct object of both verbs. The conjunction *and* is linked to the last conjoined head in these representations. This is because when there are more than two conjuncts, as in *Tom, Mary and Sally sang* or *The boy caught, cooked and ate the fish*, the conjunction occurs before the last conjunct.

It is possible to further augment the representations by adding semantic roles below the sentence. This allows one to see the interaction between grammatical relations and semantic roles quite clearly.

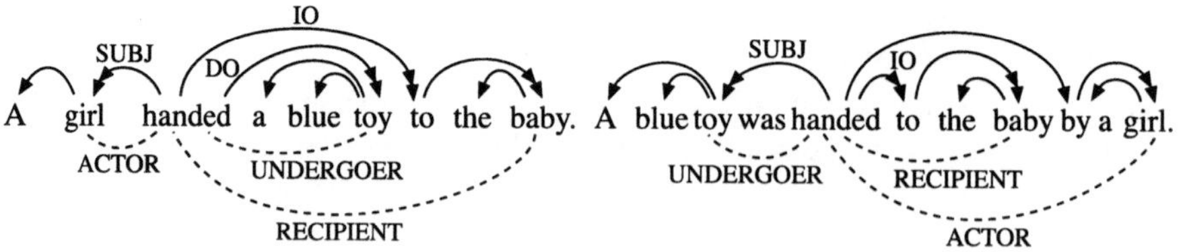
IO
SUBJ
DO
A girl handed a blue toy to the baby.
ACTOR
UNDERGOER
RECIPIENT
SUBJ
IO
A blue toy was handed to the baby by a girl.
UNDERGOER
RECIPIENT
ACTOR

Figure 3.8. *Active and passive clauses in English*

The constancy of semantic roles through changes in grammatical relations in the voice forms is made explicit in these two representations. The relationships between semantic roles and grammatical relations in different languages can readily be captured in this style of depicting dependency relations. This is illustrated in the representations of the Yidiɲ example in (2.101a) and its English translation in Figure 3.9.

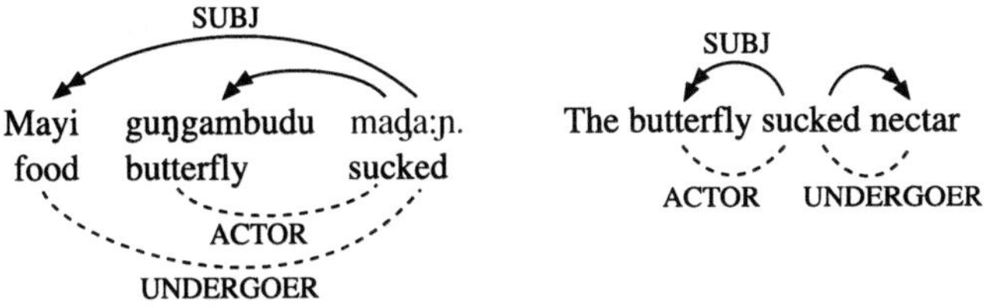

Figure 3.9. *Grammatical relations versus macroroles in Yidiɲ and English*

All of the representations thus far are of simple sentences, and it is necessary now to extend the representational schema to complex sentences. Three types will be represented: object complements (*that*-clauses), infinitival complements and relative clauses. The Malagasy object complement in (2.63a), repeated below, is diagrammed in Figure 3.10.

(3.24) Nanantena Rasoa fa nanasa ny zaza ny vehivavy. Malagasy
hoped Rasoa COMP washed the child the woman
'Rasoa hoped that the woman washed the child.'

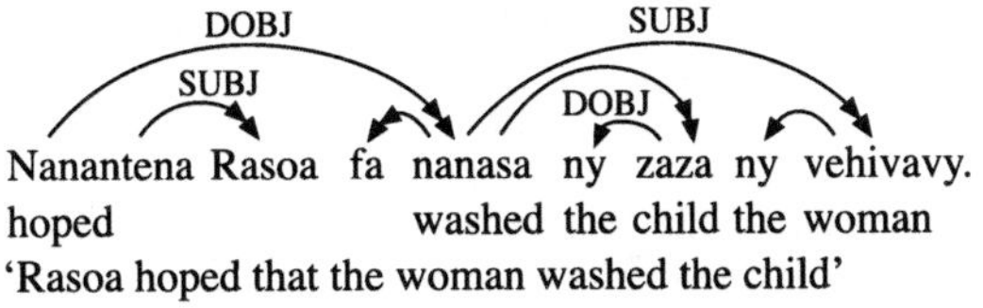

Figure 3.10. *Malagasy object complement*

In this diagram, *nanasa* 'washed' alone does not function as the direct object of *nanantena* 'hoped'; rather, the clause headed by *nanasa* is the direct object of the matrix verb.

An example from English with *tell* provides a good example of an infinitival complement, in this instance, a control construction.

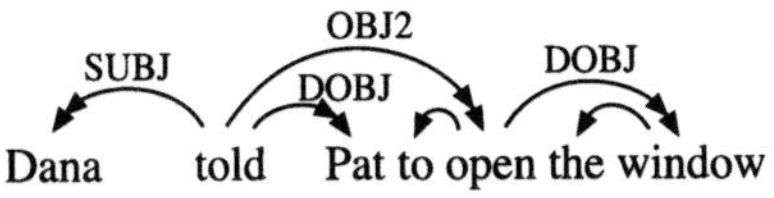

Figure 3.11. *English infinitival complement*

Here again it is the whole infinitive headed by *open* that is a dependent of *tell*, not just the verb itself. *To* serves as a marker of the infinitive; since not all English infinitives require *to*, e.g. *Mary helped John bake the cake*, it is treated as being in a unilateral dependence on the verb. This constrasts with *fa* in Malagasy, which is obligatory in all such constructions. Since this *tell* + infinitive construction is analogous to the ditransitive construction with *tell*, e.g. *Dana told Pat a story*, the infinitival complement can be treated as a secondary object (OBJ2).

Finally, the Dyirbal relative clause in (2.98b), repeated below, illustrates a relative clause construction.

(3.25) Baŋgul yaɽa-ŋgu bayi yuɽi-∅ [baŋgun ɖugumbi-ɽu baga-ŋu-∅]
NM.ERG man-ERG NM.ABS kangaroo-ABS NM.ERG woman-ERG spear-REL-ABS
buɽa-n.
see-NFUT
'The man saw the kangaroo that the woman speared.'

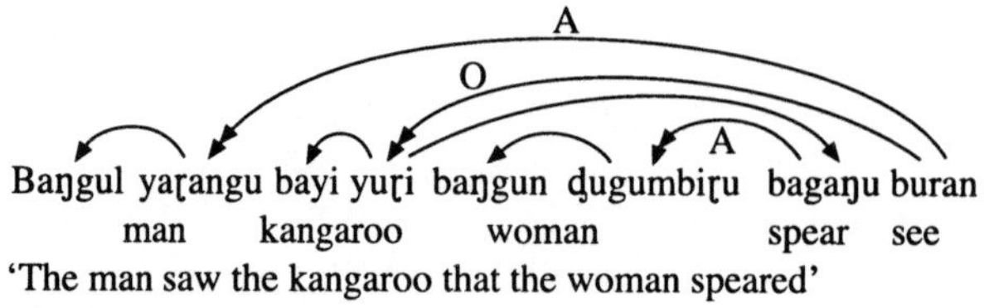

Figure 3.12. *Dyirbal relative clause*

The relative clause *baŋgun ɖugumbiɽu bagaŋu* 'the woman speared' is a dependent modifier of the head NP *bayi yuɽi* 'kangaroo' and hence is connected to it the same way as other nominal modifiers. Both of these last two constructions involve a 'missing argument', i.e. the omitted subject of the infinitive in Figure 3.11 and the head NP in Figure 3.12. The interpretation of the missing argument can be represented if the semantic roles of the arguments are given explicitly, as in Figure 3.8. The augmented representations are presented in Figure 3.13.

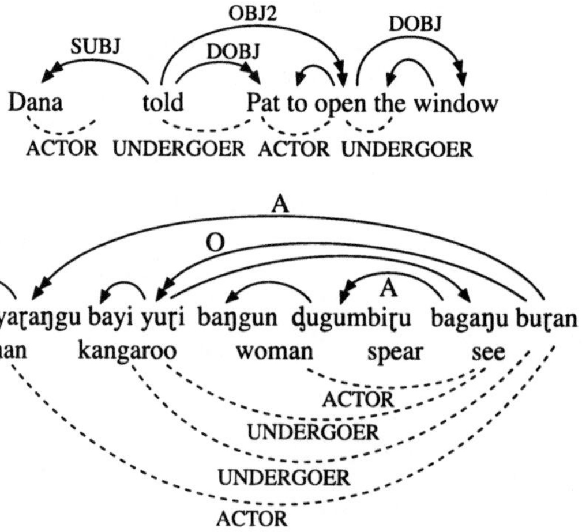

Figure 3.13. *Enhanced representations of English control construction and Dyirbal relative clause*

These diagrams make explicit that *Pat* is the actor of *open* in the control construction and that the head NP *bayi yuɽi* 'kangaroo' is the undergoer of *bagal* 'spear' in the Dyirbal relative clause.

3.3 Conclusion

In this chapter the discussion of grammatical relations in the previous chapter has expanded to the whole of the relational side of syntax. Grammatical relations are but one kind of dependency relation, and in the investigation of these more abstract relations important typological contrasts across languages have been encountered, especially that between head-marking and dependent-marking structures, which correlate with different kinds of dependency relations. The notation adopted for representing syntagmatic relations in dependency terms permits explicit expression of these important distinctions.

In the next chapter, the discussion turns to a very different way of conceiving of syntagmatic relations and of representing them, constituent-structure grammar.

Notes and suggested readings

The fundamental importance of syntagmatic and paradigmatic relations for the structure of language was first fully articulated by Saussure (1917). The primary approaches to dependency grammar include Tesnière (1953, 1959), Hays (1964), Mel'čuk (1979, 1988), Hudson (1984), Sgall, Hajičová and Panevová (1986) and Sgall and Panevová (1988). Textbook introductions to dependency grammar include Matthews (1982), Tarvainen (1991) and Brown and Miller (1991). The concept of valence was introduced independently in Tesnière (1953) and Hockett (1958); see e.g. Helbig (1971), Abraham (1978) and Allerton (1982) for extended discussion of valence. Nichols (1986) originally proposed the head-marking versus dependent-marking typological contrast. The dependency representations in section 3.2.2 follow Matthews (1982) and Payne (1993) in treating the determiner as a dependent of the noun in the NP; Hudson (1984) takes the noun to be a dependent of the determiner, which he takes to be the head, and treats the complementizer *that* and the infinitive marker *to* as heads which take the following clause or verb as a dependent.

Exercises

1. Identify the type of dependency relation (bilateral, unilateral, coordinate) that holds between or among the underlined elements in the following English sentences. [section 3.1.1]
   (1) The boys left.
   (2) Mary left.
   (3) The very tall green trees grow in the forest.
   (4) Mary and her friend live in London.
   (5) Sam put the book on the table.
   (6) Walter drinks beer.

2. Identify the (syntactic) arguments and the adjuncts in the following English sentences. Are there any examples of an NP in a clause which is a semantic argument but which is not realized as a syntactic argument? [section 3.1.2]
   (1) Chris died yesterday.
   (2) a. Sandy ate the sandwich in the kitchen.
       b. The sandwich was eaten by Sandy in the kitchen.
   (3) At the mall, Kim met two friends.
   (4) Leslie put the book on the table this morning.

3. Identify the following constructions from Apalai, a Carib language spoken in Peru and Brazil (Koehn and Koehn 1986), and Lezgian (Haspelmath 1993) as head marking or dependent marking. ('1→3' means '1sgSUBJ+3sgOBJ'.) Describe each construction and explain why it is one type or the other. [section 3.1.3]

(1) a. Taky m-ekaro-ase ey-a. Apalai
bow 2→3-give-PAST 3sg-to
'You gave the bow to him.'
b. N-anỹ-no.
3→3-catch-PAST
'He caught it.'
c. Y-pipoh-no.
1→3-hit-PAST
'I hit it.'
d. nohpo ∅-kyry-ry
woman 3-thing-POSS
'the woman's things'
d′. ∅-kyry-ry
3-thing-POSS
'his/her things'
e. y-kaparu-nu
1-club-POSS
'my club'

(2) a. Alfija-di maq̃ala-∅ kx̂e-na. Lezgian
Alfija-ERG article-ABS write-TNS
'Alfija wrote an article.'
b. Muʔminata-z Ibrahim-∅ aku-na.
Mu'minat-DAT Ibrahim-ABS see-TNS
'Mu'minat saw Ibrahim.'
c. èlectrostancijadi-n q̃enez
power.station-GEN inside
'inside the electric power station'
d. duxtur-ri-n patariw
doctor-PL-GEN to
'to the doctors'
e. külü q̃uš-ari-n pud mug
little bird-PL-GEN three nest
'three nests of little birds'
e′. pud mug
'three nests'
f. Güldestedi-n xtul
Güldeste-GEN grandson
'Güldeste's grandson.'
f′. xtul
'grandson'

4. Draw a dependency representation (syntactic relations only) for the following sentences: the Malagasy example in (2.49a), the Lakhota example in (3.19a), and the Yidiɲ example in (3.2b′). [section 3.2]

5. Represent the syntactic and semantic relations in the following sentences from the exercises in chapter 2: the German sentences in (4) and (5a) in exercise 2 (since the valence of the main verb determines the number of arguments in the clause, treat it as the head); the Malayalam sentences in (2) and (16′) in exercise 3; and the Jakaltek sentences in (4), (6) and (10a) in exercise 5 (use 'S, A, O' for the grammatical relations in the Jakaltek representations). [section 3.2]

6. Represent the syntactic and semantic relations in the following complex sentences: (2.61d′) from English, (2.63b) from Malagasy, and (1) below from Korean (Yang 1994).

   (1) Chelswu-ka kocangna-n khempwuthe-lul kochi-ess-ta.
   Chelswu-NOM broken-REL computer-ACC fix-PAST-DECL
   'Chelsoo fixed the computer that was broken.'

CHAPTER 4

Constituent structure

4.0 Introduction

In chapter 1 two distinct aspects of syntactic structure were introduced; they were labelled 'relational structure' and 'constituent structure'. The previous two chapters were devoted to relational structure, and in this chapter the focus is on the other aspect of syntactic structure, constituent structure. The constituent structure of a sentence is concerned with the units into which the words in a sentence are grouped, which are the constituents, and their hierarchical organization. Constituent structure of the kind to be discussed in this chapter is also sometimes referred to as **phrase structure**. In section 1.1, the following provisional constituent structure was given for the sentence *The teacher read a book in the library.*

(4.1) $[_{S}\,[_{NP}\,\text{The}\,[_{N}\,\text{teacher}]]\,[_{VP}\,[_{V}\,\text{read}]\,[_{NP}\,\text{a}\,[_{N}\,\text{book}]]\,[_{PP}\,[_{P}\,\text{in}]\,[_{NP}\,\text{the}\,[_{N}\,\text{library}]]\,_{PP}]\,_{VP}]\,_{S}]$

In the next section, **constituency tests** will be discussed in detail, and another method for representing constituent structure will be introduced, namely **tree** diagrams. In the analysis of the constituent structure of sentences, it is necessary to break sentences down into their various constituents and establish the form classes found in them and also to develop rules which will specify the constituent structure of sentences. Breaking sentences down into their constituents is known as **parsing**, while the specification of their structure involves the formulation of **phrase-structure rules**. In chapter 5, grammars based on phrase-structure rules will be constructed.

Constituent structure is purely **formal** in nature; that is, it is based upon the syntagmatic and paradigmatic properties of elements and groups of elements rather than their meaning. This is not to say that there may not be semantic properties associated with constituents, which there surely are. Rather, it means that the determination of constituents is based on tests which refer to the cooccurrence and substitution properties of elements and groups of elements and which make no reference to meaning.

'Constituent' and 'form class' are closely related notions. That is, lexical classes like noun, verb, etc. and the phrases they head can be considered form classes or constituents, depending upon the analytic task at hand. Formal criteria for form classes can be stated in terms of constituents' syntagmatic and paradigmatic properties. They are summarized in (4.2).

(4.2) Formal criteria for form classes

a. Internal structure: a particular form class contains certain types of elements but not others.

b. External distribution: a particular form class has a unique range of morphosyntactic environments in which it can occur.

The internal structure criterion is paradigmatic in nature: within particular types of form classes, certain types of elements may replace each other but not other types. For example, a pronoun can replace the elements in an NP but not in a PP, VP or AdjP. The external structure criterion, on the other hand, is syntagmatic in nature: each type of form class has a unique set of possibilities for cooccurring with other elements in morphosyntactic environments. For example, an AdjP can cooccur with a noun inside an NP or with a copular verb within a VP but not with an adposition in a PP. An NP, on the other hand, can occur in all three of these grammatical contexts.

In the next section the primary tests for constituency will be investigated, and constituent-structure (phrase-structure) tree representations will be introduced. In section 4.2, the notion of form class will be reexamined, and in section 4.3 a more complex schema for conceiving of constituent structure will be presented. In section 4.4 the constituent structure of some of the types of complex sentences introduced in chapter 2 will be explored, and in the final section some of the grammatical phenomena from chapter 2 will be reanalyzed in constituent-structure terms.

4.1 Constituents and their formal representation

For syntactic analysis it is necessary to have a set of tests which will permit the analyst to uncover the constituent structure of sentences of the language being studied. This is known as **immediate constituent analysis**. In addition, explicit representation of phrase structure is an important part of many theoretical approaches in syntax. In this section tests for constituency and **immediate constituent diagrams** for representing the structure of sentences will be introduced.

4.1.1 *Tests for constituency*

There are three primary tests for constituency: substitution, permutation and coordination. The substitution criterion entails that only a constituent can be replaced by another element, usually a **pro-form**, i.e. a pronoun for nouns, a **pro-VP** for VPs, or a pro-PP for a PP. In (4.3b)–(4.3e) possible substitutions in a sentence like the one in (4.3a) are given.

(4.3)

a. The new teacher read a short book in the library.

b.	She read a short book in the library.	'she' replacing 'the new teacher'
c.	The new teacher read it in the library.	'it' replacing 'a short book'
d.	The new teacher read it there.	'there' replacing 'in the library'
d′.	The new teacher read it in there.	'there' replacing 'the library'
e.	The new teacher did.	'did' replacing 'read a book in the library'

In (4.3b)–(4.3d) an NP is replaced by the appropriate pronoun, *she* in (b) and *it* in (c) and (d). The pronoun replaces the whole NP, not just the N; this can be seen in the impossibility of **the new she* or **a short it. There* can be a pro-PP, replacing a PP, as in (d), or it can be a pronoun, substituting for an NP when it is the object of a locative preposition, as in (d′). (Note that while *in/on/under/over/behind there* are all fine, **with there* is impossible.) When *there* functions pronominally, it must replace the whole NP and not just the N, as the ungrammaticality of **in the there* clearly shows. Finally, in (4.3e) *did* functions as a pro-VP and replaces the entire VP. It is a pro-VP and not a pro-verb, because it cannot replace the verb alone, as the impossibility of **The new teacher did a short book in the library* attests.

What is important for this criterion is not only the possible substitutions, as in (4.3b)–(4.3e), but the impossible ones as well. There is no possible pro-form **glarf* in English which could replace the sequence of *teacher read* in (4.3a), yielding **The new glarfed a short book in the library.* Similarly, there is no possible pro-form **wug* which could replace the sequence *read a short*, yielding **The new teacher wugged book in the library.* The possible substitutions correspond to the constituents in (4.1).

The second criterion is permutation, that is a constituent may occur in different positions in a sentence while retaining its structural unity. This can be seen in the alternative forms of (4.3a), exemplified in (4.4), (4.6), (4.7) and (4.8).

(4.4) a. In the library, the new teacher read a short book.
b. ?The library, the new teacher read a short book in.
c. *In, the new teacher read a short book the library.

In (4.4a) the PP *in the library* occurs at the beginning of the sentence; the preposition alone cannot occur at the beginning of the sentence, as in (4.4c). This is evidence that PP is a constituent. There are instances in which less than a full PP can permute, as in (4.4b), an example of preposition stranding. It is illustrated further in (4.5).

(4.5) a. The teacher gave a book to the student.
b. The student the teacher gave a book to.
b′. To the student the teacher gave a book.
c. Who did the teacher give a book to?
c′. To whom did the teacher give a book?

An important difference between the PP in (4.4a) and the one in (4.5a) is that the latter is a syntactic argument, the indirect object, while the former is an adjunct. While the conditions on preposition stranding are very complex, it is generally true that it is more acceptable with argument PPs than with adjunct PPs.

(4.6) a. A short book the new teacher read in the library.
b. *A short the new teacher read book in the library.
c. *Short book the new teacher read a in the library.
d. *Book the new teacher read a short in the library.

In the examples in (4.6), the NP following the verb, *a short book*, appears in initial position, and again this is only possible if the entire NP occurs initially; it is not possible to have just the head noun or the head noun plus one but not all of its modifiers in initial position with its (other) modifiers occurring later in the clause, as in (4.6c) and

(4.6d), nor is it possible for the modifiers to occur initially with the head noun later in the clause, as in (4.6b).

(4.7) a. The new teacher wanted to read a short book in the library, and read a short book in the library she did.
b. *The new teacher wanted to read a short book in the library, and read she did a short book in the library.
c. ?The new teacher wanted to read a short book in the library, and read a short book she did in the library.

The sentences in (4.7) involve **VP-preposing** (also known as VP-fronting), and the verb alone cannot occur in initial position, as (4.7b) shows. Interestingly, the verb plus the direct object NP seem to form a possible constituent, as (4.7c) shows; this will be discussed further below.

(4.8) a. A short book was read by the new teacher in the library.
b. *The new book was read a short by teacher in the library.
c. *A short was read book by the new teacher in the library.
d. *Book was read a short by the new teacher in the library.
e. *A short book the new was read by teacher in the library.
f. *A short book teacher was read by the new in the library.

As discussed in chapter 2, in an English passive construction the direct object NP of the corresponding active sentence appears as the subject and the subject NP of the corresponding active occurs as the object of the preposition *by*, if it occurs at all, as in (4.8a). What is relevant for this discussion is that this alternation involves whole NPs and not subparts. In (4.8b), the head noun of the erstwhile direct object NP *a short book* has replaced the head noun of the subject NP, while its modifiers remain in postverbal position; in addition, the head noun of the erstwhile subject NP appears as the object of the preposition *by*. In this example, only the head nouns have changed their positions and functions, and the result is quite ungrammatical. In the remaining examples, a head noun alone or modifiers alone have permuted, with predictable ungrammatical results. Thus, in all of the different permutations in (4.4)–(4.8), it is whole constituents that change function or position in every instance, and they are for the most part the same constituents that were identified by the substitution test in (4.3).

The final test is coordination: only constituents may be linked, usually by a coordinate conjunction, to form a coordinate structure. This is illustrated in (4.9)–(4.11).

(4.9)	a.	in the table and under the chair	$[_{PP}$ PP and PP]
	b.	on the table and the desk	P $[_{NP}$ NP and NP]
	c.	on and under the table	$[[_{P}$ P and P] NP]
	d.	*on the and under a table.	
	d′.	*on the big and under a small table	
(4.10)	a.	the happy boys and the angry girls	$[_{NP}$ $[_{NP}$ ART ADJ N] and $[_{NP}$ ART ADJ N]]
	b.	the happy boys and angry girls	ART $[_{?}$ $[_{?}$ ADJ N] and $[_{?}$ ADJ N]]
	c.	the happy boys and girls	ART ADJ $[_{N}$ N and N]
	d.	*the happy and the angry boys	

(4.11)	a.	Kim read a book at home and wrote a poem in the library.	[$_{VP}$ [$_{VP}$ V NP PP] and [$_{VP}$ V NP PP]]
	b.	Kim read a book and wrote a poem in the library.	[$_{VP}$[$_{?}$ [$_{?}$ V NP] and [$_{?}$ V NP]] PP]
	c.	Kim can read and write a poem.	[$_{V}$ V and V] NP
	d.	*Kim read a and wrote the poem.	

In the examples in (4.9)–(4.11) the whole phrase forms a coordinate PP, NP or VP in (a) and the heads form coordinate Ps, Ns and Vs in (c). In the (b) example in (4.9) coordinate NPs form a coordinate object of the preposition. In the (b) sentences in (4.10) and (4.11), on the other hand, the constituents being coordinated are neither heads nor whole phrases; they are apparently a new type of intermediate constituent; this appears to be the same constituent that the permutation identified in (4.7c). This will be discussed in section 4.3 below. Finally, all of the ungrammatical examples involve conjoining a sequence of words which is less than a full constituent, i.e. a preposition and NP modifier in (4.9d) and (4.9d′), an article plus adjective in (4.10d), and a verb plus an NP modifier in (4.11d).

One might well wonder, how many tests must a group of words pass before it can be considered a constituent? Ideally, it should pass all three, but minimally it must pass at least one. All of the constituents discussed thus far pass all three. These tests can be used to diagnose instances of **structural ambiguity**. Consider the ambiguous sentence in (4.12a).

(4.12) a. Robin decided on the train.
b. On the train, Robin decided.
c. The train was decided on by Robin.

The issue here is whether *on the train* is a constituent or not. The sentence in (4.12a) can have either of two meanings, depending upon whether *on* is analyzed as part of the **prepositional verb** *decide on*, which means 'choose', or is a preposition heading a prepositional phrase, in this case *on the train.* The two **readings** are 'Robin made the decision while on the the train' (*on* as head of PP) and 'Robin chose the train' (*decide on* as prepositional verb). The ambiguity can be resolved by the permutation test. If the PP appears at the beginning of the sentence, as in (4.12b), then only the PP reading is possible. Since only constituents can be preposed in this way, *on* must form a constituent with *the train*, and therefore the prepositional-verb reading is ruled out. If the sentence is passivized as in (c), then *on* and *the train* are not part of the same constituent but *decide* and *on* are, and therefore only the prepositional-verb meaning is possible.

In chapter 3 there were examples of discontinuous NPs; the example from Kalkatungu is repeated in (4.13).

(4.13) a. Ŋa-ci japacara-t̲u kuḷa-ji l̲aji t̲uar-∅ mal̲t̲a. — Kalkatungu
1sg-DAT clever-ERG father-ERG kill snake-ABS mob-ABS
'My clever father killed the snakes.'
b. Ŋa-ci kuḷa-ji l̲aji t̲uar-∅ mal̲t̲a-∅ japacara-t̲u.
1sg-DAT father-ERG kill snake-ABS mob-ABS clever-ERG
'My clever father killed the snakes.' (*'My father killed the clever snakes.')

In (4.13b) an adjective modifying the ergative noun *kuḷa-ji* 'father' occurs separated from it at the end of the sentence. Does this mean that *ŋa-ci japacara-ṯu kuḷa-ji* 'my clever father' is not a constituent? Not necessarily. First, it can be replaced by a pronoun, as in (4.14).

(4.14) L̲i-ji laji ṯuar-∅ maḻṯa-∅.
3sg-ERG kill snake-ABS mob-ABS
'He killed the snakes.'

Second, it can permute freely in the sentence as a unit.

(4.15) a. Ŋaci japacaraṯu kuḷa-ji l̲aji ṯuar maḻṯa.
b. Ŋaci kuḷaji l̲aji ṯuar maḻṯa japacaraṯu.
c. Ṯuar maḻṯa l̲aji ŋaci japacaraṯu kuḷaji.
d. Ṯuar maḻṯa ŋaci kuḷaji l̲aji japacaraṯu.
e. Ŋaci japacaraṯu kuḷaji ṯuar maḻṯa l̲aji.
'My clever father killed the snakes.'

Third, it can be coordinated with another NP to form a coordinate NP, as in (4.16).

(4.16) a. Ŋa-ci japacara-ṯu kuḷa-ji maṛapai-ṯu-jana l̲aji ṯuar-∅ maḻṯa-∅.
1sg-DAT clever-ERG father-ERG woman-ERG-and kill snake-ABS mob-ABS
'My clever father and the woman killed the snakes.'
b. Ŋa-ci kuḷa-ji maṛapai-ṯu-jana l̲aji ṯuar-∅ maḻṯa-∅ japacara-ṯu.
1sg-DAT father-ERG woman-ERG-and kill snake-ABS mob-ABS clever-ERG
'My clever father and the woman killed the snakes,' or 'My father and the clever woman killed the snakes.'

When the adjective appears separated from the conjoined NP, the result is ambiguous, with the adjective being interpreted as modifying either of the ergative nouns. Thus, despite the fact that the modifier does not have to occur adjacent to the noun it modifies, the NP still functions as a unit and passes the constituency tests. This shows that in some languages the elements making up a constituent do not have to occur adjacent to each other; however, the typical case is for the elements making up a constituent to be adjacent to each other.

4.1.2 *Representing constituent structure*

Thus far only labelled bracketings have been used to indicate constituency, as in (4.1), but there is an alternative way to represent constituent structure, namely a tree diagram (also known as a phrase-structure tree or immediate-constituent diagram). The essential features of a phrase-structure tree are depicted in Figure 4.1.

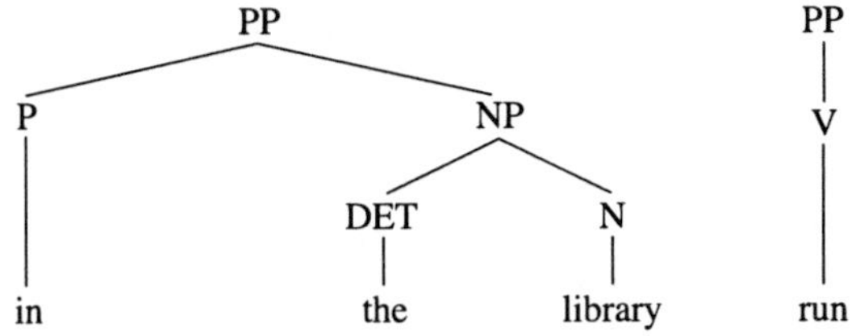

Figure 4.1. *Aspects of a phrase-structure tree*

This is the representation of the PP *in the library* and the VP *run*. The components of a constituent-structure tree are **nodes** and branches. The non-lexical nodes in Figure 4.1 are PP, P, NP, DET, N, VP, V. Branches are simply the lines connecting the nodes. Nodes may be classified in a number of ways: **branching** versus non-branching, **terminal** versus **preterminal** versus **non-terminal**, **mothers** versus **daughters**, **sisters** versus non-sisters. There are important **dominance** relations among nodes. PP immediately dominates P and NP; this means that PP is the mother node and P and NP are daughter nodes, and in addition, P and NP are sister nodes. The P node is the head daughter. Similarly, NP immediately dominates DET and N, and this entails that NP is the mother and DET and N are daughters of NP and sisters of each other. The N node is the head daughter of the NP. Branches may connect mothers and daughters only, and every daughter can have only one mother. P and either DET or N are not sisters, because they do not have the same mother node. PP also dominates DET and N; thus the PP node dominates all of the nodes within the PP. The dominance relation between PP and P or NP and between NP and DET or N is **immediate dominance**; that is, the mother nodes dominate their daughter nodes and there are no intervening nodes between them. Mother nodes always immediately dominate daughter nodes. PP dominates N but does not immediately dominate it, because the NP node comes between them, that is PP immediately dominates NP and NP immediately dominates N. In order for two nodes to be sisters, they must be immediately dominated by the same node. If a node is immediately dominated by another node, for example NP and P by PP, or DET and N by NP, then the daughters are **immediate constituents** of the mothers. In Figure 4.1, DET and N are immediate constituents of NP; NP and P are immediate constituents of PP; and V is an immediate constituent of VP. A mother node plus its daughter node(s) constitutes a **local subtree**. Branching nodes have more than one daughter; non-branching nodes have only one daughter. Hence both PP and NP are branching nodes in Figure 4.1, since each has two daughters, while VP is a non-branching node in this example; in a sentence like (4.3a), VP is a branching node, because it dominates V, NP, and PP, as in Figure 4.2 below. Finally, non-terminal nodes are nodes which dominate other nodes; preterminal nodes cannot dominate any further syntactic elements and normally dominate the lexical material in the tree. The preterminal nodes dominate the **ultimate constituents** in the structure; *in*, *the*, and *library* are the ultimate constituents of the PP, and *run* is the ultimate constituent of the VP. They are all terminal nodes.

Terminal nodes are, as noted above, filled by lexical categories. Non-terminal nodes, on the other hand, are syntactic, not lexical; hence the categories that occur in them are **syntactic categories**, not lexical categories. There is, of course, a fundamental relationship between the two; the normal situation is for the lexical item in the terminal node to be of the lexical category corresponding to the syntactic category of the preterminal node. Hence if the preterminal node is 'V', for example, then a lexical item of the lexical category 'verb' can occur as its terminal node. The four major syntactic categories correspond to the four major lexical categories: noun, verb, adjective, adposition. Since noun and verb are the most important and only universal categories, they are used as the basis for defining the other categories. Typically, two **syntactic features**, [±N] and [±V], are posited, and the combinations of these two features define the four major categories: [+N, −V] = noun, [−N, +V] = verb, [+N, +V] = adjective, and [−N, −V] = adposition. The idea behind the feature definitions of categories is to capture certain cross-categorial generalizations. For example, typically only verbs and prepositions assign case to their objects, in dependent-marking languages with case systems, and this can be captured by saying that only elements which are [–N] can be case assigners; note that the only two categories that are [–N] are verb and adposition. One might well ask, why is adjective [+N, +V] rather than [–N, –V]? Is this feature assignment arbitrary? Recall from chapter 1, however, that some languages lack adjective as a distinct lexical category, e.g. Lakhota, Quechua and Dyirbal, and in some the words corresponding to adjectives in other languages are formally verbs (Lakhota) while in some they are formally nouns (Quechua, Dyirbal). Thus, adjectives clearly have things in common with both verbs and nouns, and accordingly, it is appropriate to define them as [+N, +V]. Additional features would be required to express other syntactic categories such as adverb and complementizer.

The constituent structure of (4.3a) can be represented in the tree in Figure 4.2; the intermediate constituents found in (4.10b) and (4.11b) are being ignored for the moment.

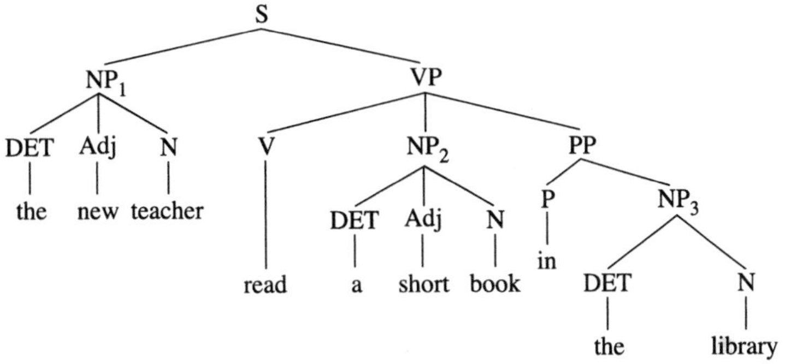

Figure 4.2. *Preliminary phrase-structure tree for (4.3a)*

It is now clear what 'being a constituent' means formally. In terms of a tree structure like this one, a group of words is a constituent if there is a single node in the tree which uniquely and completely dominates them. The sequence *the new teacher* is a constituent because the three words are uniquely and completely dominated by node NP_1. Similarly, *a short book* and *the library* are constituents because each sequence is uniquely and exhaustively dominated by a single node, NP_2 for *a short book* and NP_3 for *the library*. *In* plus *the library* form a constituent, because the PP node uniquely and completely dominates them. *Read* plus *a short book* plus *in the library* make up a constituent for the same reason: there is a single node, VP, which uniquely and exhaustively dominates them. The clause as a whole meets this condition, as there is a single node (S) which exhaustively and uniquely dominates the whole clause. There is no node uniquely and completely dominating the sequences *teacher read, read a, book in* or *in the*, and accordingly, these sequences are not constituents. Each of the constituents represented in the tree in Figure 4.1 emerged from the results of the three tests for constituency presented in this section.

The structurally ambiguous sentence in (4.12a) would have the following two immediate constituent representations.

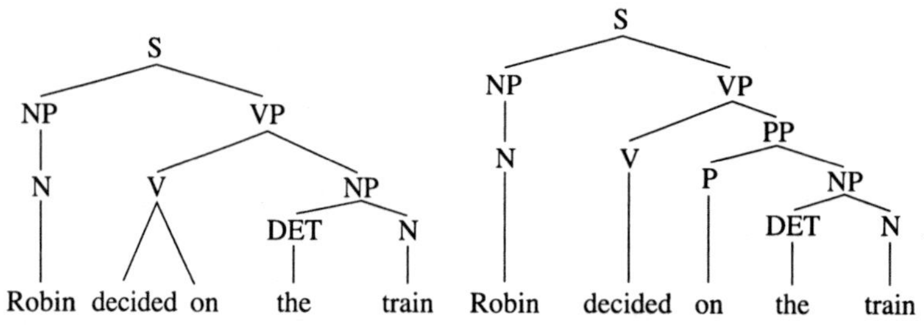

Figure 4.3. *Phrase-structure trees for the two readings of (4.12a)*

The left tree represents the prepositional-verb interpretation: *decide on* is a transitive verb and *the train* is its direct object. The right tree depicts the PP reading: *decide* is an intransitive verb, and the PP *on the train* is an adjunct locative modifier. Only the sentence represented by the left tree can have the alternative form in (4.12c), whereas only the sentence represented by the right tree can have the alternative form in (4.12b). The sequence *on the train* is a constituent only in the right tree, not in the left, while the sequence *decide on* is a constituent only in the left tree, not in the right.

Discontinuous constituents raise problems for this mode of depicting constituent structure. There have been two examples of this. The first, in chapter 3, concerned copula placement in Croatian and Serbian; it was illustrated in (3.1) from Croatian and is repeated in (4.17).

(4.17) a. Naš-a učionic-a je udobn-a. Croatian
our-FSGNOM classroom-FSGNOM be.3SGPRES comfortable-FSGNOM
'Our classroom is comfortable.'
b. Naša je učionica udobna.
our is classroom comfortable
'Our classroom is comfortable.'

The sentence in (4.17b) would have the tree representation in Figure 4.4.

It is also not clear how a sentence like (4.13b) from Kalkatungu is to be represented. One possibility is given in Figure 4.5.

While this tree captures the fact that *japacara-ṯu* 'clever' is part of the NP *ŋa-ci japacara-ṯu kuḷa-ji* 'my clever father', the majority of syntacticians who employ immediate-constituent analysis would reject this as a proper tree structure, because the branch connecting the NP and Adj crosses other branches. The same is true with respect to Figure 4.4: having the VP to V branch crossing the NP to N branch is

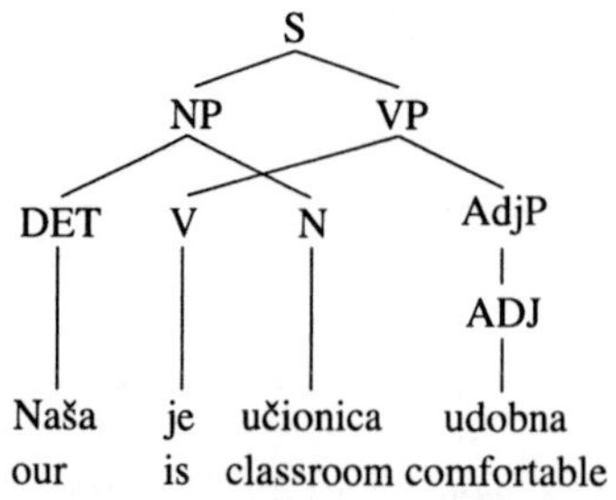

Figure 4.4. *Tree diagram for (4.17b)*

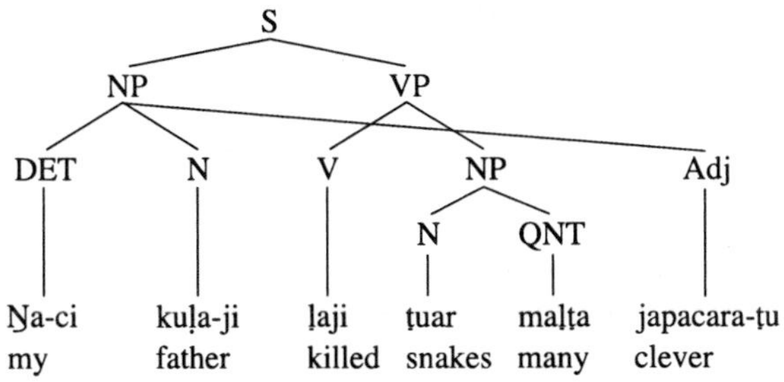

Figure 4.5. *Constituent structure of (4.13b)*

unacceptable. According to this view, branches must never cross in a tree structure (the **no-crossing condition**); in other words, constituents must consist of contiguous words or phrases, and it should be impossible for words from distinct constituents to intermingle with each other. The problem with this assumption is quite obvious: in Serbian, Croatian, Kalkatungu, Yidiɲ and other such languages, words from different constituents may be mixed together in the linear string. While discontinuous constituency may be uncommon cross-linguistically, it nevertheless occurs in a number of languages. (In contrast, preposition stranding of the English variety is much rarer cross-linguistically than discontinuous constituency of the kind illustrated here.) Thus, while the tests proposed in the previous section show that a discontinuous NP in Kalkatungu is a constituent, the standard means for representing constituent structure, phrase-structure trees, cannot readily express this, because of the widely assumed no-crossing condition. If this condition were abandoned, then there would be no problem, and the trees in Figures 4.4 and 4.5 would be perfectly legitimate.

4.2 The universality of form classes

In section 1.2 the question of the universality of lexical categories was raised, and it was argued that the distinction between noun and verb is present in the grammars of all languages, that is, is universal. What about NP and VP? Are they too universal? In order for the form class NP to be universal, it must be the case that in every language a noun plus its modifiers forms a constituent according to one or more of the tests introduced in section 4.1.1. Two problematic cases have been presented so far in this book. The first is the Croatian 'split subject NP' in (4.17b). The NP is a constituent by the permutation criterion, because if one changes the word order in the sentence, as in (4.18), the NP behaves as a unit.

(4.18) Udobn-a je nǎs-a učionic-a. Croatian
comfortable-FSGNOM be.3SGPRES our-FSGNOM classroom-FSGNOM
'Our classroom is comfortable.'

The second is the Kalkatungu example in (4.13b) in which an adjective appears separated from the noun it modifies. As discussed in section 4.1.1, the Kalkatungu NP passes all of the constituency tests, despite the occurrence of non-contiguous modifiers.

Languages with verb–subject–object word order also present a problem. Kwakwala, a Wakashan language of British Columbia, is such a language, and examples of simple sentences in Kwakwala are given in (4.19) (Anderson 1984).

(4.19) a. Yəlkʷəmas-∅-ida bəgʷanəma-x̣-a ẇats'i-s-a gʷax̣ƛux̣ʷ. Kwakwala
hurt-NOM-DEM man-ACC-the dog-INST-the stick
'The man hurt the dog with the stick.'

b. Yəlkʷəmat-səẇ-∅-ida ẇats'i-s-a bəgʷanəma-s-a gʷax̣ƛux̣ʷ.
hurt-PASS-NOM-DEM dog-INST-the man-INST-the stick
'The dog was hurt by the man with the stick.'

c. Yum̓-ux̣ʷda bəgʷanəm yəlkʷəmas-x̣-a ẇats'i-s-a gʷax̣ƛux̣ʷ.
that-DEM man hurt-ACC-the dog-INST-the stick
'That's the man who hurt the dog with the stick.'

One of the most striking features of Kwakwala morphosyntax is that case markers and NP determiners like demonstratives and articles occur as **clitics** on the preceding word in the sentence. (Clitics are stressless elements that occur phonologically attached to another form. Examples of clitics from English include the *'s* in *He's having lunch with Molly*, the possessive *'s* as in *the man I saw yesterday's house*, the *'ll* in *She'll leave tomorrow* and *n't* in *Chris isn't coming*. Pitjantjatjara *-ni* '1sgACC' in (3.6c) is also a clitic.) Accordingly, the accusative case marker *-x̣-* and the article *-a* on *bəgʷanəma* 'man' in (4.19a) signal that *ẇats'i* 'dog' is the direct object and is definite; similarly, the instrumental case marker *-s-* and the article *-a* on *ẇats'i* 'dog' indicate that *gʷax̣ƛux̣ʷ* 'stick' is an instrument semantically and definite. What looks perhaps the oddest of all is the nominative case and a demonstrative attached to the verb, but these are in fact associated with the following NP, the subject.

In all of the examples examined so far, each preterminal node dominates a word, not a part of a phonological word, as it would have to in these cases. The application of the permutation test shows, however, that the noun plus clitics on the previous word do act as a constituent. In (4.19b), the passive counterpart of (4.19a), the active direct object NP *-ida ẇats'i* 'the dog' appears as the passive subject, with its clitic modifiers now attached to the verb, and the active subject NP *-a bəgʷanəma* 'the man' appears as a unit marked by the instrumental clitic *-s-*. Similarly in (4.19c), which is the cleft construction based on (4.19a), the whole subject NP occurs in the cleft, with its determiner cliticized to the demonstrative marking the cleft, and the other NPs have retained their structural integrity after the verb. Thus despite the unusual feature of the case markers and determiners of the noun being phonologically attached to a different constituent, the noun plus modifiers does function as a constituent, passing the permutation test. Thus the constituent structure of (4.19a) would be as in Figure 4.6, following Anderson (1984).

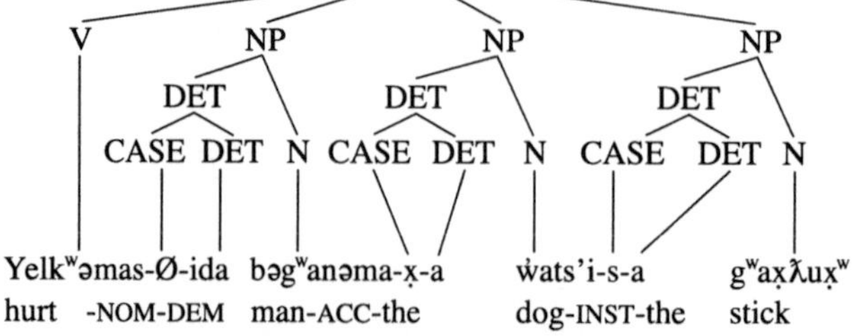

Figure 4.6. *Constituent structure of (4.19a)*

Anderson (1984) does not include a VP node in his representations of Kwakwala clause structure, and this raises the question of the universality of the form class (constituent) VP. Given that the subject NP *-ida bəgʷanəma* 'the man' comes between the verb and the direct object NP *x̣-a ẇats'i* 'the dog', it might appear that there could not be a VP in Kwakwala. Two things should be kept in mind, however. First, if the prohibition against crossing branches were abandoned, then it would be no problem uniting the verb and direct object NP in a VP. Second, simply because two elements are not adjacent in the clause does not mean that they cannot be part of the same constituent, as the discussion of Kalkatungu NPs in section 4.1.1 showed. This means that the fact that a language has very free word order, as Kalkatungu does, does not necessarily entail the non-existence of a VP in the language. In order to show that a language lacks a VP, it must be shown that the verb plus direct object NP do not act as a unit in terms of substitution, permutation and coordination.

Let's apply these three tests to clauses in Lakhota. A basic transitive clause in the language is illustrated in (4.20); the verb *naxʔų* 'hear' takes its subject and object markers as infixes.

(4.20) a. Wíyą ki igmú óta na-wíčha-∅-xʔų. Lakhota
woman the cat many stem-3plOBJ-3sgSUBJ-hear
'The woman heard many cats.'
b. Na-wíčha-∅-xʔų.
'She heard them.'

Unlike its counterpart in Kwakwala, the basic Lakhota pattern in (4.20a) poses no obvious problem for the postulation of a VP, since the direct object NP normally immediately precedes the verb. The sentence in (4.20b), on the other hand, is problematic, since it is a single phonological word. A VP includes the verb plus its direct object and excludes its subject, and in this sentence both subject and object are included, which rules it out as a VP. Moreover, it would be impossible to subdivide the word into a VP and non-VP part, since VP is a phrasal category, not a morphological category. Nevertheless, it is still necessary to apply the three tests. The first, substitution, fails, because Lakhota has no pro-VP analogous to English *do*. That is, sentences like (4.3e) are impossible in the language. If one wanted to say the Lakhota equivalent of *Kim read a book, and Pat did, too*, the verb *yawá* 'read' would have to be repeated; it could not be replaced by another verb. The second test, permutation, likewise fails, because Lakhota is strictly verb-final: the verb must be the last major constituent in the clause, and therefore there is no possibility of forming sentences analogous to (4.7) in English. The third test, coordination, also fails, because there is no possibility of conjoining just the verb and the object with another verb plus object, because the verb always carries subject marking as well. Hence sentences like (4.21), which look potentially like VP-coordination, are really S-coordination. (Like *naxʔų́* 'hear', *wąyą́ka* 'see' takes its subject and object markers as infixes.)

(4.21) Hokšíla ki sugmánitou-thąka óta na-wíčha-∅-xʔų na mathó
boy the coyote-big many stem-3plOBJ-3sgSUBJ-hear and bear
eyá wą-wíčha-∅-yąke.
some stem-3plOBJ-3sgSUBJ-see
'The boy heard many wolves and [he] saw some bears.'

This is the closest thing to VP-coordination possible in Lakhota, but because the second verb is inflected for a third person singular subject, it is really S-coordination, with 'the boy heard many wolves and he saw some bears' being a more accurate rendering of the meaning. Thus, the substitution, permutation and coordination tests fail to give any evidence of a VP constituent in Lakhota, and therefore it may be concluded that Lakhota clause structure lacks a VP. Because Lakhota and apparently Kwakwala lack VPs, then VPs, unlike NPs, cannot be universal. Languages which have VPs are often referred to as **configurational languages**, while those without VPs are termed **non-configurational languages**.

In the discussion of Croatian and Kalkatungu in section 4.1.2, the tree diagrams in Figures (4.4) and (4.5) contained VP nodes. However, it is in fact highly likely that these languages lack VP nodes in their clause structures. Whether these languages have VP nodes or not does not affect the point made there regarding discontinuous constituency; even if V were an immediate constituent of S, the subject NPs in both sentences would have a discontinuous structure.

4.3 An alternative schema for phrase structure

In the approach to constituent structure presented thus far, a phrasal constituent such as a VP, NP, or PP consists of a head V, N, or P and associated modifiers and/or objects, all of which are sisters to the head. However, in (4.10b) and (4.11b) the coordination test seemed to identify constituents that were intermediate between the N and V heads and the corresponding phrasal NP and VP. The examples are repeated in (4.22).

(4.22)	a. the happy boys and angry girls	ART $[_? [_?$ ADJ N] and $[_?$ ADJ N]]
	b. Kim read a book and wrote a poem in the library.	$[_{VP}[_? [_?$ V NP] and $[_?$ V NP]] PP]

In (4.22a) the adjective and noun seem to form a constituent, while in (b) the verb and the direct object alone seem to constitute a constituent. If the adjective plus noun form a constituent, then there must be a single node uniquely and completely dominating them, and in, for example, Figure 4.2 there is no such node in the NPs. Similarly, if the verb and the direct object form a constituent, then there must be a single node uniquely and exhaustively dominating them, and likewise in Figure 4.2 there is no such node in the VP. Is there any other evidence for these intermediate constituents?

There is a pro-form for the intermediate nominal constituent, namely, *one.* It can be a pro-NP, or a pro-noun, but it can also replace the intermediate nominal constituent as well.

(4.23)	a. Pat is eating an ice cream cone, and Robin is eating one, too.	*one* = pro-NP
	b. I liked the red scarf, but Leslie liked the green one.	*one* = pro-N
	c. I liked this red scarf, but Leslie liked that one.	*one* = pro-?

In (4.23a) *one* replaces an entire NP, *an ice cream cone*; hence it is a pro-NP. In (b) it replaces only the noun *scarf*, and therefore it is a pro-N. But in (c), it replaces the adjective plus noun combination *red scarf*, leaving the demonstrative unaffected, and in this example it is replacing the intermediate nominal constituent found in (4.22a).

The permutation test does not work for this constituent; it is impossible to permute the head noun plus an adjective independently of the determiner. The sentence in (4.22b) involves an intermediate constituent within the VP. There is a pro-form for this intermediate verbal constituent, *do so*, as in (4.24a), and it can also be identified by the coordination test, as in (4.22b), and the permutation test, as in (4.24b).

(4.24) a. Chris will eat an ice cream cone in the kitchen, and Kim will do so in the breakfast room.
b. Sally wants to eat a souvlaki, and eat a souvlaki she will tomorrow in Athens.

The proform *do so* replaces the verb plus direct object NP in (4.24a). In (b), the constituent that occurs initially in the second clause is not the whole VP but rather just the verb plus direct object NP. Thus the permutation test supports the substitution and coordination tests in identifying the intermediate verbal constituent.

How should these intermediate constituents be described? They have N and V heads, and consequently they are a kind of NP and VP. But they are themselves the head for the next phrasal constituent. What 'NP' literally means is 'a phrase with a noun head'. So let's call the intermediate nominal constituent an 'NP', which is technically correct. What then should the label be for what have been called NPs, e.g. *the red scarf*? Following this pattern, it could be called an 'NPP'; that is, it is a phrase headed by an NP, an NP-phrase. The same could be said for the verbal constituents. Since 'VP' is literally a phrase headed by a verb, then the verb plus direct object is a VP. What has been called a VP, e.g. *read a short book in the library*, is actually a VPP, a VP-phrase, i.e. a phrase headed by a VP. There are thus three levels of constituency, not just two: *scarf* N, *red scarf* NP, *the red scarf* NPP; *read* V, *read a short book* VP, *read a short book in the library* VPP.

While this way of referring to the levels of constituency is thoroughly reasonable, it is not in fact the way syntacticians have referred to them. The 'Ps' have been replaced one of three ways, e.g. $\bar{N}$, N′ or N^1. Nowadays either the second or the third notation is used; but the first one was the first to be employed, and it gave its name to the intermediate nominal constituent: **N-bar**. NPP was represented as $\bar{\bar{N}}$, N″ or N^2 and is sometimes referred to as 'N-double bar'. The same holds for the intermediate verbal constituent, **V-bar**. Since there are now two phrasal categories associated with N and V heads, a new term was developed to refer to N″ and V″; they are termed the **maximal projections** of the head, while N′ and V′ are non-maximal **projections**. Both N′ and N″ are projections of the head N, just as V′ and V″ are projections of the head V. N′ is a projection of N because it is a phrase which has N as its head, and N″ is a projection of N because it has N′ as its head, which in turn has N as its head. N is the **lexical head** of N′ and N″; N′ is the non-lexical head of N″. The same holds for V as well.

Incorporating these new constituents creates a rather different picture of sentences like (4.3a). A revised, but still preliminary, phrase-structure tree for (4.3a) is given in Figure 4.7.

This tree expresses the intermediate constituents that the tests revealed in section 4.1.1.

In NPs there are other kinds of phrases which form a constituent with the head noun, specifically certain PPs. Examples are given in (4.25).

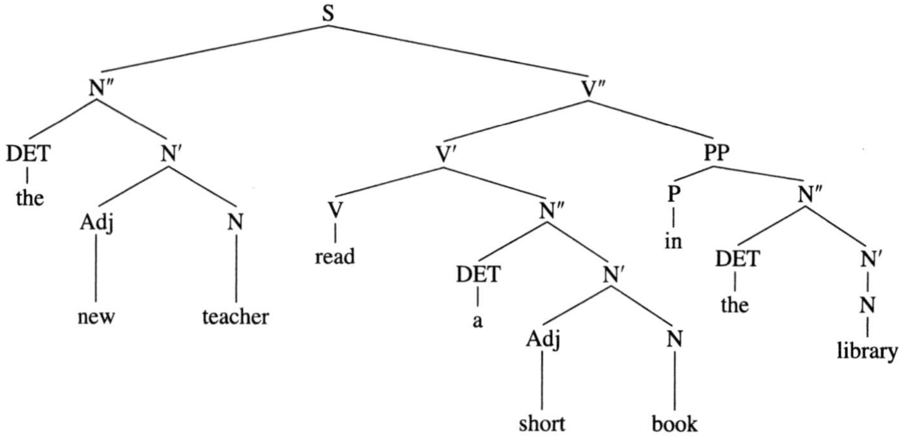

Figure 4.7. *Revised preliminary phrase-structure tree for (4.3a)*

(4.25) a. I met a tall student of linguistics, and Leslie met a short one.
b. Chris read her long proof of the theorem, but Pat only read the short one.

In (4.25a) *one* replaces *student of linguistics*, which must be an N′, while in (b) it substitutes for *proof of the theorem*, which must also be an N′. The structure of *her proof of the theorem* is given in Figure 4.8.

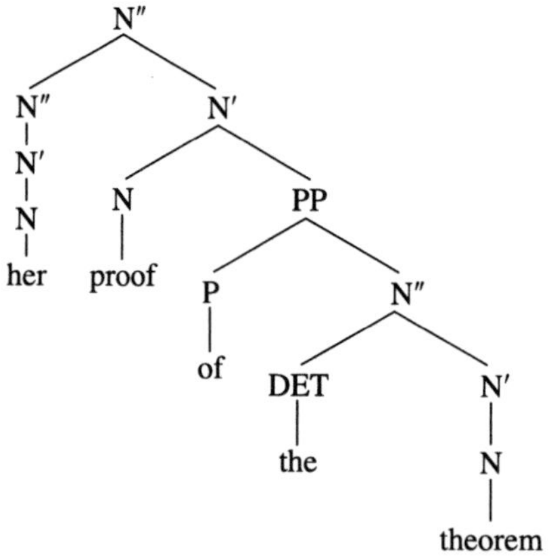

Figure 4.8. *Constituent structure of* her proof of the theorem

It has long been noted that there are fundamental similarities between NPs headed by **deverbal** nominals like *proof* and the VPs headed by the verb from which the nominal is derived, in this case *prove*. In *Kim proved the theorem*, the direct object NP *the theorem* is a sister to the V under a V′, while in the corresponding derived nominal, given in Figure 4.8, *the theorem* is part of a PP which is a sister to the N under an N′. The analogous relationships hold in the V′ *study linguistics* and the derived N′ *student of linguistics.*

Hence there is a fundamental parallelism in the structure of phrases headed by N and V. If the variable 'X' is substituted for N and V, the following general schema for

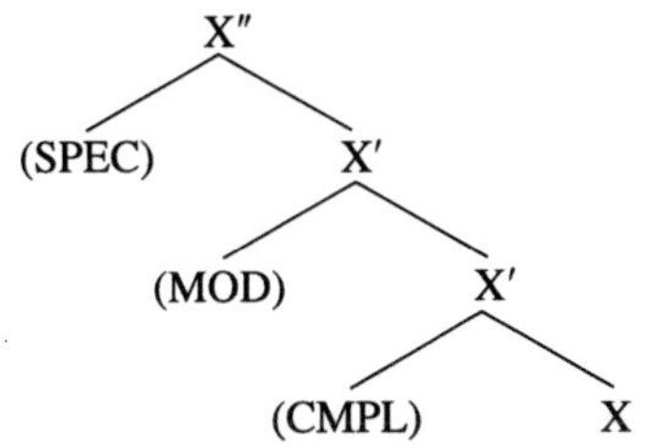

Figure 4.9. *General schema for phrase structure*

the structure of phrases emerges. ('X' stands for the lexical head of the phrase, 'SPEC' for '**specifier**', 'MOD' for 'modifier', and 'CMPL' for 'complement'.)

SPEC, MOD and CMPL are in parenthesis, because they are not always obligatory in the structure. Since 'X' is employed as a category variable and bars were originally used to indicate phrase levels, the schema in Figure 4.9 came to be known as the '**X-bar**' schema. Specifier, modifier and complement are not form classes but rather are simply labels for the function that the form class in that position in the phrase serves. Specifiers in N″ are determiners or possessors, while a tensed auxiliary verb occupies that position in a V″. The parallels between N″ and V″ can be seen clearly in the structures for *has quickly proved the theorem* and *the long proof of the theorem* in Figure 4.10.

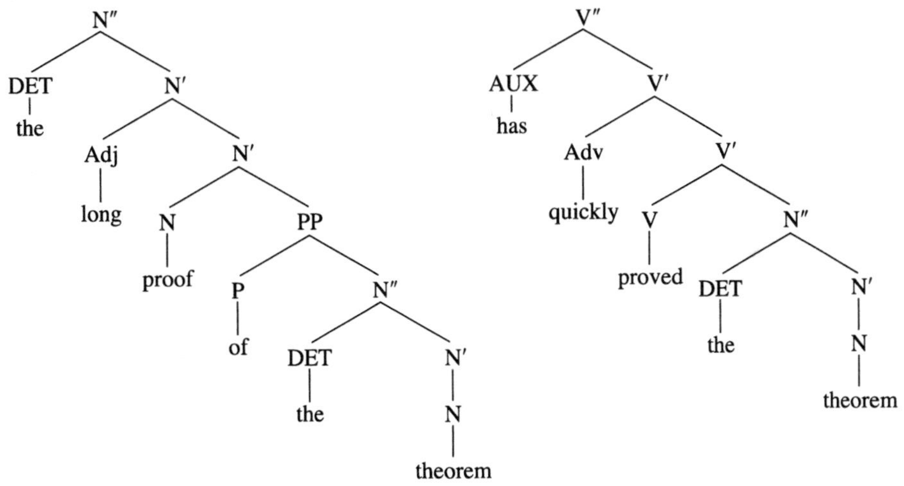

Figure 4.10. *Parallel phrase structure of N″ and V″*

The determiner *the* is the analog in the N″ of the tensed auxiliary verb *has* in the V″, and the adjectival modifier *long* is the analog in the N″ of the adverbial modifier *quickly* in the V″. Finally, both heads take complements, a PP in the case of a nominal head and an NP for a verbal head. The X-bar schema in Figure 4.9 is concerned exclusively with the hierarchical relations among the elements in an X″; the linear order of the elements at each level of structure is not dictated by the schema and can in fact vary both within and across languages. Examples of this variation will be given below and in chapter 5.

An important property of the single-bar constituents is that they can be iterated. It is well known that there can be a number of adjectives modifying a noun.

(4.26) a. this red scarf
b. this expensive red scarf
c. this beautiful expensive red scarf

The pro-N′ *one* can replace one or more of the N′s, as shown in (4.27).

(4.27) a. this one
b. this expensive one
c. this beautiful expensive one
d. this beautiful one

In (4.27a), *one* could be interpreted as replacing *red scarf*, *expensive red scarf*, or *beautiful expensive red scarf* from (4.26). In (4.27b) and (4.27c) it could be construed as replacing *red scarf* from (4.26b) and (4.26c). Finally, in (d) it could be interpreted as substituting for *expensive red scarf* from (4.26c). Since these are repetitions of the same category, namely adjective, they are all considered to be dominated by N′s. Hence the structure of (4.26c) would be tentatively as in Figure 4.11.

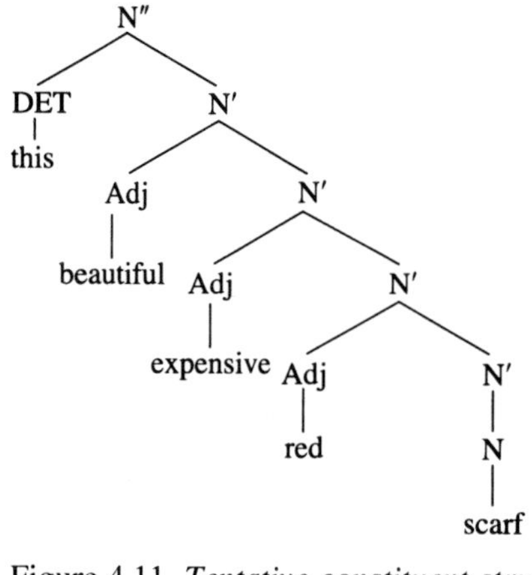

Figure 4.11. *Tentative constituent structure representation for* this beautiful expensive red scarf

The same kind of iterated single-bar structure seems to be motivated for V″. Consider the following examples.

(4.28) Sally wants to eat a souvlaki in Athens, and eat a souvlaki in Athens she will tomorrow.

The sentence in (4.24b) showed that the verb plus direct object form a constituent smaller than the maximal verb phrase, and (4.28) shows that the verb plus direct object plus PP form a constituent smaller than V″. Hence it is necessary to have two V′s: one containing the verb plus the direct object, and the second containing that V′ plus the PP *in Athens*. Figure 4.12 gives the constituent structure of the V″ *will eat a souvlaki in Athens tomorrow*.

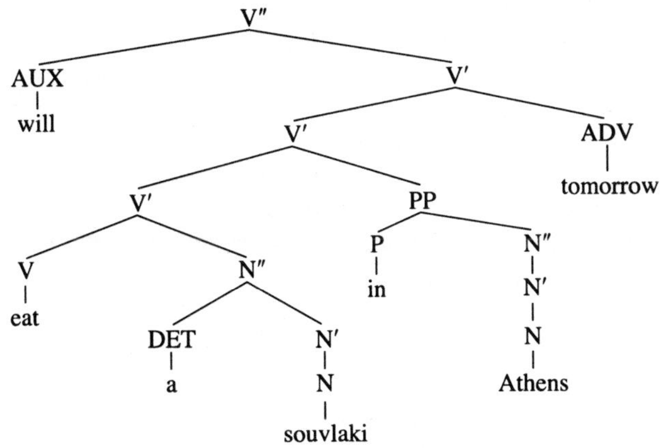

Figure 4.12. *Iterated V-bars in a V″*

The argument–adjunct contrast can be seen clearly in a tree like Figure 4.12. The NP which is a sister to the V under V′ is an argument, while the PP which is a sister to the V′ is an adjunct, along with the adverb which is a sister to the higher V′. In general, arguments are sisters to the V under the lowest V′, while adjuncts are sisters to a V′ under a higher V′.

If a verb takes a PP as an argument, like *give* or *put*, then it must be a sister to the V under the lowest V′. This can be seen from the following examples.

(4.29) a. Chris will eat an ice cream cone in the kitchen, and Kim will do so in the breakfast room.
b. *Chris will put a book on the table, and Kim will do so on the shelf.

In the kitchen is an adjunct PP in (4.29a), but *on the table* is an argument PP in (b). Hence the *do so* pro-V′ can replace the V′ *eat an ice cream cone* alone in (a) but cannot replace just *put a book* in (b). This shows that *on the table* is part of the same V′ as *put a book.* The structure of *Chris will put a book on the table in the kitchen* is given in Figure 4.13.

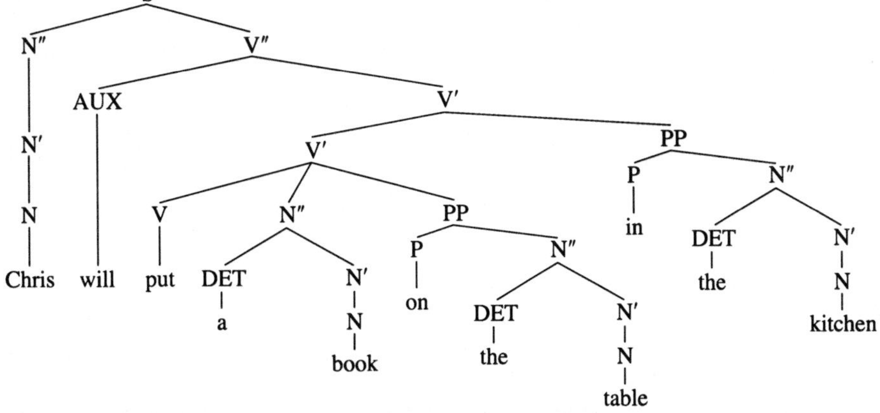

Figure 4.13. *Distinguishing argument PP from adjunct PP within V″*

When there are multiple adjuncts in a sentence, as in *Sally will eat a souvlaki in Athens tomorrow*, the V″ of which is depicted in Figure 4.12, each adjunct modifies its sister V′. In this example, *tomorrow* specifies when Sally will eat a souvlaki in Athens, while *in Athens* specifies where she will eat it. Hence the V′ *eat a souvlaki in Athens* is in the scope of modification of *tomorrow*, and the V′ *eat a souvlaki* (but not the adverbial *tomorrow*) is in the scope of modification of *in Athens.* Thus, the higher an adjunct is in the tree, the wider its scope of modification in the sentence.

This structure makes it possible to distinguish arguments from adjuncts within NP as well. The PP sister to the N under the lowest N′ is analogous to the direct-object NP under the lowest V′ in a V″. Hence one may say that the PP *of linguistics* in *student of linguistics* or the PP *of the theorem* in *proof of the theorem* is an argument of the N. (See section 3.1.1 on the valence of nouns.) In an NP like *the student of linguistics in the office*, the PP *in the office* is not a sister of the N and is under the higher N′. The fact that it is not a sister to the N under the lowest N′ can be seen in the following contrast.

(4.30) a. Dana saw the student of linguistics in the office, and I saw the one in the library.
b. *Dana saw the student of linguistics, and I saw the one of physics.

The fact that *one in the library* is grammatical in (a) but *one of physics* is ungrammatical in (b) shows that the PP *in the library* is not part of the N′ *student of linguistics* in (a) which is replaced by the pro-N′ *one.* Hence *in the office* must be outside the N′ headed by the N *student.* Thus, as in V″s, arguments are sisters to the head under the lowest N′, and adjuncts are sisters of this N′ or a higher one. The structure of *the student of linguistics in the office* is given in Figure 4.14.

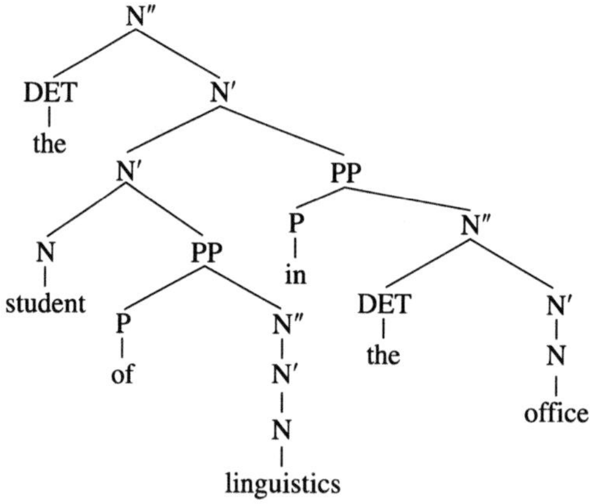

Figure 4.14. *Structural contrast between argument and adjunct within N″*

In this phrase, the PP *in the office* modifies its sister N′, specifying where the student of linguistics is.

Thus, the argument–adjunct distinction is reflected in both N″s and V″s, and it may be summarized as in Table 4.1.

Does the X-bar schema apply to other categories as well, specifically PP and AdjP? With respect to P″, what would a specifier for a P be? It has been suggested that

Table 4.1. *The argument–adjunct distinction in terms of the X-bar schema (Figure 4.9)*

Sister to X′	Adjunct
Sister to X	Argument

elements like *right* as in *right under the table* qualify as specifiers of P. Examples of modifers of P are difficult to come by, and in any case such modifiers would always be optional. Nevertheless, the specifier and complement positions can be established, and accordingly the schema can be applied to PPs, even though the norm is for there to be no specifier. The specifier of Adj is usually taken to be degree modifiers like *very, extremely, rather*, etc. Modifiers and complements of Adjs can occur in English only when the adjective is used predicatively rather than attributively. In a sentence like *The parents were very angry at the children during the party, and their friends were, too*, the adjective *angry* occurs with a specifier (*very*), a complement PP (*at the children*) and a PP modifier (*during the party*). It is not possible to have **the very angry at the children during the party parents* in English, but such phrases are possible in German. Specifiers are possible when adjectives are used predicatively and attributively, e.g. *the very expensive red scarf* (attributive) versus *the parents are very angry* (predicative). The X-bar schema thus does apply to AdjPs as well. The structures of the P″ *right under the table* and of the Adj″ *very angry at the children during the party* are given in Figure 4.15.

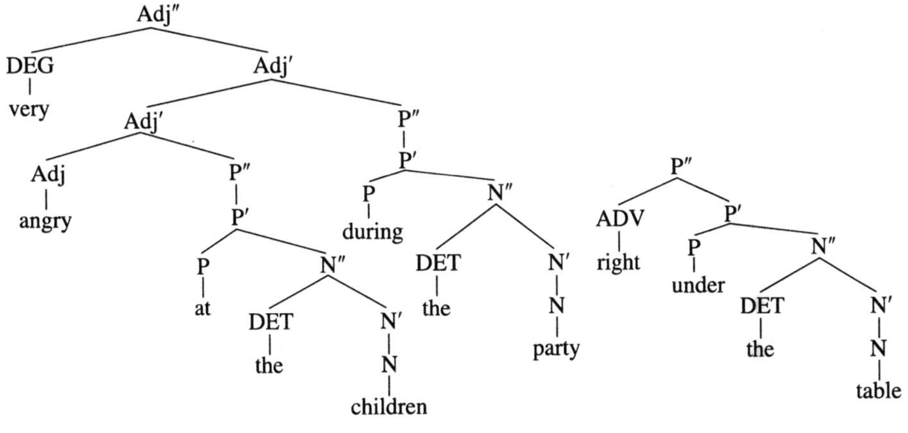

Figure 4.15. *X-bar structure of P″ and Adj″*

It is generally assumed, then, that the X-bar schema in Figure 4.9 represents the structure of all phrasal categories with a lexical head. When this schema is applied to AdjPs and PPs in (4.3a), the final revision of the tree depicting its structure appears as in Figure 4.16.

If the sentence were *The very new teacher has read an extremely short book right in the library*, then there would be specifiers for both Adj″s, for the V″, and for the P″.

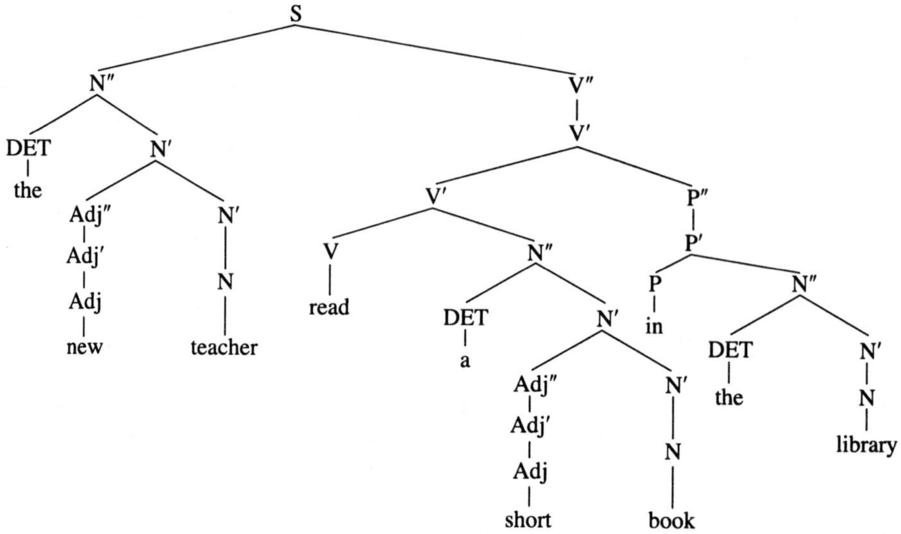

Figure 4.16. *Final revision of the phrase-structure tree for (4.3a)*

In the two Adj″s in Figure 4.16, there is only the head adjective, and yet the Adj′ level is represented. Similarly, in Figure 4.13, the N″ headed by *Chris* contains an N′, even though there are no modifiers in the phrase. Why is this apparently useless structure represented? The answer is that because it is possible to have modifiers and complements in these phrases, the structural 'slots' for them must be represented. As noted above, the sentence could have included *the very new teacher* and *an extremely short book*, and in order for those degree modifiers to occur, the full X-bar skeleton is necessary. The sentence in Figure 4.13 could have had *the tall boy* instead of *Chris*, and in that case the full structure would be needed. Hence the minimal representation of a phrasal category must contain the minimal X-bar structure: X″, X′, and X.

Throughout the discussion of constituency, coordination has been used as a test. How is it to be represented? First, the conjoined constituents normally form a constituent of the same type. Second, it is possible to coordinate constituents at all three levels of X-bar structure: X, X′, and X″. This is illustrated with the following three examples involving nominals.

(4.31)	a. the happy girls and boys	coordinate Ns
	b. the happy girls and sad boys	coordinate N′s
	c. the happy girls and the sad boys	coordinate N″s

The constituent structure of these phrases is given in Figure 4.17.

It is possible to formulate a general schema for coordination; it is given in Figure 4.18. ('^{n}', is a variable ranging over 0, 1 or 2 bars, i.e. X, X′, or X″.)

Two things must be noted immediately. First, the conjunction is optional, because, as shown in (3.5) and (3.6), it is possible to have coordination without any kind of coordinate conjunction (parataxis). Second, there may be more than two X^ns in a coordinate structure, as illustrated in the Pitjantjatjara sentences in (3.6) and their English translations, hence the '. . .'.

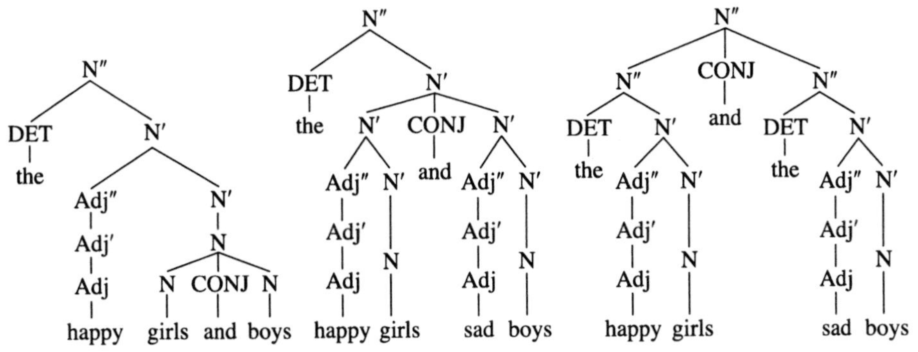

Figure 4.17. *Coordinate Ns, N′s and N″s*

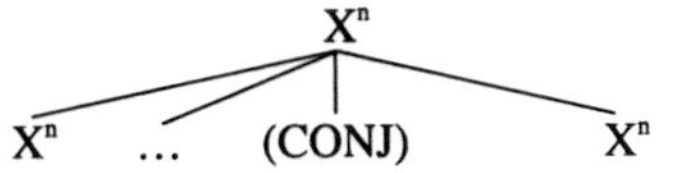

Figure 4.18. *General schema for coordination*

There is a problem with the schema in Figure 4.18. It was stated above that coordinated constituents normally form a constituent of the same type, as exemplified in (4.31) and Figure 4.17. Indeed, this is required by the schema in Figure 4.18. But there are sentences in English in which it appears that constituents from different form classes are being coordinated.

(4.32)	a. Chris is very angry and in a foul mood.	Adj″ + P″
	b. Pat completed the job rather swiftly and with great enthusiasm.	Adv″ + P″
	c. Sandy believed the report and also that the mayor was telling the truth.	N″ + S

The problem here does not affect the status of coordination as a test for constituency, because the elements being coordinated are constituents. Rather, what is problematic is the claim embodied in Figure 4.18 that the elements entering into coordination must be of the same form class. Since most syntacticians would like to maintain the schema in Figure 4.18, a variety of solutions to this problem have been proposed; a discussion of them is beyond the scope of this book.

The one major category to which the application of the X-bar schema is controversial is the clause. Syntacticians disagree as to whether the clause has a head or not, and among those who argue that it has a head, they disagree as to what it is. Since this is ultimately a theoretical issue, it will be addressed in chapter 6 in the survey of a number of contemporary theories of syntax. In this chapter and the next, the X-bar schema will not be extended to the clause.

It was mentioned earlier that the X-bar schema constrains the hierarchical structure of phrasal categories but not the linear order of the categories at each level. The order of the head and its complement may vary. If the head precedes the complement, as in the English V′ and P′ in Figure 4.16, the structure is **right-branching**. If the head follows the complement, as in the Lezgian phrases in (4.33), repeated from exercise 3 in chapter 3, the structure is **left-branching**, as shown in Figure 4.19.

(4.33) a. Mu?minata-z Ibrahim-∅ aku-na. Lezgian
Mu'minat-DAT Ibrahim-ABS see-TNS
'Mu'minat saw Ibrahim.'
b. èlectrostancijadi-n q̃enez
power.station-GEN inside
'inside the electric power station'

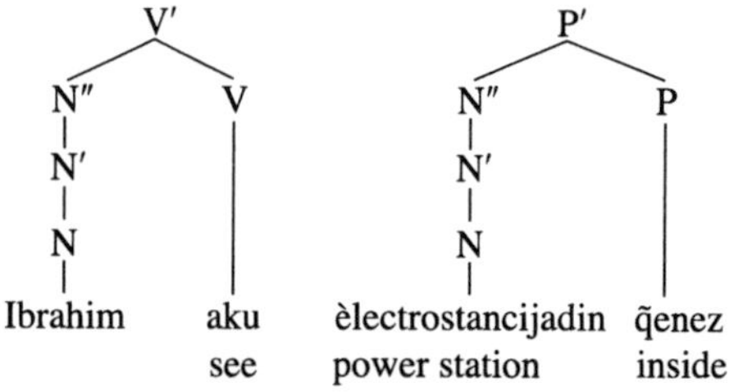

Figure 4.19. *Left-branching V′ and P′ in Lezgian*

An example of a left-branching clause can be found in (4.34) from Hindi (Narasimhan 1998); its structure is given in Figure 4.20.

(4.34) Raam sundar kapdee pahantaa hai. Hindi
Raam beautiful clothes wear AUX
'Raam wears beautiful clothes.'

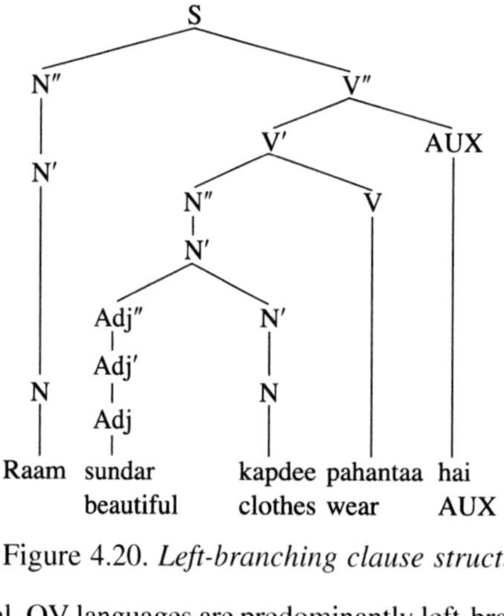

Figure 4.20. *Left-branching clause structure in Hindi*

In general, OV languages are predominantly left-branching, while VO languages are predominantly right-branching. The placement of determiners and modifiers shows some variation. Japanese and Lakhota are both SOV languages, but in Japanese demonstratives precede the head, e.g. *ano hito* 'that person', while in Lakhota they may either precede or follow, with the default position being post-head, e.g. *igmú ki lé* [cat the this] 'this cat' or *lé igmú ki* 'this cat'. Spanish, which is SVO, can have adjectives on either side of the head noun, e.g. *un gran hombre* 'a big man' (in the sense of 'important') or *un hombre grande* 'a large man' (in terms of physical size). More examples of this variation in determiner and modifier placement will be given in chapter 5.

4.4 The structure of complex sentences

Complex sentences are non-coordinate sentences that contain more than one clause or more than one VP. A number of types of complex sentence were presented in chapter 2, and three types were given dependency-grammar analyses in chapter 3. The first type to be examined is a clausal direct object, which in English is realized primarily by a *that*-clause. Examples are given in (4.35a), (4.35c) and (4.35d).

(4.35) a. Chris believed that the police arrested Kim.
b. Chris believed it.
c. That the police arrested Kim was believed by Chris.
d. Chris believed that the police arrested Kim and that it was the right thing to do.

The first question to ask is, does *that the police arrested Kim* form a constituent? The answer is 'yes', as the application of the three constituency tests in (4.35b)–(4.35d) shows. In (b) it is replaced by a proform, *it*; in (c) it occurs as a unit as the subject of a passive verb; and in (d), it can be coordinated with another *that*-clause. Hence it is a constituent. But the simple clause *the police arrested Kim* is also a constituent, and it can be one without the complementizer *that.*

(4.36) a. Chris believed the police arrested Kim.
b. Chris believed it.
c. Chris believed that the police arrested Kim and it was the right thing to do.

In (4.36a) it occurs without *that*, and in (b) it is replaced by the proform *it*; sentence (c) is perhaps the most interesting, as it and another clause are coordinated following *that.* Thus both *that the police arrested Kim* and *the police arrested Kim* are constituents. If *the police arrested Kim* is an S, then what kind of constituent is *that the police arrested Kim*? The answer is S′ (**S-bar**), which dominates the complementizer node and S. The structure of (4.35a) is given in Figure 4.21.

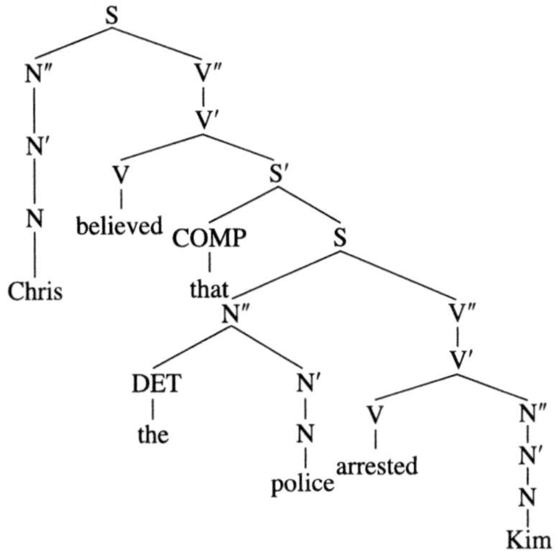

Figure 4.21. *Constituent structure of (4.35a)*

The constituent structure of the clausal direct object sentence in (4.37) from a left-branching language, Lisu (Tibeto-Burman; Hope 1974), is presented in Figure 4.22.

(4.37) Alě-nya Ása-nya ami khwa-a̱ tsɨ́ mə̱-a̱. Lisu
-NOM -NOM fields hoe-IND remember AUX-IND
'Ale remembers that Asa is hoeing fields.'

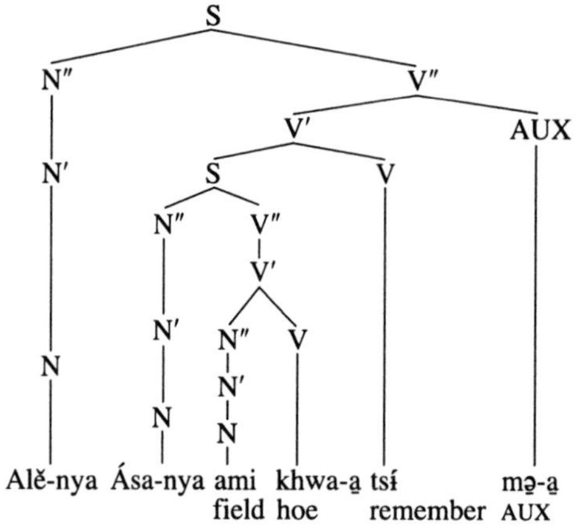

Figure 4.22. *Constituent structure of (4.37)*

Because Lisu lacks a complementizer akin to English *that* to mark embedded clauses, the object clause is an S rather than an S′ in Figure 4.22.

The next type of complex sentence is infinitival complements like *Dana persuaded Pat to open the window.* The coordination test shows that the infinitives are constituents, e.g. *Dana persuaded Pat to open the window and to close the door.* Their constituent structure is represented in Figure 4.23.

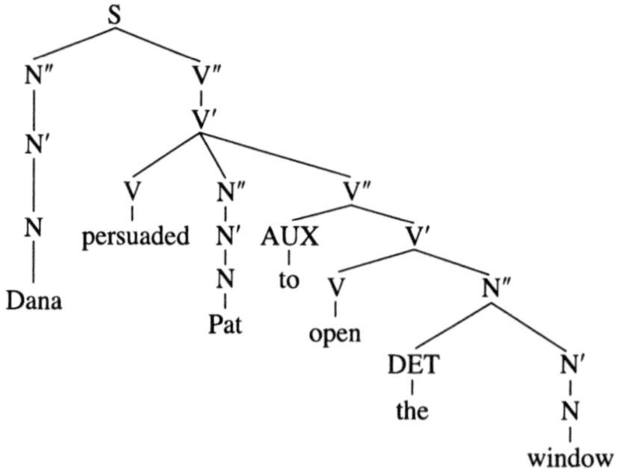

Figure 4.23. *Constituent structure of English infinitival complement*

To occurs in the specifier of V″, the place normally occupied by a tensed auxiliary verb (see Figure 4.10), and the complement V″ is a sister to the matrix V. The structural relation of the V′ to *to* in this construction is analogous to that of the S to *that* in

Figure 4.21, and it is possible to have coordinate V′s, e.g. *Dana persuaded Pat to open the window and close the door.* An example of an analogous construction from a left-branching language, Tindi, repeated from (2.74a), is given in (4.38); its structure is presented in Figure 4.24.

(4.38) Wačuła [jači hēła] q'očā hik̩'i. Tindi
brother.DAT sister.ABS see want not
'Brother doesn't want to see sister.'

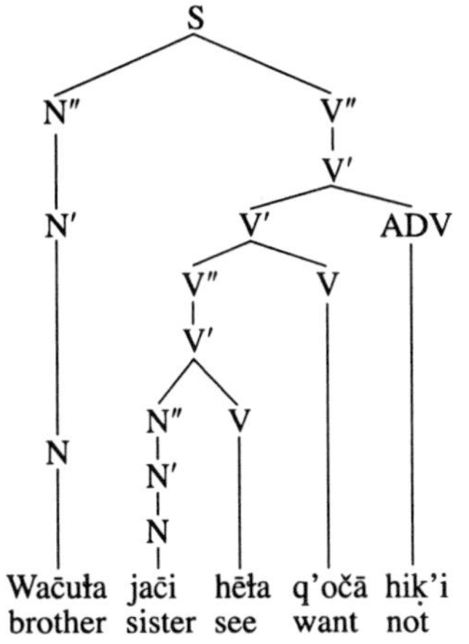

Figure 4.24. *Structure of left-branching control construction in Tindi in (4.38)*

The final construction to be analyzed is the relative clause. English relative clauses may have a complementizer *that*, as in *the man THAT I saw*, a relative pronoun, as in *the man WHO saw me*, or no marker at all, as in *the man I saw.* The relative pronoun appears in the same position in the tree as the complementizer. The constituent structure of the first two relative clauses is given in Figure 4.25; for *the man I saw*, the complementizer position would be simply empty.

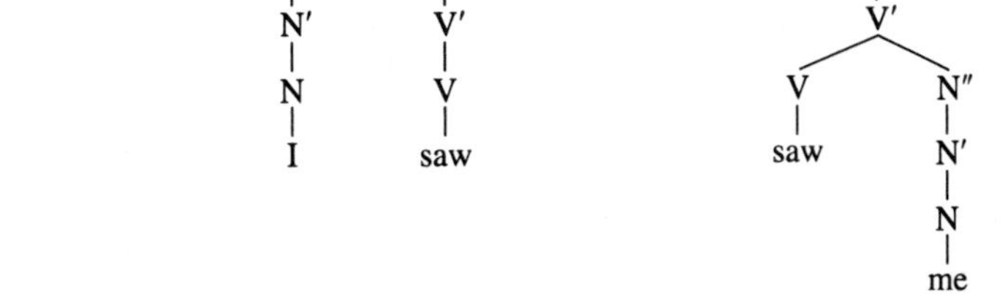

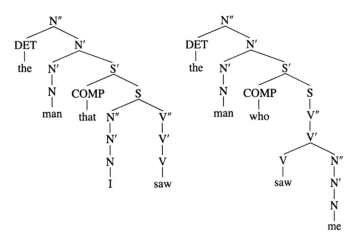

Figure 4.25. *The constituent structure of English relative clauses*

There is one N″ missing in each embedded sentence, and the head of the relative clause is interpreted as having the function of the missing NP inside the relative clause. Thus in the lefthand tree in Figure 4.25, the head NP *the man* is construed as the direct object of *saw*, i.e. as the missing N″ which is a sister to the V under the V′ in the relative clause. In the other tree, the head NP is interpreted as the subject of *saw*, i.e. as the missing N″ which is a sister to the V″ in the relative clause.

The English relative clauses in Figure 4.25 are right-branching, and Huallaga Quechua (Weber 1983) provides an example of a left-branching relative clause.

(4.39) Juan-∅ Marya-ta kañu-q allqu-ta rika-ra-n.
Juan-NOM Maria-ACC bit-REL dog-ACC see-PAST-3sg
'Juan saw the dog that bit Maria.'

In this sentence, the relative clause precedes the head noun; there is no relative pronoun, but the embedded clause is marked by the subordinator *-q*. The constituent structure of (4.39) is given in Figure 4.26.

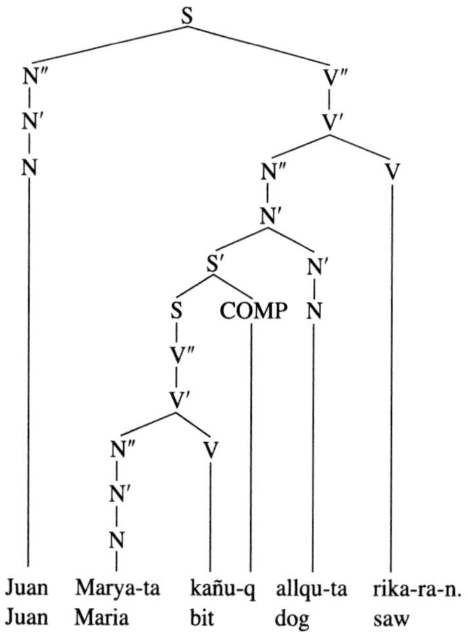

Figure 4.26. *Constituent structure of the left-branching Quechua relative clause in (4.39)*

Note that the case suffixes (*-ta* 'ACC') are not represented as occupying separate branches in the tree. This is because they are part of the morphological structure of the nouns and not independent elements. The branches of a phrase structure tree represent the syntactic structure of the sentence but not the internal morphological structure of words. This contrasts with the Kwakwala clitics in Figure 4.6, which are given separate tree branches; they are depicted differently because they are syntactically (but not phonologically) independent elements which are not part of the morphological structure of the word to which they are attached.

The English complex sentences diagrammed in this section include some of the examples which were given dependency representations in chapter 3. In the next section, the two approaches will be compared on a number of points.

4.5 Constituent structure and grammatical relations

In chapter 2 a number of grammatical phenomena were described in terms of grammatical relations, e.g. finite verb agreement in English, and the question arises as to how these phenomena could be characterized in constituent-structure terms, since there is no direct representation of grammatical relations in the tree structures introduced in this chapter. Finite verb agreement and case marking were the main coding properties of subjects discussed in chapter 2, and it is necessary to have an analysis of them in terms of constituent structure. The basic structural configuration of the clause in English and many other languages is given in Figure 4.27.

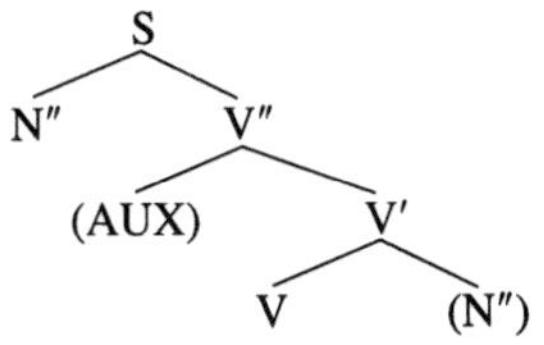

Figure 4.27. *Basic clause configuration*

The finite verb, or the finite auxiliary in the specifier of V″ position, agrees with the N″ that is a sister to the V″. Case in English is realized only on pronouns, and the nominative pronoun occurs as sister to the V″, while the accusative pronoun appears as a sister to the verb. (The discussion will be restricted to just these two possibilities.) These may be taken as initial hypotheses about English finite verb agreement and case assignment; they are summarized in (4.40). (The notation '[X, Y]' means 'the X node is immediately dominated by the Y node'.)

(4.40) a. The finite verb/auxiliary agrees in person and number with [N″, S].
b. A pronoun appears in the nominative case if it is in the position [N″, S].
c. A pronoun appears in the accusative case if it is in the position [N″, V′].

The essential feature of these rules is that they relate agreement or case to specific positions in a phrase-structure tree; they refer solely to constituent structure and make no reference to grammatical relations at all.

An important behavioral property of some terms is the ability to be the antecedent of a reflexive pronoun. In the discussion in chapter 2, constraints on the interpretation of the reflexive antecedent were captured in terms of the grammatical-relations hierarchy in (2.50). Is there a straightforward way of capturing these restrictions in terms of constituent structure? The relevant examples from English are given in (4.41).

(4.41) a. Sally$_i$ saw herself$_i$.
a′. *Herself$_i$ saw Sally$_i$.
b. Sally told Max$_i$ about himself$_i$.
b′. *Sally told himself$_i$ about Max$_i$.

The phrase-structure trees for these sentences are given in Figure 4.28.

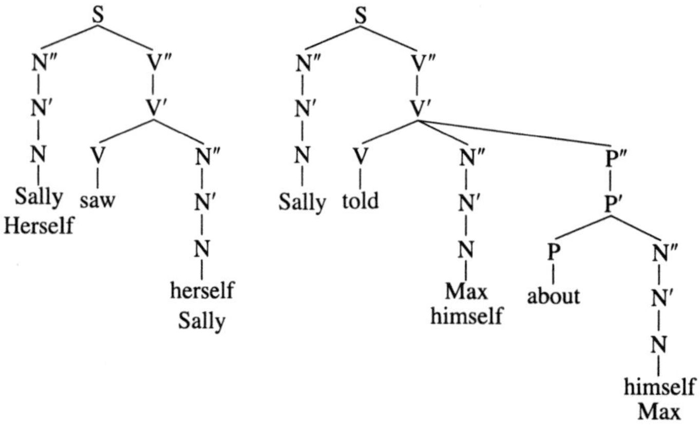

Figure 4.28. *Constituent structure of examples in (4.41)*

There is a clear pattern in both examples: in the grammatical sentences, the antecedent is 'higher in the tree' than the reflexive pronoun, and in all of the ungrammatical ones, the reflexive pronoun is higher in the tree than its antecedent. What does 'higher in the tree' mean? In (4.41a) the N″ *Sally* is immediately dominated by the S node and is a sister of V″, whereas the reflexive N″ *herself* is dominated by S and V″. Thus both *Sally* and *herself* are dominated by S, but *herself* is also dominated by V″, which does not dominate *Sally* but is, rather, its sister. The same relationship holds between *Max* and *himself* in (4.41b): *Max* is immediately dominated by V′, which also dominates *himself*, but P″, which is a sister to the N″ headed by *Max*, also dominates *himself*. The relation 'higher in the tree' is termed a **command relation**, and in the two grammatical sentences in (4.41), the antecedent commands the reflexive, while in the two ungrammatical ones, the reflexive commands its antecedent. The following rule for reflexive antecedents in (4.41) may be formulated.

(4.42) The antecedent must command the reflexive pronoun.

Thus, in (4.40) and (4.42) rules have been proposed for describing finite-verb agreement, case assignment and reflexivization in some English simple sentences, rules which refer only to the constituent structure of the sentences involved.

Implicit in these rules are constituent-structure definitions of the grammatical relations subject and direct object. Subject is the N″ immediately dominated by S (i.e. [N″, S]), and direct object is the N″ immediately dominated by V′ (i.e. [N″, V′]). Constituent-structure definitions of grammatical relations have in fact been assumed by many syntacticians since the mid-1960s. There is no corresponding structural definition of indirect object. In English, the indirect object is simply in a PP, but this is not so in languages like German, Russian and Malayalam. Consider the tree for the Russian sentence in (2.27a), repeated below.

(4.43)	Učitel'nic-a	da-l-a	knig-u	ženščin-e.	Russian
	teacher-FSGNOM	give-PAST-FSG	book-FSGACC	woman-FSGDAT	
	'The teacher gave the book to the woman.'				

The direct object (*knig-u* 'book-ACC') and the indirect object (*ženščin-e* 'woman-DAT') are both sisters of the verb under the lowest V′. Consequently, if the Russian rule

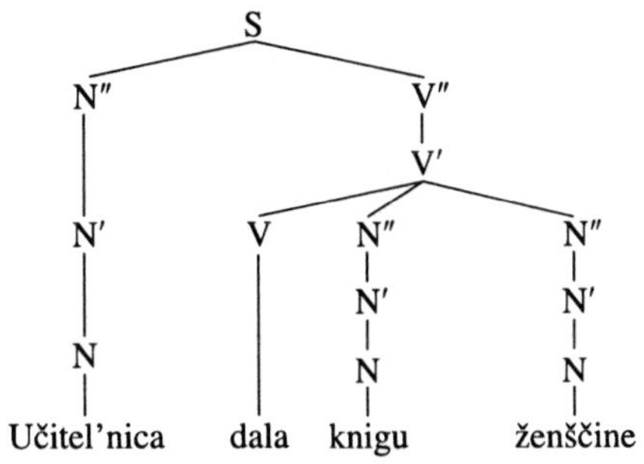

Figure 4.29. *Russian ditransitive sentence in (4.43)*

for assigning accusative case were like the one in (4.40c), then both NPs would get accusative case, which is not correct. In a tree like this one, there does not appear to be any way to structurally differentiate the direct and indirect objects. Suppose one stipulated that in languages like Russian the verb can have only one sister NP and that the indirect object had to appear as a sister to the lowest V′. This would yield the structure in Figure 4.30.

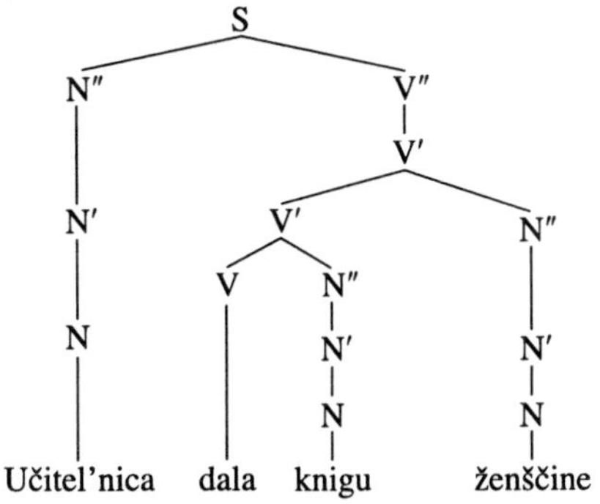

Figure 4.30. *Alternative structure for (4.43)*

While this structure distinguishes the direct and indirect objects, it suffers from two serious problems. First, it treats the indirect object as an adjunct, according to Table 4.1, despite the fact that indirect objects are terms. Second, true adjuncts bearing different cases can occur in the same position in the tree as 'woman', as in e.g. (4.44), and the original problem arises again: how does one structurally determine the correct case.

(4.44) Ženščin-a napisa-l-a pismo-∅ karandaš-em. Russian
woman-FSGNOM write-PAST-FSG letter-NSGACC pencil-MSGINST
'The woman wrote the letter with a pencil.'

This sentence would have the structure in Figure 4.30, with the adjunct *karandaš-em* 'pencil-INST' occurring in the same position as *ženščin-e* 'woman-DAT', i.e. as sister to the lowest V′. In terms of phrase structure alone, it would be very difficult, if not impossible, to account for the dative case in (4.43) and the instrumental case in (4.44) in purely phrase-structure terms. Some alternative ways of handling this will be discussed in chapter 5.

There are some additional problems with the rules in (4.40). Consider the following examples involving relative clauses.

(4.45) a. The man whom I saw was Pat's father.
b. The man who speaks Zapotec is Pat's father.
b′. The people who speak Zapotec are Pat's parents.

The subject of (4.45a) has the structure given in the lefthand diagram in Figure 4.25, while the subjects of (4.45b) and (4.45b′) have the structure presented in the righthand diagram in it. The issue in (4.45a) is the accusative case on *whom*, the relative pronoun. As the tree clearly shows, *whom* is not the sister to V under the V′, as required by the rule in (4.40c), yet it carries accusative case. Similar problems are exhibited in (4.45b) and (4.45b′): *who* is not in a position immediately dominated by the lower S and is not a sister to the V″, but it nevertheless carries nominative case and triggers finite-verb agreement in the relative clause. (Note that even if one maintained that the agreement triggers are *the man* and *the people*, the problem remains.) There are, then, examples in English which the rules in (4.40) cannot account for easily. Theories based on constituent-structure analysis must develop means to handle these basic facts; this will be discussed in chapter 6. These examples present no problem for a relationally oriented approach, since *whom* is the direct object of *saw* in (4.45a) and *who* is the subject of *speak* in (b) and (b′), regardless of its position in the sentence.

Constituent-structure-based case assignment and agreement rules such as those in (4.40) also run into problems in languages with free word order. The Russian examples from (1.2) are repeated below.

(4.46) a. Učitel'nic-a čita-et knig-u. Russian
teacher-FSGNOM read-3SGPRES book-FSGACC
b. Knigu čitaet učitel'nica.
book read teacher
c. Čitaet učitel'nica knigu.
read teacher book
'The teacher is reading the book.'
d. Ja čita-ju knig-u.
1SGNOM read-1SGPRES book-FSGACC
'I am reading the book.'
d′. *Ja čita-et knig-u.
read-3SGPRES

In Russian, the subject is in the nominative case, the direct object is in the accusative case, and the finite verb agrees with the subject, as the (d), (d′) examples clearly show. The three words in these Russian sentences can in principle occur in any order, and therefore it cannot be assumed that the NP which receives nominative case and triggers verb agreement will be in the same position in every sentence. Rules such as those in (4.40) crucially presuppose that the arguments of the verb will be in a particular position consistently, in order to receive case or act as an agreement trigger. For a sentence like (4.46c), for example, this could only be maintained if branches were allowed to cross in the tree, because the subject NP, which is a direct daughter of S, occurs between the verb and the direct object NP, which are sisters under the V′. Hence the branch connecting the subject NP to the S node would cross one of the branches coming from the V′. As mentioned in section 4.1.2, most syntacticians would not accept such a tree.

Languages like Russian are problematic for more than just the rules for case and agreement. The reflexivization rule in (4.42) requires the antecedent to be higher in the tree than the reflexive pronoun, but again, in a language with free word order, it is difficult to see that this is always the case. Consider the Russian reflexive examples in (4.47).

(4.47) a. Ivan-∅ vide-l-∅ seb-ja. Russian
Ivan-MSGNOM see-PAST-MSG self-MSGACC
b. Videl Ivan sebja.
c. Sebja Ivan videl.
'Ivan saw himself.'

All of these sentences mean 'Ivan saw himself', but it is not at all obvious that the antecedent *Ivan* commands, that is, is higher in the tree, than the reflexive *sebja*, especially in terms of standard tree diagrams without crossing branches. Tree diagrams for (4.47b) and (4.47c) which meet the command condition but violate the no-crossing condition are given in Figure 4.31.

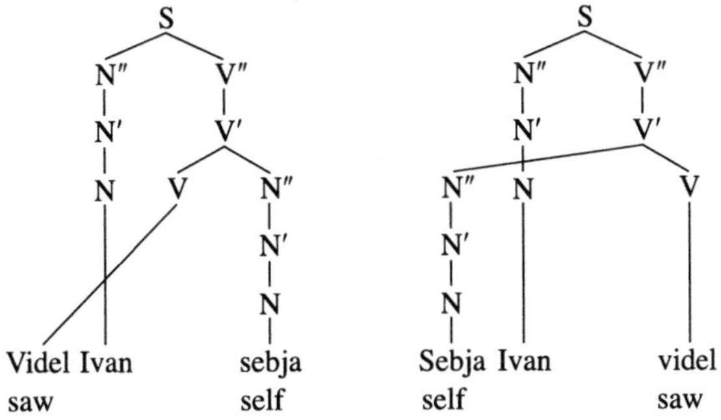

Figure 4.31. *Possible constituent-structure trees for (4.47b) and (4.47c)*

Theories which assume the no-crossing condition must come up with alternative ways of accounting for sentences like these from Russian. Again, there is no problem in relational terms: in all three the antecedent is higher on the relational hierarchy in (2.50) than the reflexive.

Grammars based on grammatical relations are a kind of dependency grammar, and it has long been known that grammars based on constituent-structure and dependency grammars are fundamentally similar in the sense that any language that can be described by a constituent-structure grammar can also be described by a dependency grammar, and vice versa. This is called **weak equivalence**; constituent-structure grammars and dependency grammars are weakly equivalent. While they both can describe the same grammatical phenomena, they do not assign the same structures to sentences. This can be readily seen through a comparison of the dependency representations in chapter 3 with the phrase-structure representations of the same sentences in chapter 4. Grammars which not only describe the same languages but also assign the same structures to the sentences of the languages are said to be **strongly equivalent**. Constituent-structure grammars and dependency grammars are thus weakly equivalent but not strongly equivalent.

The next chapter concerns the actual formulation of rules in constituent-structure and dependency grammars, as well as the role that the lexicon plays in them. With respect to constituent-structure grammars, many syntacticians use bar or prime notation only for the intermediate N′ or V′ categories and use NP and VP for the maximal projections. In the remaining chapters, this usage will be followed, and NP will be used for N″ and VP for V″.

Notes and suggested readings

For discussion of X-bar theory, see Jackendoff (1977), Radford (1988), Kornai and Pullum (1990), Borsley (1996). Its historical roots go back to Harris (1946). For discontinuous constituency, see McCawley (1982) and the papers in Huck and Ojeda (1987). On the equivalence of constituent-structure grammars and dependency grammars, see Hays (1964).

Exercises

1. Use the constituency tests from section 4.1.1 to show that the italicized elements in (1) are constituents and that the ones in (2) are not. [sect. 4.1.1]
   (1) a. Leslie *wrote a new poem* yesterday.
       b. Dana placed the watch carefully *on the bench.*
       c. *The new student* amused the chemistry class.
       d. Chris tried *to escape from the island.*
       e. *That the stock market kept going up* surprised everyone.
   (2) a. Leslie *wrote a new* poem yesterday.
       b. Dana placed the *watch carefully* on the bench.
       c. The new *student amused* the chemistry class.
       d. Chris *tried to escape from* the island.
       e. *That the stock* market kept going up surprised everyone.

2. Draw constituent-structure trees for the following English sentences; use the X-bar system developed in section 4.3. [section 4.3]
   (1) The clever new teacher amused the bored students in the class. [*in the class* is part of NP]
   (2) A very famous author has written a new book of poetry.
   (3) Dana carefully placed the watch on the table right after the meeting.
   (4) Her parents are very happy about the weather.

3. Draw constituent-structure trees for the following sentences: the Malagasy example in (2.5a), the Basque example in (2.26a), the Hungarian example in (2.27b) and the Dyirbal example in (2.31b). [section 4.3]

4. Draw constituent-structure trees for the following English sentences. [section 4.4]
   (1) Chris tried to escape from the island.
   (2) Pat had always known that Sidney would cause problems.
   (3) The man who Dana met claimed to be a spy.
   (4) The police believe Kim to have stolen the car that Leslie bought in April.

5. Draw constituent-structure trees for the following sentences: the Malagasy sentence in (2.63b), the Dyirbal sentence in (2.98b), and the ones below. [section 4.4]

   (1) Wičháša ki hokšíla ki hená mathó wą wąyą́kapi ki slolyé. — Lakhota
   man the boy the those bear a see COMP know
   'The man knows that the boys saw a bear.'

   (2) Ra:mu Kamala pa:ḍ-ina pa:ṭa winn-a:ḍu. — Telugu
   Raamu Kamala sang-REL song hear-3MSGPAST
   'Raamu heard the song which Kamala sang.'

   (3) Ali membeli ayam itu untuk perempuan yang mengirim surat itu kepada Hasan.
   Ali bought chicken DET for woman REL sent letter DET to
   'Ali bought the chicken for the woman who sent the letter to Hasan.' — Indonesian

CHAPTER 5

Grammar and lexicon

5.0 Introduction

In the previous two chapters, two different ways of representing syntactic structure were presented, dependency relations and constituent structure (phrase structure). In doing syntactic analysis, it is not enough to simply represent the syntactic structure of sentences. The goal of the syntactic analysis of a language (or set of sentences from a language) is to formulate a grammar which will specify the sentences in the data. By specifying the sentences by means of a set of rules, the analyst makes explicit the structure of the sentences and expresses generalizations about them. Two different types of rules will be presented: phrase-structure rules as part of a grammar based on constituent (phrase) structure, and relational-dependency rules as part of a grammar based on dependency relations, which includes grammatical relations.

The rules of the grammar specify the way the form classes in the language may combine, and a useful distinction may be drawn between lexical and phrasal form classes. Lexical form classes are the lexical categories discussed in chapter 1, e.g., noun, verb, adjective, adposition. Phrasal form classes are constituents like noun phrase, prepositional phrase and verb phrase, which are specified by the rules of the grammar. The elements in the lexical form classes are stored in the **lexicon**, which may be thought of as the storehouse of the words and morphemes in the language. The lexicon complements the grammar in important ways, and one of the issues to be explored in chapter 6 is the relationship between the grammar and the lexicon in different syntactic theories.

The discussion in this chapter will proceed as follows. In section 5.1 phrase-structure rules [PS-rules] will be introduced, and in the following section a lexicon for a phrase-structure grammar will be developed. Rules for a relational-dependency grammar and accompanying lexicon are presented in the section 5.3.

5.1 Phrase-structure rules

In section 4.3 the X-bar schema for phrase structure was introduced and summarized in Figure 4.9; it is repeated below.

The relations among nodes in this tree can be expressed by the following rules. ('XP' is an alternative notation for 'X″'.)

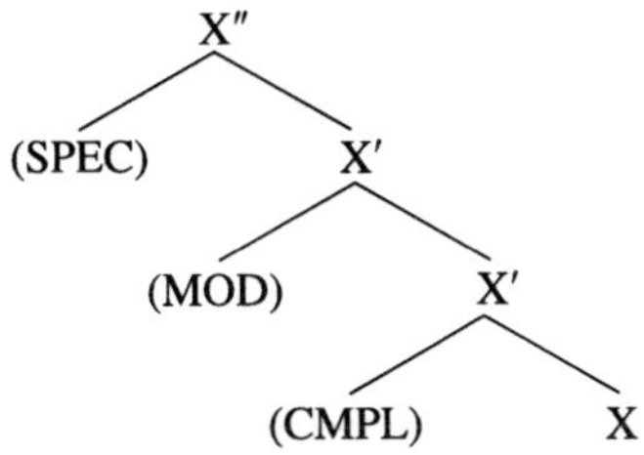

Figure 5.1. *General X-bar schema for phrase structure*

(5.1) a. XP = (SPEC) + X′
b. X′ = (MOD) + X′
c. X′ = (CMPL) + X

'SPEC', 'MOD' and 'CMPL' are functions, not form classes, and therefore a more accurate rendering in terms of form classes alone is given in (5.2), in which 'WP', 'YP' and 'ZP' stand for maximal projections headed by 'W', 'Y' and 'Z', which are variables for lexical categories.

(5.2) a. XP = (W(P)) + X′
b. X′ = (YP) + X′
c. X′ = (ZP) + X

The basic structure of the English noun phrase can be expressed as in (5.3); these rules are for 'simple' NPs, that is, NPs without sentential elements such as relative clauses.

(5.3) a. NP = (DET) + N′
b. N′ = (AdjP) + N′
c. N′ = N + (PP)

These three statements are PS-rules. The most commonly used notation, however, employs an arrow ('→') rather than the equal sign, as in (5.4).

(5.4) a. NP → (DET) + N′
b. N′ → QP + N′ [optional]
c. N′ → AdjP + N′ [optional]
d. N′ → N + (PP)

The English PS-rules specify the structure of the English NP *the three long proofs of the theorem*. Three features of this notation deserve comment. First, the parenthesis around DET and PP indicate that these constituents are optional. Second, the PS-rules expanding N′ in (5.4b) and (5.4c) are optional. It is preferable to say that these rules are optional rather than AdjP and QP are optional (i.e. N′ → (QP) + N′, N′ → (AdjP) + N′), since a literal interpretation of the latter could lead to an NP with three non-branching N′s; the minimal three-level structure can be specified by (5.4a) and (5.4d) alone. Hence they are the only obligatory rules in (5.4), and if (5.4b) or (5.4c) apply, a QP or AdjP must occur in the NP. Third, the plus (+) signals that there is a fixed order among the form classes specified in the rule, i.e., DET precedes N′, AdjP precedes N′, QP precedes N′, and N precedes PP. It should also be noted that rule (5.4c) can be repeated, in order to permit multiple adjectival modifiers as in the NP *the beautiful expensive red scarf* in Figure 4.11.

PS-rules, then, specify the constituent structure depicted in tree diagrams. The rules in (5.1)–(5.4) are formulated in terms of the X-bar schema, but PS-rules could also be formulated to specify the non-X-bar phrase-structure trees in section 4.1.2. Indeed, the development of the X-bar schema came many years after the introduction of PS-rules.

Each level of X-bar structure in the tree is represented by a rule. The constituent on the left side of the arrow is a mother node, and it immediately dominates the daughter node(s) on the righthand side of the rule. Thus in (5.4a), 'NP' is a mother node and immediately dominates DET and N′, its daughters. In (5.4b), N′ is the mother node and immediately dominates QP and N′, its daughters. In (5.4c), N′ is the mother node and immediately dominates AdjP and N′, its daughters. In (5.4d), N′ is the mother node and immediately dominates N and PP, its daughters. The correspondence between levels of structure in the tree and PS-rules can be seen in Figure 5.2. (The triangles are abbreviations for constituent structure which is irrelevant to the point at hand and is not specified.)

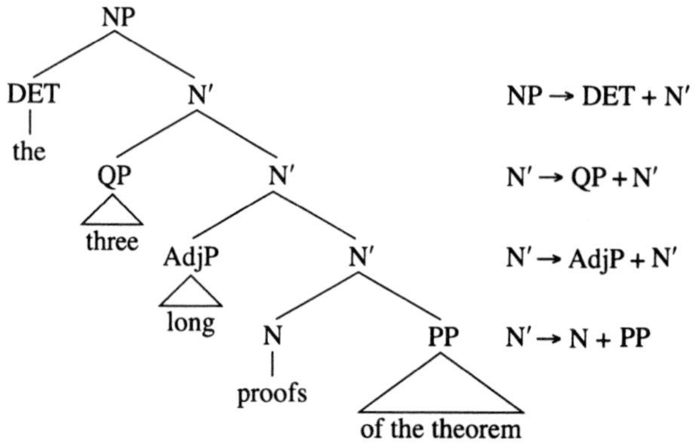

Figure 5.2. *Correspondence between constituent structure and PS-rules*

Each level of structure in a tree, that is each mother node and its daughters, is represented by a PS-rule; in other words, each PS-rule specifies a local subtree.

There are two ways to interpret the correspondence between constituent structure and PS-rules. One way is to construe the rules as instructions for drawing a tree; when understood in this sense, they are often referred to as **'rewrite rules'**. Hence on this interpretation the PS-rule in (5.4a) is understood as an instruction to rewrite NP as DET followed by N′, the one in (5.4b) as an instruction to rewrite N′ as QP followed by N′, the one in (5.4c) as an instruction to rewrite N′ as AdjP followed by N′, and the one in (5.4c) as an instruction to rewrite N′ as N followed by PP. The other way to interpret PS-rules is as constraints on possible tree structures or **node admissibility conditions**. This view takes possible tree structures as given and uses PS-rules to determine whether the structure in question is possible in the language. As an illustration of how this works, NP structure in several languages will be compared. The first to be looked at is Indonesian. The PS-rules for a simple Indonesian NP like *guru muda itu* [teacher young that] 'that young teacher' are given in (5.5).

(5.5) PS-rules for simple Indonesian NP
a. NP → N′ + (DET)
b. N′ → N′ + AdjP [optional]
c. N′ → N

As in English, determiners and adjectival modifiers are optional. Five NP structures are given in Figure 5.3. Four are compatible with the hierarchical aspect of the rules in (5.5) but differ in linear order, and one violates both the hierarchical structure and linear order specified in these rules; in other words, it violates the X-bar template in Figure 5.1, because a modifier, AdjP, dominates the specifier.

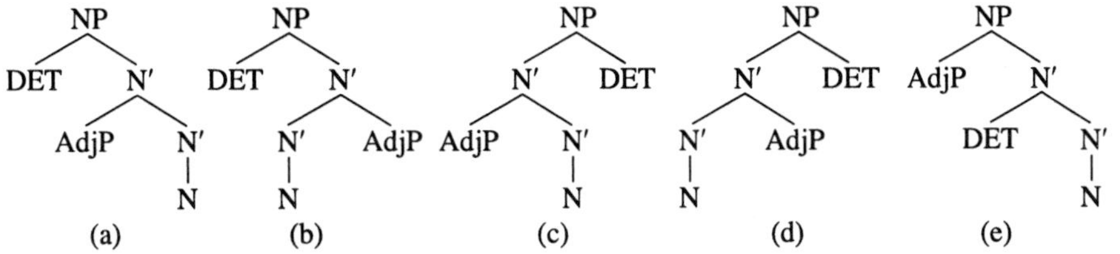

Figure 5.3. *NP structures*

Which one is a grammatical NP structure for Indonesian? In terms of the rules in (5.5), only structure (d) would be a possible Indonesian NP. Structures (a) and (b) violate rule (5.5a), while structures (a) and (c) violate rule (5.5b). Which one is a possible NP structure for English? Based on the PS-rules in (5.4), only (a) could be a possible English NP. Structures (b) and (d) violate rule (5.4b), while structures (c) and (d) violate rule (5.4a). Thus given the structures in Figure 5.3, the PS-rules in (5.4) for English and (5.5) for Indonesian admit only one of them as a potential grammatical structure in each language. This is what is meant by treating PS-rules as constraints on possible structures. Are structures (b) and (c) grammatical NP structures in some language? The answer is 'yes'. Structure (b) represents the structure of Spanish NPs like *el gato gordo* [the cat fat] 'the fat cat' or *la casa blanca* [the house white] 'the white house'. Structure (c) depicts the structure of Icelandic NPs like *rauði hestur-inn* [red horse-the] 'the red horse' (Einarsson 1945). (Spanish and Icelandic also have NPs with the structure in (a), it should be noted.) Croatian has the four possibilities in (a)–(d), e.g. *taj crveni konj* [this red horse] 'this red horse', *taj konj crveni*, *crveni konj taj* and *konj crveni taj*. The NP structure in (e) should be impossible in every language, since it violates the basic X-bar schema in Figure 5.1. However, it appears to be possible in Croatian; while *crveni taj konj* [red this horse] is considered to be stylistically marked as highly poetic, it is nevertheless possible.

It was mentioned earlier that rules like 'NP → (DET) + N′' in (5.4a) express two different pieces of information: (1) NP immediately dominates DET and N′, and (2) DET precedes N′. The first concerns immediate dominance relations among nodes, and the second is about the linear order of the daughters. Some syntacticians have suggested that each type of information should be expressed by a separate type of rule. A reformulation of the Indonesian PS-rules in (5.5) along this line is given in (5.6).

(5.6) PS-rules for simple Indonesian NP (revised)
a. Immediate dominance
1. NP → N′, (DET)
2. N′ → N′, AdjP [optional]
3. N′ → N
b. Linear precedence
Head-initial

The rules in (5.6a) are called **immediate-dominance rules** [ID-rules]. They differ from the earlier PS-rules formally only in the replacement of the plus (+) with a comma (,), which indicates that the linear order of the elements on the righthand side of the rule is not specified in the ID-rule. The ordering of the elements is provided by the **linear-precedence rule** [LP-rule] in (5.6b); in this case it states simply that each level of X-bar structure is head-initial. The N′ is the head daughter in (5.6a1) and (5.6a2), and it occurs initially, as shown in structure (d) in Figure 5.3. In the final N′-rule, (5.6a3), the head daughter is N, and it is initial (by default, since there are no other elements in the righthand side of the rule).

When PS-rules are broken down into distinct ID- and LP-rules, certain generalizations can be captured that would otherwise be missed or, at the very least, very difficult to express. The single set of ID-rules in (5.6a) describes the first four of the tree structures in Figure 5.3; the structures differ only in terms of LP-rules. Thus, instead of needing four sets of PS-rules, i.e. those in (5.4) for English, those in (5.5) for Indonesian, as well as two more sets for Spanish and Icelandic, only one set of ID-rules, those in (5.6a), and four language-specific LP-rules would be required for the specification of the (a)–(d) NP structures in Figure 5.3. This format also permits the simplification of particular grammars. For example, in English it is possible to have an adverb within the VP in two positions, either before or after the V′, as in *The lawyer quickly objected* versus *The lawyer objected quickly*. In the traditional format, two rules would be required to license these structures, V′ → AdvP + V′ and V → V′ + AdvP, whereas in the ID/LP format, only one would be needed, V → AdvP, V′. The same would be true for the Spanish NP, which can have the AdjP either before or after the noun, e.g. *un gran hombre* 'a big man' versus *un hombre grande* 'a large man'. The rule in (5.6a2) would specify both of these possibilities.

Languages like Russian with free phrase order would lack LP-rules ordering the major phrasal constituents in a clause; but they would have NP- and PP-internal LP-rules, since there is a fixed order within the NP (e.g. *et-a molod-aja učitel'nic-a* [this-FSGNOM young-FSGNOM teacher-FSGNOM] 'this young teacher' is the only possible order) and the PP (e.g. *v gostinic-e* [in hotel-FSGDAT] 'in the hotel', **gostinic-e v*). Languages with free word order like Kalkatungu (see (3.2) in section 2.1) might well have no LP-rules at all, since there seem to be no ordering constraints within the NP or within the clause.

While the formulation of ID-rules seems relatively straightforward in terms of the X-bar schema, the formulation of LP-rules can be quite complex. Consider the English NP *the three long proofs of the theorem in the book* in Figure 5.4, which contains an adjunct PP.

In order to account for this structure, it is necessary to add an additional ID-rule to the set of ID-rules based on (5.4); the revised set of ID-rules is given in (5.7).

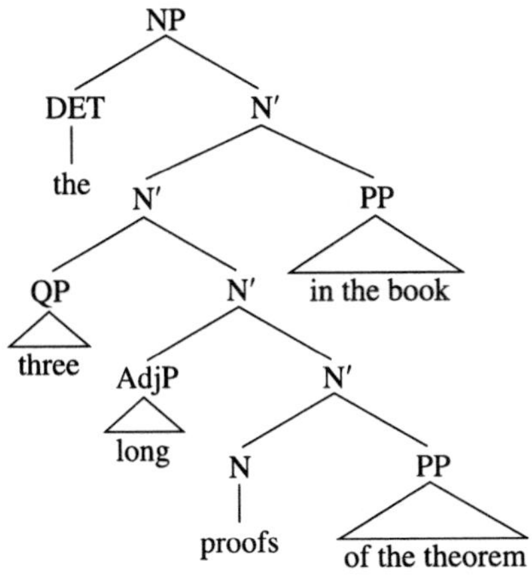

Figure 5.4. *English NP with adjunct PP*

(5.7) ID-rules for the simple English NP (revised)
a. NP → N′, (DET)
b. N′ → N′, PP [optional]
c. N′ → N′, QP [optional]
d. N′ → N′, AdjP [optional]
e. N′ → N, (PP)

The new rule is (5.7b), which **licenses** the adjunct PP *in the book* (see the discussion in section 4.3 regarding adjunct PPs in NPs). Unlike Indonesian, the English NP is not consistently head-initial; it is head-initial in the structures specified by (5.7b) and (5.7e), but is not in those permitted by (5.7a), (5.7c) and (5.7d). It appears that two LP-rules are required. The first is for the head-initial structures in (5.7b) and (5.7e); in both cases the non-head daughter is a PP, and consequently the rule is 'Head > PP', where '>' means 'linearly precedes'. The situation is more complicated in the head-final structures in (5.7a), (5.7c) and (5.7d). In both cases the pre-head constituent is a kind of modifying element, a determiner in (a), a QP in (c) and an AdjP in (d). But 'modifying element' is neither a form class nor a type of constituent, and therefore if the categories used in LP-rules are to be the same as those in the ID-rules, as they should, then this notion cannot be used in an LP-rule. There is no syntactic feature which unifies them, either, because determiner and quantifier are not among the major categories defined in terms of [±N] and [±V]. The obvious but unsatisfactory solution is to have a disjunctive characterization of the pre-head constituent, i.e. DET, QP or AdjP; this can be represented as '{DET, QP, AdjP} > Head', where '{X, Y}' means 'X or Y'. The two LP-rules can be combined into a single rule, given in (5.8).

(5.8) LP-rule for simple English NP
{DET, QP, AdjP} > Head > PP

This LP-rule and the ID-rules in (5.7) can together specify the English NPs like the ones in Figures 5.2 and 5.4.

The discussion of PS-rules thus far has been limited to NP structure, in the interest of introducing a number of basic concepts. It is now necessary to expand the discussion to include other phrase types, including clauses. Unless otherwise noted, the traditional PS-rule format in (5.4) will be used.

The PS-rules for VPs parallel those for NPs; the specifier position is occupied by a tensed auxiliary verb. As will be seen in chapter 6, the analysis of tensed auxiliary verbs varies considerably from theory to theory, and therefore the structures presented here represent only one possible analysis of them. The VP in Figure 4.10 is repeated in Figure 5.5, together with the PS-rule for each local subtree.

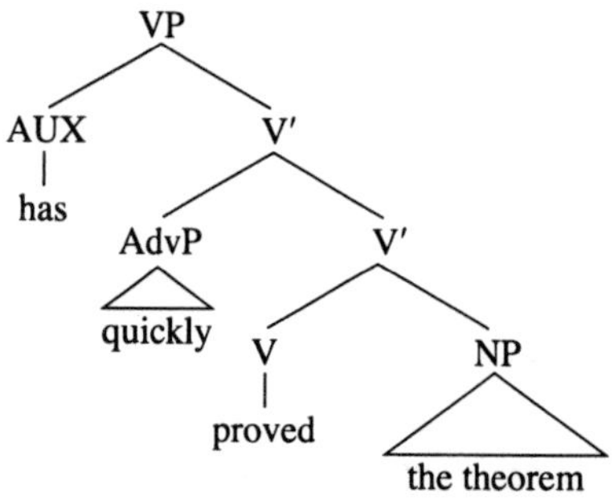

VP → AUX + V′

V′ → AdvP + V′

V′ → V + NP

Figure 5.5. *Correspondence between VP structure and PS-rules*

The structure of this VP parallels the structure of the NP in Figure 5.2, *the long proof of the theorem*, and the PS-rules licensing it are correspondingly similar. A more complex VP containing adjuncts is given in Figure 5.6, together with PS-rules.

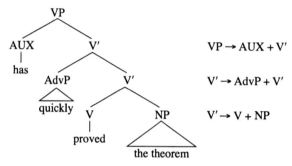

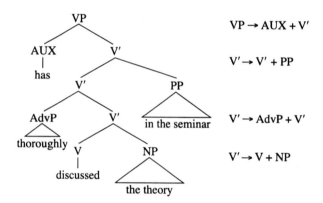

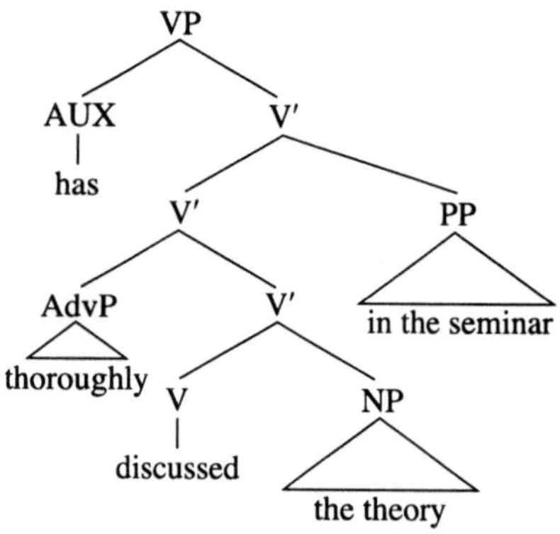

VP → AUX + V′

V′ → V′ + PP

V′ → AdvP + V′

V′ → V + NP

Figure 5.6. *English VP with adjunct PP*

This VP contains two modifiers: the adverb *thoroughly* and the adjunct PP *in the seminar*. Each is a sister to a V′ under a V′. The PP *in the seminar* is the highest adjunct in the VP, and therefore it has the remainder of the VP, i.e. *thoroughly discussed the theory*, within its scope of modification. The lowest V′, i.e. the one immediately dominating the verb, exhibits quite a number of possibilities, depending on the lexical properties of the verb. As emphasized in chapter 4 (see Table 4.1), the sisters to the V are arguments, and the sisters to a V′ are adjuncts. Examples of different V′s (immediately dominating V) together with the PS-rule for them are given in (5.9); this list is not exhaustive but does represent the major combinations.

(5.9) Some English V′ possibilities

a.	NP died	V′ → V
b.	NP is very happy.	V′ → V + AdjP
c.	NP lay on the table	V′ → V + PP
d.	NP ate a souvlaki	V′ → V + NP
e.	NP put the book on the table	V′ → V + NP + PP
f.	NP gave Tom the picture	V′ → V + NP + NP
g.	NP talked to Tom about the picture	V′ → V + PP + PP
h.	NP wiped the table clean.	V′ → V + NP + AdjP
i.	NP believes that Tom died	V′ → V + S′
j.	NP wanted to eat a souvlaki	V′ → V + VP
k.	NP told Tom that . . .	V′ → V + NP + S′
l.	NP said to Tom that . . .	V′ → V + PP + S′
m.	NP told Tom to eat a souvlaki	V′ → V + NP + VP
n.	NP vowed to Tom to eat a souvlaki	V′ → V + PP + VP

The rules in (5.9c)–(5.9n) specify the (non-subject) argument arrays of English verbs. These V′ rules can be collapsed into a single PS-rule, given in (5.10); elements in curly brackets are disjunctive alternatives, and the parenthesis around the curly brackets indicates that all of the possibilities within the curly brackets are optional.

(5.10) PS-rule for some English V′ (immediately dominating V) combinations

$$V' \rightarrow V + \left(\begin{Bmatrix} NP \\ PP \end{Bmatrix}\right) + \left(\begin{Bmatrix} NP \\ PP \\ AdjP \\ VP \\ S' \end{Bmatrix}\right)$$

With the exception of AdjP, all of the elements introduced by this rule are arguments of the verb. Collapsing the rules in (5.9) down into the single rule in (5.10) is a notational simplification only; a grammar containing the rule in (5.10) is just as complex as the one containing the individual rules in (5.9a)–(5.9n), because both (5.9) and (5.10) specify the same local subtrees.

There are five phrase types in this rule for which no PS-rules have been developed, i.e. PP, QP, AdjP, AdvP, S and S′. The X-bar structure of PPs and AdjPs was given in Figure 4.15, and the PS-rules for them are given in (5.11), along with the rules for AdvP, which takes a degree modifier like an AdjP but no other modifiers or complements. QP takes a degree modifier, e.g. *almost seven, very few*, and a PP complement, e.g. *almost eight of them.*

(5.11) a. PS-rules for AdjP
1. AdjP → (DEG) + Adj′
2. Adj′ → Adj′ + (PP)
3. Adj′ → Adj + (PP)

b. PS-rules for PP
1. PP → (ADV) + P′
2. P′ → P + NP

c. PS-rules for AdvP
   1. AdvP → (DEG) + Adv′
   2. Adv′ → ADV
d. PS-rules for QP
   1. QP → (DEG) + Q′
   2. Q′ → Q + (PP)

The structure of S′ in English was represented in Figure 4.21, and the PS-rule for it is presented in (5.12), along with the rule for S.

(5.12) PS-rule for S′
S′ → (COMP) + S
S → NP + VP

All of these PS-rules can be combined into a set of rules which license the English structures discussed in this chapter and the previous one. The V′ rule in (5.10) is given in the notation used in (5.8).

(5.13) Fragment of a PS-grammar of English

a.	S′	→ (COMP) + S	
b.	S	→ NP + VP	
c.	VP	→ (AUX) + V′	
d.	V′	→ V′ + PP	[optional]
e.	V′	→ AdvP + V′	[optional]
f.	V′	→ V + ({NP, PP}) + ({NP, PP, AdjP, VP, S′})	
g.	AdjP	→ (DEG) + Adj′	
h.	Adj′	→ Adj′ + (PP)	[optional]
i.	Adj′	→ ADJ + (PP)	
j.	PP	→ (ADV) + P′	
k.	P′	→ P + NP	
l.	NP	→ (DET) + N′	
m.	N′	→ N′ + S′	[optional]
n.	N′	→ N′ + PP	[optional]
o.	N′	→ QP + N′	[optional]
p.	N′	→ AdjP + N′	[optional]
q.	N′	→ N + (PP) + (PP) + (PP)	
r.	AdvP	→ (DEG) + Adv′	
s.	Adv′	→ ADV	
t.	QP	→ (DEG) + Q′	
u.	Q′	→ Q + (PP)	

The rules in (5.13d) and (5.13e) introduce adjuncts into the VP, while the rule in (5.13f) introduces arguments. Within the NP, rules (5.13m), (5.13o) and (5.13p) license modifiers, rule (5.13n) introduces adjuncts, and rule (5.13q) introduces arguments (cf. (3.13b) with three PP arguments within an NP).

All of the PS-rules discussed thus far have been formulated for right-branching languages. PS-rules for left-branching languages like Lezgian, Telugu, Tindi, Japanese, Lisu and Hindi would have the heads following their complements. Some of the left-branching counterparts to the PS-rules in (5.13) are given in (5.14).

(5.14) Some PS-rules for left-branching languages
a. S′ → S + (COMP)
b. S → NP + VP
c. VP → V′ + (AUX)
d. V′ → PP + V′ [optional]
e. V′ → AdvP + V′ [optional]
f. V′ → ({NP, PP, VP, S′}) + ({NP, PP}) + V
g. PP → P′
h. P′ → NP + P

These rules can specify the structures in Figures 4.19, 4.20, 4.22 and 4.24. They are basically the mirror images of the corresponding rules in (5.13), and this highlights again the usefulness of the ID/LP format. If the rules in (5.13) were written in this format, then they could apply equally to right-branching and left-branching languages; the difference in branching direction would be captured in the LP rules.

PS-rules have an important property, namely that of **recursion**. This is the property of having an instance of a phrasal form class as a constituent within the same form class; in other words, it is the ability to embed a form class within a form class of the same type. Examples in the rules above are S′ within an S′, i.e. a complement clause as in Figure 4.21, a VP within a VP, i.e. an infinitival complement as in Figure 4.23, or an NP within an PP within an NP, as in Figure 4.14. The rules in (5.13) can apply repeatedly until all instances of a phrasal constituent have been expanded (or evaluated as possible). In practice, this means that rules (5.13a)–(5.13q) are applied once, and then one goes back to the first rule that applies again and start the process of rewriting (or checking) over again.

This can be illustrated with respect to the sentence in Figure 4.21, repeated in a slightly modified form in Figure 5.7.

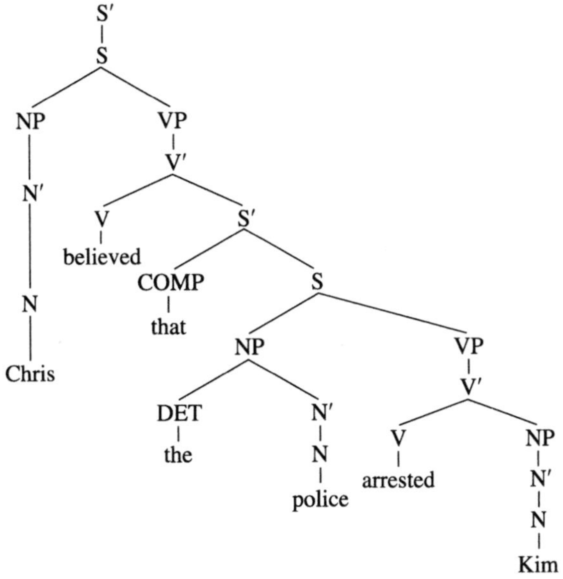

Figure 5.7. *English object complement (embedded S′)*

Since the first rule in (5.13) is 'S′ → (COMP) + S', sentences will be represented as having an S′ node, even if they are main clauses or have no complementizer if embedded. The reason why many linguists assume this to be the case will emerge in chapter 6. Rule (5.13a) licenses the first part of the tree, S′ immediately dominating S, and (5.13b) licenses the next part, S immediately dominating NP and VP. There is no tensed auxiliary verb, nor are there any AdvP or PP modifiers; hence the next two rules are irrelevant to this example. Non-branching X-bar structure which does not immediately dominate the head of any of the lexical categories is not represented in the tree. Hence rules like (5.13d), (5.13e), (5.13h), (5.13m), (5.13n), (5.13o), (5.13p) are optional. The next relevant rule is (5.13f), the one introducing the non-subject arguments of the verb; one of its possibilities is V′ → V + S′, which licenses the structure in Figure 5.7. Note that it introduces S′, the **start symbol** of the first rule, (5.13a). This, then, is an example of recursion. The only other rules pertinent to the first pass through the rules are those concerning the NP in (5.13l)–(5.13q). Thus, at the end of the first application of the rules in (5.13), the structure in Figure 5.8 has been specified.

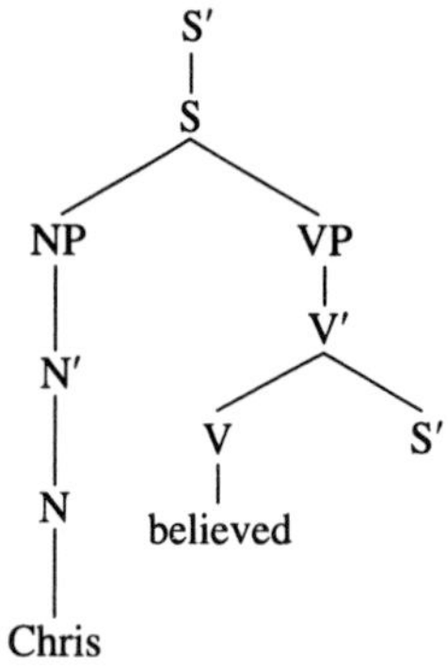

Figure 5.8. *Result of first application of PS-rules in (5.13)*

It is irrelevant whether the rules in (5.13) are conceived of as rewrite rules or as node-admissibility conditions. From the point of view of rewrite rules, only these nodes have been rewritten and this much structure specified. In terms of node-admissibility conditions, only this much of the structure in Figure 5.7 has been checked or evaluated by the rules so far.

Since S′ has been encountered, it is necessary to go back to (5.13a) and go through the rules again. The rule in (5.13a) licenses the COMP + S structure immediately dominated by S′, while the one in (5.13b) provides the basic NP–VP division of the sentence. As in the main clause, the only V′-rule that is applicable is (5.13f), which specifies V + NP as possible. The only other relevant rules are (5.13l) and (5.13q), which license the structure of the two NPs in the sentence. The result of the second application of the PS-rules in (5.13) is the complete tree structure in Figure 5.7.

It should be noted that in principle, all of the PS-rules can be conceived of as checking an entire structure at once. However, when a linguist checks a structure, it has to be done in a temporal sequence. The discussion has taken this practical perspective.

S′ is not the only node that can trigger an additional pass through the rules. In a sentence like *Dana told Pat to open the window* (the structure is given in Figure 4.21), the embedded VP *to open the window* will likewise trigger a second application of the rules, starting with the rule in (5.13c). Consider the VP structure in Figure 5.9 below.

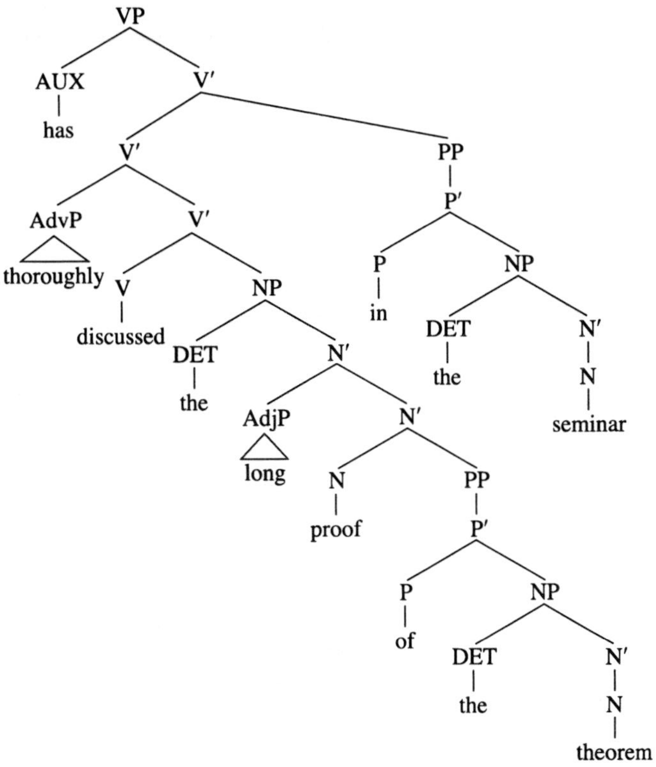

Figure 5.9. *English VP containing NP with embedded PP*

In order to specify this VP, rules (5.13c), (5.13d), (5.13e) and (5.13f) must apply, and the PP rules in (5.13j) and (5.13k) expand the PP licensed by (5.13d). There are two NPs in the structure, *the seminar* and *the long proof of the theorem*, and they are specified by the NP rules in (5.13l), (5.13p) and (5.13q). The application of (5.13q) licenses the PP *of the theorem*, and because the PP rules have already been applied, it is necessary to go through the rules again, starting with (5.13j). The second application of the rules in (5.13j)–(5.13q) yields the internal structure of the PP and the NP it contains. Because embedding is a pervasive feature of natural languages, it is necessary for the rules specifying syntactic structure to be recursive, in order to capture this important property of human language.

None of the PS-rules proposed so far can specify coordinate structures like those discussed in (4.35) and Figure 4.17. A special rule for coordination is required, which licenses the general schema for coordination presented in Figure 4.18, and it is given in (5.15).

(5.15) PS-rule for coordination
$$X^{n} \rightarrow X^{n}_{1} + \ldots + CONJ + X^{n}_{m}$$

As noted in chapter 4, '^{n}' is a variable ranging over the bar levels; the Xs on both sides of the rule must have the same bar level. The '. . .' means that there can be any number of X^{n}s in the coordinate structure; the subscripts '1' and 'm' indicate simply that there can be an in principle unlimited number of conjuncts, with 'm' being 2 or higher (the minimum number of conjuncts is two). In English the conjunction is not optional, as it is in some other languages.

The rules in (5.13) and (5.15) thus represent a significant part of a phrase-structure grammar of English. Complementing syntactic rules like these is the lexicon, the storehouse of words and morphemes in the language. It is the topic of the next section.

5.2 The lexicon and subcategorization

PS-rules specify tree structures, but what determines which words or morphemes will occupy which positions in the tree? In particular, what determines the correct cooccurrence of words in a sentence? Consider the following three V′s.

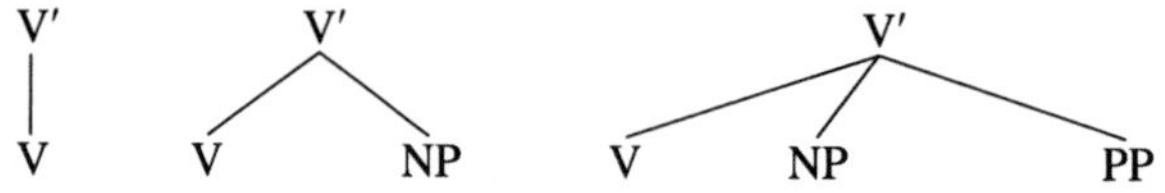

(a) (b) (c)

Figure 5.10. *Three possible English V′s*

How does one guarantee that verbs like *die* and *disappear* occur in (a) but not (b) or (c), that verbs like *own* or *devour* occur in (b) but not (a) or (c), and that verbs like *put* occur in (c) but not (a) or (b)? In other words, what rules out the following ungrammatical sentences?

(5.16) a. The frog died.
b. *The frog died the cat.
c. *The frog died the cat to the mouse.

(5.17) a. *The cat devoured.
b. The cat devoured the mouse.
c. *The cat devoured the mouse to the frog.

(5.18) a. *The boy put.
b. *The boy put the magazine.
c. The boy put the magazine on the table.

The (a) sentences have the (a) V′ in Figure 5.10, the (b) sentences have the (b) V′, and the (c) sentences have the (c) V′. The V′ in (a) is that of an intransitive verb, and accordingly intransitive verbs like *die* and *disappear* should occur in it but transitive and other verbs should not. It is possible to formulate an informal principle to the effect that intransitive verbs should occur in V′s like (a), transitive verbs in V′s like (b), and transitive verbs with a PP in V′s like (c). How would such a principle be realized formally in the kind of grammar developed in the previous section?

The first step is categorizing verbs as intransitive, transitive, etc. This information is represented in the **lexical entry** for each verb in the lexicon. The lexical entry for a **lexical item** like a verb contains phonological, semantic and syntactic information about it. The phonological information is its phonological representation. The morphological form of the lexical item in its lexical entry is the uninflected stem; hence, for example, the English verb *talk*, the form in the lexical entry would be *talk* and not *talks, talking* or *talked.* The semantic information includes its argument structure, e.g. <Patient> for *die* or <Agent Theme Recipient> for *donate* (see section 2.1). The syntactic information specifies the syntactic environment in which it occurs. What is distinctive with respect to verbs is the range of possible sisters under the immediately dominating V′, as in Figure 5.10. This is called the **subcategorization frame** of the verb, and examples of subcategorization information for *die, devour* and *put* are given in (5.19).

(5.19) Subcategorization frames for some English verbs

a. *die*	$[_{V'}\ \_\_\ ]$
b. *devour*	$[_{V'}\ \_\_\ \mathrm{NP}]$
c. *put*	$[_{V'}\ \_\_\ \mathrm{NP\ PP}]$

The '__' indicates the position occupied by the verb; in the subcategorization frame for a verb from a left-branching language, e.g. Lezgian *aku* 'see' in (4.37a), it would be at the right margin of the V′, i.e. $[_{V'}\ \mathrm{NP}\ \_\_\ ]$. The frame in (5.19a) specifies that *die* occurs in a V′ without any sister NPs; in other words, *die* is an intransitive verb. The one in (5.19b) states that *devour* occurs in a V′ with a sister NP, that is, it is a transitive verb, and the one in (5.19c) indicates that *put* occurs in a V′ with a sister NP and a sister PP. If the subcategorization frames are combined with argument-structure information, the result is the partial lexical entries given in (5.20) and (5.21), which are for the verbs in the Lezgian examples in (2.12). If an argument is represented in the semantic argument structure of the verb and it would not be the subject, then it must be in the verb's syntactic subcategorization frame. The correlation between syntactic subcategorization and semantic argument structure can be represented by subscripts.

(5.20) Partial lexical entries for some English verbs

a. *die*	$[_{V'}\ \_\_\ ]$ <Patient>
b. *devour*	$[_{V'}\ \_\_\ \mathrm{NP}_1]$ <Agent Patient$_1$>
c. *put*	$[_{V'}\ \_\_\ \mathrm{NP}_1\ \mathrm{PP}_2]$ <Agent Theme$_1$ Location$_2$>

(5.21) Partial lexical entries for the Lezgian verbs in (2.12)

a. *gišin-* 'hungry'	$[_{V'}\ \_\_\ ]$ <Experiencer>
b. *agaq'-* 'reach'	$[_{V'}\ \mathrm{NP}_1\ \_\_\ ]$ <Theme Goal$_1$>
c. *aku-* 'see'	$[_{V'}\ \mathrm{NP}_1\ \_\_\ ]$ <Experiencer Stimulus$_1$>
d. *kx̂e-* 'write'	$[_{V'}\ \mathrm{NP}_1\ \_\_\ ]$ <Agent Patient$_1$>

In (5.20b), the identical subscripts on 'NP' and 'Patient' signal that the NP which is the sister to the V under the V′ is semantically a patient. Similarly, in (5.20c) the identical subscripts indicate that the NP which is the sister to the V under the V′ is semantically a theme and that the NP in the PP is semantically a recipient. The unsubscripted thematic relation is that of the subject. The same is true in the partial lexical entries for some Lezgian verbs in (5.21). This is only one way of expressing the relationship between the syntactic subcategorization properties of a verb and its semantic argument structure. Syntactic theories differ substantially with respect to how they capture this relationship, and it will be one of the topics to be explored in chapter 6.

The informal principle constraining the occurrence of verbs can now be made more precise as in (5.22).

(5.22) The subcategorization principle
A verb (or other lexical head) can only occur in a syntactic environment which matches its subcategorization frame.

The subcategorization frame in (5.19a) matches the V′ in (a) but not in (b) or (c) in Figure 5.10, and therefore *die* can only occur in (a), following the subcategorization principle. Hence the sentences in (5.16b) and (5.16c) are ungrammatical because they violate this principle. The frame in (5.19b) matches the V′ in (b) but not in (a) or (c) in Figure 5.10, and accordingly *devour* can only occur in (b). Finally, the frame in (c) matches the V′ in (c) but not in (a) or (b), and consequently *put* can only occur in (c). Thus, subcategorization information in the lexical entries for verbs plus the subcategorization principle in (5.22) provides an answer to the question raised at the beginning of this section and accounts for the ungrammaticality of the starred sentences in (5.16)–(5.18).

Subcategorization frames in languages like English do not contain any information regarding subjects or adjuncts. This is because 'having a subject' is not a distinctive property of verbs; all verbs take a subject, and accordingly what is distinctive is whether they take a sister NP or sister NP + PP, etc. However, this crucially presupposes that the language has a VP, which structurally distinguishes the subject from the sisters to the verb. In non-configurational languages like Kwakwala, Lakhota and Dyirbal, which lack a VP, the subject is a sister to the verb and therefore must be included in the verb's subcategorization frame. Partial lexical entries for the Kwakwala verb *yəlkʷəmas-* 'hurt' in (4.19a), the Lakhota verb *naxʔų* 'hear' in (4.20b), and the Dyirbal verb *buṛal* 'see' in (2.98) are given in (5.23).

(5.23) Partial lexical entries for verbs from non-configurational languages
a. *yəlkʷəmas-* 'hurt' [$_S$ __ NP$_1$ NP$_2$ (NP$_3$)]
<Agent$_1$ Patient$_2$ (Instrument$_3$)>
b. *naxʔų* 'hear' [$_S$ (NP$_1$) (NP$_2$) AFF$_2$+AFF$_1$+__]
<Experiencer$_1$ Stimulus$_2$>
c. *buṛal* 'see' [$_S$ NP$_1$, NP$_2$, __]
<Experiencer$_1$ Stimulus$_2$>

Lakhota and Dyirbal present two interesting twists. Lakhota is a head-marking language, and in (4.20b) the clause consists of a single phonological word, *nawíčhaxʔų* 'she/he heard them'. The arguments are realized by the bound markers on the verb, and therefore they are what are represented in the subcategorization frame ('AFF'). For sentences with overt NPs like (4.20a), the NPs are represented as optional in the lexical entry. In a Dyirbal clause with a transitive verb, the three elements can occur in any order, and therefore the ID/LP format is most appropriate for rendering the subcategorization properties of Dyirbal verbs; in (5.23c), NP_1, NP_2 and V are unordered with respect to each other. The same would be true with respect to Russian verbs (see (1.2), (4.47)).

Adjuncts are always optional and can occur with virtually any verb, and therefore they too are not distinctive. In the phrase-structure trees in chapter 4, both the subject and any adjuncts are outside of the V′ headed by the verb; it contains the distinctive subcategorization information. As discussed in section 3.1.2, the distinction between arguments and adjuncts is not always obvious. Consider the status of instrumental PPs, as in the English examples in (3.8), repeated below.

(5.24) a. The boy broke the window (with a rock).
a′. The rock broke the window.
b. The girl ate the pasta (with a fork).
b′. *The fork ate the pasta.

The *with*-PPs are optional in both (5.24a) and (5.24b), but there is nevertheless a big difference between them: the instrumental argument can be subject with a transitive verb like *break* but not with one like *eat*, as the examples in (5.24a′) and (5.24b′) show. As argued in chapter 3, the fact that *the rock* can be the subject in (5.24a′) indicates that it must be an argument of the transitive verb *break*, whereas *a fork* is an adjunct with *eat*. Partial lexical entries for these two verbs are given in (5.25).

(5.25) a. *break* $[_{V'}$ __ NP_1 $(PP_2)]$
<(Agent) $Patient_1$ $(Instrument_2)$>
If the agent is unrealized, the instrument is obligatory.
b. *eat* $[_{V'}$ __ $NP_1]$
<Agent $Patient_1$>

Another piece of evidence in favor of the argument status of the instrument with *break* and its adjunct status with *eat* is that the *with*-PP is possible with *eat* regardless of whether it is transitive or intransitive (*The girl ate with a fork*), but it is impossible with *break* when it is intransitive (**The window broke with the rock*). The fact that the instrument is the subject when the agent is unrealized follows from the hierarchy in (2.20a).

What about adjuncts in languages lacking VP? Because Kwakwala has no VP, for example, the argument–adjunct contrast cannot be signalled syntactically by having adjuncts being daughters of higher V′s as in configurational languages like English and Malagasy. Rather, since all XPs in a clause are sisters of V, adjuncts will be those XPs not included in the argument structure of the verb, and because they are not in the verb's argument structure, they will not be included in its subcategorization frame.

Lexical heads from all lexical categories have subcategorization information in their lexical entries, and it is restricted to information about potential sisters under the immediately dominating X′ in configurational languages. In this discussion, the focus will be exclusively on verbs.

Verbs which take infinitival complements or *that*-clauses would have them specified in their subcategorization frame. Examples are given in (5.26) from English and (5.27) from Lisu and Tindi, which are left-branching languages.

(5.26) a. Chris forced Pat to open the window. $[_{V'}$ __ NP VP]
b. Dana believes that Pat opened the window. $[_{V'}$ __ S′]
c. Kim convinced Leslie that Pat opened the window. $[_{V'}$ __ NP S′]

(5.27) a. *tsɨ́* 'remember' (in (4.37)) $[_{V'}$ S __] Lisu
b. *q'očā* 'want' (in (4.38)) $[_{V'}$ VP __] Tindi

Some verbs have more than one subcategorization frame, as illustrated in (5.28).

(5.28) a. Chris ate pizza. $[_{V'}$ __ NP]
a′. Chris ate. $[_{V'}$ __]
b. Kim gave the picture to Pat. $[_{V'}$ __ NP PP]
b′. Kim gave Pat the picture. $[_{V'}$ __ NP NP]
c. Kim convinced Leslie that Pat opened the window. $[_{V'}$ __ NP S′]
c′. Kim convinced Leslie to open the window. $[_{V'}$ __ NP VP]

The transitivity alternation with *eat* is usually described in terms of the direct object being optional, and this can be represented in the lexical entry by putting the NP in the subcategorization frame in parenthesis, i.e. $[_{V'}$ __ (NP)]. Verbs like *convince* could be handled by specifying S′ and VP as alternatives, i.e. $[_{V'}$ __ NP {S′, VP}]. The problem posed by verbs like *give* is more significant, because the mapping between thematic relations and syntactic arguments is different in the two forms, as shown in section 2.2.2.2, and different theories propose different solutions to it; it will be discussed in chapter 6 as part of the discussion of syntactic theories and the role of the lexicon in them.

The lexical entry for a verb contains information about its phonological, morphosyntactic and semantic properties, and these properties are often idiosyncratic to the particular verb, e.g. its phonological shape, its meaning. When a verb has a grammatically significant idiosyncratic feature, it may be represented in its lexical entry as well. Consider the following three German verbs.

(5.29) a. Die Frau hat den Mann gesehen. German
the.FSGNOM woman has the.MSGACC man seen
'The woman saw the man.'
b. Die Frau hat den Männer-n geholfen.
the.FSGNOM woman has the.MPLDAT men-DAT helped
'The woman helped the men.'
c. Die Frau hat ihr-es tot-en Vater-s
the.FSGNOM woman has 3SGF.POSS-GEN dead-MSGGEN father-GEN
gedacht.
remembered
'The woman reverently remembered her dead father.'

Regular transitive verbs in German take accusative direct objects, as with *sehen* 'see' in (5.29a) and in the examples in exercise 2 in chapter 2. Nominative and accusative case marking are handled by the rules in (4.40), which refer to phrase-structure configurations. A small number of verbs are irregular and take a dative or genitive second argument, e.g. *helfen* 'help' in (5.29b) and *gedenken* 'remember reverently' in (5.29c). How could one account for this in a grammar of German? One possibility would be to indicate the case irregularity in the lexical entry for each verb. This is illustrated in (5.30).

(5.30) a. *sehen* 'see' [$_{V'}$ NP$_1$ __]
<Experiencer Stimulus$_1$>

b. *helfen* 'help' [$_{V'}$ NP$_1$ __]
<Agent Patient$_1$>
[DAT]

c. *gedenken* 'remember reverently' [$_{V'}$ NP$_1$ __]
<Experiencer Stimulus$_1$>
[GEN]

The case feature is assigned to the semantic argument in the argument structure. One reason for doing this is that when verbs like this passivize, the argument retains its idiosyncratic case, even though it may no longer be VP-internal, as in (5.31).

(5.31) a. Den Männer-n wurde von der Frau geholfen.
the.MplDAT men-DAT became by the.FSGDAT woman helped
'The men were helped by the woman.'

b. Ihr-es tot-en Vater-s wurde gedacht.
the.FSGPOSS-GEN dead-MSGGEN father-GEN became remembered
'Her dead father was remembered reverently.'

The patient of *helfen* 'help' appears in the dative case and the stimulus of *gedenken* 'remember reverently' appears in the genitive case in the passive, and this is readily accounted for by specifying that this argument bears a special case regardless of its syntactic position. Case features in a lexical entry like those in (5.30) override (or take precedence over) the general case-marking rules in the language, for example, those like (4.40).

In section 2.1 verbs in Avar and Lezgian were discussed which take dative and locative arguments. The examples in (2.11) from Avar showed that regular transitive verbs take ergative agents and absolutive patients, that perception and cognition verbs take their perceiver and cognizer arguments in the locative case, and that emotion verbs take their experiencer in the dative case. The sentences in (2.12) from Lezgian showed that while agents and patients with transitive verbs appear in the ergative and absolutive cases, just as in Avar, perception, cognition, emotion and internal-experience verbs take their experiencer in the dative case. Partial lexical entries for the Lezgian verbs were presented in (5.21). Is the mechanism of case features tied to thematic relations the appropriate way of handling the situation in Avar and Lezgian? Should a dative-case feature be attached to the experiencer arguments with *gišin-* 'hungry' in (5.21a) and *aku-* 'see' in (5.21c)? Should a locative case feature be attached to the perceiver argument in the lexical entry of the Avar verb *wix̄-* 'see' in (2.11b)? While this is certainly a possible approach, it suffers from the following serious drawback. In German only a handful of verbs take dative or genitive second arguments; it is not a general pattern in the language. In Avar and Lezgian, on the other hand, these case patterns are not idiosyncratic properties of handfuls of verbs; rather, perceiver and cognizer arguments in Avar normally appear in the locative case, while experiencer arguments in Lezgian normally bear dative case. Hence assigning a case feature to every lexical entry in these languages which has an experiencer, perceiver or cognizer argument would be missing important generalizations about case marking in the languages. In order to express these generalizations, case-marking rules like the following would be needed.

(5.32) a. Some case rules in Avar:
1. Perceivers and cognizers carry locative case.
2. Experiencers of emotion verbs carry dative case.
b. A case rule in Lezgian:
Experiencers carry dative case.

These rules would operate in addition to the general rules assigning ergative and absolutive case. Thus there seem to be two kinds of case rules: rules like those in (4.40) which assign nominative and accusative case or ergative and absolutive case and which are based on phrase-structure configurations, and those like the ones in (5.32) which are based on thematic relations. One may therefore distinguish between 'structural case' (as in (4.40)) and 'semantic case' (as in (5.32)). As with case features, the semantic case rules take precedence over the structural case rules.

This brings us back to a problem raised in section 4.5 regarding the phrase-structure-based treatment of dative and instrumental case. It was noted there that there was no obvious structural way to distinguish the NP receiving accusative case from one receiving dative case if both were sisters to V, as in Figure 4.29, or to distinguish the NP receiving dative case from one receiving instrumental case if they were sisters to V′, as in Figure 4.30. The distinction between structural case and semantic case provides a possible solution. If, in Russian, all recipients received dative case and all instruments received instrumental case, then rules analogous to (5.32b) could be proposed to handle dative and instrumental case assignment in Russian. In a structure like Figure 4.29, the structural case rules would assign nominative to the NP immediately dominated by S and accusative to both NPs which are sisters of the verb. However, the semantic case rule for recipients ('Recipients carry dative case') would override the structural rule and ensure that the recipient, in this instance *ženščin-* 'woman', appears in the dative case. The same kind of rule would make sure that *karandaš-* 'pencil' occurs in the instrumental case in (4.44). Hence in phrase-structure based grammars, the distinction between structural and semantic case is very important.

5.3 Relational-dependency rules and lexicon

In chapter 3 dependency grammar was introduced, along with a way of representing the dependencies among the elements in a sentence. Dependency grammarians have typically not proposed rules specifying dependency structures the way phrase-structure-oriented syntacticians have postulated phrase-structure rules as in section 5.1, but it is possible to formulate such rules. They would need to specify three things: heads, the dependents (if any) of the head, and the grammatical relation or dependency holding between the head and its dependent(s). In place of the '$\rightarrow$' of PS-rules, '$\Rightarrow$' meaning 'has as unilateral dependent(s)' and '⇛' meaning 'has as bilateral dependent(s)' can be used in the relational-dependency rules [RD-rules]. Examples of some RD-rules for English are given in (5.33).

(5.33) Some RD-rules for English (preliminary formulation)
a. V ⇛ N_{SUBJ}, (N_{DOBJ}), (N_{OBJ2}), (P_{IOBJ}), (P_{OBL})
b. V $\Rightarrow$ (P(s)), (ADV(s))
c. P ⇛ N
d. N $\Rightarrow$ (DET), (Q) (ADJ(s)), (P(s))

There is nothing corresponding to a V′ in a relational-dependency representation, and the distinction between arguments and adjuncts for English emerges from the contrast between bilateral and unilateral dependencies. Because English is a dependent-marking language, the verb and its arguments are in a bilateral dependence, but adjuncts, which are always optional, are in a unilateral dependence with the verb. Accordingly, the rule in (5.33a) specifies the arguments of the verb, while the one in (5.33b) introduces adjuncts.

These rules specify only the dependents of the heads but not their linear sequence; that would be given by a separate set of LP-rules, analogous to those discussed in section 5.1., e.g. SUBJ > V > DOBJ > IOBJ > OBL for English. The relational-dependency representation of the English sentence *A girl handed a blue toy to the baby* given in Figure 3.2 can be specified by these rules. Figure 3.2 is repeated below, in Figure 5.11.

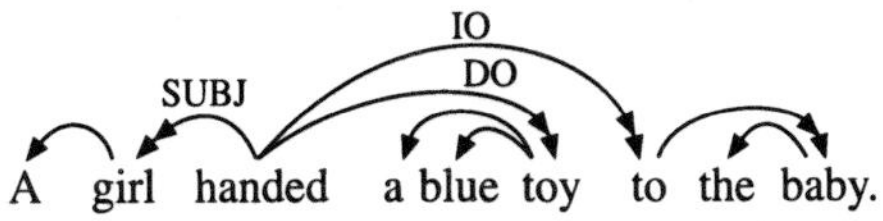
IO
SUBJ
DO
A girl handed a blue toy to the baby.

Figure 5.11. *Relational-dependency representations of English sentence*

The verb *handed* is the head of the clause, and it takes a number of term dependents. They are listed in its lexical entry as its subcategorization frame. However, because this is a relational-dependency grammar, not a phrase-structure grammar, the subcategorization information must be stated in relational, not phrase-structure, terms. Consequently, the verb is subcategorized on the basis of the dependents specified in RD-rule (5.33a), which involves bilateral dependencies only. This means that the subject is included in the subcategorization frame, since it is a relational 'sister' to the verb just like the direct object and other objects. Hence the subcategorization frame for the verb *hand*, along with those for *die*, *devour*, and *put* would be as in (5.34).

(5.34) Relational subcategorization frames for some English verbs

a. *die*	[N_{SUBJ}]
b. *devour*	[N_{SUBJ} N_{DOBJ}]
c. *hand*	[N_{SUBJ} N_{DOBJ} P_{IOBJ}], [N_{SUBJ} N_{DOBJ} N_{OBJ2}]
d. *put*	[N_{SUBJ} N_{DOBJ} P_{OBL}]

The subcategorization principle in (5.22) applies in a relational-dependency grammar, just as in a phrase-structure grammar. In the lexicon for a phrase-structure grammar, the subcategorization frames for *hand* and *put* would be the same, i.e. [$_{V'}$ __ NP PP], but they are not identical in terms of relational subcategorization, because the grammatical relations of the NP in the PP are not the same with the two verbs; it is an indirect object with *hand* but an oblique object with *put*.

Girl, *toy* and *to* in Figure 5.11 are licensed by the rule in (5.33a); there are no adjuncts in the sentence. The object of *to*, *baby*, is specified by the rule in (5.33c), which states that a preposition may have a noun as a bilateral dependent. Finally, the modifiers of the three nouns are licensed by the rule in (5.33d), which specifies the modifiers as being unilateral dependents of the head nouns. Thus, each dependency represented by an arrow in Figure 5.11 is a function of one of the RD-rules in (5.33), just as each level of X-bar structure in a phrase-structure tree is a function of a PS-rule.

The RD-rules in (5.33) permit combinations of terms and non-terms that do not in fact occur in English, e.g. *subject + secondary object + indirect object. How are impossible combinations ruled out? The answer is: they are ruled out by the subcategorization principle. There could only be a sentence containing a subject, secondary object and indirect object in English if there were a verb which was subcategorized for this set of terms. But no such English verb exists, and consequently the ungrammaticality of this combination follows from the subcategorization principle. The same holds for a phrase-structure grammar as well. The impossible combinations allowed by rule (5.10) would be excluded because there is no English verb with a subcategorization frame matching such combinations, e.g. *V + PP + AdjP or *V + PP + NP.

The distinction between unilateral and bilateral dependencies shows up in the typological contrast between head-marking and dependent-marking languages discussed in chapter 3 (see Table 3.4 for summary). Swahili is a head-marking language, and the RD-rules specifying clause structure for it will be rather different from those for English, a dependent-marking language. The Swahili example in (5.35) is a slightly simplified version of (3.16); the noun modifiers have been omitted, as their dependence on the head is the same as in English (unilateral).

(5.35) Wa-tu wa-na-vi-nunua vi-ti duka-ni. Swahili
2-person 2-PRES-8-buy 8-chair store-18
'The people are buying the chairs in the store.'

This sentence contains two terms, the subject *watu* 'people' and the direct object *viti* 'chairs', and an adjunct, *dukani* 'in the store'. A relational-dependency representation for (5.35) is given in Figure 5.12.

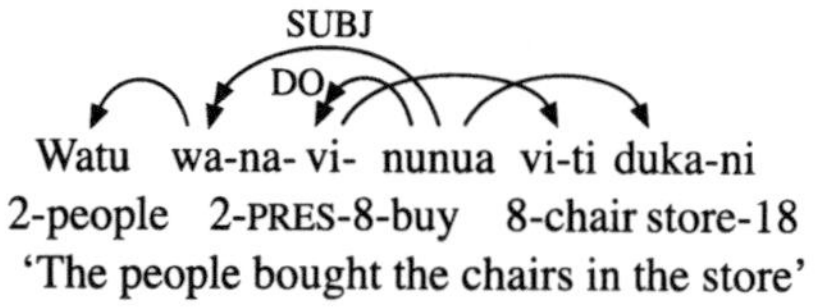
SUBJ
DO
Watu wa-na- vi- nunua vi-ti duka-ni
2-people 2-PRES-8-buy 8-chair store-18
'The people bought the chairs in the store'

Figure 5.12. *Relational-dependency representation of (5.35)*

It was pointed out in section 3.1.3 that in head-marked constructions only the head may occur; the dependents are options. Hence the obligatory part of (5.35) is *wanavinunua* 'they are buying them', and in order for the verb to constitute a complete sentence it must bear subject and, if appropriate, direct object affixes. These affixes, *wa-* 'class 2' and *-vi-* 'class 8', are therefore in a bilateral dependence with the verb. The independent NPs *watu* 'people' and *viti* 'chairs' are licensed by these affixes on the verb, and accordingly they are in a unilateral relationship with them. Finally, the adjunct *dukani* 'in the store' modifies the whole clause, and consequently it is in a unilateral dependence with the head of the clause, the verb. These are the dependencies that are represented in Figure 5.12. RD-rules specifying them are given in (5.36).

(5.36) Some RD-rules for Swahili
a. V $\Rrightarrow$ AFF_{SUBJ}, $(\text{AFF}_{\text{DOBJ}})$
b. V $\Rightarrow$ (N(s)), (P(s))
c. AFF $\Rightarrow$ (N)
d. P $\Rrightarrow$ N
e. N $\Rightarrow$ (DET), (ADJ(s))

The RD-rule in (5.36a) licenses the minimal Swahili clause, *wanavinunua* 'they are buying them'. The one in (5.36b) permits adjuncts to occur; in (5.35) the adjunct is a noun with a locative class suffix, but in earlier Swahili examples, e.g. (2.83), there are adjunct PPs. Independent nouns licensed by the argument-marking affixes on the verb are specified by RD-rule (5.36c). The rules for PPs and NPs are the same for both types of languages.

Thus, the typological contrast between dependent-marking languages, such as English, and head-marking languages, such as Swahili, emerges clearly from the differences in the RD-rules in (5.33) and (5.36) and is reflected in the difference between the RD-diagrams in Figures 5.11 and 5.12. This contrast is difficult to capture in purely phrase-structure terms. Clauses in English and Swahili would be assigned essentially the same structure, and the affixes on the verb would be treated as agreement by means of rules like (4.40a), which could be extended to include object agreement (i.e., 'The finite verb agrees in person, class and number with [NP, S] and [NP, V′]').

The RD-rules in (5.33) and (5.36) must be expanded to capture the structure of complex sentences. In order to make the rules recursive, it is necessary to introduce V as one of the dependents of the verb in (5.33a). A tentative reformulation of the rules is given in (5.37).

(5.37) Tentative reformulation of some RD-rules for English
a. V ⇛ N_{SUBJ}, (N_{DOBJ}), (V_{DOBJ}), (N_{OBJ2}), (V_{OBJ2}), (P_{IOBJ}), (P_{OBL})
b. V ⇛ (P(s)), (ADV(s))
c. P ⇛ N
d. N ⇛ (DET), (Q), (ADJ(s)), (P(s))

'V_{DOBJ}' licenses direct object clauses as in *Chris believed that the police arrested Kim*, and 'V_{OBJ2}' permits the occurrence of an infinitival complement as in *Dana told Pat to open the window*. There is an obvious redundancy in (5.37a): the rule licenses both N and V direct objects and secondary objects. It is also possible to have clauses or infinitives as subjects, as illustrated in (5.38).

(5.38) a. That the stock market kept going up surprised everyone.
b. To open the window now would be a terrible mistake.

The subject in (5.38a) is a *that*-clause, while the subject in (b) is an infinitive. It appears, then, that the grammatical relations of subject, direct object and secondary object can be realized by a construction headed by a noun or a verb. Rather than having both, for example, 'N_{DOBJ}' and 'V_{DOBJ}' in the RD-rules, which is redundant, it would be preferable to simply specify the grammatical relations and have a separate statement to the effect that the three grammatical relations can be instantiated by either noun-headed or verb-headed constructions. Thus the rule in (5.39a) replaces (5.33a) and (5.37a), and the statement in (b) permits nominal, clausal or infinitival realization of the relations specified in (a).

(5.39) a. V ⇛ SUBJ, (DOBJ), (OBJ2), (P_{IOBJ}), (P_{OBL})
b. SUBJ, DOBJ, OBJ2 = {N, V}

If a term is realized by a verb-headed construction, then the rules must apply recursively, in order to license the dependents of the verb in it.

This revision of the RD-rule in (5.33a) suggests that the subcategorization frames in (5.34) require revision as well. The primary change would be dropping the 'N' from the specification of the three grammatical relations of subject, direct object and secondary object. The revised subcategorization frames from (5.34) are given in (5.40), together with argument-structure information.

(5.40) Partial lexical entries for some English verbs

a. *die*	[SUBJ$_1$] <Patient$_1$>	
b. *devour*	[SUBJ$_1$ DOBJ$_2$] <Agent$_1$ Patient$_2$>	
c. *hand*	[SUBJ$_1$ DOBJ$_2$ P$_{IOBJ\text{-}3}$], <Agent$_1$ Theme$_2$ Recipient$_3$>,	[SUBJ$_1$ DOBJ$_2$ OBJ2$_3$] <Agent$_1$ Theme$_3$ Recipient$_2$>
d. *put*	[SUBJ$_1$ DOBJ$_2$ P$_{OBL\text{-}3}$] <Agent$_1$ Theme$_2$ Location$_3$>	

Basic case marking rules in an RD-grammar would refer directly to grammatical relations. Examples of basic rules for accusative and ergative systems are given in (5.41).

(5.41) RD-case marking rules

a. Accusative system
   1. SUBJ carries nominative case.
   2. DOBJ carries accusative case.
   3. IOBJ carries dative case.

b. Ergative system
   1. S, O carry absolutive case.
   2. A carries ergative case.
   3. IOBJ carries dative case.

Case determined by these rules would be the equivalent of structural case in a RD-grammar. Note that the problem of distinguishing direct from indirect object for case assignment does not arise in a RD-grammar. Rules for semantic case, to handle oblique objects of various kinds, for example instruments, locations, would be exactly like those in (5.32), and idiosyncratic case can be handled in terms of case features attached to thematic relations in lexical entries, as in (5.30).

For verbs which occur in both simple clauses and complex constructions, e.g. *try* (*Chris tried the window* versus *Chris tried to open the window*) or *tell* (*Kim told Dana a joke* versus *Kim told Dana to open the window*), these two possibilities can be handled by specifying in the lexical entry for the verb that a particular grammatical relation can be realized by a noun-headed or a verb-headed construction. This is illustrated in (5.42).

(5.42)	a. *try*	[SUBJ DOBJ]	DOBJ = {N, V}
	b. *tell*	[SUBJ DOBJ OBJ2]	OBJ2 = {N, V}

There is another possibility with *tell*, namely, a *that*-clause for the secondary object, as in *Kim told Dana that Pat opened the window.* Both *that*-clauses and infinitives are verb-headed constructions, and nothing in the information in (5.42) signals that both are possible with *tell* but only a VP is possible with *try.* The simplest way to express this contrast is by adding a syntactic feature, [±finite]; a [+finite] verb-headed construction would be a *that*-clause (even if the *that* happened to be omitted), while a [–finite] verb-headed construction would be an infinitival or participial (e.g. *Chris tried opening the window*) complement. Revised partial lexical entries for these verbs are given in (5.43).

(5.43) a. *try* [SUBJ DOBJ] DOBJ = {N, V [–finite]}
b. *tell* [SUBJ DOBJ OBJ2] OBJ2 = {N, V [±finite]}

It is necessary to add an RD-rule which permits markers of complement constructions, i.e. *to* with infinitives or *that* with clauses in English. Such a rule is given in (5.44).

(5.44) V ⇒ (CLM)

'CLM' stands for 'clause-linkage marker', and the dependence is unilateral: with complement clauses functioning as direct or secondary object, *that* is often omitted, and not all verbs which take an infinitival complement require *to*, e.g. *Chris made Pat (*to) leave, Kim saw Pat (*to) leave.* Verbs which require a clause-linkage marker on their complement could carry a feature [+CLM] along with [±finite]. A revised set of RD-rules for English is given in (5.45).

(5.45) Some RD-rules for English (revised)
a. V ⇛ SUBJ, (DOBJ), (OBJ2), (P_{IOBJ}), (P_{OBL})
b. V ⇒ (CLM), (P(s)), (ADV(s))
c. P ⇛ N
d. N ⇒ (DET), (Q), (ADJ(s)), (P(s))
e. SUBJ, DOBJ, OBJ2 = {N, V}

If the terms are all realized by noun-headed constructions, then the result is a simple clause. If any of them is instantiated by a verb-headed construction, then the rules apply recursively in order to license the embedded infinitive or clause. A relational-dependency diagram for *Dana told Pat to open the window* is presented in Figure 5.13. Because the secondary object is realized by an infinitive, (5.45a) applies again, licensing the direct object *the window.* The rule in (5.45b) also applies, specifying the clause-linkage marker, in this case *to.*

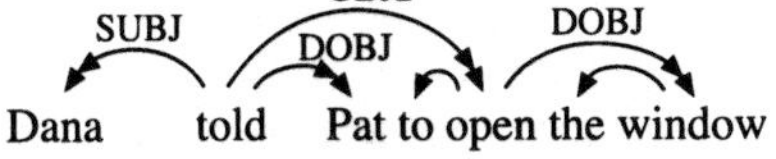

Figure 5.13. *Relational-dependency representation of infinitival complement*

In order to license a finite *that*-clause object complement like *Chris believed that the police arrested Kim,* the same rules would apply as in the previous example. However, the second application of (5.45a) would license both a subject and a direct object, and (5.45b) would permit the occurrence of *that.* The resulting diagram is given in Figure 5.14.

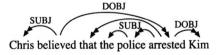

Figure 5.14. *Relational-dependency representation of* that-*clause complement*

Finally, it is necessary to add a rule licensing coordinate structures of the kind illustrated in Figure 3.7 from English. It is shown in (5.46).

(5.46) RD-rules for coordination
a. $X = X_1 \ldots \cup X_m$
b. $X_m \Rrightarrow$ CONJ

The first rule states that a head may be realized by any number of coordinated like heads, while the second specifies that the conjunction is in a bilateral relationship with the last of the coordinated heads. That the coordination is linked to the last element can be seen when three or more elements are coordinated, as in *Chris, Pat, Dana and Kim went to the beach*. The addition of these rules makes possible the following representations for *The boy and the girl sang* and *The boy cooked and ate the fish*, taken from Figure 3.7.

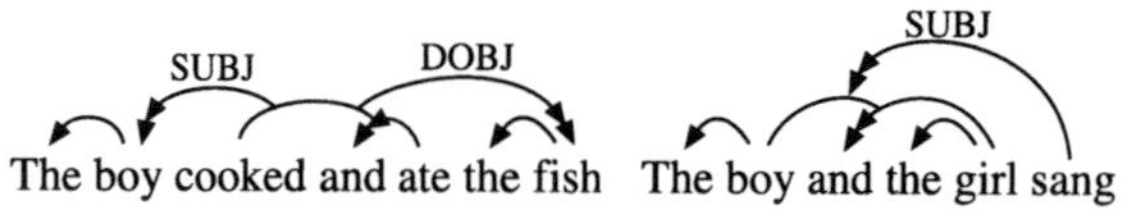
SUBJ
DOBJ
SUBJ
The boy cooked and ate the fish
The boy and the girl sang

Figure 5.15. *Revised representations for coordinate constructions*

The last element in the coordination is in a bilateral dependence with the conjunction *and*, and the two of them are in a coordinate dependence with the other member of the construction. The resulting coordinate N or V functions the same way as a single N or V in the sentence.

5.4 Concluding remarks

In this chapter rules which specify, or **generate**, the structures introduced in chapters 3 and 4 have been developed. They enable the analyst to formulate a grammar which expresses generalizations about the data under consideration. For the X-bar constituent structures of chapter 4, phrase-structure rules are used, and for the relational-dependency structures of chapter 3, relational-dependency rules are used. In addition to these syntactic rules, the notion of subcategorization information in the lexicon was introduced, in order to permit the expression of important syntactic properties of verbs and other lexical items. Subcategorization information is combined with the semantic argument-structure information from section 2.1 to create partial lexical entries for verbs.

PS- or RD-rules work together with the lexicon to make possible the specification of the syntactic structures in a language. There is more to a grammar than just PS- or RD-rules, however. In chapter 2 a number of principles governing different grammatical phenomena were formulated with reference to the grammatical relations hierarchy in (2.50), and in section 4.5 rules for subject-finite verb agreement, case marking, and reflexive antecedents were formulated in terms of constituent-structure configurations. Just how to formulate such rules and principles is one of the primary concerns of different syntactic theories, and in the next chapter the approaches to these phenomena taken by four syntactic theories will be presented. The purpose of the chapter is not to give comprehensive introductions to the theories; rather it is to show how the concepts and analytic constructs introduced in chapters 2 to 5 are combined in different ways in the various theoretical frameworks in the pursuit of a range of theoretical goals.

Notes and suggested readings

For discussion of phrase-structure rules, see Chomsky (1957, 1965), Jackendoff (1977), Gazdar (1982), Radford (1988) and Borsley (1996). McCawley (1968a) first proposed interpreting PS-rules as node admissibility conditions rather than as rewriting rules. On the ID/LP format for PS-rules, see Gazdar and Pullum (1981), Gazdar (1982), Gazdar, *et al.* (1985) and Borsley (1996). **Generalized Phrase Structure Grammar** [GPSG] is a theory which attempts to describe natural language syntax using a phrase structure grammar (Gazdar, *et al.* 1985). It introduced a number of innovations into syntactic theory, e.g. the ID/LP format for PS-rules, and it reinvigorated the study of the mathematical properties of natural languages. On subcategorization and the lexicon, see Chomsky (1965), Jackendoff (1972), Radford (1988) and the papers in Bresnan (1982a). For discussion of relational-dependency grammars similar to the one developed herein, see Vater (1975), Matthews (1982) and Hudson (1984, 1990).

Exercises

1. Write a phrase-structure grammar, using the format in (5.13), for the following Cantonese data (Matthews and Yip 1994). Treat classifiers (glossed 'CL') as a type of modifier under N′. Treat *ge* (glossed 'LNK') as a kind of specifier in the AdjP; a degree modifier would be a sister to the highest A′. Don't represent the aspect endings on the verbs in your rules. Draw tree structures for (3), (5) and (10). [section 5.1]

(1) Ngohdeih yám-jó hóu dō būi chàh.
1pl drink-PRFV very many CL tea
'We drank many cups of tea.'

(2) Kéuih sihk-jó leuhng wún faahn.
3sg eat-PRFV two CL rice
'She ate two bowls of rice.'

(3) Gó go léuihyán sung-jó nī sāam fan hóu leng ge láihmaht béi ngóh.
that CL woman send-PRFV this three CL very nice LNK gift to 1sg
'That woman sent these three very nice gifts to me.'

(4) Ngóh sung-jó leuhng fan láihmaht béi gó go léuihyán.
1sg send-PRFV two CL gift to that CL woman
'I sent two gifts to that woman.'

(5) Gó go nàahmyán hái nī gàan yīýn jouhsih.
that CL man at this CL hospital work
'That man works at this hospital.'

(6) Nī go léuihyán hái Yīnggwok yáuh pàhngyáuh.
this CL woman at England has friend
'This woman has friends in England.'

(7) Ngóh gwa gó leuhng fūk sān ge wá hái godouh.
1sg hang that two CL new LNK picture at there
'I'm hanging those two new pictures there.'

(8) Kéuih hái jáudim chēutbihn dáng ngóh.
3sg at hotel outside wait 1sg
'She awaits me outside the hotel.'

(9) Ngóh waih léih cheung séu gō.
1sg for 2sg sing CL song
'I'll sing a song for you.'

(10) Kéuih hái chyùhfóng fong-jó dō dī yéh hái tói seuhngmihn.
3sg in kitchen put-PRFV many CL thing at table top
'She put many things on the table in the kitchen.'

2. Reformulate the grammar developed in exercise 1 in the ID/LP format. [section 5.1]

3. Write a phrase-structure grammar, using the format in (5.13), for the following Malagasy data (Keenan 1976a). Formulate partial lexical entries for the verbs, giving the syntactic subcategorization frame only for each verb. Draw tree diagrams for (3) and (5). [section 5.2]

(1) Manasa ny lamba amin-ny savony ny vehivavy.
washes the clothes with-the soap the woman
'The woman washes the clothes with the soap.'

(2) Nahita ny vehivavy (izay) manasa ny lamba amin-ny savony Rasoa.
saw the woman (COMP) washes the clothes with-the soap
'Rasoa saw the woman who is washing the clothes.'

(3) Nahita Rasoa ny vehivavy (izay) manasa ny lamba amin-ny savony.
saw the woman (COMP) washes the clothes with the soap
'The woman who is washing the clothes with the soap saw Rasoa.'

(4) Toa manasa lamba Rasoa.
seem wash clothes
'Rasoa seems to be washing clothes.'

(5) Nanantena ny vehivavy ho nanasa ny zaza Rasoa.
hoped the woman COMP washed the child
'Rasoa hoped the woman to have washed the child.'

(6) Mikasa hanasa ny zaza ny vehivavy.
intends wash the child the woman
'The woman intends to wash the child.'

4. Reformulate the grammar developed in exercise 3 in the ID/LP format. [section 5.1]

5. Explain the ungrammaticality of the following English sentences. [section 5.2]

(1) *The bicycle which the boy did not put the car in the garage got wet in the rain.
(2) *Max slept the rock.
(3) *The businessman sent.
(4) *The book lay.

6. Formulate partial lexical entries for the verbs in the Cantonese sentences in exercise 1. Give the syntactic subcategorization frame and argument structure for each verb. [section 5.2]

7. Formulate a phrase-structure grammar for sentences (1)–(21) from Malayalam in exercise 3 from chapter 2. Use either the traditional or ID/LP format; is there any reason to prefer one over the other? Formulate case-marking rules and partial lexical entries for the verbs; give the syntactic subcategorization frame and argument structure for each verb. Explain how your grammar accounts for the grammaticality of (2′) and (15′) and the ungrammaticality of (3′), (6′), (7′) and (15″). Give tree diagrams for (2′), (4), and (9″). [section 5.2]

8. Formulate a relational-dependency grammar for the Cantonese data in exercise 1. Give both RD-rules, following the format in (5.45), and LP rules. Formulate partial lexical entries for

the verbs in RD-terms; give the syntactic subcategorization and argument structure for each verb. Draw RD-representations for (3), (5) and (10). [section 5.3]

9. Formulate a relational-dependency grammar for sentences (1)–(21) from Malayalam in exercise 3 from chapter 2. Give both RD-rules, following the format in (5.45), and LP rules. Formulate case-marking rules and partial lexical entries for the verbs in RD-terms; give the syntactic subcategorization and argument structure for each verb. Explain how your grammar accounts for the grammaticality of (2′) and (15′) and the ungrammaticality of (3′), (6′), (7′) and (15″). Give RD-representations for (2′), (4), and (9″). [section 5.3]

10. Having formulated phrase-structure and relational-dependency grammars for the data from Cantonese and Malayalam, compare the strengths and weaknesses of each approach. What problems arise in trying to apply one but not the other approach to a given set of data? Is there any reason to prefer one approach to the other? [section 5.3]

CHAPTER 6

Theories of syntax

6.0 Introduction

In the past four chapters the basic concepts and analytic tools employed in syntactic analysis have been introduced, and in this chapter the focus turns to theories of syntax. Every syntactic theory treats some concepts as being of central importance and others as being of lesser or no importance, and every theory likewise makes use of a unique set of analytic tools. The emphasis in this chapter is on different combinations of concepts and tools that are found in a variety of theories. This is not a comprehensive survey of contemporary theories; that is far beyond the scope of this book. Rather, the focus is on looking at four theories which exhibit distinct combinations of of the notions introduced in the previous chapters. The theories to be discussed are Relational Grammar [RelG], **Lexical-Functional Grammar** [LFG], the Government-Binding [GB] version of **Principles and Parameters** Theory, and Role and Reference Grammar [RRG].

The points of comparison among the theories are the following:

1. How syntactic structure is represented (relational structure only, constituent structure only or both)
2. How grammatical relations are treated
3. The role of the lexicon, including how subcategorization information is handled and the notion of argument structure assumed
4. Treatment of morphosyntactic phenomena (in simple sentences only)
   a. Case assignment and finite verb agreement
   b. Grammatical-relations-changing constructions such as passive and dative shift
   c. WH-question formation.

A brief summary of the theoretical goals of each framework will also be presented.

One thing all of these theories share is a commitment to being fully explicit and rigorous and to being a theory in which syntacticians can formulate grammars capable of accounting for all and only the grammatical sentences of the language under study. Such a grammar is called a **generative grammar**, and in this general sense, all of these theories are theories of generative grammar. (There is a narrower sense of the term which is associated primarily with Principles and Parameters theories.)

The discussion begins with RelG in section 6.1. The discussion then turns to LFG in section 6.2, to GB in section 6.3 and to RRG in section 6.4. A summary of the similarities and differences among the theories is presented in section 6.5, and in section 6.6 other contemporary theories are briefly discussed.

6.1 Relational Grammar

The fundamental question which RelG seeks to answer is typological in nature: 'in what ways do natural languages differ, and in what ways are they all alike?' (Perlmutter 1980: 195). A crucial part of the answer, from a RelG perspective, involves the grammatical relations subject, direct object and indirect object. They are **primitive** notions of the theory, in terms of which rules, principles and constraints are formulated; they are not derivative of any other concepts. Non-terms are labelled in terms of their semantic function, e.g. instrument, benefactive, locative, etc.

Clause structure is represented in terms of grammatical relations. This type of representation is called a 'relational network'. Its primary concern is the presentation of the grammatical relations in the sentence and not dependency relations in general. Example (3.15a) from Russian, repeated below in (6.1), would be given the relational network in Figure 6.1; in a relational network, grammatical relations are represented by numbers, with 1 = subject, 2 = direct object and 3 = indirect object, and 'P' stands for 'predicate'.

(6.1) a. Molod-aja učitel'nic-a da-l-a nov-uju Russian
young-FSGNOM teacher-FSGNOM give-PAST-FSg new-FSGACC
knig-u star-oj ženščin-e.
book-FSGACC old-FSGDAT woman-FSGDAT
b. Novuju knigu dala molodaja učitel'nica staroj ženščine.
c. Staroj ženščine novuju knigu dala molodaja učitel'nica.
d. The young teacher gave a/the new book to a/the old woman.

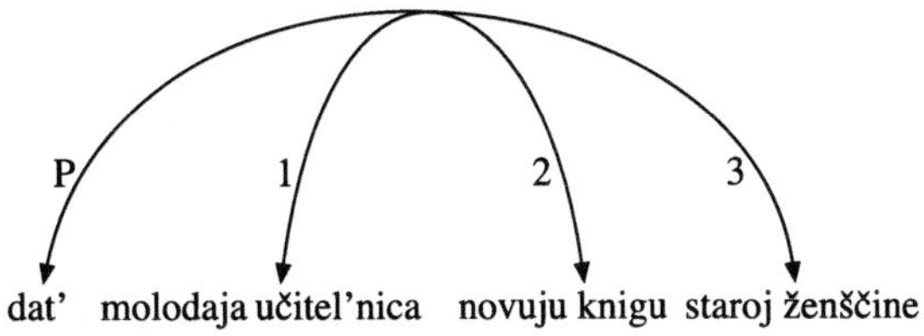

Figure 6.1. *Relational network of the Russian sentences in (6.1)*

(*Dat'* is the infinitive form of 'give' in Russian.) There would be one relational network for all of the word-order variants in (6.1), since the grammatical relations of the terms is the same in each sentence. The English translation in (6.1d) would have the same relational representation, as given in Figure 6.2.

A relational network is thus an abstract representation of the Russian and English sentences in (6.1). It does not represent the actual form of the sentences; this is clearest in the English example in Figure 6.2. Sentences with the same relational structure in different languages would get the same representation in RelG, despite the overt morphosyntactic differences among the languages, for example fixed versus free word order, occurrence versus lack of case marking on terms.

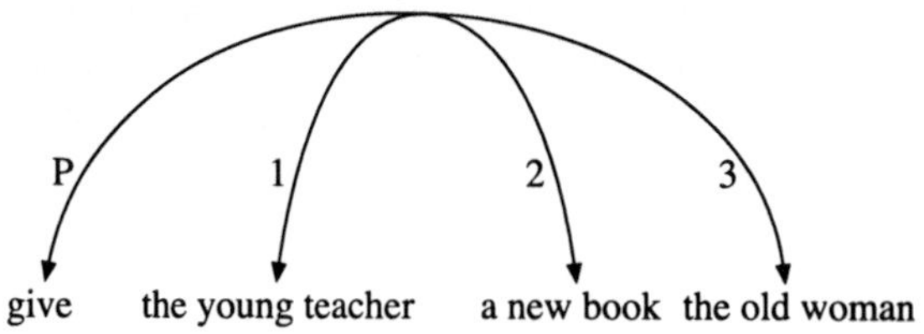

Figure 6.2. *Relational network for (6.1d)*

With respect to the lexicon, there has been little work explicitly done on it in RelG. Relational grammarians assume that there is a lexicon, containing lexical entries for verbs and other elements, and each lexical entry contains subcategorization information (stated relationally) together with a list of the verb's thematic relations, as in (5.40). The theory initially assumed a universal mapping between thematic relations and grammatical relations: agent to 1, patient or theme to 2, recipient to 3. This was known as the Universal Alignment Hypothesis (Perlmuter and Postal 1983, but see Rosen 1984).

Case assignment and finite verb agreement are stated in terms of grammatical relations. Rules for Russian to handle sentences like (6.1) are formulated in (6.2).

(6.2) Rules for case assignment and finite verb agreement

1. Case
   a. 1 receives nominative case.
   b. 2 receives accusative case.
   c. 3 receives dative case.
2. Finite verb agreement: the finite verb agrees with the 1 in e.g. person and number.

The exact agreement features would vary from language to language, and even within languages; in Russian, for example, in the present tense the verb agrees with the subject in person and number, while in the past tense it agrees in gender and number (contrast (4.43) with (4.46)). These rules would apply to Russian and any other language with a nominative–accusative case system and finite verb agreement with the subject.

WH-question formation is handled in a relatively simple manner. In a WH-question like *What did Pat buy?*, the WH-word *what* functions as the direct object (2) of the verb *buy*. In order to express this, the notion of 'overlay arc' is proposed in Perlmutter and Postal (1983); the question function can be overlaid over a more basic grammatical relation, yielding the relational network in Figure 6.3.

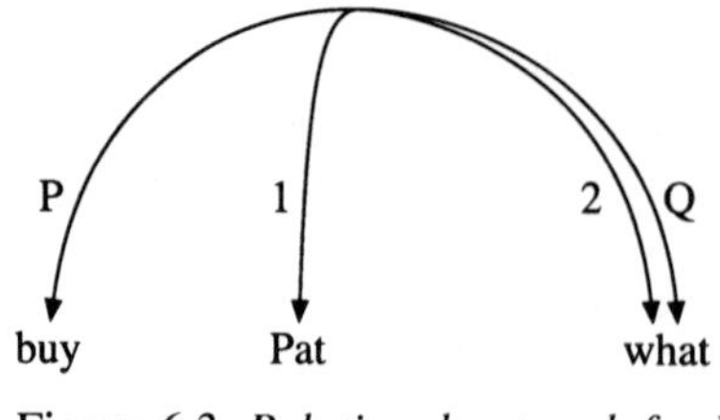

Figure 6.3. *Relational network for WH-question*

As noted earlier, this is a very abstract representation; the fact that WH-words appear in a special clause-initial position is not represented at all.

The analysis of grammatical-relations-changing phenomena like passive and dative shift is at the heart of RelG, and indeed the first major paper on the theory proposed a universal characterization of passive (Perlmutter and Postal 1977). Consider the active and passive sentences in (6.3).

(6.3) a. Pat ate the apple.
b. The apple was eaten by Pat.

It was mentioned above that RelG assumes a consistent, universally valid, mapping between thematic relations and terms, and this mapping holds in (6.3a) but not in (6.3b), in which the patient (*the apple*) is subject and the agent (*Pat*) is an oblique non-term. How can sentences like this be reconciled with the Universal Alignment Hypothesis? The RelG answer is to posit that sentences may have more than one level of syntactic representation, and only the initial representation has to conform to this assumption. In the case of the passive sentence in (6.3b), this would mean that the initial representation would be the same as that of the sentence in (6.3a), and then the application of the passive rule would change the initial direct object into a derived subject and the initial subject into an oblique non-term. RelG postulates a special grammatical relation for arguments which have lost their term relations and been made into non-terms, like the initial subject in a passive construction; it is called a **chômeur** (which is French for 'unemployed person'). The initial subject (agent) in a passive construction is, then, technically a 1-chômeur ($\hat{1}$). The relational network for (6.3b) is given in Figure 6.4.

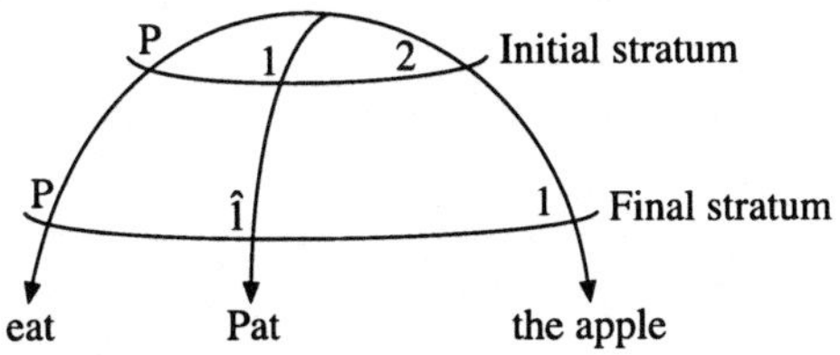

Figure 6.4. *Relational network for a passive construction*

In the initial representation, called the initial **stratum**, the proposed correlation between thematic relations and grammatical relations holds. If this were the only stratum, then the sentence would appear as (6.3a). If the passive rule is invoked, then there is a second stratum, in which the initial 1 is a 1-chômeur and the initial 2 a 1, and the realization of this relational network is (6.3b). The formal representation for the passive rule is given in (6.4).

(6.4) Passive in RelG: $2 \rightarrow 1$

There is a general principle, called the Chômeur Law, which states that when a term has its grammatical relations usurped in a stratum, it becomes a chômeur. Hence, when the initial 2 becomes 1 in a non-initial stratum, the initial 1 must become a 1-chômeur.

Dative shift presents a similar problem for the Universal Alignment Hypothesis. It is exemplified in (6.5).

(6.5) a. The young teacher gave a new book to the old woman.
b. The young teacher gave the old woman a new book.

In (6.5a), the agent is 1, the theme is 2, and the recipient is 3. In (6.5b), on the other hand, the recipient is 2 and the theme is no longer a 2, according to the RelG analysis; the theme is a 2-chômeur. Hence it is necessary to posit two strata for (6.5b), just as for (6.3b); the first represents the relational structure of (6.5a). The relational network for (6.5b) is given in Figure 6.5.

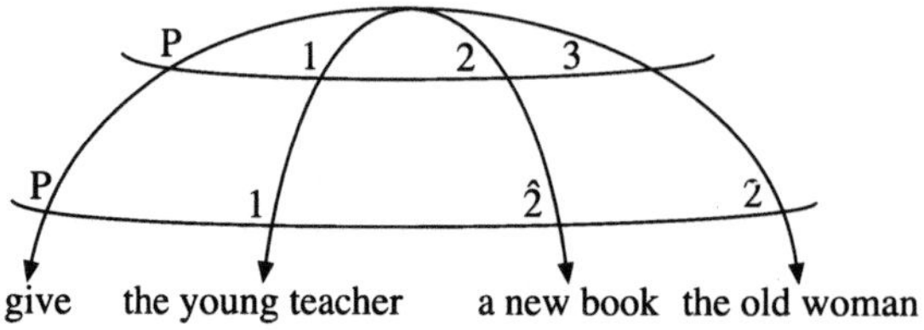

Figure 6.5. *Relational network for dative shift*

Dative shift is referred to as '3-to-2 advancement' in RelG and is formulated as '3 → 2'. Since the old woman is a 2 in the second stratum, passive can be used to make it a 1, yielding (6.6).

(6.6) The old woman was given a new book by the young teacher.

The relational network for this sentence is given in Figure 6.6.

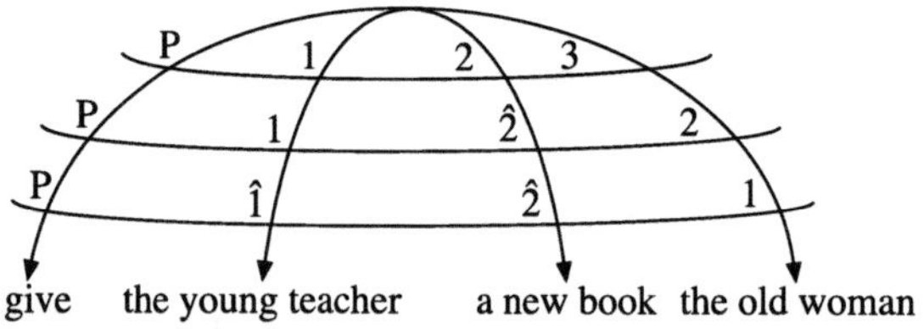

Figure 6.6. *Relational network for dative shift + passive*

There are three strata in Figure 6.6: an initial stratum, reflecting the Universal Alignment Hypothesis, an intermediate stratum reflecting dative shift, and a final stratum reflecting passive. Of the three terms in the initial stratum, the initial 3 winds up as a final 1, while the other two each appear as a chômeur of the appropriate type in the final stratum.

The idea of multiple, **derivational**ly-linked syntactic representations for a sentence goes back to **transformational grammar** [TG] (Chomsky 1957, 1965). TG was a constituent-structure-based theory, unlike RelG, employing phrase-structure rules of the kind discussed in chapter 5 and **transformations**, which are rules mapping one phrase-structure configuration into another. PS-rules would specify the basic forms of sentences, e.g. (6.3a) and (6.1d). The output of the PS-rules was referred to as the '**deep structure**' of the sentence; the initial stratum in RelG corresponds to the deep structure of TG. Dative shift and passive are classic examples of transformational rules, and they would apply to derive (6.3b) from (6.3a), (6.5b) from (6.5a) and (6.6) from (6.5b). (The structures posited in TG are more abstract than the actual English sentences in these examples in various respects, but this may be ignored for the purposes of this discussion.) Like their RelG counterparts, transformations are construction-specific, i.e.

each major construction in a language is described by a different rule. The output of the application of transformations was called the '**surface structure**' of the sentence; its analog in RelG is the final stratum. The organization of TG is given in Figure 6.7.

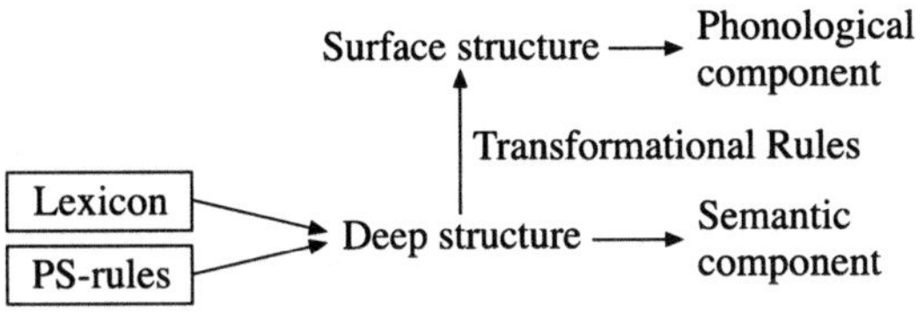

Figure 6.7. *Organization of TG (Chomsky 1965)*

PS-rules of the kind discussed in chapter 5 specify the constituent structure of a possible sentence, and lexical items from the lexicon are inserted; this yields the deep structure, which is interpreted in the semantic component to give the meaning of the sentence. Transformational rules apply to the deep structure to derive the surface structure, which is the input to the phonological component, which specifies the phonological properties of the sentence.

A simplified sketch of the TG derivation of (6.6) is presented in Figure 6.8. This derivation parallels the one summarized in the multistratal relational network in Figure 6.6: the deep structure corresponds to the initial stratum, the intermediate representation is derived from it by the dative shift transformation, and the surface structure, which corresponds to the final stratum, is derived from the intermediate representation by the passive transformation and by rules which correctly inflect the finite verb or auxiliary in terms of tense and agreement and give the main verb (if it is not finite) its appropriate form.

One of the major motivations for positing transformations is to capture systematic relationships in syntax. For example, for virtually every passive sentence in a language there is a corresponding active sentence, and the same constellation of predicate and semantic arguments (in terms of thematic relations) occurs in both. Hence they are not two random, unrelated patterns in the syntax. Rather, there is a systematic relationship between active and passive constructions in English and many other languages, and this relationship should be captured in some way in the grammar of the language. In a similar vein, there is a systematic relationship between the declarative and interrogative forms of sentences, i.e. NP + (AUX) + V (. . .) versus AUX + NP + V (. . .), and this too needs to be expressed. Transformations were the first device developed in modern linguistic theory capable of capturing generalizations like these, and every theory must account for systematic relationships like these in some way. Transformational analysis was first developed by Harris (Harris 1956, 1957), and Chomsky, who was Harris' graduate student, took these ideas and developed TG.

Virtually no syntacticians work in this type of TG today, but it is nevertheless of great historical significance in terms of the development of syntactic theory since the 1960s. All four of the theories discussed in this chapter are related historically to TG, and RelG and GB are direct descendents of it (see Figure 6.45). They are also the only two theories which posit multiple derivationally related syntactic representations for sentences. RelG, in its initial stages, took the transformational rules of TG and

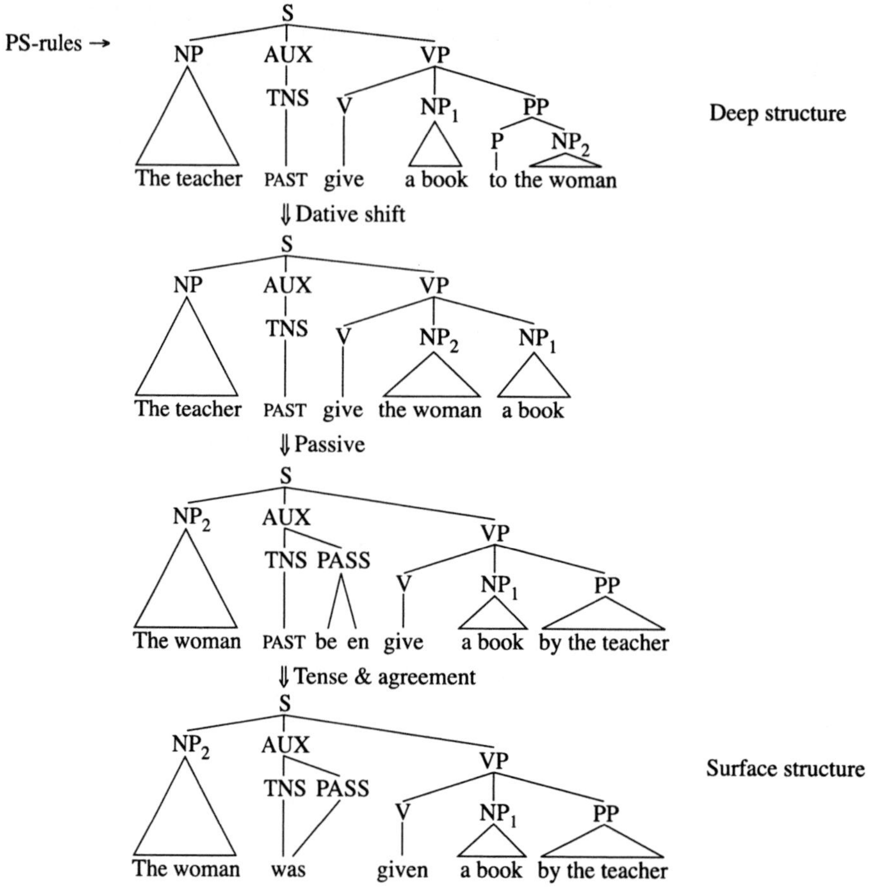

Figure 6.8. *TG derivation of (6.6)*

reformulated them in terms of grammatical relations. GB posits transformation-type rules, as will be shown in section 6.3, which link the abstract **underlying** syntactic representation of a sentence to the GB analogue of surface structure; these rules differ in certain important respects from the transformations of TG, however. The other theories, LFG and RRG, posit neither abstract underlying syntactic representations nor transformations or transformational-type syntactic rules. Hence they use rather different devices to account for phenomena such as passive and dative shift; this will be a major focus in the discussion of these theories below.

One of the motivations for the reformulation of transformations as relational rules was to overcome one of the inherent shortcomings of TG rules. Since transformations were stated in terms of constituents, they were necessarily language-specific. For example, the TG passive rule looked something like NP_1 – AUX – V – NP_2 – X ⇒ NP_2 – AUX+PASS – V – X – *by*+NP_1 ('X' is a variable denoting possible additional but irrelevant material in the clause); its operation is illustrated in Figure 6.8. While this might be the correct rule for English, it could not be extended to other languages, since it has many English-specific features, i.e. the order of elements, the existence of an AUX node, the preposition *by*. This rule would not work for the Malagasy passive in (2.4b) the Kwakwala passive in (4.19b), or the Japanese passive in (2.77). The transformations describing those constructions would also have many language-specific features, and consequently the rules in each language would be different. The RelG rule in (6.4) is not subject to these limitations, because it refers to grammatical relations and not to language-specific structures, and consequently it would be valid for all four of them. Hence the RelG approach permits the expression of important cross-linguistic generalizations about syntactic constructions, something that was very difficult in TG.

If RelG were just a relational analogue of TG, then one would expect to find rules like those in (5.45) specifying the initial strata of sentences, analogous to the PS-rules which specify the deep structures of sentences in TG. But no such rules are postulated in RelG. What, then, determines the form of the initial strata of sentences? The syntax–semantics alignment principles, e.g. agent should be initial 1, etc. Like node-admissibility conditions in a phrase-structure grammar, this hypothesis rules out initial strata which do not satisfy it. In terms of it, (6.1d), (6.3a) and (6.5a) are possible **well-formed** initial strata in English, while (6.3b), (6.5b) and (6.6) are excluded as possible well-formed initial strata, because they do not satisfy the Universal Alignment Hypothesis. In a similar vein, passive and 3-to-2 advancement (dative shift) are not conceived of as deriving one stratum from another, like transformations in TG in Figure 6.8, but rather as constraints on possible successive strata in a relational network. Thus while Figures 6.4 to 6.6 represent well-formed relational networks, the one in Figure 6.9 does not.

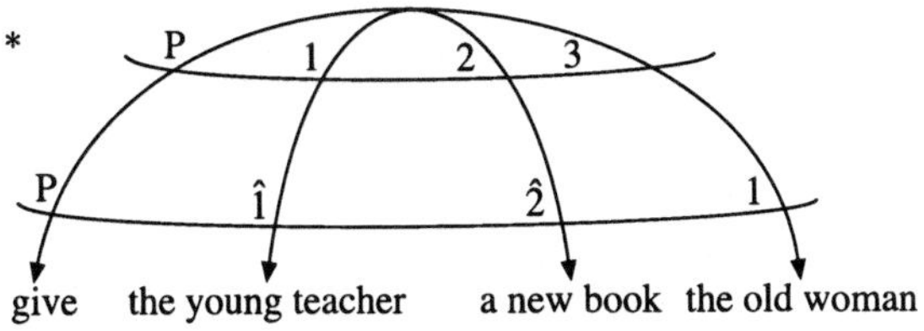

Figure 6.9. *An ill-formed relational network*

Even if there were a rule of '3-to-1 advancement' in English, which there is not, this relational network would still be ill-formed, because there is nothing that would account for the 2-chômeur in the final stratum. Hence this relational network is ill-formed. Thus, RelG is a constraint-satisfaction theory, that is, a theory in which rules are treated as constraints on possible structures (and derivations, in RelG), analogous to the node-admissibility-condition interpretation of PS-rules, rather than as rules which derive one structure from another, analogous to TG transformations.

RelG postulates a number of general principles constraining possible relational networks and hence possible syntactic structures in human languages. Some of the most important ones, called 'laws' in RelG terminology, are given in (6.7) (Perlmutter 1980).

(6.7) Some RelG laws

a. Stratal Uniqueness Law: there can be no more than one instance of a particular term relation in a given stratum.

b. Final 1 Law: there must be a 1 in every final stratum.

c. 1 Advancement Exclusiveness Law: there can be only one advancement to 1 in a clause.

The first two principles codify the traditional ideas that there can be only one subject, direct object and indirect object in a clause and that every clause has a subject. The first, however, restricts that condition to individual strata and not to clauses as a whole. It allows RelG to handle apparent problems like the Tagalog examples in chapter 2 which appeared to have two subjects; the relevant examples from (2.97) are repeated in (6.8).

(6.8) a. ang bigas-na b-in-ili ng babae para sa kaniyang sarili Tagalog
NOM rice-LNK UND-bought NTL woman for DAT 3sgGEN self
'the rice that the woman bought for herself'
b. B-in-ili ng babae ang bigas para sa kaniyang sarili.
UND-bought NTL woman NOM rice for DAT 3sgGEN self
'The woman bought the rice for herself.'

In the relative clause in (6.8a), the reflexivization test picks out *babae* 'woman' as subject, because it is the antecedent of the reflexive, while the relativization test picks out *bigas* 'rice' as subject, because it is the missing NP interpreted to be the same as the head noun. The RelG solution to this problem can be seen in the relational network for (6.8b) in Figure 6.10.

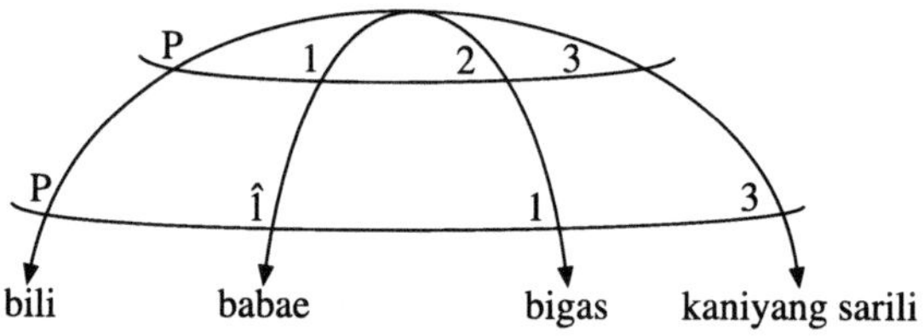

Figure 6.10. *Relational network for (6.8)*

There are two subjects in relational network: the initial 1 is *babae* 'woman', and the final 1 is *bigas* 'rice'. This does not violate the Stratal Uniqueness Law, because the two 1s are on different strata. The RelG analysis of (6.8) would be, then, that it is the initial 1 which is the antecedent of the reflexive and it is the final 1 which is the missing argument corresponding to the head of the relative clause. Hence the two subjects in (6.8) in Tagalog actually are 1s on different strata.

The 1 Advancement Exclusiveness Law rules out relational networks like the following.

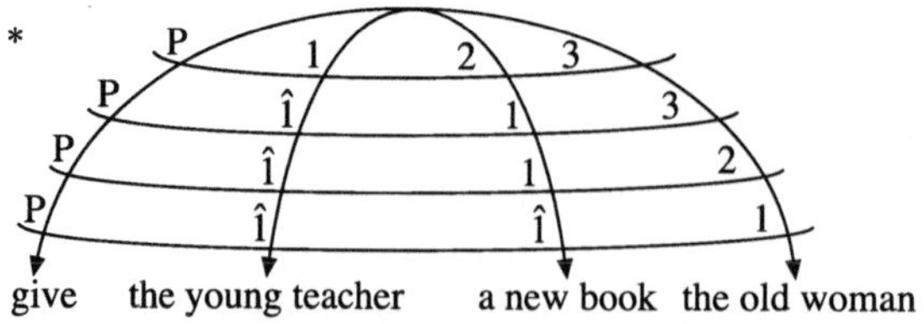

Figure 6.11. *Relational network ruled out by 1 Advancement Exclusiveness Law*

The initial stratum is the same as in Figures 6.5 and 6.6. Passive (2 → 1 advancement) licenses the second stratum, in which the initial 2 is a 1 and the initial 1 a 1-chômeur. In the third stratum, 3 → 2 advancement licenses the 2 in that stratum. In the final stratum, passive has applied again to advance the derived 2 to 1. The sentence that results from this is given in (6.9).

(6.9) *The old woman was given by the young teacher by a new book.

The ungrammaticality of (6.9) is explained in terms of the 1 Advancement Exclusiveness Law: passive has applied twice, resulting in two advancements to subject in a single clause and thereby violating this law.

The Final 1 Law has important consequences in concert with the Universal Alignment Hypothesis. In section 2.1 it was shown that some intransitive verbs take a patient as their single argument, e.g. *The glass shattered*, whereas others take an agent, e.g. *The dog barked.* The Universal Alignment Hypothesis requires that the initial stratum with *shatter* have an initial 2 and the one with *bark* an initial 1. The claim that some intransitive verbs have an initial 1 and others an initial 2 is called the '**Unaccusative Hypothesis**' (Perlmutter 1978). The intransitive verbs with an initial 2 are called '**unaccusative** verbs', while those with an initial 1 are called '**unergative** verbs'. The initial stratum with unergative verbs is a possible final stratum, but this is not the case with unaccusative verbs; if it were the only stratum, then the Final 1 Law would be violated. Hence with unaccusative verbs, the initial 2 must be advanced to final 1, in order to satisfy the Final 1 Law. This is represented in the relational networks in Figure 6.12.

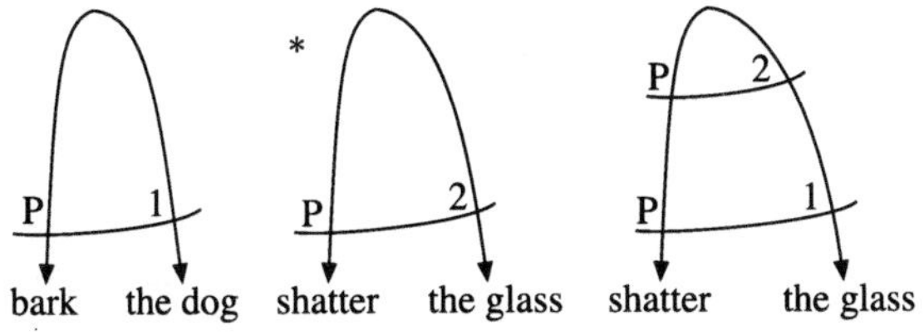

Figure 6.12. *Relational networks for unergative and unaccusative verbs*

Thus, 2 → 1 advancement applies in both passive clauses and clauses with unaccusative verbs, and it is obligatory in clauses with unaccusative verbs, because of the Final 1 Law.

In chapter 2, intransitive verbs like *bark* and *shatter* were described as having actor (agent) and undergoer (patient) subjects, respectively; given that RelG recognizes thematic relations theoretically, why does it posit the contrasting syntactic derivations in Figure 6.12 rather than simply distinguish between actor and undergoer subjects of intransitive verbs directly? The answer lies in another important concept inherited from TG, namely the **autonomy of syntax**. One of the major claims of TG was that syntax is autonomous; this means that the syntactic component of grammar includes only syntactic categories and relations (e.g. NP, subject) and excludes semantic notions like actor and patient. Furthermore, syntactic rules can make reference only to these same syntactic categories and relations. As an example of this restriction, consider the Tagalog example in (6.8a). In section 2.3.1 it was analysed in terms of the actor NP being the controller of the reflexive and the nominative NP being the omitted argument in the relative clause. Replacing 'nominative NP' with final 1, it is possible to reformulate this as 'the actor is the controller of the reflexive and the head of the relative clause must be interpreted as the final 1 in the relative clause'. Such a formulation violates the principle of the autonomy of syntax, however, since it refers to both a semantic role (actor) and a syntactic relation (final 1), and it is therefore impossible in RelG. Since the Universal Alignment Hypothesis requires that the initial stratum be universally predictable from the argument structure of the verb, the grammatical relations in the initial stratum act as syntactic copies of the thematic relations in the argument structure, and because they are syntactic, not semantic, the rules of the syntax can refer to them. Hence the proper RelG analysis of (6.8a) involves reference to the initial 1, not the actor argument, even though they are the same NP. In this way the autonomy of syntax can be preserved. Of the four theories in this chapter, RelG and GB vigorously maintain the autonomy of syntax, LFG is less committed to it, and RRG rejects it altogether.

Researchers using RelG proposed a number of important cross-linguistic generalizations based on the relational hierarchy in (2.50). Its strength was the analysis of syntactic phenomena which affected the relational structure of sentences, but this was at the same time its greatest weakness theoretically. Many of the most important syntactic phenomena which have figured in the theoretical debates of the last twenty-five years have little, if anything, to do with grammatical relations, e.g. intrasentential pronominalization, extraction phenomena in languages like English, and accordingly, RelG has nothing to say about them. It has influenced a number of different theories (see Figure 6.45), and one theory has developed directly out of it, **Arc Pair Grammar** (Johnson and Postal 1980). Arc Pair Grammar is a highly formalized version of RelG which includes not only clausal grammatical relations but also NP-internal relations, like the relational-dependency grammar sketched in section 5.3. It also tried to account for grammatical phenomena beyond those involving grammatical relations.

The next theory to be discussed, LFG, is an interesting combination of phrase structure grammar and some ideas from RelG together with a strong emphasis on the role of the lexicon in grammar.

6.2 Lexical-Functional Grammar

Like RelG, Lexical-Functional Grammar developed out of classical transformational grammar, but unlike RelG, it rejects the notion of abstract underlying syntactic representations and transformational rules. Like RelG, it is a constraint-satisfaction theory. LFG is a member of a group of contemporary theories which have the following properties: (1) they do not posit abstract underlying syntactic representations (i.e. they are **monostratal**); (2) they emphasize the explicit representation of morphosyntactic information by means of syntactic features; (3) the lexicon plays a very significant role; and (4) they employ **unification** as a central mechanism in the grammar. The other theories of this type include **Head-driven Phrase Structure Grammar** [HPSG] and Construction Grammar. LFG will be taken as representative of this general approach, and the others will be discussed briefly in section 6.6.

In chapter 1 the distinction between relational structure and constituent structure was introduced, and a unique feature of LFG is that it is concerned with both types of structure and provides two syntactic representations for each sentence: **c-structure** (short for constituent structure), which represents the constituent structure of the sentence, and **f-structure** (short for **functional structure**), which represents the relational structure of the sentence. Grammatical relations are called 'grammatical functions' in LFG. LFG makes extensive use of syntactic features, and its analyses of grammatical-relation-changing phenomena like passive and dative shift crucially involve the lexicon.

Because LFG assigns two representations to each sentence, it is easy to represent how individual languages differ structurally and what they have in common at the same time. Consider the following sentences from four languages, all of which mean 'Juan sees a dog.'

(6.10) a. Juan sieh-t ein-en Hund. — German
Juan.NOM see-3sgPRES a-ACC dog
b. Ẓ̌-leʔele ẓ̌wa bekoʔ. — Yateé Zapotec
PRES-see Juan dog
c. Juan-i kay-lul po-n-ta. — Korean
Juan-NOM dog-ACC see-PRES-IND
d. Mang-ida biang si Juan. — Toba Batak
ACTIVE-see dog PN Juan

While each language would have a different c-structure, they would all have the same f-structure, since in each 'Juan' is the subject and 'dog' is the direct object. This is illustrated in Figure 6.13.

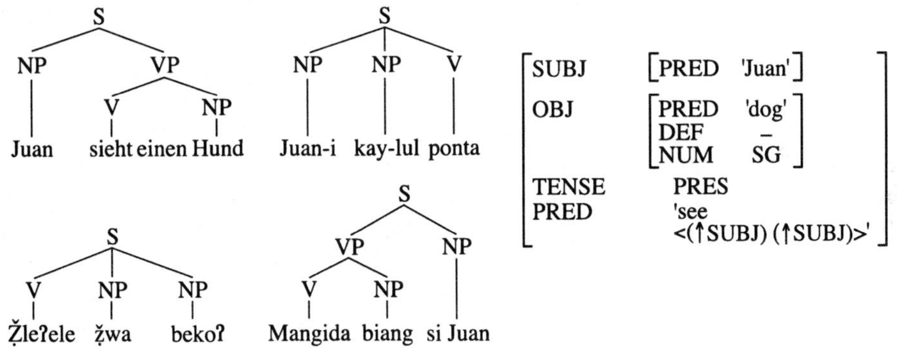

Figure 6.13. *C-structure and f-structure representations for 'Juan sees a dog'*

The only difference in the f-structures across the four languages would be the lexical items supplying the values for the 'PRED' functions, e.g. German *Hund*, Zapotec *bekoʔ*, Korean *kay*, Toba Batak *biang*, and English *dog*. The c-structures in Figure 6.13 are simplified; more complete c-structures will be given below. As exemplified in the c-structure for (6.10b), (6.10c), LFG does not assume that VP is a universal property of clauses; rather, it posits VPs only when they can be motivated by the constituency tests discussed in chapter 4.

The LFG inventory of grammatical functions is not the same as the RelG inventory of grammatical relations. The grammatical functions posited for simple sentences are given in Figure 6.14, adapted from Bresnan (1982b).

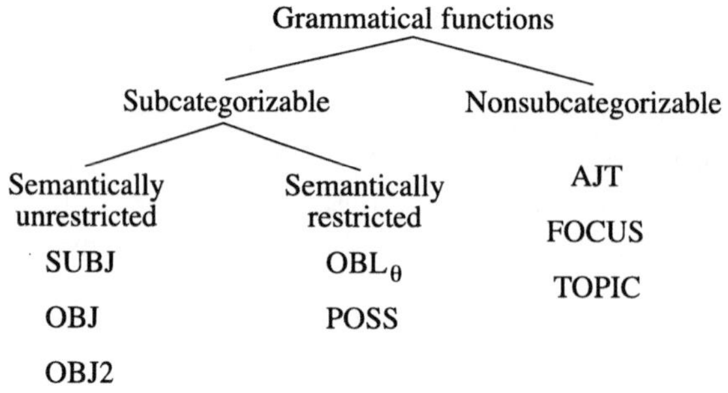

Figure 6.14. *Grammatical functions in simple sentences*

The fundamental division in this taxonomy is between those grammatical functions that can be part of a verb's subcategorization and those that cannot be. With respect to subcategorizable functions, there is a distinction between semantically unrestricted functions and semantically restricted functions. The semantically unrestricted functions are subject (SUBJ), direct object (OBJ) and secondary object (OBJ2); they are semantically unrestricted because arguments bearing a variety of thematic relations can have these functions. In section 2.2.1 it was shown that subjects can be agents, experiencers, instruments, patients, themes, recipients, etc., depending on the choice and voice of the verb, and similarly direct objects can be themes, patients, instruments, recipients, etc., depending upon the verb. The secondary object with *give* (in *Chris gave Pat the book*) would be a theme, while the one with *show* (in *Chris showed Pat the book*) would be a stimulus. The semantically restricted grammatical functions, as the name implies, are associated with particular thematic relations, e.g. recipient, instrument or benefactive, or semantic functions, e.g. possessor (POSS). The traditional indirect object in *Chris gave the book to Pat* is analyzed as an OBL_{θ} in LFG, as is the *with* PP in *He cut the bread with a knife* and the locative PP with verbs like *put*. There is nothing in Figure 6.14 which directly corresponds to indirect object (3) in RelG. The nonsubcategorizable functions are adjunct [AJT], **TOPIC** and **FOCUS**. 'Adjunct' is used in the same sense as in chapters 3 and 4. The terms 'topic' and 'focus' are normally used to refer to discourse functions; roughly speaking, the topic element denotes an entity that has in some way already been established in the discourse context, usually by prior mention, and the focus is information about one or more topical participants that is new in the context. This can be illustrated by the following question–answer pair.

(6.11) a. Q: What happened to John?
b. A: He got arrested.

The question in (6.11a) establishes the referent of the NP *John* as the topic, and as befits its topical status, the referent is referred to by an unstressed pronoun in the answer. The focal part of the answer is the predicate *got arrested*, which is the new information about the referent of *John*. Focus is often talked about in terms of being a **comment** about a topic. In (6.11b), *he* expresses the topic and *got arrested* is the comment or focus. In LFG, the terms 'TOPIC' and 'FOCUS' are used to describe specific functions which NPs or PPs may have outside the clause; in other words, they are treated as grammatical functions. This is illustrated in (6.12).

(6.12)	a. Montreal I'd like to visit some day.	*Montreal* = TOPIC
	b. What did Chris give Pat?	*What* = FOCUS

In (6.12a) *Montreal* is the TOPIC and *I'd like to visit some day* is a comment about it. In the WH-question in (6.12b), *what* is a FOCUS, because WH-words are always focal in nature; *what* stands for the information that the speaker wants to get from the addressee. In possible answers to the question, e.g. *He gave her a new sweater*, the part replacing *what* (i.e. *a new sweater*) is focal.

The representation of relational structure in LFG is also rather different from that in RelG, as a comparison of Figures 6.1 and 6.16 readily reveals. An f-structure represents dependencies in terms of attribute–value matrices. Syntactic heads are represented by the elements labelled 'PRED' in the f-structure; the verb *see* is the head of the entire matrix f-structure in Figure 6.13, and *Juan* and *dog* are the heads of the subsidiary f-structures. Each grammatical relation is represented as an attribute or feature which takes an f-structure as its value, hence the term 'attribute–value matrix'. The grammatical relation 'object' has as its value *a dog*, and this is represented by a subsidiary f-structure which itself contains three attributes or features: definiteness, whose value is '–', number, whose value is 'singular', and predicate, whose value is 'dog'. The attribute 'tense' has the value 'past'. The value of 'PRED' for the matrix f-structure is the verb *see*, which takes two term arguments as represented by its subcategorization frame. The f-structure for the Russian example in (6.13) is given in Figure 6.15.

(6.13)	Učitel'nic-a	da-l-a	knig-u	ženščin-e.	Russian
	teacher-FSgNOM	give-PAST-FSg	book-FSgACC	woman-FSgDAT	
	'The teacher gave a book to the woman.'				

```
[ SUBJ     [ PRED  'učitel'nica-' ]
           [ GEND  FEM            ]
           [ NUM   SG             ]
           [ CASE  NOM            ]

  TENSE    PAST
  ASPECT   PERFECTIVE
  PRED     'dat'
             <(SUBJ) (OBJ) (OBJ2)>'

  OBJ      [ PRED  'knig-'        ]
           [ GEND  FEM            ]
           [ NUM   SG             ]
           [ CASE  ACC            ]

  OBJ2     [ PRED  'ženščin-'     ]
           [ GEND  FEM            ]
           [ NUM   SG             ]
           [ CASE  DAT            ]  ]
```

Figure 6.15. *F-structure of Russian example in (6.13)*

In the Russian f-structure, *učitel'nic-* 'teacher', *knig-* 'book' and *ženščin-* 'woman' are the dependents (terms) of the head *dat'* 'give'. The case, number and gender features of each are represented in the subsidiary f-structure which serves as the value of a grammatical function.

What is the relationship between the c-structure and f-structure of a sentence? A glance at Figure 6.13 leads to the conclusion that a c-structure cannot be derived uniquely from an f-structure, since a number of different c-structures can be related to a single f-structure. If there were information in the c-structure concerning grammatical functions, on the other hand, then it would be possible to derive an f-structure from a c-structure. However, the phrase-structure trees in Figure 6.13 contain no consistent representation of grammatical functions; while the subject is the sister to the VP and the object is the sister to the verb within the VP in German and Toba Batak, both the subject and object are sisters of the verb in Korean and Yateé Zapotec. LFG solves this problem by adding **functional annotations** to the tree. Revised c-structures with functional annotations for the Yateé Zapotec and German sentences are given in Figure 6.16.

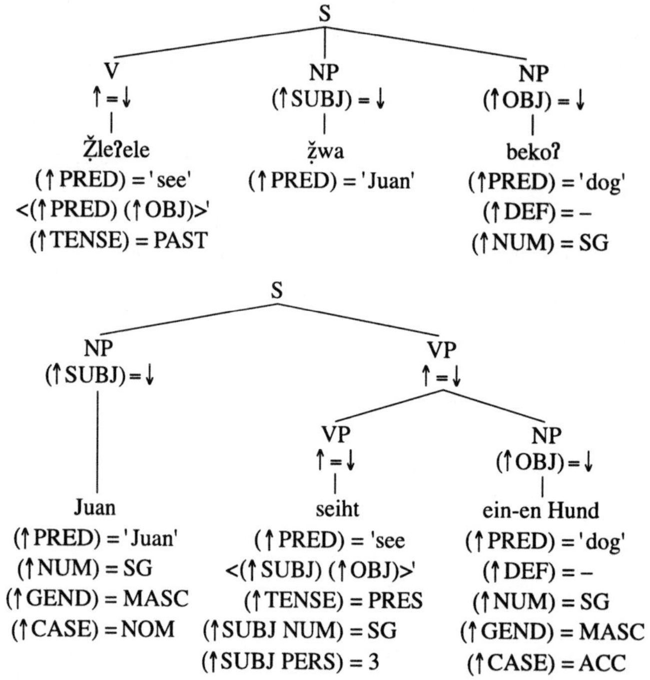

Figure 6.16. *Enhanced c-structures for (6.10b) and (6.10c)*

LFG represents all relevant grammatical information explicitly, using functional annotations. '(↑GF) = ↓' indicates that the head of the XP (which '↓' points to) has the specified grammatical function with respect to its mother node (which '↑' points to). In the German c-structure, '(↑SUBJ) = ↓' signals that *Juan* 'Juan-NOM' is the subject of the sentence, while '(↑OBJ) = ↓' indicates that *ein-en Hund* 'a-ACC dog' is the object of its mother node, the VP. The VP in turn carries the notation '↑ = ↓', which means that features passed to it from its daughters are passed on to be features of its mother node, the S node; hence *einen Hund* is the object of the sentence as a whole. The V *sah* 'saw' is the head of the VP, and all of its features are passed up to the VP and on to the sentence as a whole. Hence the sentence as a whole has past tense and indicative mood. The same is true in the Yateé Zapotec c-structure, despite the lack of a VP node.

How do c-structures get these functional annotations? They are part of the PS-rules that generate the c-structures. The basic PS-rules for the Yateé Zapotec and German examples in (6.10) are given in (6.14).

(6.14) a. Some LFG PS-rules for Yateé Zapotec

S → V NP (NP)
↑ = ↓ (↑SUBJ) = ↓ (↑OBJ) = ↓

b. Some LFG PS-rules for German

S → NP VP
(↑SUBJ) = ↓ ↑ = ↓

VP → V NP
↑ = ↓ (↑OBJ) = ↓

These rules will specify the c-structures in Figure 6.16. The information under each of the terminal nodes comes from the lexical entries for each morpheme. For example, the Yateé Zapotec verb *ẓ̌leʔele* 'sees' is composed of *ẓ̌-* 'present tense' and *-leʔele* 'see', and consequently '(↑PRED) = 'see <(↑SUBJ) (↑OBJ)>' comes from the lexical entry for *-leʔele* and '(↑TENSE) = PRES' comes from the lexical entry for *ẓ̌-*. The lexical entries for nouns such as *Juan, Hund* and *bekoʔ* contain grammatically relevant information, e.g. person, number, gender. The lexicon and lexical entries will be discussed further below.

It is now possible to describe case assignment and finite verb agreement in LFG. Consider the simple Croatian example in (6.15).

(6.15) Iren-a živ-i u Zagreb-u. Croatian
Irena-FSGNOM live-3SGPRES in Zagreb-MSGLOC
'Irena lives in Zagreb.'

The PS-rules to generate this sentence are given in (6.16), and the resulting c-structure is presented in Figure 6.17.

(6.16) PS-rules for some simple clauses in Croatian

a. S → NP V (NP) (PP)
(↑SUBJ) = ↓ ↑ = ↓ (↑OBJ) = ↓ (↑OBL$_\theta$) = ↓

b. PP → P NP
(↑OBJ) = ↓

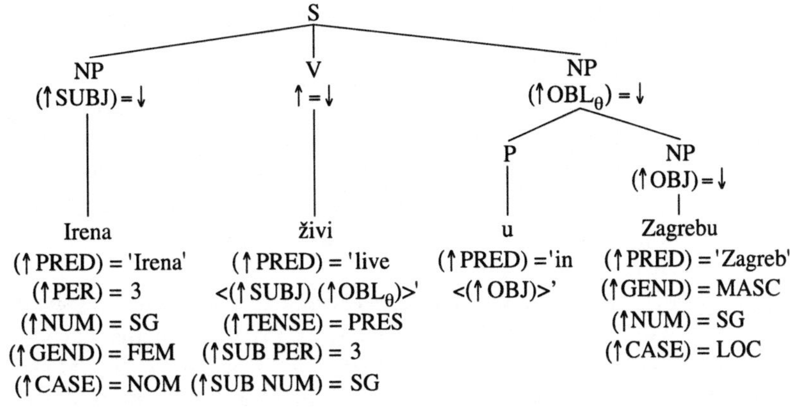

Figure 6.17. *C-structure of (6.15)*

Case is assigned by the verb and the preposition, with the subject receiving nominative case and the preposition *u* assigning locative case to its object. The agreement features of the subject NP *Irena* must not conflict with the agreement features of *-i*, the suffix expressing tense and the person and number of the subject on the verb. In this sentence they do not, and the result is grammatical. If the verb were *živim* 'I live', with the feature '(↑PER) = 1', the resulting sentence **Irena živim u Zagrebu* would be ungrammatical, due to the conflict between the person feature of the subject and the person feature on the verb. This process of having syntactic features move up the tree and combine is called **unification**: features may unify if they do not contain conflicting information. In this example, the agreement features of the subject must not conflict with the agreement features of the verb, in order for their features to unify, and a grammatical sentence results only when the relevant features in the structure unify properly.

Given a c-structure with functional annotations, it is now possible to project an f-structure from it. The c-structure in Figure 6.17 can be projected into the f-structure in Figure 6.18.

$$\begin{bmatrix} \text{SUBJ} & \begin{bmatrix} \text{PRED} & \text{'Iren-'} \\ \text{GEND} & \text{FEM} \\ \text{PER} & 3 \\ \text{NUM} & \text{SG} \\ \text{CASE} & \text{NOM} \end{bmatrix} \\ \text{TENSE} & \text{PRESENT} \\ \text{PRED} & \text{'živjeti <(SUBJ) (OBL}_{\theta}\text{)>'} \\ \text{OBL}_{\theta} & \begin{bmatrix} \text{PRED} & \text{'u<(OBJ)>'} \\ \text{OBJ} & \begin{bmatrix} \text{PRED} & \text{'Zagreb-'} \\ \text{GEND} & \text{MASC} \\ \text{NUM} & \text{SG} \\ \text{CASE} & \text{LOC} \end{bmatrix} \end{bmatrix} \end{bmatrix}$$

Figure 6.18. *F-structure of (6.15)*

The NP *Irena* is the subject in (6.15), and the features associated with it in Figure 6.17 appear as the subsidiary f-structure supplying the value of the attribute 'SUBJ' in Figure 6.18. Similarly, the PP functioning as OBL_{θ}, *u Zagrebu* 'in Zagreb', has the preposition *u* as its head, represented as a 'PRED' function, and then its object, *Zagrebu*, is represented as a subsidiary f-structure containing the features associated with it in the c-structure in Figure 6.17. The head of the clause is the 'PRED' of the matrix f-structure; its value is the verb plus its subcategorization information; the tense feature is represented, but the agreement features are not. Thus, the f-structure in Figure 6.18 is projected from the c-structure in Figure 6.17, with the information in the functional annotations in the c-structure being realized as subsidiary f-structures specifying the values of the major functions in the c-structure.

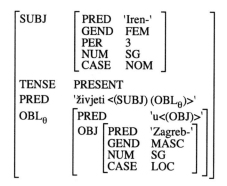

F-structures are subject to two important constraints: the Completeness Condition and the Coherence Condition. The first condition states that an f-structure must be complete, i.e. all of the functions in it must be satisfied. In Figure 6.18, the SUBJ function is satisfied by the subsidiary f-structure representing the NP *Irena*, the OBL_{θ} function is satisfied by the subsidiary f-structure representing the PP *u Zagrebu*, and the OBJ function in it is satisfied by the subsidiary f-structure representing *Zagrebu*. In addition, the verb *živjeti* 'live' is subcategorized for two grammatical functions, SUBJ and OBL_θ, and since the matrix f-structure contains both of these functions, the subcategorization properties of the main predicate are satisfied. Hence the f-structure in Figure 6.18 is complete. The second condition specifies that each subcategorizable grammatical function in the f-structure must be subcategorized for by one of the predicates. In Figure 6.18, the SUBJ and OBL_θ the main verb for functions are subcategorized, and the preposition *u* subcategorizes for an OBJ. Hence the f-structure in Figure 6.18 is coherent. Examples of incomplete and incoherent f-structures are given in Figure 6.19.

$$
{}^{*}\begin{bmatrix}
\text{TENSE} & \text{PRESENT} \\
\text{PRED} & \text{'živjeti <(SUBJ) (OBL}_\theta\text{)>'} \\
\text{OBL}_\theta & \begin{bmatrix} \text{PRED} & \text{'u<(OBJ)>'} \\ \text{OBJ} & \begin{bmatrix} \text{PRED} & \text{'Zagreb-'} \\ \text{GEND} & \text{MASC} \\ \text{NUM} & \text{SG} \\ \text{CASE} & \text{LOC} \end{bmatrix} \end{bmatrix}
\end{bmatrix}
\qquad
{}^{*}\begin{bmatrix}
\text{SUBJ} & \begin{bmatrix} \text{PRED} & \text{'Iren-'} \\ \text{GEND} & \text{FEM} \\ \text{PER} & 3 \\ \text{NUM} & \text{SG} \\ \text{CASE} & \text{NOM} \end{bmatrix} \\
\text{TENSE} & \text{PRESENT} \\
\text{PRED} & \text{'živjeti <(SUBJ) (OBL}_\theta\text{)>'} \\
\text{OBJ} & \begin{bmatrix} \text{PRED} & \text{'knjig-'} \\ \text{GEND} & \text{FEM} \\ \text{NUM} & \text{SG} \\ \text{CASE} & \text{ACC} \end{bmatrix} \\
\text{OBL}_\theta & \begin{bmatrix} \text{PRED} & \text{'u<(OBJ)>'} \\ \text{OBJ} & \begin{bmatrix} \text{PRED} & \text{'Zagreb'} \\ \text{GEND} & \text{MASC} \\ \text{NUM} & \text{SG} \\ \text{CASE} & \text{LOC} \end{bmatrix} \end{bmatrix}
\end{bmatrix}
$$

Figure 6.19. *Impossible f-structures*

The left f-structure is incomplete, because the SUBJ grammatical function in the subcategorization frame of the verb is not satisfied. Croatian is a so-called 'pro-drop' language (see section 3.1.3), and this means that a sentence like *živi u Zagrebu* 'He/she lives in Zagreb' is perfectly grammatical. However, the left f-structure is not the f-structure for this sentence, because it does have a subject, which is expressed by the *-i* '3sgPRES' suffix on the verb. The f-structure of the 'pro-drop' sentence would be almost the same as the one in Figure 6.18, except that 'PRED *Iren-*' would be replaced by 'PRED PRO', and there would be no gender feature. The right f-structure is incoherent, because the OBJ function filled by *knjigu* 'book' does not correspond to a subcategorized grammatical function of the matrix verb. Note that the c-structure corresponding to the right f-structure could be generated by the PS-rules in (6.16); nothing in those rules prevents the specification of **Irena živi knjigu u Zagrebu* 'Irena lives the book in Zagreb'. The sentence is nevertheless ruled out as ungrammatical, because there is no possible f-structure corresponding to it that could satisfy the Coherence Condition. In LFG, the major grammatical constraints are stated on f-structures, and this in turn rules out ungrammatical c-structures.

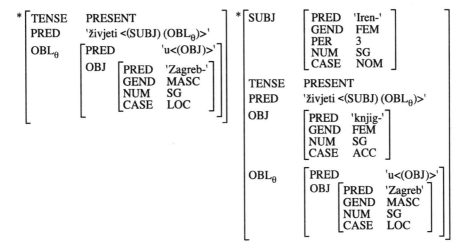

The lexicon is very important in LFG, and this is reflected in the term 'lexical' in the name of the theory. The lexical entry for a verb contains, among other information, its subcategorization and argument structure; the pairing of a subcategorization frame and an argument structure is referred to as a **lexical form**. The lexical forms for Yateé Zapotec *-le?ele* 'see' from (6.10b), Russian *dat'* 'give' from (6.13), and Croatian *živjeti* 'live' from (6.15) are given in (6.17).

(6.17) a. *-le?ele* 'see <(↑SUBJ) (↑OBJ)>' — Yateé Zapotec
EXP THEME

b. *dat'* 'give <(↑SUBJ) (↑OBJ) (↑OBJ2)>' — Russian
AGENT THEME RECIPIENT

c. *živijeti* 'live <(↑SUBJ) ($\uparrow OBL_\theta$)>' — Croatian
THEME LOCATIVE

An important feature of LFG is that the subcategorization properties of verbs are stated in relational rather than constituent-structure terms (i.e. in terms of grammatical functions). The Completeness and Coherence Conditions refer crucially to subcategorization information, and since it is formulated in terms of grammatical functions, they can only be satisfied by a well-formed f-structure.

Changes in grammatical functions, as in passive and dative shift, are stated in LFG in terms of changes in the lexical forms of verbs. The passive rule takes the argument that is the OBJ in the active voice and makes it the SUBJ of the output verb; the argument that is the SUBJ in the active voice is either omitted or appears as an OBL_θ of the output verb. Rules such as these that apply in the lexicon are called **lexical rules.** The rule is formulated in (6.18a), and its effect on the English verb *break* is illustrated in (6.18b).

(6.18) a. Lexical rule for passive:
SUBJ → $\emptyset/OBL_\theta$
OBJ → SUBJ

b. 'break <(↑SUBJ) (↑OBJ)>' → 'broken <($\uparrow OBL_\theta$)/∅ (↑SUBJ)>'
AGENT PATIENT → AGENT PATIENT

The rule in (a) changes the grammatical functions that the verb is subcategorized for and relinks the thematic relations: agent is linked to SUBJ in the active, but patient is linked to SUBJ in the passive, while the agent is either omitted (represented by '∅') or linked to OBL_θ. The rule also affects the morphology of the verb; in English, it changes the verb into its past participle form, the form which cooccurs with the auxiliary verb *be* in the passive construction. If the rule applied to Kwakwala *yəlkʷəmat-* 'hurt' in (4.19a) to derive the passive form in (4.19b), it would add the passive morpheme *-səẇ*, yielding *yəlkʷəmat-səẇ* 'hurt-PASS'. An example of a passive sentence from English is given in Figure 6.20; both structures have been simplified, and the representation of the tensed auxiliary verb in the c-structure is much simpler than the standard LFG analysis.

Dative shift is also handled by a lexical rule. It is formulated in (6.19a), and its application to the English verb *give* is stated in (6.19b).

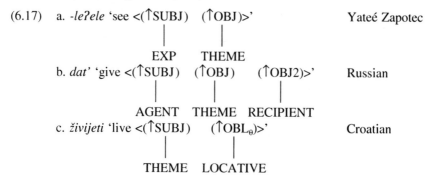

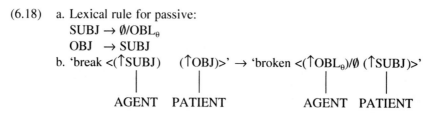

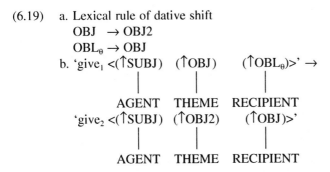

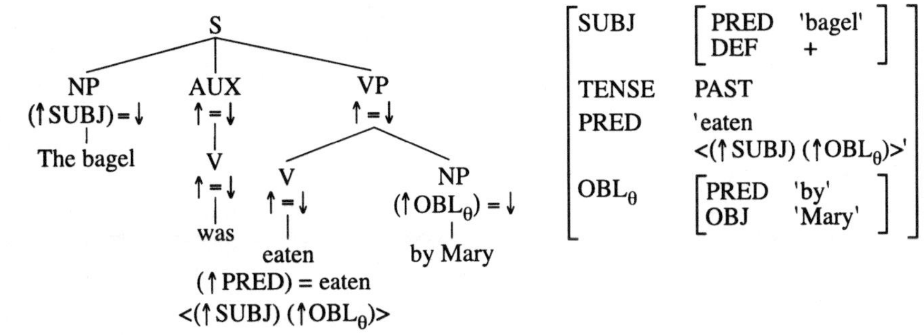

Figure 6.20. *C-structure and f-structure of English passive sentence*

(6.19) a. Lexical rule of dative shift

OBJ $\rightarrow$ OBJ2

OBL_θ $\rightarrow$ OBJ

b. 'give$_1$ <(↑SUBJ) (↑OBJ) (↑OBL_θ)>' $\rightarrow$

AGENT THEME RECIPIENT

'give$_2$ <(↑SUBJ) (↑OBJ2) (↑OBJ)>'

AGENT THEME RECIPIENT

The two versions of *give* can be referred to as *give$_1$* (plain) and *give$_2$* (dative-shifted); with *give$_1$* the theme is the OBJ and the recipient is the OBL_θ, whereas with *give$_2$* the recipient is the OBJ and the theme is the OBJ2. Each can be the input to the passive rule in (6.18), yielding the two possible passive forms with *give*, i.e. *The book was given$_1$ to Chris by Pat* and *Chris was given$_2$ the book by Pat.*

LFG thus offers a different way of capturing systematic linguistic phenomena, namely rules in the lexicon. RelG and TG posit derivationally linked syntactic representations and syntactic rules (advancements in RelG, transformations in TG) which map one syntactic representation (a stratum in a relational network in RelG, a phrase-structure tree in TG) into another and capture systematic relationships found in passive and dative shift. The LFG approach captures these systematic relationships by relating active verbs to passive verbs and plain verbs to dative-shifted verbs in the lexicon. Hence in LFG these relationships are expressed in the lexicon rather than in the syntax, as in the other two theories. These approaches are summarized in Table 6.1.

Recent work in LFG has moved away from treating grammatical relations as primitives and reformulated the lexical rules for passive and dative shift. This new development,

Table 6.1. *Ways of capturing systematic relationships in grammar*

Theory	Passive	Dative shift
Transformational Grammar	Syntactic transformation	Syntactic transformation
Relational Grammar	Syntactic advancement rule	Syntactic advancement rule
Lexical-Functional Grammar	Lexical rule	Lexical rule

called ‘lexical mapping theory’ [LMT] (Bresnan and Kanerva 1989, Bresnan 1994), defines the four primary grammatical functions in terms of two features, [±r] for ‘semantically restricted’ and [±o] for ‘object’ (see Figure 6.14). In terms of these features, SUBJ = {[−r], [−o]}, OBJ = {[−r], [+o]}, OBJ2 = {[+r], [+o]}, and OBL_θ = {[+r], [−o]}. Certain thematic relations have intrinsic values, e.g. agent is [−o] and theme/patient is [−r], and then their default values are [−r] for agent and [+o] for theme/patient. If nothing changes the defaults, then the agent is the SUBJ and the theme/patient is the OBJ. The lexical rule for passive overrides the defaults, changing agent to [+r]. This means that the agent will be realized as an OBL_θ, {[+r], [−o]}. There is a well-formedness condition to the effect that every clause must have a SUBJ (the LFG analogue of the RelG Final 1 Law), the theme/patient, which is [−r], appears as the SUBJ ({[−r], [−o]}). Dative shift is handled by an analogous change of features affecting the OBL_θ and the OBJ. The decomposing of grammatical functions into syntactic features is an attempt to place relation-changing lexical rules on a firmer theoretical foundation.

The final phenomenon to be discussed is WH-question formation. The grammatical function FOCUS plays a central role in the LFG account of these phenomena. For a language like English, the PS-rules specifying the relevant clause patterns are given in (6.20).

(6.20) Some annotated PS-rules for English

a. S′	→	(XP)	S		
		(↑FOCUS) = ↓	↑ = ↓		
b. S	→	(AUX)	NP	VP	
		↑ = ↓	(↑SUBJ) = ↓	↑ = ↓	
c. VP	→	V	(NP)	(NP)	(PP)
		↑ = ↓	(↑OBJ) = ↓	(↑OBJ2) = ↓	($↑OBL_\theta$) = ↓

Simplified c- and f-structures for *What did Pat buy?* are given in Figure 6.21.

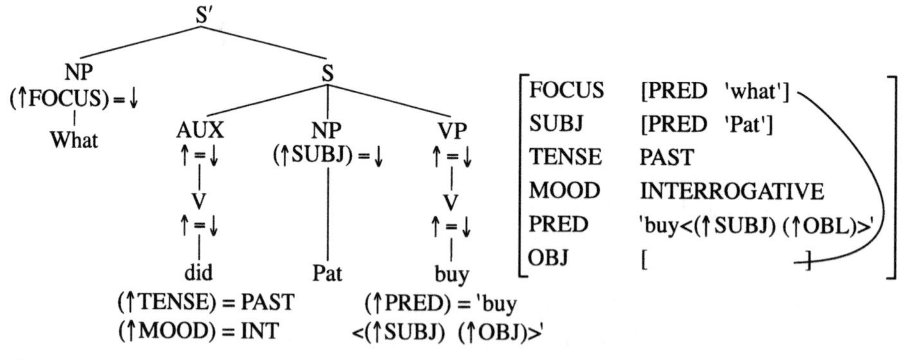

Figure 6.21. *C-structure and f-structure for a WH-question in English*

The f-structure is projected from the c-structure, and it appears to be incomplete; nothing appears to satisfy the OBJ function of *buy*. There is, however, an extra, unsubcategorized grammatical function in the f-structure, namely the FOCUS NP *what*. If its PRED is interpreted as also being the PRED satisfying the OBJ function, then the f-structure would be complete and the sentence grammatical. Thus the FOCUS XP is allowed to satisfy an unsatisfied function. If there were no unsatisfied functions, then the resulting f-structure would be incoherent, because there would be no way to interpret the FOCUS NP, as in **What did Pat buy the book?* Similarly, if there were two unsatisfied functions, then the occurrence of a FOCUS NP could not save the f-structure from being incomplete, as in **Where did Pat put?* Thus, LFG uses the grammatical function of FOCUS and an extended notion of completeness to account for long-distance dependencies like WH-questions in English. This approach to long-distance dependencies is called 'functional uncertainty' (Kaplan and Zaenen 1989).

Research in LFG has had a number of different emphases, including the study of the lexicon and the development of a psychologically plausible, empirically testable theory of language production and comprehension, and like RelG, there has been a great deal of work on languages other than English and the familiar Indo-European languages.

6.3 Government-Binding Theory

Government-Binding Theory (Chomsky 1981, 1986) is one of the approaches that falls within the Principles and Parameters family of theories. It is a direct descendent of TG, and like TG it posits multiple, derivationally linked levels of syntactic representation. The overall organization of GB is given in Figure 6.22 (cf. Figure 6.7).

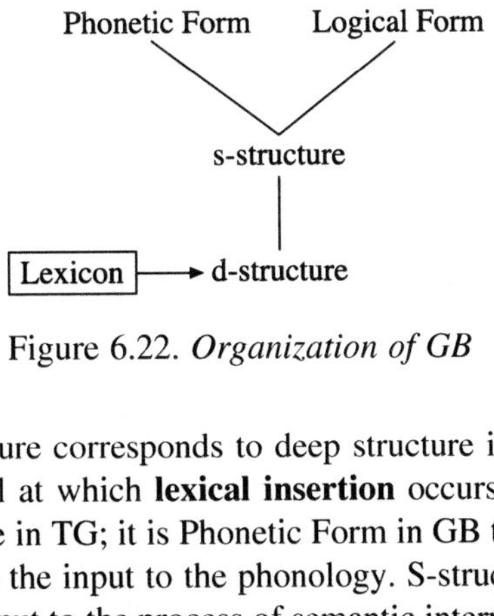

Figure 6.22. *Organization of GB*

D-structure corresponds to deep structure in TG and the initial stratum in RelG. It is the level at which **lexical insertion** occurs. S-structure is more abstract than surface structure in TG; it is Phonetic Form in GB that corresponds to surface structure in TG, and it is the input to the phonology. S-structure is mapped into **Logical Form**, which is the input to the process of semantic interpretation. Whereas deep structure is what is interpreted semantically in TG, d-structure is not the input to semantic interpretation in GB. A comparison of Figure 6.7 with Figure 6.22 reveals that there is no reference to PS-rules in GB; this will be clarified below.

GB strives to be a theory of universal grammar, and consequently the principles it proposes are intended to be linguistic universals, that is, universal properties of the grammars of human languages. Variation across languages is expressed in terms of **parameters**, e.g. the **pro-drop parameter** which characterizes languages like Latin in which subjects can be dropped and those like English in which they cannot. Further examples of parametric variation will be noted below. It is not claimed, however, that the principles of the theory and parameters can account for all of the grammatical sentences in a language. Rather, the sentences that are accounted for in this way constitute **core grammar**; for example, the matrix-coding as subject phenomena ('raising to subject') in (2.55a) and (2.55a′) are considered to be part of core grammar, while matrix-coding as object phenomena ('raising to object') in (2.55b) and (2.55b′) are not. It is core grammar that has been the primary focus of Principles and Parameters research.

All Principles and Parameters theories employ some type of X-bar constituent structure for the representation of syntactic structure at all levels, including Logical Form. While both LFG and GB assume that lexical categories head full X-bar projections, GB makes the additional assumption that grammatical categories like tense and complementizer also head full X-bar structures. This leads to the general clause structure in Figure 6.23.

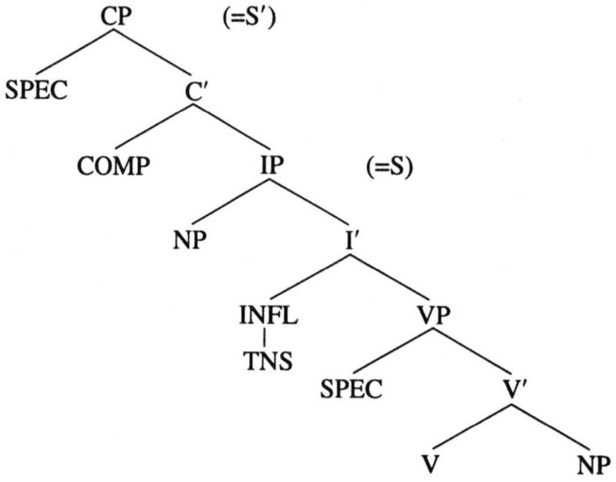

Figure 6.23. *General X-bar structure for clauses*

The tense and agreement morphemes are the main constituents of **INFL**, which is short for 'inflection'. Its complement is the VP, and its maximal projection is **IP** (inflection phrase), which is equivalent to S in Figure 4.27. COMP is the home of complementizers in complex sentences, and its maximal projection is **CP** (complementizer phrase), which is equivalent to S′. Two of the three specifier positions are important: the subject occurs in the specifier position under IP, and WH-words in WH-questions and relative clauses occur in the specifier position under CP. An important claim in GB is that this is the hierarchical structure of every clause in every human language. Languages obviously differ in terms of word order, for example, Malagasy XPs are head-initial, while Japanese XPs are head-final. This is captured in terms of a parameter, the **head parameter**, which give the possible orders of heads within XPs.

Only two grammatical relations are recognized in GB, subject and direct object, and they are derived from the constituent structure configuration in Figure 6.23. Subject is defined as the NP immediately dominated by IP (abbreviated as '[NP, IP]'), and direct object is defined as the NP immediately dominated by V′ (i.e. '[NP, V′]') (cf. (4.40)). In other words, the subject is in the SPEC of IP position, while the direct object is the sister to the verb under the V′. Traditional indirect objects as in *Pat gave the book to Chris* are treated simply as the object of a preposition. In the GB literature the subject is usually referred to as the **'external argument'**, i.e. the argument that is external to the VP, and the direct object is usually termed the **'internal argument'**, i.e. the argument that is internal to the VP.

The lexicon plays an important role in GB. Subcategorization information in lexical entries is stated in constituent-structure terms, as in (5.19). Thematic relations are called 'theta roles' in GB (often abbreviated as 'θ-roles'), and the argument structures containing them are termed 'theta grids'. The mapping between theta roles and syntactic positions is governed by the GB-analog of the Universal Alignment Hypothesis of RelG, the Uniformity of Theta Assignment Hypothesis (Baker 1988). It states that the universal default realization of an agent argument is as an external argument and that a theme or patient argument occurs as an internal argument.

One of the most important principles in GB concerns the relationship between the subcategorization properties of verbs and the constituent structures in which they occur. The subcategorization principle in (5.20) requires that the syntactic environment in which a verb or other head occurs match its subcategorization frame, and GB extends this by requiring that the subcategorization properties of verbs be satisfied at *all* levels of syntactic representation, i.e. d-structure, s-structure and Logical Form. This requirement is called the '**Projection Principle**', and it has profound consequences for how the theory works. It demands that if a verb, e.g. *kill*, takes an internal argument in its subcategorization frame, then it must have an internal argument at d-structure, s-structure and Logical Form. There are sentences involving *kill* which appear to lack an internal argument, e.g. *The rabbit was killed by the coyote* and *What did the coyote kill?*, and consequently the question arises as to how such sentences can be reconciled with this principle; this issue will be discussed below. Since verbs are subcategorized for their sisters under the V′, the Projection Principle is silent with respect to the occurrence of subjects. The **Extended Projection Principle** subsumes the Projection Principle and adds the requirement that all predicates must have subjects; in structural terms, it means that all VPs must be associated with an external argument.

It was noted above that there are no PS-rules in Figure 6.23, unlike Figure 6.7, and the Projection Principle, along with the X-bar schema, makes it possible to eliminate PS-rules as an independent component of grammar. There is an inherent redundancy between PS-rules like (5.13f) and the information contained in subcategorization frames in the lexical entries of verbs. This redundancy exists because the PS-rules specify the possible V′s in which verbs can occur. Since the subcategorization principle requires the identity of syntactic environment (specified by a PS-rule) and subcategorization frame, the same information must be expressed in the PS-rule (e.g. V′ → V + NP) and in the lexical entries for verbs which can occur in the particular constituent structure configuration (e.g. $[_{V'}$ __ NP]). Theoreticians generally abhor redundancies, and in GB, PS-rules are eliminated. How, then, are d-structures created? They are projected from the subcategorization information in the lexicon, and the resulting structures must adhere to the X-bar schema. This accounts for VPs, PPs, NPs and AdjPs, all of which are headed by lexical categories; what about IP and CP? GB assigns subcategorization properties to grammatical categories like INFL and complementizer; that is, INFL would be subcategorized for a VP complement ($[_{I'}$ __ VP]), while complementizers would be subcategorized for an IP complement (e.g. *that* $[_{C'}$ __ IP]). Given this analysis of these grammatical categories, the entire clause structure in Figure 6.23 can be projected from the information in the subcategorization frames of lexical and grammatical categories in the lexicon.

Like the other theories discussed in the chapter and unlike its predecessor TG, GB is a constraint-satisfaction theory, and the Projection Principle and the X-bar schema are two of the principles that must be satisfied. Two others that are very important for this discussion are given in (6.21).

(6.21) a. **Theta Criterion**: each θ-role can be assigned to one and only one argument, and each argument can be assigned one and only one θ-role.
b. **Case Filter**: every NP must be assigned Case.

The first states that there can be only one agent, one theme, one recipient, etc., per clause, and furthermore that a given argument can bear only one of these roles. It is impossible for a single NP to be interpreted as agent and patient simultaneously, e.g. *Sam hit* cannot mean 'Sam hit himself'. Verbs and adpositions assign θ-roles to their internal argument position; when the external argument position receives a θ-role, it is assigned by the VP as a whole. An important point is that θ-roles are assigned to specific positions in the tree, and NPs are interpreted as having that role by virtue of occupying the position. One might wonder how the Theta Criterion is compatible with the principle of the autonomy of syntax, since it appears to involve semantic relations. However, θ-roles have no real semantic content and are in effect syntactic copies of semantic thematic relations; moreover, nothing in the Theta Criterion refers to any possible semantic content of the θ-roles, and it states only that each argument should receive one, etc., and says nothing about which particular θ-roles they should be.

With respect to the Case Filter, GB distinguishes between abstract Case (with a capital 'C') and morphological case (with a lower case 'c'). There are only two abstract Cases, nominative and accusative, and they are assigned to the external and internal arguments, respectively. This is claimed to be true for English and Cantonese, even though verbs in these languages do not assign any morphological case to their full NP arguments and for morphologically ergative languages in which the morphological cases do not parallel the abstract Cases. This is why it is termed 'abstract Case'. Morphological case, which may be assigned by verbs and adpositions, also satisfies the Case Filter; the cases discussed in chapter 2 count as morphological cases in GB. Case assignment, be it abstract or morphological, is structurally based. The case assigner must govern the NP to which case is assigned. **Government** is defined as follows: X^0 governs YP iff the first maximal projection dominating X^0 also dominates YP and no maximal projection intervenes between X^0 and YP.

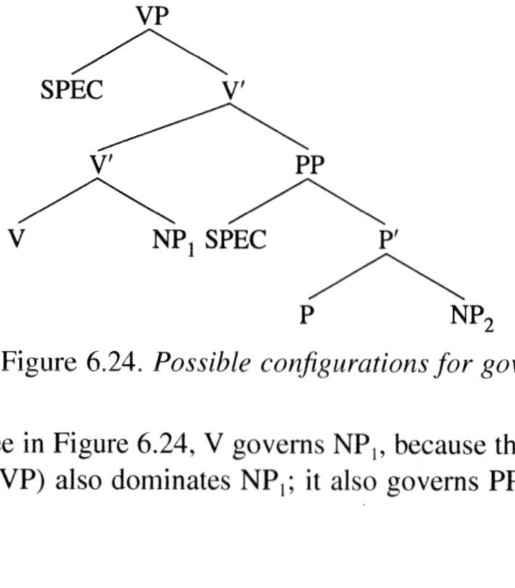

Figure 6.24. *Possible configurations for government*

In the tree in Figure 6.24, V governs NP_1, because the first maximal projection dominating it (VP) also dominates NP_1; it also governs PP, for the same reason. Moreover, no maximal projection intervenes between V and NP_1 and PP. However, V does not govern NP_2, because even though VP dominates both V and NP_2, there is a maximal projection (PP) which intervenes between V and NP_2, i.e. PP dominates NP_2 but not V. P governs NP_2. In terms of the clause in Figure 6.23, INFL governs the external argument, and if it contains tense, it assigns nominative Case to the external argument position. The verb, if it is transitive, assigns accusative Case to the internal argument position, which it governs (cf. (4.45)). Prepositions assign morphological case to their internal object, which they govern. The structural assignment of Case and θ-roles is summarized in Figure 6.25.

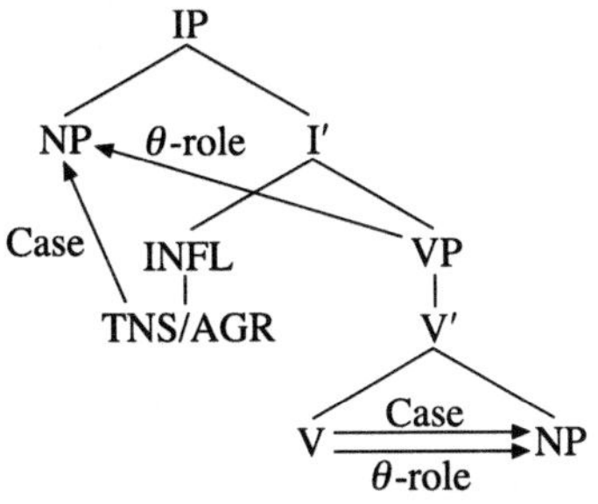

Figure 6.25. *Case and θ-role assignment in GB*

Finite verb agreement is handled in a similar fashion. INFL is assumed to contain both a tense morpheme and an agreement morpheme with the appropriate person, number and other features (usually abbreviated as 'AGR'). It governs the external argument, and the subject NP and AGR must have identical features.

The analysis of passive in GB is rather different from that in the other theories. To begin with, there is no 'passive rule' in GB; in fact, there are no construction-specific rules of any kind. As discussed in section 6.1, TG had construction-specific rules, which were also language-specific, and rules such as those are problematic in the context of GB's goal of being a theory of universal grammar. The approach taken by RelG, i.e. reformulating the rules in terms of grammatical relations so as to make them valid cross-linguistically, is impossible in GB, since it treats grammatical relations as being derivative of constituent structure. Hence GB abandons construction-specific rules altogether and postulates that what appears to be the working of construction-specific rules is in fact the interaction of a number of universal principles. Passive is a textbook case of this interaction. To begin with, the verb in a passive sentence is listed in the lexicon as a passive verb, e.g. *eat* and *eaten* would be separate lexical entries with different subcategorization frames and theta grids, as in (6.22).

(6.22)	a. *eat*	$[_{V'}$ __ NP]	<Agent Patient>
	b. *eaten*	$[_{V'} [_{V'}$ __ NP] ($[_{PP}$ *by* $NP_i])]$	<(Agent$_i$) Patient>

Eaten is analyzed as related to *eat*, and both are therefore analyzed as having an internal argument, to which each assigns the theta role of patient, following the Uniformity of Theta Assignment Hypothesis. *Eaten*, however, licenses an optional PP headed by *by*, and the NP in the *by*-PP realizes the agent argument of the verb; because this assignment violates the above constraint, it must be indicated in the lexical entry.

(The optional PP is in a higher V′ since it is an adjunct.) All information about the two verbs would not be repeated in both entries; all information common to both would appear only in the *eat* entry, and then the *eaten* entry would be related to it by means of a lexical redundancy rule, which links the active and passive entries for every verb. A lexical redundancy rule does not derive one entry from another, like the LFG lexical rule in (6.18a), but rather links two related lexical entries, allowing them to share information about the lexical items. The d-structures of *Pat ate the snack* and *The snack was eaten by Pat* are given in Figure 6.26; they are projected from the lexical entries in (6.22), following the Extended Projection Principle and the X-bar schema. Note that there is no subject NP in the d-structure for the passive sentence; this is because lexical items cannot be inserted into a position in a tree to which a θ-role is not assigned. The VP headed by the passive verb *eaten* cannot assign a θ-role to the external argument, because both of its θ-roles are assigned to NPs within the VP.

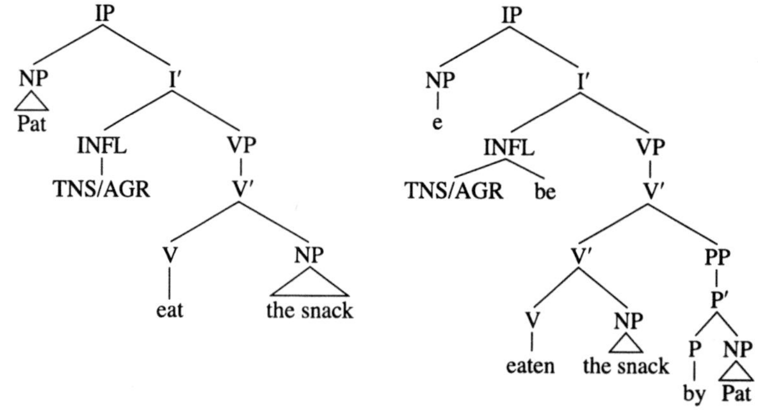

Figure 6.26. *D-structures of active and passive sentences*

In the derivation of the active sentence, tensed INFL assigns nominative Case to the external argument *Pat*, and the transitive verb *eat* assigns accusative Case to the internal argument *the snack*. Furthermore, the verb *eat* assigns the θ-role patient to the internal argument, and the VP assigns the θ-role agent to the external argument. Thus, the Projection Principle, X-bar schema, Case Filter and Theta Criterion have all been satisfied in the active sentence. In the derivation of the active sentence in Figure 6.26, the verb *eat* would move to the head of INFL position, in order for it to merge with the tense and agreement morphemes there; this is how a finite verb gets its tense and other inflections. The s-structure of *Pat ate the snack* is given in Figure 6.27.

The situation is crucially different in the passive sentence. The verb *eaten* assigns the θ-role patient to the internal argument, and as specified in its lexical entry, the θ-role agent is assigned to the object of the preposition *by*. Hence the Theta Criterion is satisfied. What about Case? The NP *Pat* is assigned case by the preposition *by*. One of the important properties of passive verbs is that they cannot assign accusative Case, something only active voice transitive verbs can do. Hence *eaten* cannot assign Case to its internal argument. If the NP *the snack* remains in internal argument position, the Case Filter would be violated. How can a Case Filter violation be avoided? The external argument position is empty, and INFL contains tense; hence if the NP *the snack* could

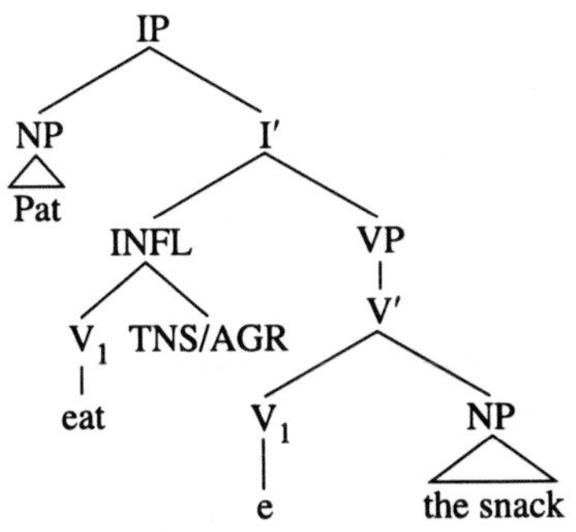

Figure 6.27. *S-structure of* Pat ate the snack

move to external argument position, it could receive nominative Case from tensed INFL, thereby satisfying the Case Filter. GB posits a universal rule of **NP-movement**; it is a maximally general rule, stating simply that an NP can move anywhere. While the rule itself is unconstrained, it is subject to the principles discussed so far, plus the **Structure-Preservation Constraint**, which states that a rule cannot change the constituent structure of a clause. This means that in the right tree in Figure 6.26, there is only one place that the NP *the snack* can move to, namely, the empty external argument position. If the NP in internal argument position moves to external argument position, however, then why is the resulting structure not a violation of the Projection Principle? The answer is that when the NP moves, the structural position from which it moved remains, and in addition, the moved NP is **coindexed** with the position from which it moved. The resulting structure is given in Figure 6.28.

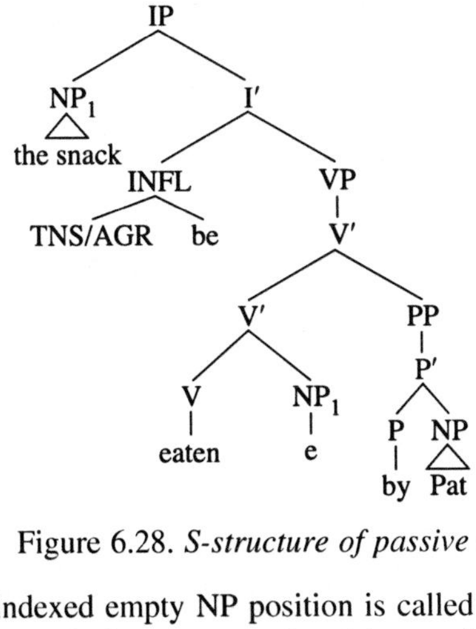

Figure 6.28. *S-structure of passive sentence* The snack was eaten by Pat

The coindexed empty NP position is called a **trace**, and the moved NP plus its trace constitute a **chain**, represented as {*the snack*$_1$, e$_1$}. The coindexing relation between the moved NP and its trace is considered to be an instance of **binding**, analogous to the relation between a reflexive element and its antecedent (see section 4.5). In particular, a moved NP must command its trace, just as an antecedent must command the reflexive pronoun it binds (see (4.42)). The principles governing coindexing between a moved element and its trace or a reflexive and its antecedent constitute **Binding Theory** in

GB. Since the command requirement entails that the moved element be higher in the tree than its trace, this means that movement can only be 'up the tree', i.e. to a higher position in the tree.

A chain counts as a single argument for the purposes of the Case Filter and the Theta Criterion. The Case Filter is satisfied, because the chain is assigned nominative Case by the tensed INFL, and the Theta Criterion is satisfied, because it is assigned one θ-role by the verb *eaten.* Thus, passive constructions are accounted for without invoking a construction-specific or language-specific passive rule. The only thing passive-specific about the analysis is the lexical entry for a passive verb; all other elements in the analysis are general, universal principles: the Projection Principle, the X-bar schema, the Structure-Preservation Constraint, the Case Filter, the Theta Criterion, the Binding principles and the rule of NP-movement.

The rule of NP-movement is also invoked in the analysis of unaccusative verbs, which were mentioned in the discussion of RelG. The Uniformity of Theta Assignment Hypothesis requires that an intransitive verb taking a patient argument, e.g. *shatter* as in *the glass shattered*, must have its argument in internal argument position at d-structure. Hence the d-structure of *the glass shattered* would look like the passive d-structure in Figure 6.26, minus the *by*-PP. In order to satisfy the Case Filter, the NP *the glass* would have to move from its d-structure position where it cannot get Case, due to the intransitivity of *shatter*, to the external argument position, where it can receive Case from the tensed INFL. This is analogous to the RelG analysis summarized in Figure 6.12, although the motivation for the movement in GB is completely different from the motivation for the advancement in RelG.

Dative shift is treated lexically in GB: there are two versions of, for example, *give*, each with different subcategorization properties. As with passive and active verbs, there is a lexical redundancy rule linking the two verbs and allowing the two lexical entries to share information.

The final phenomenon to be examined is WH-questions. As mentioned earlier, the WH-word in a WH-question ends up in the specifier of CP position. The d- and s-structures of *What did Pat buy?* are given in Figure 6.29.

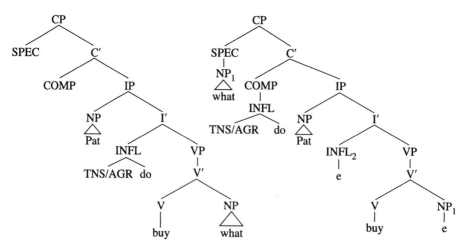

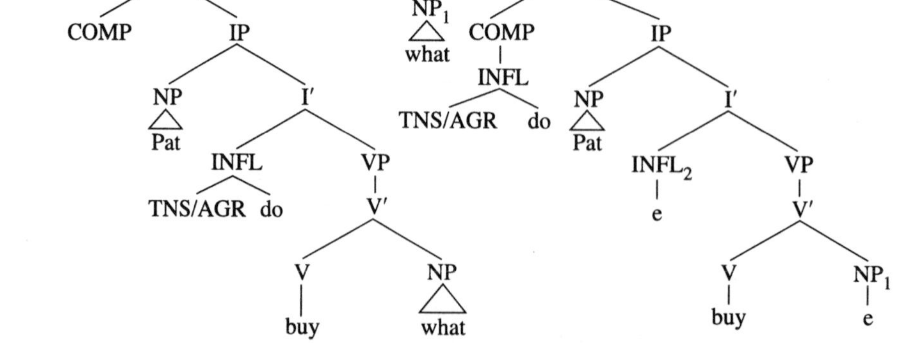

Figure 6.29. *D-structure and s-structure of WH-question in English*

Two movements are involved in the derivation of this sentence. The WH-word *what* moves from its internal argument position in d-structure to [SPEC, CP], leaving a co-indexed trace behind. The movement rule in this instance is known as **WH-movement**. It has somewhat different properties from NP-movement; the two will be contrasted below. The second movement involves the auxiliary verb *do* plus its tense and agreement inflection; it is moved from the head of INFL position to the head of COMP position, leaving a trace. This is how subject–auxiliary inversion is handled in GB. This rule, which may be called 'verb movement', can move a verb, which is a head, only to another empty head position, because of the Structure-Preservation Constraint, and the only empty head position is the head of COMP. NP-movement and WH-movement, on the other hand, affect only maximal projections, and therefore the moved NP or WH-XP must move to an open position for maximal projections, which is [SPEC, IP] or [SPEC, CP].

The s-structure tree in Figure 6.29 satisfies all of the principles discussed so far. The Projection Principle is satisfied, because the trace in the V′ reflects the subcategorization of *buy*, and the X-bar schema and Structure-Preservation Constraint are also obeyed. The Theta Criterion is fulfilled, because the chain {*what*$_1$, e$_1$} is assigned a single θ-role by *buy*, and the VP assigns a θ-role to *Pat*. The structure does not violate the Case Filter, because the chain {*what*$_1$, e$_1$} receives accusative Case from *buy*, and the external argument *Pat* is assigned nominative Case by the tensed INFL. In addition, both moved elements command their traces, as required by Binding Theory.

The three movement rules posited in GB each have distinct properties, as do their traces. They are summarized in Table 6.2.

Table 6.2. *Movement rules and their traces in GB*

Rule	Type moved	Trace [+Case]
NP-movement	XP	No
WH-movement	XP	Yes
Verb movement	X^0	does not apply

Because lexical items can appear in d-structure only in positions to which a θ-role is assigned, due to the Projection Principle, all XP traces are in θ-role-receiving positions [θ-positions], and all movement is to non-θ-positions. Movement from one θ-position to another would violate the Theta Criterion, because the chain would be assigned two θ-roles. NP-movement moves XPs from positions in which they would not receive Case to one in which they can receive Case, and this means that NP-movement can only move an XP to a Case-receiving, non-θ-position, and the only position meeting this description is the [SPEC, IP] position with a verb whose VP does not assign a θ-role to its external argument. The verbs in this class include passive and unaccusative verbs. The traces left by NP-movement are called **NP-traces**, and they are [–Case, +θ]. WH-movement, on the other hand, moves an XP to [SPEC, CP], which is outside of the IP and therefore cannot in principle be governed by a Case-assigning head. Hence the only way for a chain created by WH-movement to comply with the Case Filter is to have its trace be Case-marked, and this is in fact what happens. **WH-traces** always occur in Case-receiving positions, and they are therefore [+Case, +θ]. Verb movement moves a verbal X^0 to a lexically unfilled head position, leaving a trace; since it is a verb, the issues of Case and θ-roles are irrelevant. These three movement rules have complementary properties, and so they are treated in GB as variants of one general movement rule, **Move α**, which states simply 'move α (any category) anywhere'. While the formulation of the rule is maximally general, it is subject to all of the principles and constraints discussed above, and consequently the range of possible movements that can satisfy all of the principles and constraints is extremely limited.

In the late 1980s the idea that grammatical categories like tense and complementizer could head full X-bar projections was extended to all grammatical categories. With respect to noun phrases, the determiner became the head of a determiner phrase [DP], with NP as its complement. (It was noted at the end of chapter 3 that some dependency theories take the determiner to be the head and the noun the dependent.) With respect to the clause, INFL was broken up into its constituent morphemes, each of which headed a different X-bar projection. In the tree diagram in Figure 6.30, tense phrase [TP], aspect phrase [ASPP], subject agreement phrase [AGR_SP] and object agreement phrase [AGR_OP] are represented. Object agreement was introduced because of languages like Lakhota and Swahili. In addition to the splitting up of INFL, it was proposed that the subject (external argument) be generated inside the VP in the specifier position; this came to be known as the VP-internal-subject hypothesis. The revised conception of clause structure is given in Figure 6.30.

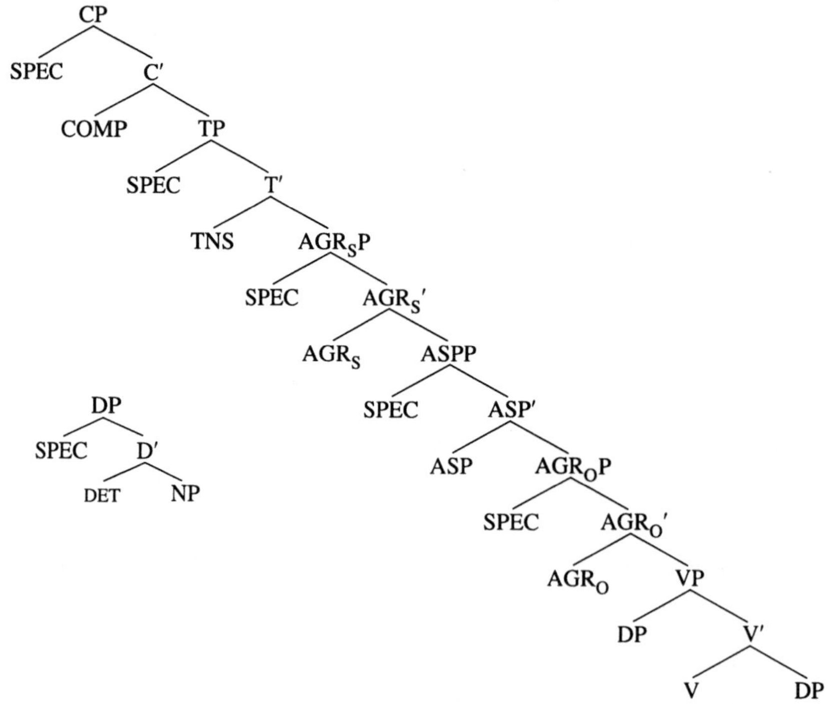

Figure 6.30. *Extended functional projections in the clause*

It should be noted that there is some variation in the literature as to whether TP dominates AGR_SP or AGR_SP dominates TP. TP will be taken to be the complement of C for this discussion.

What does the derivation of a simple sentence like *Pat saw Chris* look like? The three lexical items would be inserted into positions within the VP at d-structure. Nominative case is associated with TP, and accusative case with AGR_O. Subject agreement is associated with AGR_S; since English lacks object agreement, there is no morphology associated with AGR_O, but, as noted above, it is involved with accusative case. The external argument *Pat* would raise to SPEC of AGR_S to leave its agreement features and then raise further to SPEC of TP to receive nominative case. The internal argument *Chris* would raise to SPEC of AGR_O to receive accusative case. The verb *see* would raise to head of AGR_O, because it is transitive and takes an accusative object, then to head of AGR_S to receive subject agreement, and finally to head of TP to receive tense. The resulting tree structure is given in Figure 6.31.

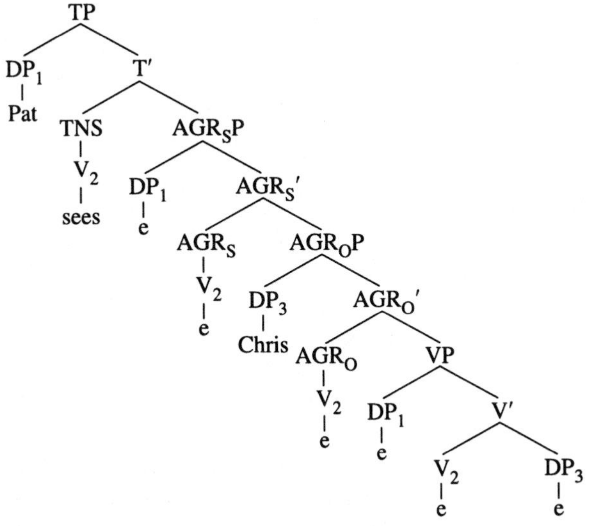

Figure 6.31. *S-structure of* Pat sees Chris

In the earlier version of GB, the only movement is a sentence like this would be the verb moving to INFL to get tense and agreement inflection, as noted above (see Figure 6.27); the NPs *Pat* and *Chris* would be in the same structural positions in both d- and s-structure. The situation is strikingly different in Figure 6.31: in this s-structure, all three lexical items occupy different structural positions in s-structure from the ones they occupy in d-structure.

In the 1990s a new type of Principles and Parameters approach arose, the Minimalist Program (Chomsky 1992, 1995, 1998). It is termed 'minimalist' because it posits only two levels of representation, Phonetic Form and Logical Form. Chomsky argues that these are the only levels of representation that are conceptually necessary, Logical Form being the level that interfaces with the intentional–conceptual cognitive systems which are involved in the interpretation of sentences, and Phonetic Form being the level that interfaces with the articulatory–perceptual systems that underlie the actual production of speech. The organization of the Minimalist Program is given in Figure 6.32.

While the Minimalist Program retains the general 'Y' structure of GB, both d-structure and s-structure are missing as well-defined levels of representation. From TG

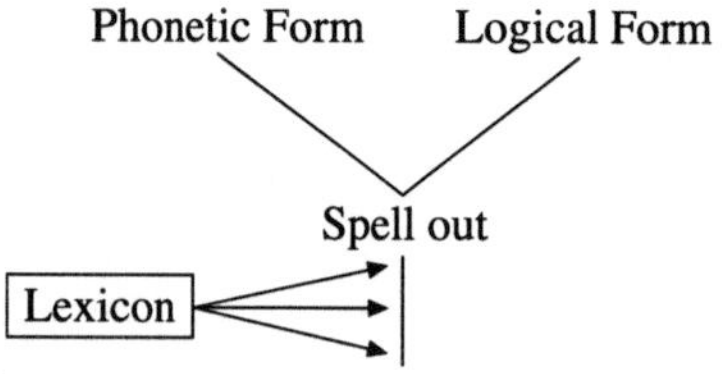

Figure 6.32. *Organization of the Minimalist Program*

to GB there was always a level of representation at which lexical insertion occurs *in toto*, and it is to that representation that transformational rules or Move α apply. Once these syntactic rules have started applying during a derivation, no further lexical insertion is possible. However, in the Minimalist Program lexical insertion is interspersed with the application of syntactic rules. (This was a salient feature of **Generative Semantics** analyses (McCawley 1968b, 1971; Lakoff 1971), something which Chomsky argued vehemently against in the 1960s and 1970s; see Pullum 1996) Hence there is no level of representation corresponding to the TG deep structure or GB d-structure. S-structure is also no longer a well-defined level, because the principles and constraints that applied there in GB, for example, the Case Filter, are argued to apply at Logical Form. It is replaced by 'Spell-Out', the point in the derivation at which no more lexical items can be inserted into the sentence and no more overt syntactic rules may apply. Whether Spell-Out happens only once or happens repeatedly during a derivation is a point of controversy within the theory. A copy of the structure goes to Phonetic Form and ultimately into the articulatory–perceptual interfaces, while another copy goes to Logical Form for the checking of various well-formedness conditions, for example, Theta Criterion and Case Filter, and ultimately to the intentional–conceptual interfaces for semantic interpretation.

In keeping with its minimalist tone, phrase structure is simplified to what is termed 'bare phrase structure', in which only the nodes actually utilized in a sentence are represented in a tree. This leads to much simpler phrase structure trees than those found in GB. A leading idea of the Minimalist Program is that morphology drives syntax; that is, morphological features (some abstract) have to be satisfied, analogous to how the Case Filter drives the application of Move α with passive and unaccusative verbs. A simple example of this is WH-movement. COMP may be [±WH], and if it is [+WH], then a WH-word must be moved to its specifier position in order to satisfy the feature. Case is no longer assigned but rather is checked, and the case-receiving NP must be in the specifier position of the case-determining head in order for its case to be checked, as in Figure 6.31.

Chomsky (1995) argues that the derivational mechanism of syntax (what he calls 'C_{HL}', the computational procedure for human language that derives Logical Form and Phonetic Form), is invariant across languages, and therefore that all apparent differences among languages are lexical in nature. This invariant syntax has become the focus of work in the Minimalist Program, and Chomsky (1998) terms it 'narrow syntax'; it is a more restricted version of core grammar. Because narrow syntax is invariant across languages, it excludes many of the syntactic phenomena which have been central to syntactic theory, both Principles and Parameters theories and others, over the last few decades, for example, binding. These phenomena are excluded because they exhibit significant cross-linguistic variation.

For syntacticians working within the general Principles and Parameters framework, the Minimalist Program is something of a departure from GB, and the two approaches are competitors within that general framework. Many syntacticians have found the notion of a theory of universal grammar composed of a single general rule, Move α, along with a small set of universal principles with limited parametric variation, very appealing, and there has been a great deal of work done using the GB framework.

One of the most important motivations for research in this framework is the goal of developing a theory of grammar which can accurately characterize native speakers' knowledge of their language and which can be the foundation for an account of how children acquire language. Chomsky maintains that the principles of syntax are so abstract and that there is insufficient evidence in the input for the child to induce them from the language to which it is exposed, and he concludes that language acquisition is possible only because human beings are born with an autonomous cognitive system devoted to language, the central component of which is the autonomous syntactic system. The universal grammar composed of principles and parameters is simultaneously the language-acquisition device that makes language acquisition possible. Thus for Chomsky, not only is syntax autonomous, but language is itself an autonomous mental faculty.

6.4 **Role and Reference Grammar**

A fundamental question motivating the development of Role and Reference Grammar has been 'how can the interaction of syntax, semantics and discourse-pragmatics in different grammatical systems best be captured and explained?' Early work in RRG concentrated on the analysis of Lakhota, Tagalog and Dyirbal, and because of this cross-linguistic point of departure, many of the analyses proposed in RRG are strikingly different from those put forth in the other three theories.

The first starting point can be seen clearly in the way RRG represents syntactic structure. RRG maintains that a theory of clause structure should capture all of the universal features of clauses without imposing features on languages in which there is no evidence for them. This assumption rules out, for example, VP as a universal feature of clauses. RRG rejects both grammatical-relations-based representations, such as those in RelG and LFG, and X-bar-type constituent-structure representations, because, it is argued (see Van Valin and LaPolla 1997), neither type is universally valid. The universality of grammatical relations will be discussed below. The problems which lead to the rejection of X-bar-type constituent structure include the structure of head-marking languages, discontinuous constituency of the type found in South Slavic and Australian languages, and languages with completely grammatically unconstrained (i.e. 'free') word order. Despite the great diversity of human languages, there are universal features of clause structure: all languages distinguish structurally between predicating and non-predicating elements, on the one hand, and, among the non-predicating elements, between those that are semantically arguments of the predicating element and those that are not. This may be represented schematically as in Figure 6.33.

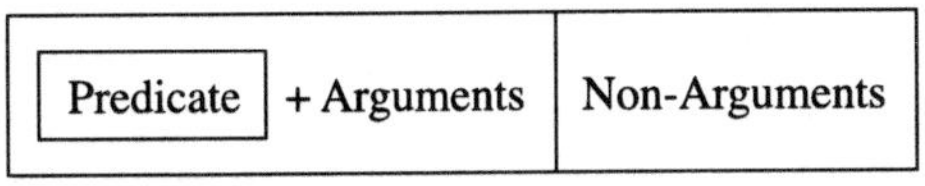

Figure 6.33. *Universal oppositions underlying clause structure*

The syntactic unit containing the predicate is termed the **nucleus**, the unit containing the nucleus plus the arguments of the predicate in the nucleus is called the **core**, and the unit encompassing the non-arguments (adjuncts) is labelled the **periphery**. Clauses are thus conceived of as having a **layered** structure, each layer being motivated semantically. A simple example from English with its layered structure is given in Figure 6.34, and the semantic basis of the structure is laid out in Table 6.3.

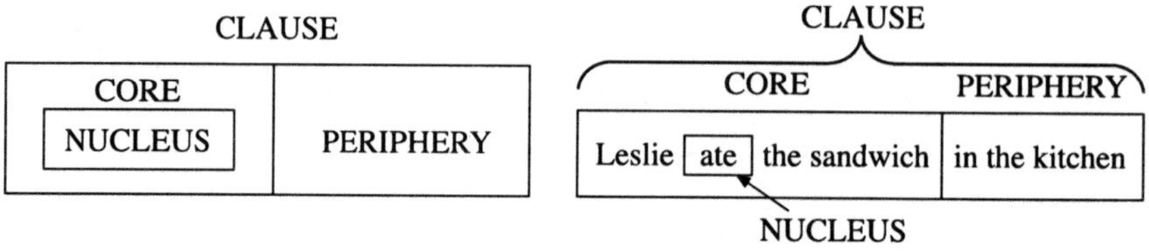

Figure 6.34. *Layered structure of the clause*

Table 6.3. *Semantic units underlying the syntactic units of the layered structure of the clause*

Semantic element(s)	Syntactic unit
Predicate	Nucleus
Argument in semantic representation of predicate	Core argument
Non-arguments	Periphery
Predicate + Arguments	Core
Predicate + Arguments + Non-arguments	Clause (= Core + Periphery)

Nucleus, core and periphery are universal features of clauses; every language manifests them. Tree diagrams representing clauses in English and Lakhota are given in Figure 6.35.

In the English example, *Scully*, *the photo* and *Mulder* are core arguments, and *at the office* and *yesterday* are adjuncts in the periphery. The arrow linking the periphery to the core indicates that the periphery is an optional modifier of the core. Lakhota is a head-marking language, and consequently in the RRG analysis the bound pronominal affixes on the verb count as the core arguments; this can readily be seen in the fact that *nawíčhayaxʔųkte* 'You will hear them' is a complete sentence on its own (the verb *naxʔų́* 'hear' takes its actor and undergoer affixes as infixes). The independent NP *mathó ki hená* 'those bears' is within the clause but outside the core and is in apposition to *wičha-* '3plUndergoer' (cf. the analysis of head-marking languages in section 3.2). The layered structure of the clause is the same in English and Lakhota; the primary difference is that the core arguments are instantiated by free morphemes in English but by bound morphemes in Lakhota. NPs and PPs have layered structures analogous to that of clauses, but they will not be discussed here.

The elements *did* and *not* are not attached to anything in the English tree. They are grammatical morphemes, and such morphemes, which are called **operators** in RRG, are represented in a different projection of the clause from the predicate, arguments and adjuncts. The operators relevant to this discussion are **aspect** (e.g. **perfective, imperfective, progressive, perfect**), negation, tense and **illocutionary force** (i.e. whether the

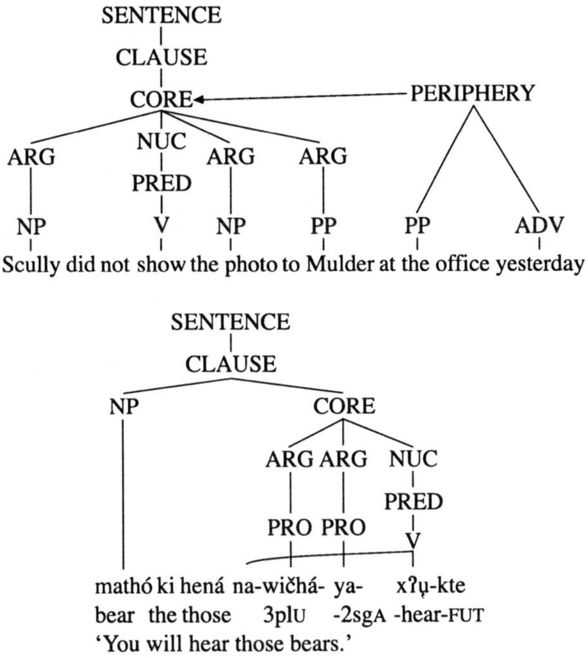

Figure 6.35. *Layered structure of clauses in English and Lakhota*

utterance is a question, statement or command). Operators have scope over different layers of the clause: aspect is a nuclear operator, modifying the predicate only, tense and illocutionary force are clausal operators, and negation can be an operator modifying any of the three layers. The scope of an operator is a function of its meaning; for example, tense expresses a deictic relation between the time of the event referred to in the clause and the speech time, and therefore tense must have clausal scope. The formal representation of the operators in the sentences in Figure 6.35 is given in Figure 6.36.

In the English example both tense and illocutionary force are connected to *did*; this is because illocutionary force in English is signalled by the position of the tense morpheme in the (main) clause (core-medial tense = declarative, core-initial tense = interrogative, absence of tense = imperative). In the Lakhota example, the question particle *he* has been added, so that there is an explicit illocutionary force operator. Interestingly, the linear order of the morphemes expressing the operators (with respect to the verb) reflects their scope; that is, if all of the operator morphemes occur on the same side of the verb, the morphemes expressing nuclear operators will be closer to the verb than those expressing core operators, and they in turn will be closer to the verb than those expressing clausal operators. This is the case in both trees in Figure 6.36. In tree diagrams like these, the upper projection is called the 'constituent projection', and the lower one the 'operator projection'. The RRG system of representing clause structure thus combines aspects of both dependency and constituent structure approaches: it represents constituents, but some of the labels for the constituents are relational (e.g. ARGument), while modifiers are represented explicitly as such (e.g. peripheral adjuncts, operators).

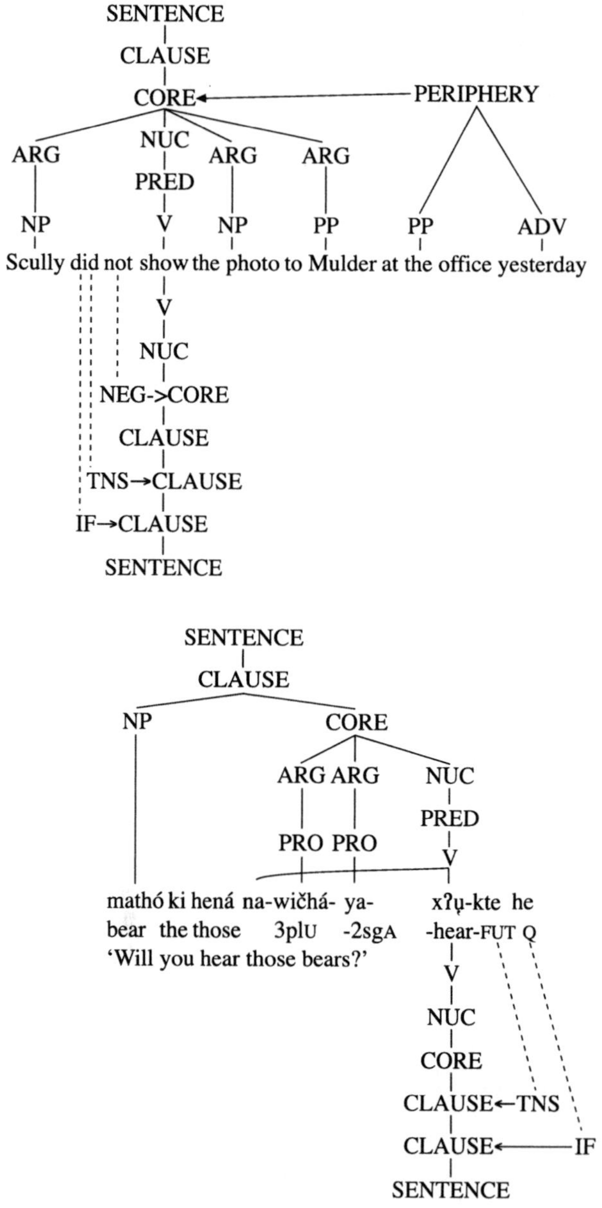

Figure 6.36. *The representation of operators in RRG*

All of the elements of the constituent projection discussed so far are universal, but there are some additional, non-universal elements. The one which is relevant to this chapter is the precore slot [PrCS], which is the position in which WH-words occur in WH-questions in languages like English and Malagasy. It is illustrated in Figure 6.39 below.

RRG posits only a single syntactic representation for each sentence, which corresponds to the overt form of the sentence; there are neither abstract representations like f-structure in LFG nor underlying levels of representation as in TG, RelG and GB. It is in many respects the original 'minimalist' theory, since it has postulated only a single syntactic representation and a single semantic representation from its inception in the late 1970s. There is a direct mapping between the semantic representation and the syntactic representation; this is depicted schematically in Figure 6.37.

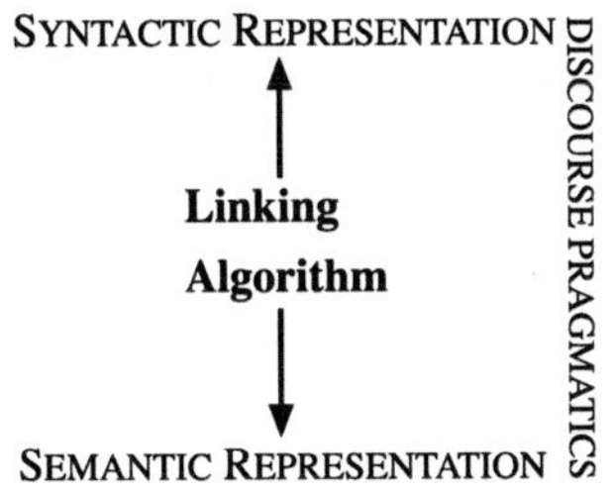

Figure 6.37. *The organization of RRG*

The linking algorithm which effects the mapping works both from the syntax to the semantics and from the semantics to the syntax. Discourse-pragmatics plays a role in the mapping; languages vary in terms of where and how it affects the linking, and this is a major source of cross-linguistic variation in grammatical systems. Discourse-pragmatics is represented primarily in terms of the focus structure of the sentence. Roughly speaking, focus structure is the division of a sentence into topical and focal parts (see (6.11) and the discussion regarding it in section 6.3). The theory assumes the universal typology of focus structure types proposed in Lambrecht (1994). RRG adds a projection to the clause which represents the potential focus domain, i.e. the part of the sentence in which focus can occur, and the actual focus domain, i.e. the part of the sentence which is the focus. In the trees in Figure 6.38, the dotted lines in the focus structure projection delimit the potential focus domain, while the triangle indicates the actual focus domain.

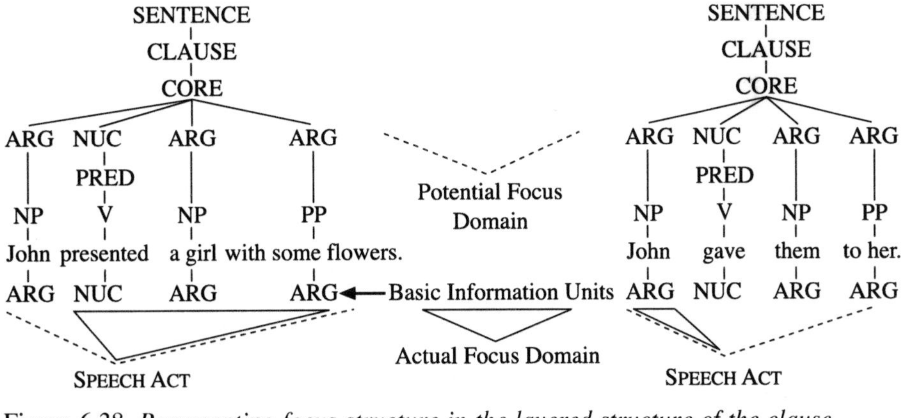

Figure 6.38. *Representing focus structure in the layered structure of the clause*

The first sentence is a traditional topic–comment structure in which the subject is the topic and the predicate (nucleus plus post-nuclear constituents) is focal. The second

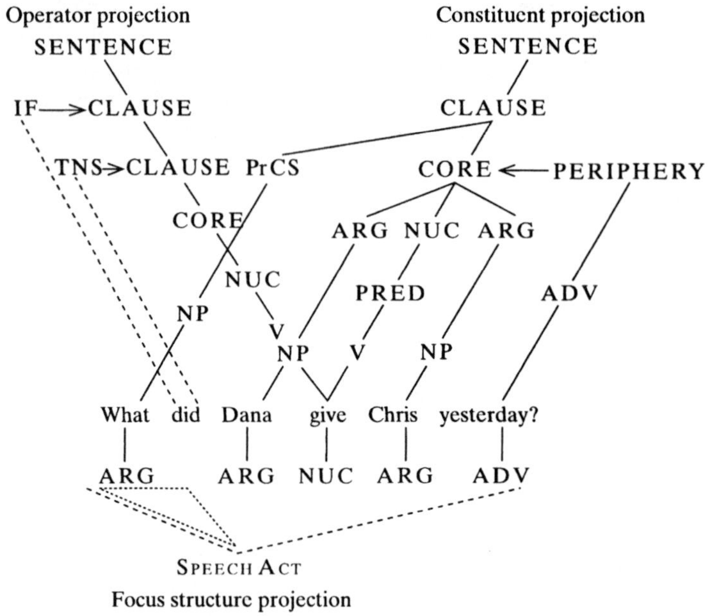

Figure 6.39. *Constituent-, operator-, and focus-structure projections of the clause*

represents narrow, contrastive focus on the subject. The three projections may be combined into a single representation, as in Figure 6.39.

Since this is a WH-question, the focus is the WH-word, which appears in the precore slot. Note the lack of an empty NP position in the core; the analysis of WH-questions in RRG will be discussed in more detail below.

The semantic representation of a sentence is based on the lexical representation of verbs. Unlike some of the other theories, the lexical entry for a verb does not contain a list of thematic relations. RRG uses a system of **lexical decomposition** for representing aspects of the meaning of verbs and other predicates; examples of the representations are given in (6.23).

(6.23) Lexical representations for some English verbs in RRG

a. *broken*	**broken′** (y)	[e.g. *the glass is broken*]
a′. *break*	BECOME **broken′** (y)	[e.g. *the glass broke*]
a″. *break*	[**do′** (x, ∅)] CAUSE [BECOME **broken′** (y)]	[e.g. *the boy broke the glass*]
b. *dead*	**dead′** (y)	
b′. *die*	BECOME **dead′** (y)	
b″. *kill*	[**do′** (x, ∅)] CAUSE [BECOME **dead′** (y)]	
c. *cool*	**cool′** (y)	[e.g. *the soup is cool*]
c′. *cool*	BECOME **cool′** (y)	[e.g. *the soup cooled*]
c″. *cool*	[**do′** (x, ∅)] CAUSE [BECOME **cool′** (y)]	[e.g. *the breeze cooled the soup*]

d. *sing* **do′** (x, [**sing′** (x, y)])
e. *run* **do′** (x, [**run′** (x)])

The predicates in the (a), (b) and (c) examples are all **stative**, i.e. they depict states rather than actions. The verbs in the (a′), (b′) and (c′) examples all signal changes of state, while those in (a″), (b″) and (c″) refer to caused changes of state. Change-of-state verbs are called ‘accomplishment verbs’ in RRG, and caused change-of-state verbs are termed ‘causative accomplishment verbs’. The verbs in (d) and (e) are activity verbs, since they denote actions which lack an inherent endpoint. To the right of each verb or predicate is its lexical representation or ‘logical structure’. A plain **pred′** indicates a stative predicate, while **do′** is a part of the logical structure of all activity predicates; ‘**do′** (x, ∅)’ is an unspecified activity. ‘BECOME’ indicates change over time, hence change of state when combined with a stative predicate. ‘CAUSE’ signals a causative relation between two predicates. The logical structure in (6.23a″) forms the basis of the semantic representation of a sentence like *the boy broke the glass*; the representation that is the input to the linking algorithm for the mapping from semantics to syntax is given in (6.24).

(6.24) [**do′** (the boy, ∅)] CAUSE [BECOME **broken′** (the glass)]

The interpretation of this logical structure is that some unspecified activity done by the boy causes the glass to become broken.

The lexical entry for each verb and other predicating element contains its logical structure, and for most this is all that is required. In particular, there is no syntactic subcategorization information in the entry at all. The subcategorization frame of a verb indicates its transitivity, and transitivity in RRG is expressed in terms of the number of semantic macroroles a verb takes. (The semantic macroroles, actor and undergoer, were introduced in section 2.1.) An intransitive verb takes one macrorole (it can be either actor or undergoer), and a transitive verb takes both of them. There are general principles which predict the transitivity of a verb from its logical structure; there are irregular verbs, and for them the number of macroroles is specified in the verb's lexical entry.

The discussion in this section will focus on the linking from semantics to syntax, since that parallels the analyses in the other theories most closely. The grammatical phenomena listed in section 6.0 are handled in terms of the semantics-to-syntax mapping. The first step is the constitution of the semantic representation of the sentence, and this involves accessing the logical structure of the predicate in the lexicon and replacing the variables in it with referring expressions, as in the logical structure in (6.24). The next step is determining which argument is actor and which is undergoer, if the logical structure contains two or more arguments. This selection is based on the Actor–Undergoer Hierarchy, which is given in Figure 6.40; it is similar to the hierarchies in (2.20).

ACTOR ⟶				⟵ UNDERGOER
Arg of DO	1st arg of **do′** (x, ...	1st arg of **pred′** (x,y)	2nd arg of **pred′** (x,y)	Arg of state **pred′** (x)

[‘⟶’ = increasing markedness of realization of argument as macrorole]

Figure 6.40. *The Actor–Undergoer Hierarchy*

('DO' will not be discussed, as it is not germane to the major issues in this chapter.) Unlike the hierarchies in (2.20) which refer to thematic relations, this hierarchy refers to the argument positions in logical structures. The leftmost argument in the hierarchy will be selected as actor, and the rightmost as undergoer. With respect to the logical structure in (6.24), *the boy* will be the actor, since it is the first argument of **do′**, and *the glass* will be the undergoer, since it is the single argument of **broken′** (y). This is a very simple example. As noted in sections 2.1 and 2.2.2.2, there is only one possible choice for actor with every verb, but some verbs allow more than one candidate for undergoer, e.g. English *give, send, present, supply* and many others (see (2.78)–(2.83) for examples from English and Swahili). The logical structure for *give* is presented in (6.25).

(6.25) [**do′** (Chris, ∅)] CAUSE [BECOME **have′** (Pat, the glass)]

The default undergoer assignment is *the glass*, since it is the second argument of **have′** (y, z) and therefore outranks *Pat*, the first argument of **have′** (y, z). However, this verb permits a selection that violates the hierarchy: it is possible to select *Pat* as undergoer. The default selection yields the sentence in (6.26a), while the alternative selection results in (6.26b), assuming a simple active voice clause (more on this below).

(6.26) a. Chris gave the glass to Pat.
b. Chris gave Pat the glass.

This is, of course, the dative-shift alternation, and it is handled in RRG in terms of alternative choices for undergoer. In (6.26a), *Pat* is a non-macrorole oblique core argument, while in (6.26b) *the glass* is a non-macrorole direct core argument.

Once the selections for actor and undergoer have been made, the arguments are then mapped into the syntax. There are two considerations here: the selection of the appropriate clause structure, and the selection of the privileged syntactic argument ('subject'). The clause structures in Figures 6.35 and 6.36 are not generated by the equivalent of PS-rules in RRG; rather they are stored as a set of basic syntactic templates in what is called 'the syntactic inventory', a syntactic analogue to the lexicon. In Figure 6.41, the precore slot template is combined with a core template to form the clause structure in Figure 6.39. There are general principles governing the selection of the appropriate syntactic template, given the logical structure of the predicate and certain information about the linking, for example, whether a passive or WH-question is involved, since both of these affect the number of core-argument positions in the clause.

RRG has a very different view of grammatical relations from the other theories. Because of the phenomena discussed in section 2.3 (Philippine systems, syntactic ergativity), the theory does not attribute cross-linguistic validity to the traditional grammatical relations of subject, direct object and indirect object, and therefore does not employ them as theoretical or analytical constructs. Rather, it adopts a construction-specific conception of grammatical relations and postulates only a single one, which is called the 'privileged syntactic argument'. 'Construction-specific' means that a privileged argument may be identified for each construction; the first column in Table 2.3 (p. 59) summarizes the privileged arguments in the constructions discussed there. This notion subsumes syntactic **pivots**, which are the omitted NP in a control or conjunction-reduction construction or the matrix-coded NP in a matrix coding construction, and controllers, which are the triggers for verb agreement, the antecedents of reflexives and the controller of the omitted argument in a conjunction–reduction construction (see

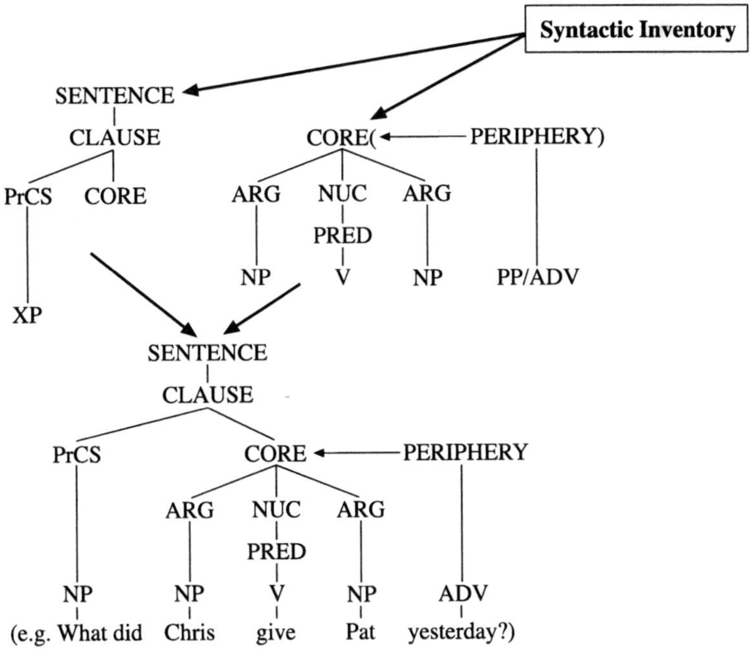

Figure 6.41. *Combining syntactic templates from the syntactic inventory*

Table 2.3). Since privileged syntactic argument is a construction-specific grammatical relation, no conflict arises if a single sentence contains two different constructions with distinct privileged syntactic arguments, as in the Tagalog example in (6.8a): the actor *ng babae* 'the woman' is the controller of the reflexivization construction, and the undergoer *ang bigas* 'the rice' is the pivot of the relative clause construction. No notion corresponding to direct object is posited; the properties of direct objects in Table 2.4 are handled primarily in terms of the notion of undergoer in RRG.

There is a hierarchy governing the selection of privileged syntactic arguments. It is given in (6.27) and corresponds to the actor part of the Actor–Undergoer Hierarchy.

(6.27) Privileged syntactic argument selection hierarchy:
arg of DO > 1st arg of **do′** > 1st arg of **pred′** (x, y) > 2nd arg of **pred′** (x, y) > arg of **pred′** (x)

The selection principles for syntactically accusative constructions and syntactically ergative constructions are given in (6.28); they refer to the hierarchy in (6.27).

(6.28) Privileged syntactic argument selection principles:
a. Syntactically accusative constructions: highest ranking macrorole is default choice.
b. Syntactically ergative constructions: lowest ranking macrorole is default choice.

Given a transitive verb with an actor and an undergoer, the actor will be the highest ranking macrorole and the undergoer the lowest ranking, because of the Actor–Undergoer Hierarchy. If the verb is intransitive, then the macrorole counts as both the highest and lowest ranking, since it is the only one. In a language like English or German in which virtually all constructions are syntactically accusative, (6.28a) means that the actor will be the default choice for 'subject', i.e. the privileged syntactic argument. In the syntactically ergative constructions in languages like Yidiɲ and Dyirbal, (6.28b) means that the default choice for pivot or controller will be the undergoer. Languages with voice constructions allow the default choice to be overridden: a passive construction permits the undergoer to be the privileged syntactic argument, whereas in an antipassive construction the actor is the privileged syntactic argument (cf. Table 2.5). The universal statements of passive and antipassive are given in (6.29). (By 'universal' is meant that if a language has a passive or antipassive construction, it will have to conform to this characterization; it does not mean that every language has one of these constructions.)

(6.29) Universal characterizations of voice oppositions:
  a. Passive: ~A = Privileged syntactic argument (A receives non-canonical coding)
  b. Antipassive: A = Privileged syntactic argument (U receives non-canonical coding)

('Non-canonical coding' includes being omitted, being an adjunct in the periphery, or occurring in an oblique case; these are language-specific features of the constructions.) The privileged syntactic argument in passive is characterized as '~A' rather than as 'U', because in some languages non-undergoers can have this function in a passive, e.g. Japanese (see (2.77)), Kinyarwanda (see (2.84)). In antipassive constructions, on the other hand, the actor is always the privileged syntactic argument. Malagasy, Kwakwala and Tagalog have additional voice forms which allow non-macrorole arguments to be the privileged syntactic argument. The syntactic split in Yidiɲ involving pronouns (accusative syntax) versus full NPs (ergative syntax) illustrated in (2.104) can be captured in terms of both of the principles in (6.28) being operative in the grammar: constructions involving pronouns use (6.28a), while constructions involving full NPs use (6.28b).

The linking system may be summarized as in Figure 6.42. An important feature of it is that it divides naturally into two phases, one universal and one language-specific.

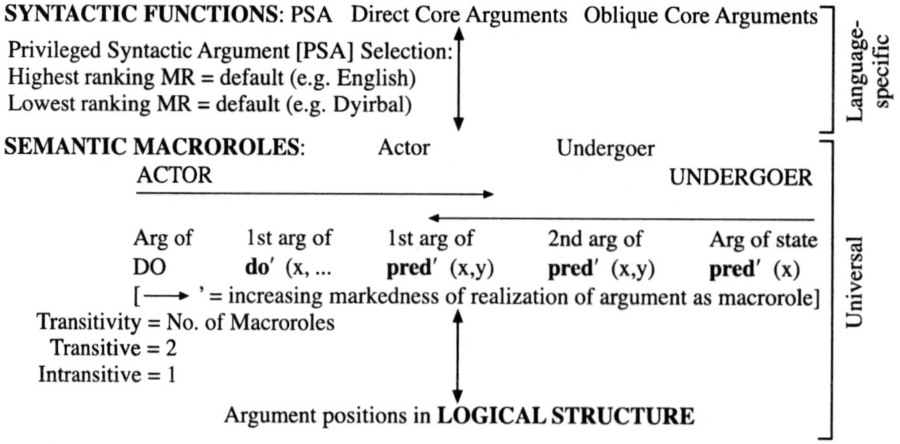

Figure 6.42. *Summary of the RRG linking system*

The purely semantic phase, involving logical structures and macrorole selection, is virtually universal; there is very little cross-linguistic variation in this phase. The primary example of this variation is whether languages allow variable linking to undergoer or not; English and Swahili do, but most languages do not. The locus of significant cross-linguistic diversity is the syntactic phase of the linking; as was shown in chapter 2, there is considerable variation across languages in terms of how semantic arguments are treated syntactically, the contrast between accusative and ergative syntax being a major instance of this variation.

English is an accusative language, and therefore given the logical structure in (6.24) and the selection of *the boy* as actor and *the glass* as undergoer, the default linking is for *the boy* to be the privileged syntactic argument, following (6.28a). The privileged syntactic argument occurs in the core-initial argument position, while the undergoer occurs immediately after the nucleus. Non-macrorole arguments (if any) follow it, followed by adjuncts in the periphery. If the non-default linking were made, then the undergoer *the glass* would be the privileged syntactic argument and occupy the core-initial position, while the actor *the boy* would optionally appear as an adjunct in the periphery in a PP headed by *by*. The semantic representation is the same in both linkings. These two linkings are diagrammed in Figure 6.43.

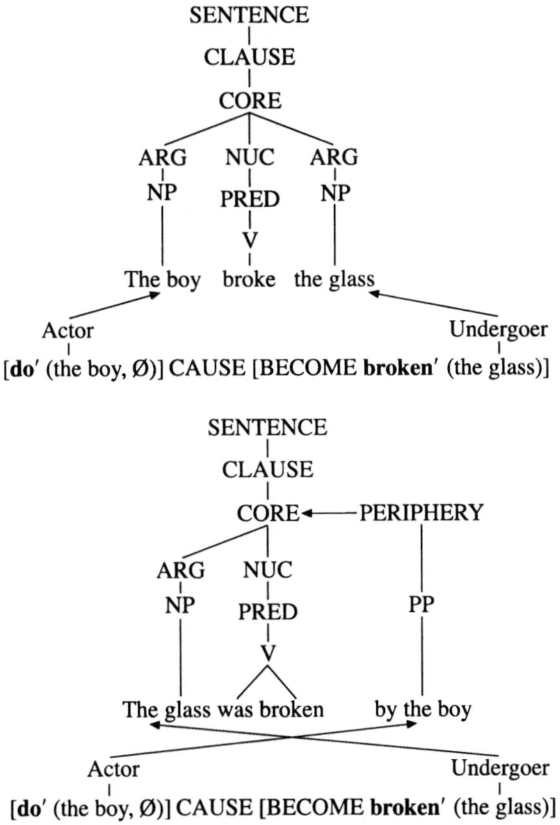

Figure 6.43. *Active and passive linkings from the logical structure in (6.24)*

The linking algorithm is subject to the Completeness Constraint, which says that everything in the semantic representation must be realized in the syntax, and conversely, everything in the syntax must be linked to an argument position in a logical structure in the semantic representation. This is the RRG analog of the Completeness and Coherence Conditions in LFG. This rules out a linking between the logical structure in (6.24) and the sentence *The glass broke*, because the actor NP *the boy* is not realized in the syntax. Conversely, it rules out a linking between *The boy broke the glass* and the logical structure BECOME **broken′** (x), because one of the two arguments in the sentence cannot be linked to the semantic representation.

Case assignment and verb agreement rules refer to the hierarchy in (6.27). The rules for accusative languages are presented in (6.30) and (6.31).

(6.30) Case assignment rules for direct core arguments in German, Russian and Telugu:
a. Assign nominative case to the highest-ranking core macrorole argument.
b. Assign accusative case to the other core macrorole argument.
c. Assign dative case to non-macrorole direct-core arguments (default).

(6.31) Finite verb agreement in German, English and Russian:
The finite verb agrees with the highest-ranking macrorole argument in the core.

Note that the formulation of passive and antipassive in (6.29), the case assignment rules in (6.30), and the agreement rule in (6.31) all refer to semantic macroroles; these are clear examples of syntactic rules referring to semantic notions, and they illustrate that in RRG syntax is not autonomous. The application of these rules can be illustrated with respect to the Russian sentence in (6.1), repeated below without the adjectives; its logical structure is given in (6.32b).

(6.32) a Učitel'nic-a da-l-a knig-u ženščin-e. Russian
teacher-FSGNOM give-PAST-FSG book-FSGACC woman-FSGDAT
'The teacher gave a/the book to a/the woman.'
b. [**do′** (učitel'nic-, ∅)] CAUSE [BECOME **have′** (ženščin-, knig-)]

Russian does not permit variable linking to undergoer, and accordingly only the default macrorole assignments obtain: *učitel'nic-* 'teacher' is the actor, and *knig-* 'book' is the undergoer. (6.32a) is active voice, and accordingly the actor *učitel'nic-* is the highest-ranking macrorole. Following (6.30a), it receives nominative case. The other macrorole is the undergoer *knig-*, and following (6.30b), it receives accusative case. The third argument, *ženščin-* 'woman', is a non-macrorole core argument, and accordingly it receives dative case, following (6.30c). The agreement rule in (6.31) states that the finite verb should agree with the actor (*učitel'nic-* 'teacher'), which is correct.

The final phenomenon to be analyzed is WH-question formation. The WH-word is linked directly to the precore slot; there is no empty NP position inside the core, that is, no traces as in GB. This is illustrated in the left linking diagram in Figure 6.44. The interpretation of the WH-word in the precore slot is equally straightforward; the linking from syntax to semantics in a WH-question is depicted in the right linking diagram in Figure 6.44.

In English, as in Malagasy, Tagalog, German, Icelandic and many other languages, a WH-word in a WH-question is linked directly to the precore slot, as in the left diagram. In a language with case-marked WH-words, for example, German, no special provisions

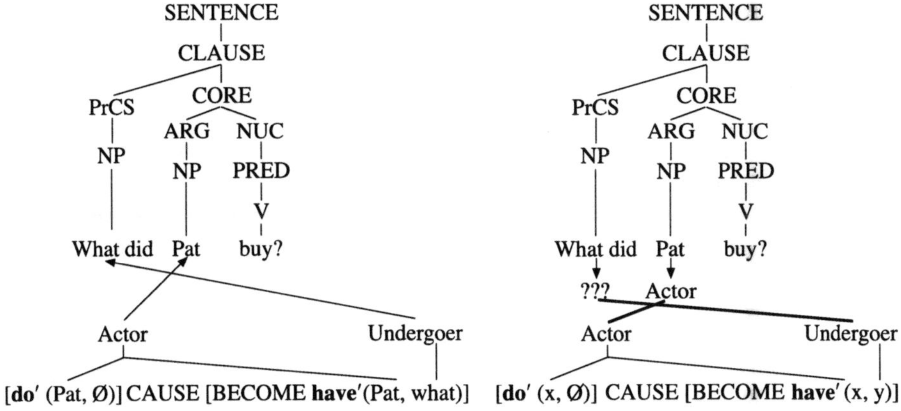

Figure 6.44. *Linking between semantics and syntax in a WH-question*

need to be made for the case marking of WH-words in the precore slot, because the case rules in (6.30) would assign the appropriate case, depending upon whether the WH-word is an actor, undergoer, or non-macrorole direct-core argument.

The syntax-to-semantics linking algorithm depends upon extracting as much information as possible from the overt morphosyntactic properties of the elements in the sentence. *What*, for example, formally carries no clues to its function; it can be interpreted as an actor, as in *What scared the dogs?*, as an undergoer, as in *What did Pat buy?*, or a non-macrorole argument, as in *What did you put the leftover soup in?* This is why '???' is under it in the right diagram. The voice of the verb, active, signals that the privileged syntactic argument is an actor; since *Pat* is the NP in the core-initial, pre-nuclear privileged syntactic argument position in English, it must be an actor. The logical structure of the verb *buy* is retrieved from the lexicon, and since it has only two distinct arguments, it can easily be determined which argument would have to be the actor and which the undergoer, following the hierarchy in Figure 6.40: the *x* argument would have to be the actor, and the *y* argument the undergoer. Given the information gleaned from the morphosyntactic properties of the sentence and the information derived from the logical structure plus the Actor–Undergoer Hierarchy, it is possible to conclude that the NP *Pat* must be interpreted as the *x* argument in the logical structure. There is nothing in the morphosyntactic form of the sentence that entails that *what* is the *y* argument. However, there is one unlinked argument in the syntax, *what*, and one unlinked argument position in the logical structure, *y*. The Completeness Constraint demands that everything in the syntax be linked, and the element in the precore slot must therefore be linked to the remaining argument position, thereby satisfying the Completeness Constraint and yielding the correct interpretation of the sentence. English presents one of the most challenging syntax-to-semantics linking situations involving WH-words in the precore slot, for the reason noted above. The linking is much simpler in languages like German and Russian in which WH-words are case-marked, since case gives a major clue as to their function, and it is trivial in languages like Malagasy, Kwakwala and Tagalog in which the WH-word must always be the privileged syntactic argument of the clause; in such languages the function of the WH-word is always directly recoverable from the voice of the verb.

Table 6.4. *Summary of ways of capturing systematic relationships in grammar*

Theory	Passive	Dative shift	Long-distance dependence
TG	Syntactic transformation	Syntactic transformation	Syntactic transformation
RelG	Syntactic advancement rule	Syntactic advancement rule	Overlay arc
LFG	Lexical rule	Lexical rule	Functional uncertainty
GB	Move α, NP-trace	Different verbs	Move α, WH-trace
RRG	Variable linking to PSA	Variable U selection	Direct linking LS ↔ PrCS

RRG thus presents different ways of capturing systematic relationships in syntax from those of the other theories. Table 6.4 represents an expansion of Table 6.1 to include GB, RRG and treatments of long-distance dependencies.

The RRG analyses presented in this section are in many ways quite distinct from those of the other three theories, and this is a function of the rather different starting points, both empirical and conceptual, that RRG assumes. Work in the theory has not been concentrated solely on issues of universal grammar and linguistic typology. Like linguists working in LFG, researchers in RRG are very interested in how it would fit into a psychologically plausible theory of language comprehension and production. As with those working in the Principles and Parameters framework, there is great interest in the question of language acquisition, although work in RRG does not assume the existence of an autonomous language acquisition device.

6.5 Summary

The purpose of this chapter has been to explore the different combinations of concepts and analytic tools from chapters 2 to 5 in different syntactic theories, and in order to explicate some of the features of particular theories it has been necessary to refer back to features of TG. The general picture regarding the development of these four theories can be summarized as in Figure 6.45.

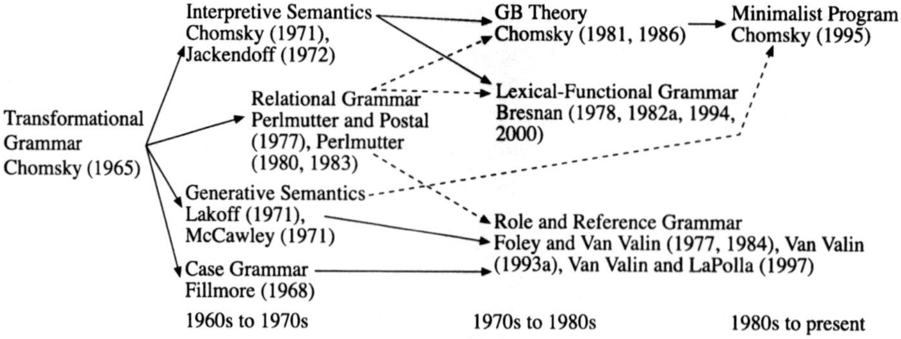

Figure 6.45. *Historical development of the theories discussed in this chapter*

(The solid arrows indicate direct development, while the dashed arrows signal influence.) Interpretive Semantics (also knows as the **Extended Standard Theory**), Generative

Semantics and **Case Grammar** are all direct descendents of TG, and they are in turn the direct ancestors of all of the theories discussed in this chapter except RelG. The most theoretically divisive issue arising out of the development of TG was the autonomy of syntax; Interpretive Semantics maintained it, while Generative Semantics and Case Grammar rejected it. Interpretive Semantics differed from TG in that semantic interpretation was no longer restricted to deep structure; features of surface structure could also play a role in semantic interpretation (see Figure 6.7). Generative Semantics and Case Grammar both rejected the autonomy of syntax, but in different ways. Generative semanticists held that there was no syntactic deep structure underlying sentences; rather, an abstract semantic representation replaced deep structure, and transformational rules applied to derive the surface syntactic structure from it. Case Grammar postulated that the underlying form of sentences was an array of thematic relations (called 'case roles' or '**deep cases**' in the theory), and these were mapped into the surface syntactic form by transformational rules.

The discussion in this chapter has focussed on the specific issues listed in section 6.0 and repeated below.

1. How syntactic structure is represented (relational structure only, constituent structure only, or both)
2. How grammatical relations are treated
3. The role of the lexicon, including how subcategorization information is handled and the notion of argument structure assumed
4. Treatment of morphosyntactic phenomena (in simple sentences only)
   a. Case assignment and finite verb agreement
   b. Grammatical-relations-changing constructions such as passive and dative shift
   c. WH-question formation.

Two points emerged with respect to the issue of the representation of syntactic structure. The first is the one mentioned in point 1, whether constituent structure or relational structure is the basis for the description of clause structure, and the second is new, namely, how many levels of syntactic representation a theory posits. With respect to the first point, two theories (LFG, GB) employ some version of the X-bar schema for representing constituent structure, while two (RelG, LFG) make use of an abstract representation of grammatical relations. LFG uniquely assigns two structural representations to each sentence, one for its constituent structure (c-structure) and one for its relational structure (f-structure). The RRG notion of the layered structure of the clause is a hybrid of the two types of representations; it depicts constituent structure (albeit not following the X-bar schema) but also includes some relational-dependency notions. The second point divides the theories more sharply. While all of them are descendents of TG directly or indirectly, only two maintain the distinction between surface and underlying syntactic structure that was the hallmark of TG, namely RelG and GB. The other two reject the notion of abstract underlying syntactic structure and use a variety of means to account for the phenomena which have been cited as requiring an analysis in terms of multiple levels; the prime example discussed in this chapter is long-distance dependencies.

The second issue concerns the treatment of grammatical relations. RelG and early LFG treat them as primitives; more recent versions of LFG do not. GB treats them as derivative of phrase-structure configurations and recognizes only two, subject (external argument) and object (internal object). It is no accident that GB posits only two abstract Cases, nominative and accusative, and that they are assigned to the external and internal arguments, respectively. RRG has the most distinctive analysis of grammatical relations. It rejects the traditional Indo-European based grammatical relations and takes a construction-specific view of the phenomena discussed in chapter 2. From this perspective, it is necessary to postulate only a single syntactic relation, the privileged syntactic argument of the construction in question.

The lexicon plays a very important role in some theories and has almost no role in others. The lexicon is most important in LFG, GB and RRG. In LFG verbs are subcategorized relationally, i.e. in terms of the grammatical functions they govern. The early version of LFG treats passive and dative shift in the lexicon by means of lexical rules operating on the lexical forms of verbs. Lexical forms contain a verb's subcategorization information and argument structure, stated in terms of a list of thematic relations. In LMT the lexical rules change the feature composition of the grammatical functions in order to achieve the same effects as the earlier lexical rules. GB has a lexical analysis of dative shift, treating the alternating verbs as distinct lexical entries related by a lexical redundancy rule. There is also a lexical component to its treatment of passive, as passive and active verbs are likewise treated separately and linked by a redundancy rule. Subcategorization information is stated in constituent-structure terms, and it is projected into the syntax via the Projection Principle. The argument structure of a verb is represented by a θ-grid, a list of θ-roles. RRG dispenses with syntactic subcategorization and lists of thematic relations altogether; the semantic representation of a verb in a lexical entry is its logical structure, which is a decompositional representation, and subcategorization is done semantically in terms of the number of semantic macroroles a verb takes. Dative shift is handled in the lexical phase of the linking in terms of variable undergoer selection. RelG assumes a lexicon with lexical entries containing relational subcategorization information and a list of thematic relations for argument structure; all grammatical phenomena are handled outside of the lexicon in the syntax.

The treatment of morphosyntactic phenomena, the final point, concerns case and agreement, on the one hand, and passive, dative shift and WH-question formation, on the other. The various accounts of the latter phenomena are summarized in Table 6.4 and need not be repeated here. It is worth noting that passive is treated syntactically in RelG and RRG (albeit in different ways), lexically in LFG and a combination of syntactic and lexical analysis in GB; dative shift, on the other hand, is treated syntactically only in RelG, while the other theories handle it lexically in some way. Long-distance dependencies are uniformly treated syntactically. Why does this contrast exist? The answer is that passive and dative shift are lexically governed phenomena, which WH-questions and other long-distance dependencies are not. **Lexical government** means that the construction in question is only possible with certain lexical items and not others. Dative shift is a prime example of this, because only some verbs, e.g. *give*, *send*, *show* but not *donate*, allow it. Passive is likewise lexically governed, because passive is not possible with every transitive verb in, for example English, although it is a much more general phenomenon than dative shift; this accounts for the fact that more approaches treat it syntactically than treat dative shift syntactically. WH-questions are not lexically governed at all; it is always possible to form a WH-question of some kind in a simple sentence, regardless of what the verb in the sentence is. Hence there is no basis for treating them lexically, and they are consistently handled syntactically.

The treatments of case and agreement generally follow the constituent-structure or relational-structure emphasis of the theory. RelG states case and agreement rules in terms of grammatical relations, while RRG formulates them in terms of semantic macroroles and the privileged syntactic-argument-selection hierarchy. LFG treats them in terms of matching features of the verb with features of the subject and other arguments, and GB defines them in terms of the same structural configurations used to define grammatical relations.

The points of comparison among the four theories are summarized in Table 6.5.

Table 6.5. *Summary of theories*

Theory	Representation of syntactic structure	Treatment of grammatical relations	Lexical information	Morphosyntactic phenomena (Table 6.3)
Relational Grammar	Relational network of grammatical relations Multistratal	Primitives	Relational subcategories Thematic relations	All are analyzed in terms of grammatical relations
Lexical-Functional Grammar	X-bar syntax (c-structure) Attribute-feature matrix for grammatical functions (f-structure)	Primitives (early) Derived from features (LMT)	Relational subcategories Thematic relations Lexical rules	Handled in lexicon or in f-structure
Government-Binding Theory	X-bar syntax Multiple, derivationally linked levels	Derived from phrase-structure configurations	Constituent structure subcategorization, θ-grid Lexical redundancy rules	Universal principles subject to parametric variation Move-α
Role and Reference Grammar	Projection grammar Layered structure of the clause, NP, PP	Rejects traditional grammatical relations Construction-specific	Lexical decomposition, macrorole selection	Linking algorithm involving syntax, semantic discourse-pragmatics

6.6 Other syntactic theories

The discussion in sections 6.1 to 6.4 presented brief sketches of four syntactic theories, but the current theoretical situation in syntax is much more complex. There are a number of important syntactic theories not discussed thus far, and it will be possible to give only a brief mention of them here.

Head-driven Phrase Structure Grammar [HPSG] (Pollard and Sag 1987, 1994; Sag and Wasow 1999) is a monostratal, unification-based theory in which the lexicon plays a crucial role; it is closer to LFG than to any of the other theories in Table 6.5. Considerable information about the grammatical properties of lexical heads is represented in the lexical entries of the heads in the lexicon (hence the name of the theory) and in the feature structures instantiating the heads in trees. It employs a theory of argument structure involving verb-specific semantic relations (see Figure 2.2). In addition, it incorporates a grammatical-relations hierarchy to account for certain grammatical phenomena, for example, reflexivization. Unlike LFG, it posits only a single representation for each sentence, and the constituent structure tree contains all of the information contained in the separate f-structures and c-structures in LFG. This is illustrated in the simplified tree structure in Figure 6.46 for *They sent us a letter* (Sag and Wasow 1999). The use of feature structures to represent the syntactic nodes in a tree was pioneered by GPSG. *Us* and *a letter* are given abbreviated representations, due to space limitations.

In this figure, 'SYN' = syntactic properties of the word or phrase, 'SEM' = semantic properties of the word or phrase, 'SPR' = specifier, 'COMPS' = complements, and 'RESTR' = restriction ('a list of conditions that the situation or individual has to satisfy for the expression to be applicable to it' (Sag and Wasow 1999: 106)), i.e. its semantic

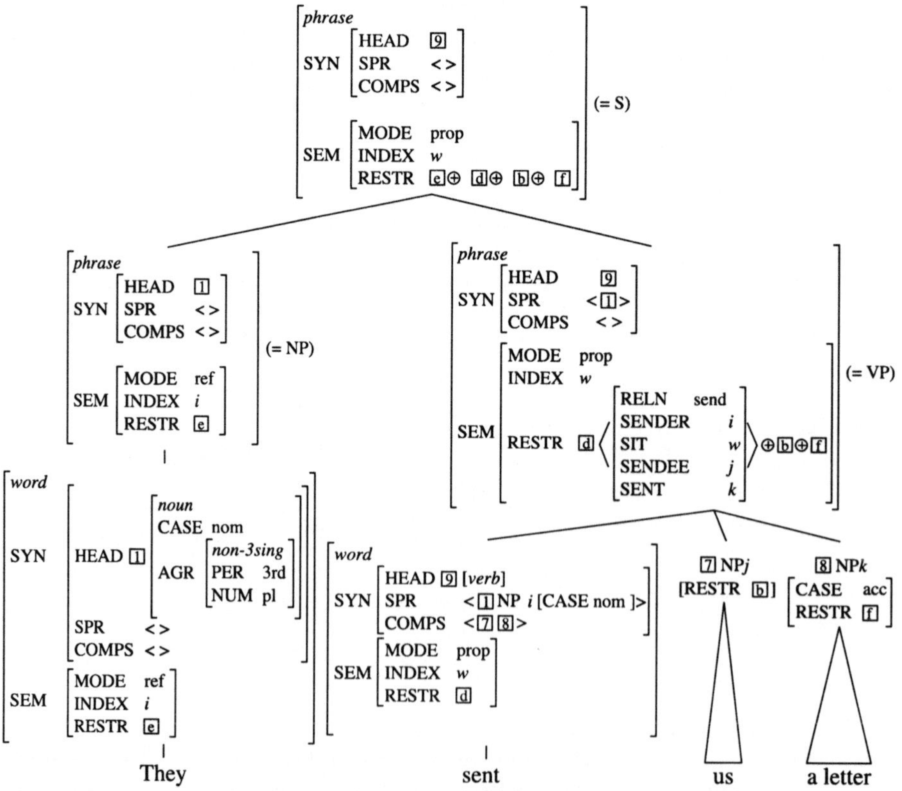

Figure 6.46. *HPSG representation of* They sent us a letter

properties. The subcategorization of a head is expressed by its COMPS list; the verb *sent* takes two complements, which are represented by the boxed numbers 7 and 8 (called 'tags' in HPSG), which are also found on the two NPs following it. Its subject is expressed by the SPR feature, which has as its value a nominative case NP with the tag '1', the same tag carried by the VP-external NP in the tree. The indexes *i, j* and *k* refer to the argument structure of *sent*, as depicted by the feature structure with the *d* tag in the semantics part of the VP node feature structure. It is inherited from the feature structure of the verb *sent* (note the *d* tag in the RESTR feature of the semantic part of its feature structure). The COMPS list in the VP node is empty, signalling that the subcategorization feature of *sent* has been satisfied by the two NPs in the VP. The RESTR of the VP contains the RESTR tags for *sent*, *us* and *a letter.* The SPR feature still contains the tag '1'. At the S node, however, the specifier feature is empty, indicating that it has been satisfied by the VP-external NP with the tag '1'. The RESTR feature of the S node contains the RESTR tags for the three NPs and the verb in the clause. Thus, syntactic and semantic information flows up the tree, satisfying the requirements of the heads and yielding a grammatical sentence. If, for example, there had been only one NP in the VP, then the COMPS feature of *sent* would be unsatisfied, and the sentence would be ungrammatical. Thus the HPSG equivalents of the LFG Completeness and Coherence Conditions are satisfied directly in the constituent structure tree, rather than in a separate f-structure as in LFG. HPSG has attempted to deal with a broad range of cross-linguistic data, and it has been widely used by computational linguists for **natural-language processing**.

Cognitive Grammar (Langacker 1987, 1991; Lakoff 1987) developed out of Generative Semantics and adopts the position that syntax, semantics and discourse-pragmatics cannot be separated from each other but rather are manifestations of a single linguistic symbolization process, which has its roots in human cognitive processes. Construction Grammar (Fillmore 1988, Fillmore *et al.* 1988, Goldberg 1995) emphasizes the crucial role of grammatical constructions in syntax, in opposition to the GB view that denies constructions any theoretical status. It makes extensive use of feature structures to represent the morphosyntactic, semantic and pragmatic features of constructions, and in this respect it is similar to LFG and HPSG. **Functional Grammar** (Dik 1978, 1989, 1997) is concerned with the interaction of syntax, semantics and discourse-pragmatics in grammar, and it shares a great deal with RRG; there has been a very productive exchange of ideas between the two theories. It was heavily influenced by RelG, Generative Semantics and Case Grammar, and like RelG it posits only abstract, relationally based representations of syntactic structure, but like LFG and RRG and unlike RelG, it is a monostratal theory. Also like RelG, LFG and RRG, it has a strong typological orientation. Finally, **Autolexical Syntax** (Sadock 1991) posits distinct semantic, morphological and phonological representations of sentences, in order to capture mismatches between, for example, syntax and morphology like the clitic case markers in Kwakwala that occur phonologically on the 'wrong' word. It uses features to represent relevant grammatical information, as in LFG and HPSG. The relation of these representations to each other is somewhat analogous to that of the projections in RRG (see Figure 6.39).

In addition to the syntactic theories which linguists use, there are also what may be called 'formalizations' of grammatical principles, rules and operations. Two which are of particular significance in contemporary syntactic discussion are **tree-adjoining**

grammars and optimality theory. Tree-adjoining grammars (Joshi 1985, Kroch and Joshi 1987) combine local phrase-structure subtrees into larger tree structures. It is essentially the method of composition used in the Minimalist Program. An item is taken from the lexicon, e.g. a verb, and a local subtree is projected from it, following the X-bar schema. Then another lexical item is taken from the lexicon, this time a common noun. A local subtree is projected from it, following the X-bar schema, yielding an NP, and then its local subtree is combined with the local subtree headed by the verb to form a VP with the NP as the internal argument. Then another lexical item is accessed, its local subtree is projected, and it is added to the structure. This process is repeated until the entire tree structure is assembled. Given this procedure, it is clear why there is no level of d-structure in the Minimalist Program. A process analogous to this is used in RRG in combining syntactic templates to create complex syntactic structures; the constituents in this case are those of the layered structure of the clause, not X-bar syntax; it is illustrated in Figure 6.41. The other formalization is optimality theory, which, despite its name, is not a theory. It is, rather, a way of organizing the rules, principles and constraints of a theory. It treats all rules, etc., as constraints which are hierarchically ranked and violable. A violation of a higher-ranked constraint is more significant than that of a lower-ranking constraint. The constraints are assumed to be universal, and cross-linguistic variation is derived from the different rankings that different languages impose on them. Since optimality theory is just a way of organizing grammatical principles, rules and constraints, the theoretical constructs to be ranked must come from a substantive syntactic theory, and in fact all four of the theories discussed in this chapter have had analyses done in an optimality theory format: RelG (Legendre, *et al.* 1993), LFG (Bresnan 1998), GB (Grimshaw 1997) and RRG (Nakamura 1997).

The final theoretical contrast to be mentioned is that between formalists and functionalists. Roughly speaking, formalists strongly uphold the autonomy of syntax and employ a range of formal devices in seeking to describe and explain linguistic phenomena. RelG, GPSG and GB are all examples of formalist approaches. In general, they work within the conceptual framework originally proposed in TG by Chomsky, even if they make use of very different formal description devices. Functionalists, on the other hand, tend to reject the autonomy of syntax and seek to explain linguistic phenomena with respect to semantics, discourse-pragmatics, language processing and/or human cognitive processes. LFG, RRG and Functional Grammar are all examples of functionalist approaches, although they are atypical in that they make extensive use of formal representations and explicit formulations of rules and principles. Many functionalists emphatically reject any kind of symbolic notation or explicit formulation of rules and principles.

6.7 Conclusion

This book began with a characterization of syntax as 'the ways in which words, with or without appropriate inflections, are arranged to show connections of meaning within the sentence' (Matthews 1982: 1), and in the course of it the striking cross-linguistic variation in these ways of arranging words have been presented. In order to analyse the rich range of syntactic phenomena presented by human languages, syntacticians have developed an arsenal of analytic tools, which were introduced in chapters 2 to 5. Since the late 1950s linguists have not been content to stop at describing languages, although this remains an important, difficult and highly valuable enterprise, and they have proposed theories to explain syntactic phenomena. Given the diversity and complexity of syntactic phenomena, it is perhaps not surprising that a diverse array of theories has been put forward in the last forty years. The discussion in this chapter is but a brief overview of the theoretical richness of the field, and the next step for someone interested in syntax is to explore one or more of these theories in depth.

Notes and suggested readings

The literature in syntactic theory is huge, and only a few references for each theory will be given here. The best source for up-to-date bibliographies for most theories is the internet; there are web sites which contain not only constantly updated lists of works relating to a theory but often also have recent papers which can be downloaded. The best way to locate the relevant web sites is through the Linguist List web site (http: //linguistlist.org/), which has a page devoted to theory-related web sites and links to them.

The core readings in RelG are collected in the *Studies in Relational Grammar* volumes (Perlmutter 1983, Perlmutter and Rosen 1984, Perlmutter and Joseph 1990). Blake (1990) presents a general introduction to RelG, with some comparison to other theories.

The foundational works in LFG appear in Bresnan (1982a); Sells (1985) and Horrocks (1987) include introductions to the early version of LFG. Bresnan (2000) is a comprehensive presentation of the current version of the theory.

GB encompasses the widest range of competing analyses of syntactic phenomena within a single framework, and it has the most books and articles devoted to it. Introductions to early versions of GB can be found in Sells (1985) and Horrocks (1987). Textbooks devoted to later versions of the theory include Cowper (1992), Napoli (1993), Haegeman (1994) and Culicover (1997). Radford (1997a, b) presents introductions to the Minimalist Program.

With respect to RRG, Van Valin (1993a) is a collection of papers applying the theory to a number of syntactic problems in a range of languages. Introductions to RRG can be found in Van Valin and LaPolla (1997) and Yang (1998).

For a history, both theoretical and sociological, of the development of contemporary linguistics from the 1950s to the 1980s, see Newmeyer (1986). For discussion of the 'formalist' versus 'functionalist' contrast, see the papers in Darnell, *et al.* (1998), Newmeyer (1998) and Van Valin (2000).

Exercises

1. Give an analysis of the Malayalam sentences in (1)–(21), (26)–(27), and (29)–(31) from exercise 3 in chapter 2 in each of the four theories discussed in this chapter. Give a set of PS-rules to specify the structures; if the theory does not use PS-rules, explain how syntactic structures are specified and give examples. Give lexical entries for all of the verbs in the data, following the format for each theory. Formulate a set of case-marking rules, and explain how the passive sentences would be treated. State how each theory would explain the ungrammaticality of the starred examples. Give syntactic representations in each theory for (1), (2), (9) and (27).

2. Give an analysis of the following Icelandic sentences in each of the four theories discussed in this chapter. Give a set of PS-rules to specify the structures; if the theory does not use

PS-rules, explain how syntactic structures are specified and give examples. Ignore the internal structure of NPs in your rules. Give lexical entries for all of the verbs in the data, following the format for each theory. Formulate a set of case-marking and finite-verb agreement rules, and explain how the passive sentences and WH-questions would be treated. Give syntactic representations in each theory for (1), (4), (8) and (11).

(1) Hann sá þá.
3sgM.NOM see.3sgPAST 3plM.ACC
'He saw them.'

(2) Hún hjálpa-ð-i þeim.
3sgF.NOM help-PAST-3sg 3plDAT
'She helped them.'

(3) Sigga mun sakna hans.
Sigga.FSGNOM will miss 3sgM.GEN
'Sigga will miss him.'

(4) Ég sýn-d-i henni bílinn.
1sgNOM show-PAST-1sg 3sgF.DAT car.MSGACC.DEF
'I showed her the car.'

(5) Sigga skila-ð-i peningunum til hennar.
Sigga.FSGNOM return-PAST-3sg money.MSGDAT.DEF to 3sgF.GEN
'She returned the money to her.'

(6) Strákurinn dansa-ð-i í garðinum.
boy.MSGNOM.DEF dance-PAST-3sg in park.MSGDAT.DEF
'The boy danced in the park.'

(7) Jón tók bókina.
John.MSGNOM take.3sgPAST book.FSGACC.DEF
'John took the book.'

(8) Bókin var tekin af Jóni.
book.FSGNOM.DEF be.3sgPAST taken by John.MSGDAT
'The book was taken by John.'

(9) Peningunum var skilað til hennar af Siggu.
money.MSGDAT.DEF be.3sgPAST returned to 3sgF.GEN by Sigga.FSGDAT
'The money was returned to her by Sigga.'

(10) Hvers mun Sigga sakna?
who.GEN will Sigga-FSGNOM miss
'Who will Sigga miss?'

(11) Hvað sýn-d-i Sigga henni?
what show-PAST-3sg Sigga.FSGNOM 3sgF.DAT
'What did Sigga show her?'

3. Having formulated partial grammars for the data from Icelandic and Malayalam in each of the theories, compare the strengths and weaknesses of each approach. What problems arise in trying to apply each theory? What does each theory seem to handle very easily?

References

Abraham, Werner, ed. 1978. *Valence, semantic case, and grammatical relations.* Amsterdam and Philadelphia: John Benjamins.
Allerton, D. J. 1982. *Valency and the English verb.* London: Academic Press.
Anderson, Stephen. 1976. On the notion of subject in ergative languages. In Li (1976), 1–24.
1984. Kwakwala syntax and the Government-Binding theory. In Cook, Eung-Do and Donna Gerdts, eds., *Syntax and Semantics* vol. XVI: *The syntax of Native American languages*, 21–75. Orlando: Academic Press.
Andrews, Avery. 1985. The major functions of the noun phrase. In T. Shopen, ed., *Language typology and syntactic description*, vol. I, 62–154. Cambridge University Press.
Archangeli, Diane and D. Terence Langendoen, eds. 1997. *Optimality Theory: an overview.* Oxford: Blackwell.
Asher, R. E. and T. C. Kumari. 1997. *Malayalam.* London and New York: Routledge.
Barac-Kostrenčić, Višnja, Miljenko Kovačićek and Sonja Lovasić. 1993. *Učimo hrvatski.* Zagreb: Centar za strane jezike i Šolska knjiga.
Baker, Mark. 1988. *Incorporation.* University of Chicago Press.
Bauer, Laurie. 1988. *Introducing linguistic morphology.* Edinburgh University Press.
Berman, Ruth. 1978. *Modern Hebrew structure.* Tel Aviv: University Publishing.
Bhat, D. N. S. 1991. *Grammatical relations: the evidence against their necessity and universality.* London and New York: Routledge.
Blake, Barry. 1977. *Case marking in Australian languages.* Canberra: Australian Institute of Aboriginal Studies.
1979. *A Kalkatungu grammar.* (Series B, no. 57) Canberra: Pacific Linguistics.
1990. *Relational Grammar.* London and New York: Routledge.
Bloomfield, Leonard. 1933. *Language.* New York: Holt.
Borsley, Robert. 1996. *Modern phrase structure grammar.* Oxford: Basil Blackwell.
Bowe, Heather. 1990. *Categories, constituents and constituent order in Pitjantjatjara.* London and New York: Routledge.
Bresnan, Joan. 1978. A realistic transformational grammar. In M. Halle, J. Bresnan and G. Miller, eds., *Linguistic theory and psychological reality*, 1–59. Cambridge, MA: MIT Press.
1982b. Control and complementation. In Bresnan (1982a), 282–390.
1994. Locative inversion and the architecture of universal grammar. *Language* 70.1: 72–131.
1998. Explaining morphosyntactic competition. In M. Baltin and C. Collins, eds., *Handbook of contemporary syntactic theory.* Oxford: Blackwell Publishers.
2000. *Lexical-Functional Grammar.* Oxford: Basil Blackwell.
Bresnan, Joan, ed. 1982a. *The mental representation of grammatical relations.* Cambridge, MA: MIT Press.

Bresnan, Joan and Jonni M. Kanerva. 1989. Locative inversion in Chicheŵa: a case study of factorization in grammar. *Linguistic Inquiry* 20.1: 1–50.
Brown, Keith and Jim Miller. 1991. *Syntax: a linguistic introduction to sentence structure* (2nd edn). New York: Harper Collins Academic.
Černý, Václav. 1971. Some remarks on syntax and morphology of verb in Avar. *Archiv Orientalni* 39: 46–56.
Chomsky, Noam. 1957. *Syntactic structures* (Janua linguarum 4). Gravenhage: Mouton.
1965. *Aspects of the theory of syntax*. Cambridge, MA: MIT Press.
1971. Deep structure, surface structure, and semantic interpretation. In Steinberg & Jakobovits (1971), 183–216.
1981. *Lectures on government and binding*. Dordrecht: Foris.
1986. *Barriers*. Cambridge, MA: MIT Press.
1992. A minimalist program for linguistic theory. *MIT Occasional Papers in Linguistics*, No. 1. Cambridge, MA: MIT.
1995. *The minimalist program*. Cambridge, MA: MIT Press.
1998. Minimalist inquiries: the framework. *MIT Occasional Papers in Linguistics*, No. 15. Cambridge, MA: MIT.
Chung, Sandra. 1978. *Case marking and grammatical relations in Polynesian*. Austin: University of Texas Press.
Cole, Peter and Jerrold Sadock, eds. 1977. *Syntax and semantics*, vol. VIII: *Grammatical relations*. New York: Academic Press.
Comrie, Bernard. 1978. Ergativity. In Winfred P. Lehmann, ed., *Syntactic typology*, 329–94. Austin: Texas Press.
1989. *Language universals and linguistic typology* (2nd. edn). University of Chicago Press.
Corbett, Greville, Norman Fraser, and Scott McGlashan, eds. 1993. *Heads in grammatical theory*. Cambridge University Press.
Cowper, Elizabeth. 1992. *A concise introduction to syntactic theory*. University of Chicago Press.
Craig, Colette. 1977. *The structure of Jacaltec*. Austin and London: University of Texas Press.
Croft, William. 1991. *Syntactic categories and grammatical relations*. Chicago and London: University of Chicago Press.
Culicover, Peter. 1997. Principles and parameters: an introduction to syntactic theory. Oxford University Press.
Dahm-Draksic, Tracy. 1997. A Role and Reference Grammar analysis of case–marking in Croatian. MA Project. Buffalo: State University of New York.
Darnell, Michael, Edith Moravcsik, Frederik Newmeyer, Michael Noonan and Kathleen Weatley, eds. 1998. *Functionalism and formalism in linguistics* (2 volumes). Amsterdam: John Benjamins.
Derbyshire, Desmond and Geoffrey Pullum, eds. 1986. *Handbook of Amazonian languages*, vol. I. Berlin: Mouton de Gruyter.
Derbyshire, Desmond and Geoffrey Pullum. 1991. Object-initial languages. *IJAL* 47: 193–214.
Dik, Simon. 1978. *Functional Grammar*. Amsterdam: North-Holland.
1989. *The theory of Functional Grammar, part 1*. Berlin: Mouton de Gruyter.
1997. *The theory of Functional Grammar, part 2*. Berlin: Mouton de Gruyter.
Dixon, R. M. W. 1972. *The Dyirbal language of North Queensland*. Cambridge University Press.
1977a. Where have all the adjectives gone? *Studies in Language* 1: 19–80.
1977b. *A grammar of Yidiɲ*. Cambridge University Press.
1979. Ergativity. *Language* 55.1: 59–138.
1994. *Ergativity*. Cambridge University Press.
Dowty, David, Robert Wall and Stanley Peters. 1980. *Introduction to Montague semantics*. Dordrecht: Reidel.

Driever, Dorothea. 1976. *Aspects of a case grammar of Mombasa Swahili.* Hamburg: Helmut Buske Verlag.
Dryer, Matthew. 1983. Indirect objects in Kinyarwanda revisited. In Perlmutter (1983), 129–40.
1986. Primary objects, secondary objects, and antidative. *Language* 62: 808–45.
Durie, Mark. 1985. *A Grammar of Acehnese.* Dordrecht: Foris.
1987. Grammatical relations in Acehnese. *Studies in Language* 11: 365–99.
Einarsson, Stefán. 1945. *Icelandic: Grammar, texts, glossary.* Baltimore: Johns Hopkins University Press.
Faltz, Leonard. 1978. On indirect objects in universal grammar. *CLS* 14: 76–87.
Fillmore, Charles. 1968. The case for case. In Emmon Bach and Robert Harms, eds., *Universals in linguistic theory*, 1–88. New York: Holt, Reinhart and Winston.
1977. The case for case reopened. In Cole and Sadock (1977), 59–82.
1988. The mechanisms of 'Construction Grammar.' *BLS* 14, 35–55.
Fillmore, Charles, Paul Kay and Mary Catherine O'Connor. 1988. Regularity and idiomaticity in grammatical constructions: The case of *let alone*. *Language* 64: 501–38.
Foley, William and Robert Van Valin, Jr. 1977. On the viability of the notion of 'subject' in universal grammar. *BLS* 3: 293–320.
1984. *Functional syntax and universal grammar.* Cambridge University Press.
Gary, Judith and Edward Keenan. 1977. On collapsing grammatical relations in universal grammar. In Cole and Sadock (1977), 83–120.
Gazdar, Gerald. 1982. Phrase structure grammar. In Pauline Jacobson and Geoffrey Pullum, eds., *The nature of syntactic representation*, 131–86. Dordrecht: Reidel.
Gazdar, Gerald and Geoffrey Pullum. 1981. Subcategorization, constituent order and the notion of 'head'. In T. Hoekstra, H. van der Hulst and M. Moortgat, eds., *The scope of lexical rules*, 107–23. Dordrecht: Foris.
Gazdar, Gerald, Ewan Klein, Geoffrey Pullum and Ivan A. Sag. 1985. *Generalized Phrase Structure Grammar.* Cambridge, MA: Harvard University Press.
Givón, Talmy. 1979. *On understanding grammar.* New York: Academic Press.
Goldberg, Adele. 1995. *Constructions: a construction grammar approach to argument structure.* University of Chicago Press.
Grimshaw, Jane. 1997. Projection, heads and optimality. *Linguistic Inquiry* 28: 373–422.
Groot, Casper, de. 1989. *Predicate stucture in a Functional Grammar of Hungarian.* Dordrecht: Foris.
Haegeman, Liliane M. V. 1994. *Introduction to Government and Binding theory* (2nd edn). Oxford and Cambridge, MA: Basil Blackwell.
Harris, Alice, 1981. *Georgian syntax.* Cambridge University Press.
Harris, Zellig. 1946. From morpheme to utterance. *Language* 22: 161–83.
1956. Introduction to transformations. *Transformations and discourse analysis papers 2.* Linguistics Dept., University of Pennsylvania. Reprinted in Z. Harris, *Papers in structural and transformational linguistics*, 383–89. Dordrecht: Reidel, 1970.
1957. Cooccurrence and transformation in linguistic structure. *Language* 33: 283–340.
Haspelmath, Martin. 1993. *A grammar of Lezgian.* Berlin: Mouton de Gruyter.
Hays, David G. 1964. Dependency theory: a formalism and some observations. *Language* 40: 511–25.
Helbig, Gerhard, ed. 1971. *Beiträge zur Valenztheorie.* The Hague: Mouton.
Hellan, Lars. 1988. *Anaphora in Norwegian and the theory of grammar.* Dordrecht: Foris.
Hinnebusch, Thomas J. 1979. Swahili. In T. Shopen, ed., *Languages and their status*, 209–93. Cambridge, MA: Winthrop.
Hockett, Charles. 1958. *A course in modern linguistics.* New York: Macmillan.
Hope, Edward. 1974. *The deep syntax of Lisu sentences. Pacific Linguistics* series B-no. 34. Canberra: Pacific Linguistics.

Hopper, Paul J. and Sandra A. Thompson. 1984. The discourse basis for lexical categories in universal grammar. *Language* 60: 703–52.

Horrocks, Geoffrey. 1987. *Generative grammar.* London: Longmans.

Huck, Geoffrey and Almerindo Ojeda, eds. 1987. *Syntax and semantics* vol. XX: *Discontinuous constituency*. New York: Academic Press.

Hudson, Richard. 1984. *Word Grammar.* Oxford: Basil Blackwell.

1990. *English Word Grammar.* Oxford: Basil Blackwell.

1993. So-called 'double objects' and grammatical relations. *Language* 68: 251–76.

Jackendoff, Ray S. 1972. *Semantic interpretation in generative grammar.* Cambridge, MA: MIT Press.

1976. Toward an explanatory semantic representation. *Linguistic Inquiry* 7: 89–150.

1977. *X-bar syntax.* Cambridge, MA: MIT Press.

1990. *Semantic structures.* Cambridge, MA: MIT Press.

Jacobsen, William H. 1979. The noun and verb in Nootkan. *The Victoria Conference on Northwestern Languages* (*British Columbia Provincial Museum Heratige Record* 4), B. S. Efrat, ed., 83–155. Victoria: British Columbia Provincial Museum.

Johnson, David and Paul Postal. 1980. *Arc Pair Grammar.* Princeton University Press.

Joshi, Aravind K. 1985. Tree-adjoining grammars: how much context-sensitivity is required to provide reasonable structural descriptions? In D. Dowty, L. Karttunen and A. Zwicky, eds., *Natural language parsing*, 206–50. Cambridge University Press.

Kaplan, Ronald and Joan Bresnan. 1982. Lexical-Functional Grammar: A formal system for grammatical representation. In Bresnan (1982a), 173–281.

Kaplan, Ronald and Annie Zaenen. 1989. Long-distance dependencies, constituent structure, and functional uncertainty. In M. Baltin and A. Kroch, eds., *Alternative conceptions of phrase structure*, 17–42. University of Chicago Press.

Keenan, Edward L. 1976a. Remarkable subjects in Malagasy. In Li (1976), 247–301.

1976b. Towards a universal definition of 'subject'. In Li (1976), 305–33.

Keenan, Edward L. and Bernard Comrie. 1977. Noun phrase accessibility and universal grammar. *Linguistic Inquiry* 8: 63–99.

Kibrik, A. E. 1985. Toward a typology of ergativity. In Nichols and Woodbury (1985), 268–323.

1997. Beyond subject and object: toward a comprehensive relational typology. *Linguistic Typology* 1: 279–346.

Kimenyi, Alexandre. 1980. *A Relational Grammar of Kinyarwanda* (*University of California Publications in linguistics* 91). Berkeley: University of California Press.

Koehn, Edward and Sally Koehn. 1986. Apalai. In Derbyshire and Pullum (1986), 33–127.

Kornai, András and Geoffrey Pullum. 1990. The X-bar theory of phrase structure. *Language* 66: 24–50.

Kroch, Anthony and Aravind K. Joshi. 1987. Analyzing extraposition in a tree adjoining grammar. In Huck and Ojeda (1987), 107–49.

Kroeger, Paul. 1993. *Phrase structure and grammatical relations in Tagalog.* Stanford: CSLI.

Kuipers, Aert. 1974. *The Shuswap language.* The Hague: Mouton.

Kuno, Susumu. 1973. *The structure of the Japanese language.* Cambridge, MA: MIT Press.

Laka, Itziar. 1997. *The Basque language.* University of the Basque Country. Available on the Internet (http://www.ehu.es/grammar/).

Lakoff, George. 1971. On generative semantics. In Steinberg and Jakobovits (1971), 232–96.

1987. *Women, fire, and dangerous things.* University of Chicago Press.

Lambrecht, Knud. 1994. *Information structure and sentence form.* Cambridge University Press.

Langacker, Ronald. 1987. *Foundations of Cognitive Grammar*, vol. I. Stanford University Press.

1991. *Foundations of Cognitive Grammar*, vol. II. Stanford University Press.

Legendre, Géraldine, William Raymond and Paul Smolensky. 1993. An optimality–theoretic typology of case and grammatical voice systems. *BLS* 19: 464–78.

Li, Charles, ed. 1976. *Subject and topic*. New York: Academic Press.

Manning, Christopher. 1996. *Ergativity: argument structure and grammatical relations*. Stanford: CSLI.

Matthews, Peter. 1982. *Syntax*. Cambridge University Press.

Matthews, Stephen and Virginia Yip. 1994. *Cantonese: a comprehensive grammar*. London: Routledge

McCawley, James. 1968a. Concerning the base component of a transformational grammar. *Foundations of Language* 4: 243–69.

1968b. Lexical insertion in a transformational grammar without deep structure. *CLS* 4: 71–89.

1971. Where do noun phrases come from? In Steinberg and Jakobovits (1971), 217–31.

1982. Parentheticals and discontinuous constituent structure. *Linguistic Inquiry* 13: 91–106.

Mel'čuk, Igor. 1979. *Studies in dependency syntax*. Ann Arbo, MI: Karoma.

1987. *Dependency syntax: theory and practice*. Albany: State University of New York Press.

Michaelis, Laura. 1993. On deviant case marking in Latin. In Van Valin (1993a), 311–73.

Mohanan, K. P. 1982. Grammatical relations and clause structure in Malayalam. In Bresnan (1982a), 504–89.

Moravcsik, Edith A. and Jessica R. Wirth. 1980. *Current approaches to syntax* (*Syntax and semantics* 13). New York: Academic Press.

Müller-Gotama, Franz. 1994. *Grammatical relations: a cross-linguistic perspective on their syntax and semantics*. Berlin: Mouton de Gruyter.

Nakamura, Wataru. 1997. A constraint-based typology of case systems. PhD dissertation, Buffalo, State University of New York.

Napoli, Donna Jo. 1993. *Syntax: theory and problems*. Oxford University Press.

Narasimhan, Bhuvana. 1998. A lexical semantic explanation for 'quirky' case marking in Hindi. *Studia Linguistica* 52: 48–76.

Newmeyer, Frederick. 1986. *Linguistic theory in America* (2nd edn). Orlando: Academic Press.

1998. *Language form and language function*. Cambridge, MA: MIT Press.

Nichols, Johanna. 1986. Head-marking and dependent-marking grammar. *Language* 62: 56–119.

Nichols, Johanna and Anthony Woodbury, eds. 1985. *Grammar inside and outside the clause*. Cambridge University Press.

Nida, Eugene. 1946. *Morphology: the descriptive analysis of words* (2nd edn). Ann Arbor: University of Michigan Press.

Palmer, Frank R. 1994. *Grammatical roles and relations*. Cambridge University Press.

Parker, Gary J. 1969. *Ayacucho Quechua grammar and dictionary*. The Hague: Mouton.

Payne, Doris L. 1986. Basic constituent order in Yagua clauses: implications for word order universals. In Derbyshire and Pullum (1986), 440–65.

Payne, John R. 1993. The headedness of noun phrases: slaying the nominal hydra. In Corbett, *et al.* (1993), 114–39.

Perlmutter, David. 1978. Impersonal passives and the unaccusative hypothesis. *BLS* 4: 157–89.

1980. Relational Grammar. In Moravcsik and Wirth (1980), 195–229.

Perlmutter, David, ed. 1983. *Studies in Relational Grammar 1*. University of Chicago Press.

Perlmutter, David and Brian Joseph, eds. 1990. *Studies in Relational Grammar 3*. University of Chicago Press.

Perlmutter, David and Paul Postal. 1977. Toward a universal characterization of passivization. *BLS* 3: 394–417.

1983. Some proposed laws of basic clause structure. In Perlmutter (1983), 81–128.

1984. The 1-Advancement Exclusiveness Law. In Perlmutter and Rosen (1984), 81–125.

Perlmutter, David and Carole Rosen, eds. 1984. *Studies in Relational Grammar 2*. University of Chicago Press.

Pollard, Carl and Ivan Sag. 1987. *Information-based syntax and semantics.* Stanford: CSLI.
1994. *Head-driven Phrase Structure Grammar.* University of Chicago Press.
Prakasam, V. 1985. *The syntactic patterns of Telagu and English: A study in contrastive analysis.* Hyderabad: Central Institute of English.
Pullum, Geofrey. 1996. Nostalgic views from Building 20. *Journal of Linguistics* 32: 137–48.
Radford, Andrew. 1988. *Transformational grammar: a first course.* Cambridge University Press.
1997a. *Syntactic theory and the structure of English.* Cambridge University Press.
1997b. *Syntax: a minimalist introduction.* Cambridge University Press.
Rosen, Carol. 1984. The interface between semantic roles and initial grammatical relations. In Perlmutter and Rosen (1984), 38–77.
Sadock, Jerrold. 1991. *Autolexical syntax.* University of Chicago Press.
Sag, Ivan and Thomas Wasow. 1999. *Syntactic theory.* Stanford: CSLI.
Saussure, Ferdinand de. [1917] 1959. *Course in general linguistics*, Charles Bally and Albert Sechehaye, with Albert Riedlinger, eds. New York: McGraw-Hill Book Co.
Schachter, Paul. 1976. The subject in Philippine languages: actor, topic, actor–topic, or none of the above. In Li (1976), 491–518.
1977. Reference-related and role-related properties of subjects. In Cole and Sadock (1977), 279–306.
Schachter, Paul, ed. 1984a. *Studies in the structure of Toba Batak* (*UCLA Occasional Papers in Linguistics* 5). UCLA Department of Linguistics.
Schachter, Paul. 1984b. Semantic-role-based syntax in Toba Batak. In Schachter (1984a), 122–49.
Schachter, Paul. 1985. Parts-of-speech systems. In T. Shopen, ed., *Language typology and syntactic description*, vol. I, 1–61. Cambridge University Press.
Sells, Peter. 1985. *Lectures on contemporary syntactic theories.* Stanford: CSLI.
Sgall, Petr and Jarmila Panevová. 1988. Dependency syntax: a challenge. *Theoretical Linguistics* 15: 73–86.
Sgall, Petr, Eva Hajičová and Jarmila Panevová. 1986. *The meaning of the sentence in its semantic and pragmatic aspects*, Jacob L. Mey, ed. Dordrecht and Boston, MA: Reidel.
Siewierska, Anna. 1991. *Functional Grammar.* London: Routledge.
Spencer, Andrew. 1991. *Morphological theory.* Oxford: Basil Blackwell.
Steinberg, Danny and Leon Jakobovits, eds. 1971. *Semantics.* Cambridge University Press.
Swadesh, Morris. 1939. Nootka internal syntax. *IJAL* 9: 77–102.
Tarvainen, Kalevi. 1991. *Einführung in die Dependenzgrammatik.* Tübingen: Max Niemeyer Verlag.
Tesnière, Lucien. 1953. *Equisse d'une syntaxe structurale.* Paris: Klinksieck.
1959. *Eléments de syntaxe structurale.* Paris: Klinksieck.
Underhill, Robert. 1976. *Turkish grammar.* Cambridge, MA: MIT Press.
Van Valin, Robert Jr. 1981. Grammatical relations in ergative languages. *Studies in Language* 5: 361–94.
Van Valin, Robert Jr., ed. 1993a. *Advances in Role and Reference Grammar.* Amsterdam and Philadelphia, PA: John Benjamins.
1993b. A synopsis of Role and Reference Grammar. In Van Valin (1993a), 1–164.
2000. Functional linguistics. In Mark Aronoff and Jamie Rees-Miller, eds., *The Handbook of Linguistics*, 319–36. Oxford: Basil Blackwell.
Van Valin, Robert Jr. and Randy LaPolla. 1997. *Syntax: structure, meaning & function.* Cambridge University Press.
Vater, Heinz. 1975. Toward a generative dependency grammar. *Lingua* 36: 121–45.
Vitale, Anthony. 1981. *Swahili syntax.* Dordrecht: Foris.
Weber, David J. 1983. *Relativization and nominalized clauses in Huallaga (Huanuco) Quechua.* University of California Publications in Linguistics 103. Berkeley: University of California Press.

Welmers, William. 1973. *African language structures.* Berkeley: University of California Press.

Wilkins, David P. 1989. Mparntwe Arrernte (Aranda): studies in the structure and semantics of grammar. PhD dissertation, Australian National University.

Wölck, Wolfgang. 1987. *Pequeño breviario Quechua.* Lima: Instituto de Estudios Peruanos.

Yang, Byong-seon. 1994. *Morphosyntactic phenomena of Korean in Role and Reference Grammar: psych-verb constructions, inflectional verb morphemes, complex sentences, and relative clauses.* Seoul: Hankuk Publishers.

Yang, Byong-seon. 1998. *Role and Reference grammar kaylon.* Seoul: Hankuk Publishers.

Language index

Subject index

Lightning Source UK Ltd.
Milton Keynes UK
18 November 2009

146409UK00001B/3/A

9 780521 635660